Lib

projecting migration

Nonfictions is dedicated to expanding and deepening
the range of contemporary documentary studies.
It aims to engage in the theoretical conversation
about documentaries, open new areas of scholarship,
and recover lost or marginalised histories.

General Editor, Professor Brian Winston

projecting migration

TRANSCULTURAL DOCUMENTARY PRACTICE

Edited by Alan Grossman and Áine O'Brien

 WALLFLOWER PRESS LONDON AND NEW YORK

First published in Great Britain in 2007 by
Wallflower Press
6 Market Place, London W1W 8AF
www.wallflowerpress.co.uk

A catalogue for this book is available from the British Library

ISBN 978-1-905674-04-6

Book design by Rob Bowden Design

Printed and bound in Poland; produced by Polskabook

CONTENTS

ACKNOWLEDGEMENTS

The realisation of this book and its accompanying DVD-ROM is the product of a genuinely collective effort and series of productive collaborations across disciplines and geographical borders. We would like to express our gratitude to the following for their support and interest in helping guide this ambitious project through to completion:

The contributing authors and media practitioners for their responsiveness, participation and patience at various stages during the book's production; the Digital Media Centre, Dublin Institute of Technology (DIT), in particular Evin McCarthy, for his time, skills and inspirational authorship of the DVD; the commissioning editor of Wallflower Press, Yoram Allon, for recognising the value of a DVD as a necessary and innovative component of the book and Rob Bowden, for his imagination in the book's design; the Faculty of Applied Arts, DIT, for their longstanding commitment and financial support of this project; Hamid Naficy, for his appreciation of the imbrication of theory and practice in the representation of trans-localised migrant identities; finally, Janet Davies, for her careful editing, intelligence and constructive comments.

NOTES ON CONTRIBUTORS

Harry Brown is a journalist and Lecturer in the School of Media, Dublin Institute of Technology, Ireland.

David B. Coplan is Professor and Chair in Social Anthropology, University of the Witwatersrand, Johannesburg, South Africa.

Alan Grossman is a Lecturer in Ethnographic Media Production, Centre for Transcultural Research and Media Practice, Dublin Institute of Technology, Ireland.

Anthony Haughey is an artist and research fellow at Interface, the Centre for Research in Art, Technologies and Design, Ulster University, Belfast, UK.

Glenn Jordan is Reader in Cultural Studies, Cardiff Centre for Creative and Cultural Industries, University of Glamorgan, Wales, UK, and Director, Butetown History and Arts Centre, Cardiff.

Roshini Kempadoo is a Senior Lecturer in Digital Media Production, School of Social Sciences, Media and Cultural Studies, University of East London, UK.

Roberta McGrath is a Reader in History and Criticism of Photography, School of Creative Industries, Napier University, Scotland, UK.

Hamid Naficy is John Evan Professor of Communications, School of Communications, Northwestern University, USA.

Áine O'Brien is a Senior Lecturer and Director of the Centre for Transcultural Research and Media Practice, Dublin Institute of Technology, and the Forum on Migration and Communications (FOMACS).

Chinedu Onyejelem is co-founder and editor of Ireland's first multicultural newspaper Metro Eireann.

Rossella Ragazzi is a Senior Researcher in the University of Tromso Ethnographic Museum, Norway.

Graeme Rodgers is a social anthropologist and Research Fellow, Refugee Studies Centre, University of Oxford, UK.

Jayce Salloum is a Vancouver-based media artist, social activist and curator.

Andy Spitz is a South African independent filmmaker and Social Impact Assessment consultant.

Lawrence Taylor is Professor and Head of Anthropology, National University of Ireland.

Gei Zantzinger is Director of Constant Spring Productions, Inc., an A/V company that collaborates with independent artists.

GUIDELINES FOR DVD-ROM

The DVD-ROM included is designed as an essential and integrated component of this book, offering the reader a viewing source of all moving image, photographic, audio and pdf materials referenced in the introduction and each of the eleven chapters. We would encourage the reader therefore to work closely with both text and DVD media content simultaneously.

The book's cross-links to the DVD-ROM are embedded within chapters, designated by a corresponding numerical DVD reference, together with one or more of a combination of the following descriptive media types: video, photo, audio and pdf. These cross-links may also appear in chapter footnotes. While appearing in sequential order, authors will occasionally refer back to previously cited DVD references, retaining the numerical and medium specificity of the cross-link.

Double-clicking on the **ProjectingMigration.exe** (PC) or **ProjectingMigration** (Mac) icon launches the contents menu of the DVD-ROM in which the introduction, chapter titles and authors are presented; clicking on a selected chapter activates its submenu. On the PC the DVD-ROM will auto-launch once the disc has been recognised by the system; there is no auto-launch on the Mac. The DVD-ROM can be exited on either PC or Mac by using the **quit** button found in the top right-hand corner.

Layout and navigation structure of chapter submenu:

– The **references** section is automatically selected, providing a corresponding list of numbers (and titles) of DVD references cited in each chapter, together with their written colour-coded media types: video (blue); photography (yellow); audio (green); pdf (red). Click on a reference to open its media content. Navigate between references via **previous** and **next** or by clicking on **references**. Note that the stage size is fixed and cannot be enlarged to full screen.

– Click on the **figures** option to browse sequentially numbered illustrations used in chapters. These are reproduced for convenience of the reader to view figures in their original format and are presented as a slideshow sequence. The dropdown titles of chapter figures appear only when the cursor is placed on the image; this same principle applies when viewing series of photographs in references.

– The **author biography** option contains photographs of authors, together with brief biographical statements.

– Click on **chapters** to return to contents menu.

Minimum requirements: Windows 2000 or later; Mac OS X; DVD-ROM Drive; monitor resolution 800 x 600; and desktop speakers.

ON THE GLOBAL INTER-, MULTI- AND TRANS-

Hamid Naficy

Globalisation and displacement are the Janus faces of our contemporary late-modern condition; one necessitates the other. We are living in an interrelated world that increasingly favours horizontality over verticality, multiplicity over singularity, routes over roots, and network over nation. This has brought on the ascendance of the terms that denote connectivity and interconnectivity – horizontal, vertical and transverse – in the realms of culture, media, technology and society, giving new meanings to such prefixes as inter, multi and trans that emphasise transitive and rhizomatic relations, collaboration, transition, mobility, synergy and synchronicity. Thus, nowadays in the fields of culture and media we commonly come across such 'inter' terms as international, interstitial, intermedia, interactive, intertextual, intercultural, interdisciplinary, interethnic, intersensory and intersubjective, such 'multi' terms as multimedia, multilingual, multinational, multifocal, multisited and multicultural, and such 'trans' terms as transnational, transborder, transgender, transcultural, translational and transitional. The internet itself, which condenses and embodies these terms and their attending concepts and practices in its very ontology, is a perfect emblem and medium of our time.

Projecting Migration: Transcultural Documentary Practice and the accompanying DVD, containing a range of still and moving audiovisual materials, together constitute a fine example and artefact of this inter-, multi- and trans-dimensionality of our current cultural moment and of film and media studies as a discipline. It is a collaborative project, co-edited by two media scholar-practitioners, Alan Grossman and Áine O'Brien, whose task as editors went well beyond the traditional practice of editing manuscripts containing a few still visuals. Not only the book and DVD but also several individual chapters are collaborative, taking advantage of the synergy that this lateral process offers media-makers and critics. In addition, *Projecting Migration* is one of the first comprehensive projects to successfully tackle a key problem that has dogged film and media studies scholarship and pedagogy from the start: how to quote moving audiovisual materials textually (in print) and orally (in class). For decades film scholars and instructors were forced to rely on extensive scene description, dialogue quotation, film frames, or roughly cued films or videos for their publications and teaching. *Projecting Migration* solves the problematic of quotation; but it goes beyond that by offering a multimedia package in which the audiovisual is not just supplementary or illustrative but primary and constitutive of the arguments presented in and across chapters.

The project's integrated multimedia design and intertextuality has a repercussion not only for authoring but also for reading, as it transforms the traditional act of simply reading a self-contained book to a more complex generative activity involving reading, listening, watching and interacting. In Roland Barthes' terms, it transforms the book into a text in whose construction the readers actively participate. The use of digital video technology by the subjects in some chapters to record their own conditions further blurs the boundary separating author from subject, creating both opportunities and pitfalls for media-makers, ethnographers and media scholars. Not only the book and DVD in their design and architecture, but also the chapter authors in their writings and audiovisual materials invoke in one version or another the various inter-, multi- and trans-dimensional concepts and practices.

Moreover, their chapters contain interdisciplinary, practice-driven media making, media criticism and media theory, which are brought to bear on exploring a vital and complex issue of our time: the lives and times of diverse displaced persons, migrants, refugees, nomads, stateless persons, émigrés and exiles, from South Africa to North America, who have been roaming the world in recent years in search of new homes and new opportunities. According to the United Nations High Commissioner of Refugees, even though the number of refugees decreased in 2005, the total number of asylees, refugees, stateless persons and displaced persons worldwide is large, currently standing at nearly 21 million (http://www.unhcr.org/basics.html). If the number of émigrés, exiles and diasporic subjects were to be added, however, collectively they would constitute a formidable global population that endures and thrives in conditions of unprecedented mobility and transitionality. Several of the authors, themselves migrants, explore the displaced populations from which they come, while others examine migrant constituencies to which they do not belong, introducing fascinating tensions in their contributions.

Globalisation and mediation are another Janus-faced feature of our contemporary times, one necessitating the other. While the means of transportation generally take us away to other lands, the communication media reconnect us to earlier places and times, connect us to new places and times, and help us re-imagine new possibilities. With media-saturated globalisation, imagination has taken wings as never before. Indeed, it has become a daily fact of life. Epistolary structuration – whether it involves letters, e-mail, telephone, photographs, voice recording, or film and video – is one aspect of the internalisation of the imagination in this age of globalised dispersion and distraction. All migrant literary, artistic and cinematic formations today are driven by epistolarity and network connectivity of one sort or another, both in content and form. Today's displaced populations, like their predecessors who built the film, media, journalism and entertainment empires of the various countries to which they relocated – are highly media-conscious and media-savvy, not only as consumers but also as producers of the media. Such mediated connectivity allows, indeed encourages, the new displaced populations to break out of the hermeticity of their physical enclaves – national, ethnic, religious, racial or class, which bound previous émigré generations – to create other alternative affiliations and rhizomatic connections with individuals and communities not their own.

However, two important caveats regarding our contemporary globalisation, dispersion and mediation are in order to prevent us from flying into stratospheric weightlessness and irrelevancy. The network – the combined discursive formations of globalisation, dispersion and mediation – has not so much replaced the nation as supplanted it in some real sense and displaced it in certain psychological ways. As some of the contributions demonstrate, the physical borders remain in place and are in full force despite the paroxysm of premature celebration by proponents of corporate globalisation and postmodernity. In fact, in tandem with the globalisation of capital and the mobility of peoples and goods, the integrity, security, sovereignty and protection of physical borders have assumed heightened attention, budgets and resources. Increasingly, ethnic, religious, tribal and national borders have hardened into sacrosanct and highly militarized edifices over which passive but intrusive surveillance-driven cold wars, as well as active and particularistic lethal hot wars, are being waged throughout the world. Likewise, border crossings have become cathected places of fear and terror, where international passengers must provide proofs of their identities in the form of tamper-proof, digitised and holographed passports and identity papers, where they are subjected to racial, ethnic, political, religious and national profiling, fingerprinting, mug shots, biometric readings, dog sniffing and other forms of discriminatory, disciplinary and sometimes racist security and intelligence data gathering. The inter-, multi- and trans-dimensional worldviews and theories, which generally celebrate the liberatory possibilities of globalisation, must come to terms with these actual, material border realities, which tend to be authoritarian and panoptic. In addition, they must constantly be checked against the tendency of the modern mass media and cultures to revel in surface tensions and fashionable differences while disregarding the festering wounds and the deep, historical differences. Indeed, one of the grave challenges of our age as media-makers and scholars is how to reconcile synchronicity with historicity, how to maintain differences and specificity in the face of the global machines and machinations that obliterate these for economic and political profits.

INTRODUCTION
Alan Grossman and Áine O'Brien

It becomes ever more urgent to develop a framework of thinking that makes the migrant central, not ancillary, to the historical process ... It begins by regarding movement, not as an awkward interval between fixed points of departure and arrival, but a mode of being in the world.
– Paul Carter (cited in Moorehead 2006: 283)

Appearance *is* knowledge, of a kind. Showing becomes a way of saying the unsayable. Visual knowledge (as well as other forms of sensory knowledge) provides one of our primary means of comprehending the experience of other people. Unlike the knowledge communicated by words, what we show in images has no transparency or volition – it is a different knowledge, stubborn and opaque, but with a capacity for the finest detail.
– David MacDougall 2006: 5–6

There is no institutionalized world of 'documentary studies', [although] I argue for the emergence of just such an interdisciplinary field of inquiry, in which a range of theoretical and methodological approaches converge and in which the object can be photography, film, video, and the digital arts as vehicles of historical representation.
– Michael Renov (1999: 324–5)

REPRESENTING MIGRATION: THE TRANSDISCIPLINARY CHALLENGE

The underlying impetus for this volume dates back to a conference in 2001, purposely staged outside the familiar confines of the academic institution in the Project Arts Centre, Dublin, titled 'Migration and Location: Visual Media Research'. Responding to the accelerated economic growth of the 1990s, transforming Ireland from a country of net-emigration to net-immigration, with 'one of the fastest growing immigrant populations in Europe in the early years of the twenty-first century' (IOM World Migration 2005: 13), the conference brought together media and art practitioners, academics, NGOs, trade union activists, policy makers, and members of immigrant constituencies in the context of comparative non-fiction media production work from both within and outside Ireland. Several contributors to this book (Naficy, Haughey, Ragazzi, McGrath, Taylor and Hickey) participated in this inaugural event.[1] The overarching objective of the conference was to foreground documentary media production as a valuable and contributory evidence-based transdisciplinary research formation, with the capacity both to inform and impact on the very substance of immigration policy-related research in Ireland and beyond, arguably too reliant on quantitative methods of data collection. Looking back at this initial forum, we are struck by parallel efforts within the social sciences to establish similarly oriented frameworks in the field of migration studies (Brettell & Hollifield 2000; Papastergiadis 2000; Castles 2001; Vertovec 2004), most clearly outlined in a European Science Foundation 'Forward Look Report for the Humanities':

> Transdisciplinarity is not a name in itself; it is a necessity in the investigation of complex phenomena such as migration, culture identity and transnationality which cannot be encompassed by single disciplines. The simple juxtaposition of researchers who carry out parallel studies on the same topic, each in his own discipline will not be enough to yield innovative results. There is a pressing necessity for complementarity in the use of data – collection methods and analyses of findings.[2]

This forceful statement signifies a clear recognition of the difficulties of exploring the phenomenon of migration from the safe confines of any one discipline, proposing instead a dialogue across fields of study and their critical intermixing. This is precisely what, ambitiously, we set out to do in this volume: to bring together a range of documentary media projects on the topic of migration with a view to moulding that very 'complementarity' of research across the social sciences and the humanities and, hopefully, to steer the dialogue toward a critical axis, constituted in the dynamic domain of non-fiction media production. For in many respects, migration challenges the researcher/practitioner to constructively abandon their disciplinary comfort zones, to both listen and look carefully at what is, in practice, a multifaceted and global phenomenon. A related programmatic intervention, supporting the nexus between empirical, theoretical and practice-led research on the thematic of 'Diasporas, Migration and Identities' (2005) – initiated by the Arts and Humanities Research Council (UK) for a period of five years – is further testimony to an epistemological opening in the study of transnational mobility and diasporic belonging, necessitating the cross-fertilisation of research methods and strategies of representation.[3] With hindsight the 2001 'Migration and Location' conference's use of the colloquial phrase 'Visual Media' elides the emphatic overlay of the aural and tactile senses, always interwoven in the mediation, performance and reception of any given medium. For as William Mitchell argues, 'all media are, from the standpoint of sensory modality "mixed media"' (2005: 257). The predominance of the visual over other sensory modalities has long been critiqued in an anthropology of the senses in which C. Nadia Seremetakis (1994a) examines their cultural role in the construction of social meaning, and Paul Stoller (1997) speaks to the question of sensuous epistemologies (see Feldman 1991 and Taussig 1993). The use of the phrase *Projecting Migration* in this volume's title does not merely suggest the projection and exhibition of 'mixed media' artefacts. It is more importantly intended to signify, proactively rather than literally, an imagining of the present and toward the future, in which the performative dimensions of human and social processes of migration are both recognisable and accessible through the prism of documentary media production.

The representational practices and methodological considerations informing our initial engagement with the everyday complexities of transnational migration took the form of a short performative documentary film, titled *Silent Song* (2000).[4] In the making of this film about an exiled Kurdish refugee musician residing in Scotland, we became aware of the extent to which the lived experience of migration is not always fully accessible through the limitations of textual and word-based knowledge. Following on from our filmic and written attempt to represent Kurdish lyrical protest through the terrain of acoustic migration (see Grossman & O'Brien 2006), we wish further to explore in this volume just how the research application of still, moving image and sound technologies can adequately frame the material conditions and contingencies, motivations and transnational affiliations shaping the everyday lived reality of migrants, their families and extended communities. How, for example, can documentary representation effect a critical comparative reading of new and established zones of transnational migration, resisting the televisual compulsion to render such sites transparent? How do images documenting population movement and re-settlement migrate within and across archival formations? How is it possible to re-imagine and construct 'living' archives enjoining the past and present? What intersubjective relationships are possible when image makers, exploring the temporal and spatial co-ordinates of migration across varied locations and public spheres, initiate different modes of collaborative production and fieldwork practices in their research imaginaries?

These are but a selection of key questions underpinning this integrated book/DVD-ROM anthology, comprising contributions from scholars/practitioners working in and across diverse transnational field sites and media formats – film, video, photography, radio and new media.[5] *Projecting Migration* foregrounds the potential and merits of documentary practice as a mode of engagement with the material and embodied dimensions of migration and new modes of citizenship, together with the changing conditions of place, locality and globalisation.[6] The emphasis throughout is not on the reading and reception of media and cultural texts, intertextually legible images, sounds and objects, central to the 'emergence of visual culture as a transdisciplinary and cross-methodological field of inquiry' (Rogoff 1998: 16).[7] Rather, it is concerned with collaborative processes and transdisciplinary methods of research and representation conducted across the arts, humanities and social sciences, from preproduction to postproduction, thinking through and with sounds and images, and the intersubjective relations surrounding the (ethnographic) assemblage and dissemination of media and art practice across a range of exhibition formats and settings.

Building on long-established formalised and experimental modes of visual representation in the creative arts, there has, significantly, been a growing interest in the last decade in the application of visual research methods across the humanistic social sciences (Prosser 1998; Emmison & Smith 2000; Banks 2001; Pink 2001; Rose 2001; Grimshaw 2002). This development has been a function of both disciplinary expansionism into applied research contexts allied to technological developments – for example, the advent of lightweight still and moving image digital cameras and desktop video editing systems – facilitating innovative and flexible fieldwork approaches in ethnographically-mediated production and its representation (Henley 2000; MacDougall 2001; Pink *et al.* 2004; Harper 2005; Pink 2006).[8] And yet, within this ongoing commitment to the merits of media practice in the production of new knowledge and fieldsites, interpretative output is often limited to a written multilayered contextualisation and pictorial illustration of the use of visual and digital technologies and their resulting artefacts whether CD-ROM, DVD, video, photography or hypermedia; seldom does the writer/practitioner point to a 'media object', inviting the reader to move simultaneously and laterally into a parallel performative space.[9] In the chapters that follow, guided by our editorial imperative to purposely interrupt reflective discussion by recourse to media representation of research materials on the DVD-ROM, readers will detect resonances of a longstanding debate in visual anthropology in which David MacDougall (1998) and Lucien Taylor (1996; 1998) among others, underscore the distinction between the visual as a *medium* rather than an *object* of analysis.[10] As MacDougall writes:

> A concept of deep reflexivity requires us to read the position of the author in the very construction of the work, whatever the external explanations may be. One reason for this is that the author's position is neither uniform nor fixed, and expresses itself through a multileveled and constantly evolving relation with the subject … One of the difficulties involved in placing much confidence in external reflexivity is that the author is poorly placed to define the terms in which the work should be read. The things that matter most are likely to be those in which the author is most deeply implicated. (1998: 89)

For MacDougall, reflexivity is both an implicit and an intrinsic part of the form and structure of the work, whether intentionally registered or not; explanatory, in contrast to 'deep reflexivity', is, therefore, what the practitioner offers in the form of secondary insights after the 'event', so to speak. A primary aim of *Projecting Migration* is to move beyond the predominance of a unidimensional register and, in so doing, align the book's writerly reflection with the reflexive dimensions inherent in the media content presented on the DVD–ROM. The collection of chapters and accompanying DVD-ROM, conceived as a thoroughly integrated resource of media referenced in the text, does not set out to provide a geographically representative sample of global migration flows nor deliberately point to emergent and transformative spaces of 'migrant transnational practices' (Vertovec 2004: 9). Instead, the contributions instantiate a range of media practice interventions in a select number of research sites across Ireland, the UK, Caribbean, the US, Mexico, Southern Africa, Lebanon, France and the former Yugoslavia. Collectively, the projects address the interconnected phenomena and thematics of economic and forced migration, border crossings, uprootings, diasporic history and memory, migration and childhood, the transnational family, post-conflict landscapes, oral culture and migrant youth culture. What results, therefore, *in and through the practice*, are a series of transdisciplinary dialogues between cultural theorists and media practitioners working in the areas of visual and cultural anthropology, media and visual cultural studies, art practice and independent documentary production. The work incorporates longitudinal creative documentary made for television and outreach audiences; ethnographic film for both an academic and primary/secondary school audience; a development-related video project; photographic and video fieldwork translated into art installation format for exhibition; a photographic public archival project for publication; multimedia installations designed for virtual and site-specific exhibition; and photographic/oral history publications and exhibitions for local migrant communities.

Short of reproducing the richness of the varied media content in its material fullness, as experienced in the 'live' viewing and listening contexts of radio, television, cinema, art gallery or archive, the media presented on the DVD-ROM nevertheless retains a qualitative fidelity to the specificity of work generated. It offers a strategic selection of textually cross-referenced video extracts, photographs, installations/exhibition materials, an inter-active multimedia piece, audio files and pdf interview transcripts. Indicative of different research methods allied to technological specificities defining modes of creative practice, the combined body of work reveals a productive unevenness, with some projects already completed and reflected upon retrospectively, while others are currently being 'thought through', exhibiting marked signs of stylistic and theoretical rawness as they move toward completion; the varying levels of form and content are further manifest in disparate levels of project funding, which in turn shape modes of production and undoubtedly ideologies of the aesthetic.

SITUATING MIGRATION STUDIES AND DOCUMENTARY PRACTICE: INTERSECTING CONCERNS

As a transdisciplinary object of study, migration with its 'diversity of paths and . . . com-plexity of forms of movement' (Papastergiadis 2000: 23) challenges researchers to engage creatively with settled, mobile and temporarily-located constituencies, experiences of ex-ile and historical and contemporary diasporas. There is now an established theoretical focus within migration studies in response to the emergence of accelerated migration flows since the late 1980s, what theorists call the 'new age of migration' (Castles & Miller 1998), otherwise described as 'transmigration' or 'transnationalism' (Glick Schiller et al. 1992; Basch et al. 1994; Kearney 1995; Smith & Guarnizo 1998; Grillo 2001; Castles 2002), in which transnational social, cultural and political networks and affiliations are produced and sustained across national borders. For as Ayse Caglar notes, 'migrants construct and reconstitute their lives as simultaneously embedded in more than one society' (2001: 607).[11] Roger Rouse's pioneering ethnographic fieldwork in the early 1980s on the mi-gration of Mexican migrants from Aguililla, Michoacán to Redwood City, California not only anticipates such a focus, but further enacts a cross-disciplinary conversation between cultural anthropology, geography and cultural studies. For Rouse the bi-polar model of migration from country of origin to country of destination (dominating the social scienc-es into the 1980s), is radically overturned by the contradictory socio-spatial conditions wrought by transnational capitalism and the accompanying reconfiguration of 'spatially extended relationships' along the continuum of a 'transnational migrant circuit' (2002: 162). Spaces stretching from either side of the US/Mexico border are thus linked through familial, social and economic ties, comprising multiple yet interconnected networks and locations in which migrant constituencies have settled (even if temporarily), and where the continuous, nevertheless disaggregated contours, of the circuit mark out new cartog-raphies of migration. Irit Rogoff refers to this, in a separate context, as moving beyond a feeling of loss for a sense of 'seamless emplacement', toward an understanding of location as a 'site of performativity and of criticality rather than a set of naturalised relations be-tween subjects and places' (2004: 88). Our use of the term 'transcultural' in this book's title is, therefore, symptomatic of this understanding of location as a site of 'performativity' in the manner posited by Rogoff or in the 'circuit' presented by Rouse, where subjects no longer retain a sense of place or sustain an intrinsic connection to a specific location. The 'trans' in the transcultural further evokes what Crispin Thurlow describes as:

moving *through* and *across* cultural systems, in whatever way they may be constituted or conceived … [a] fluidity of these systems, their porous boundaries and
constantly reorienting expressions, as well as the conceptual spaces that open up
between traditionally defined cultural systems – the putative 'Third Space' of Homi
Bhabha (1994) and the borderlands of Gloria Anzaldúa (1987) – that emerge between shifting patterns of sociocultural organization and practice. (2006)

In the combined discussion developed throughout the chapters, and further evidenced in
the range and media content featured on the DVD-ROM, this volume argues that transcultural documentary production facilitates a deeper understanding of the lived, contradictory and at times ephemeral conditions shaping the lives of migrant subjects. For as David
MacDougall notes, a 'transcultural perspective accommodates cultural shift, movement,
and interchange, which more adequately fits the experience of many Westerners as well as
populations often identified as indigenous, migrant, or diasporic' (1998: 261). The prevailing focus within the social sciences to address the everyday realities of migration through
qualitative research, one focused on the nuances and structural realignments produced
within and across national borders, surely requires an expansive conceptual and methodological frame. Non-fiction media production scholarship, we maintain, is advantageously
positioned, as the DVD-ROM material hopefully demonstrates, to render publicly visible
and audible the spatialized daily rhythms and routines, political agencies, socio-economic
and familial cultural relations and linkages depicted by Luis Guarnizo (1997) and Steven
Vertovec (2004) as configuring the 'habitus of migrant transnationalism'.

Mediated through an engagement with differing levels of migrant social integration
and exclusion, civic and political participation, class and gendered processes, together
with the concrete implications surrounding the legal status of migrants in countries of
both residence and origin, documentary practice is methodologically capable of critically re-framing, through an integrated micro and macro analysis of 'everyday life', the
'accumulation of singular actions and … alternative and [collective] resistant practices'
(Highmore 2002: 11). The concept of 'habitus' (Bourdieu 1977, 1990), signifying the accumulation of culturally conditioned dispositions performed by social actors in the course
of their everyday life has, however, different sociological connotations to the notion of
the 'everyday' as a theoretical orientation. While 'habitus' infers a socio-cultural, indeed
somatic and psychological, habituation by subjects within their daily lives, the 'everyday'
functions as both 'problematic' and 'meta-field'. As Ben Highmore puts it referring to
Henri Lefebvre, the everyday lies outside the parameters of the human sciences yet simultaneously traverses them. The study of the 'everyday' thus fuses both the particular
and the general, in so far as the particular evokes 'the agency of individuals in daily life,
forms of resistance or non-conformity to social structures, a stress on feeling and experience', while the general delineates the 'social structures, institutions and discourses as a
domain of power determining the everyday' (2002: 5). In positing a critical convergence
of 'habitus' and the 'everyday', we advocate a media practice-based response to what Arjun
Appadurai calls the 'optical challenges posed by the global' (2000: 3) that demand a 'new
architecture [pedagogy] for producing and sharing knowledge about globalisation' (2000:
18), elicited from the bottom up – alternatively described as transnationalism and globalization 'from below' (Guarnizo & Smith 1998; Portes 1998).[12]

In this volume many of the contributors attempt to 'see' and 'hear' the grounded realities of migration in its multidimensionality, re-placing the research-contrived notion of a single-sited ethnographic field with a negotiation of multi-localities and spatio-temporal practices. Reflecting on a 'multi-sited' research trajectory intrinsic to the field of migration studies, since it is inherently concerned with identity formation in a shifting and relational local-global framework, Marcus proposes modes of enquiry necessarily designed

> around chains, paths, threads, conjunctions, or juxtapositions of locations in which the ethnographer establishes some form of literal, physical presence, with an explicit, posited logic of association or connection among sites that in fact defines the argument of the ethnography ... a revival of a sophisticated practice of [avant-garde] constructivism. (1995: 105)

Marcus's account of a 'multi-sited research imaginary' (1998: 3) was both instructive and provocative in shaping the design of our own film fieldwork in Ireland and the Philippines (2003–06). In a longitudinal and comparative two-part documentary film project, we ethnographically observed, both with and without the camera, the gradual, nevertheless forceful and tangible, participation of migrant subjects in Irish civil society formations, working with and alongside NGOs. The project's overriding problematic, worked through at the level of practice and its theoretical inflection, is how to situate migrant subjectivity, its collectivised political instantiation and performance against the concrete restrictions of Irish government immigration policies, which distinguish between 'high-skilled' visa holders – for example, overseas nurses – at liberty to change jobs and therefore not prey to government quotas, and so-called 'low-skill' work permit holders – such as domestic workers – subject to temporary and bonded labour work permits.[13]

In Part 1 of the project titled *Here To Stay* (2006), we foreground Filipino nurse Fidel Taguinod, who was part of the first contingent of nurses recruited from the Philippines in 2000 to work at a teaching hospital in Dublin.[14] Through a sustained period of observational film work on the hospital ward, we depict Fidel's managerial competence, his everyday working relations with patients, consultants, Irish and overseas staff from India, Nigeria and South Africa; a perspective hitherto absent in broadcast representations of the health service with its increasing reliance on the international recruitment of overseas nurses, evidencing nursing shortages throughout developed countries and giving rise to crucial concerns surrounding the need for ethical recruitment policies (Buchan 2000).

Here To Stay is not entirely 'observational' in the strict visual anthropological measure of its application; the integrity of the long sequence is at times deliberately transgressed through cutaways and edits, thus dramatising emergent areas of concern for migrant workers and their families, with a view to reaching mixed audiences including new migrant constituencies and immigration policy makers. For example, tracking the mobilisation of the Overseas Nurses Section within the Irish Nurses Trade Union (INO) from its inception, with Fidel as President, provided a way to portray the dynamics of migrant-led political activism and how trade unionism develops in a rapidly expanding multiracial society. The rough assembly footage of the section's inauguration [DVD REF 1: VIDEO] reveals collectivised migrant agency at work in its negotiation with an INO representative, conveying a transcultural exchange based on recognition of both differences and shared goals and agendas. In filming the evolution of political process over time, through documentation of critical debates in Section meetings and his participation in migration NGO and union conferences, we followed Fidel as he acquired a position of leadership, mediating between different stakeholders, including hospital employers, government immigration officials and fellow migrants. Fidel's expression of his migrant cultural politics is further observed through the everyday performance of his gay identity, or to invoke the Tagalog term, *bakla*, a self-formation 'concerned with the manipulation of surface appearances', through dramaturgical cross-dressing, for example, involving the 'scripting of divergent selves, each of which is embedded in a specific social situation and network of social relationships' (Manalansan IV 2003: 16). For Fidel, alias 'Miss Diva Manila', the negotiation of Filipino and Irish sexual and gender traditions, specifically '*bakla* and gay ideologies' (2003: ix), is enacted fluidly, indeed transculturally, across domestic, work and public contexts; this is illustrated in his strategic use of the first 'Alternative Miss Philippines' beauty pageant in Ireland (2004) as a vehicle to promote migrant labour participation in union politics. [DVD REF 2: VIDEO]

CHAPTER OUTLINES AND THEMATIC HORIZONS

Five chapters of *Projecting Migration* engage with the politics and practice of 'seeing' and the construction of archives of migration, either exploring archival collections (McGrath) or examining the process of building 'living archives' through documentary photography, installation fieldwork and multimedia practice (Kempadoo, Jordan, Haughey and Salloum). The tension between 'seeing' and 'constructing' is central throughout, as the 'past' is rearticulated in what C. Nadia Seremetakis calls a brushing off of dust: 'the perceptual waste material formed by historical-cultural repression of sensory experience and memory' (1994b: 222). The concept of the 'living archive' (Bailey & Boyce 2001: 87) suggests a re-imagining of past and present, expanding the narrative boundaries of archival formations to transitory, site-specific spaces, where the exchange between practitioner and audience is staged through temporary re-enactments of a history of the present.

In 'History Read Backward: Memory, Migration and the Photographic Archive', Roberta McGrath reconfigures images and material artefacts from the archives of the Mitchell Library, Glasgow and the National Archives of Scotland, Edinburgh into a 'multi-sited' project in which the boundaries of the collection are transgressed; photography, film, letters, public reports and other discursive documents are radically juxtaposed, tracing parallels and disjunctures between past and present migrant narratives. Echoing Stuart Hall's concept of the archive as a 'field of ... rupture, significant breaks, transformations, new and unpredicted departures' (2001: 90), the photographic images and written texts documenting labour migration in and out of Scotland between 1841 and 1949 jostle with and are startlingly similar to accounts of the 'management' of migration in contemporary Britain. For McGrath, the prevailing paranoia about and increasing 'control' of migrants have a stratified dialectical history which, traceable across the labyrinthine layers of the archive, effects a traversal mode of enquiry in her search for sensory memory, 'experiential fragments, deferred emotions and lost objects' (Seremetakis 1994a: 215). Constructing a mode of situated knowledge through embodied research, McGrath advocates 'active passivity' (Kracauer 1969: 84), an ethics of reading within visual culture, where the researcher – in a reversal of the subject/object dichotomy of reading/imposing meaning on the image – waits patiently for the photograph to speak (should it so choose), revealing a mode of knowledge 'constructed by a form of acquaintance' (MacDougall 1998: 77). In this scenario, the researcher explores an accretion of meanings long subdued, regulated by nationalist histories and mythological narratives of emigration/immigration.

In 'Back Routes: Historical Articulation in Multimedia Production' Roshini Kempadoo transposes the documentary photographic image on to a digital aesthetic, offering a critique of technologies and practices underpinning colonial archival collection. In this virtual landscape multiple spatio-temporal frames are manipulated to coexist within the same image plane, invoking both Nicholas Mirzoeff's notion of diasporic 'intervisuality' (2000: 7) and Johannes Fabian's concept of coeval time (1983). For the Caribbean and Caribbean British subject (indeed for the spectator/user in the gallery space), the logic of the 'indexical' (and the archive) is directly challenged in this reconstruction of narratives of slavery and the legacies of empire. Via a digital process of simultaneous projection, competing yet mutually linked stories are seen and heard describing the provenance of a sixteenth-century curiosity, the Drake Cup, which symbolises the material embodiment of the slave trade and colonial commercial enterprise. Kempadoo appropriates the cup, currently archived as an English 'national treasure', and juxtaposes two stories: in one a valuations expert records the history of craftsmanship; in the 'other', the brutality of the transatlantic crossing is imagined through the 'voice' of an elderly Caribbean woman. Inscribed in both this counter narrative and the 'virtual cup' is a direct rebuke of dominant heritage lore.

Whereas Kempadoo, for historical reasons, eschews documentary photographic realism, Glenn Jordan, while fully appraised of its potential to stereotype and historically misrepresent, embraces it. In 'Presenting Themselves Before the Camera: The Somali Elders Project in Cardiff', he produces a diasporic archive which merges oral history, collaborative ethnography and humanist portraiture, performing the role of photographer and author in an overtly self-reflexive stance. As curator, cultural critic and photographer at Butetown History and Arts Centre, located in one of the UK's oldest established sites for inward migration and the formation of multi-ethnic communities, Jordan intertwines history with photographic realism in the context of public archival and community politics. Photographic subject and photographer are intricately linked by their mutual migrant histories and through the research process itself: a sustained ethnographic project with male members of the Somali community resulting in a series of 'constructed biographies'. Portraits, for Jordan, are 'co-productions', since as Dai Vaughan notes, 'every photograph … is a portrait signed by its sitter' (1999: 58). The doubling of image and life story interrupts a too easy consumption of the portrait as 'essence', challenging the spectator to move across narrative frames, where the life stories, 'always artificial, variable and partial' (Portelli 1998: 72), lead us to a more complex understanding and recognition of an established migrant community in Wales.

The exploration of 'photographic realism' and the archive continues in Anthony Haughey's 'Imaging the Unimaginable: Disputed Territory', an art-practice project centred on post-conflict landscapes across Europe, particularly the effects of forced migration in the former Yugoslavia. As documentary photographer and installation artist, Haughey refuses to abandon photography's power to witness, document and translate the lived realities of the aftermath of war. Implicit in his practice are echoes of photographic debates on the status of the 'real', together with transdisciplinary exchanges between ethnography and art practice which, despite Hal Foster's caution against the blind spots of a 'quasi-anthropological paradigm' practised by artists (1996: 196), facilitates a methodological challenge to produce what Alan Sekula calls a truly social documentary, 'framing the crime, the trial, the system of justice and its official myths' (1999: 122). Resulting in a more 'expansive' (Clifford 2003: 24) ethnography, Haughey (mirroring McGrath's 'active passivity') waits/watches for a 'gesture' to lead him to a chain of associations inscribed on the land in the documentation of ambivalent referents ('Destroyed Files, Sarajevo, 1999'); heard in the audio recordings of survivors' testimony; chronicled (in a looped-video) in the forensic examination of missing persons' clothing. The installation space as visual ethnographic site is thus for Haughey the ultimate examination of whether the 'viewer' is able (or willing) to suspend disbelief and enter into a wholly reconstructed transnational fieldwork location, which stubbornly and ethically holds out for the persistence of evidence and testimony.

In 'sans titre/untitled: Video Installation as an Active Archive', the 'field' functions 'as habitus rather than [as] place, a cluster of embodied dispositions and practices' (Clifford 1997: 69), providing Jayce Salloum with a way of exploring 'interstitiality' in and across diverse sites of migration, shaped by subjects who, living under conditions of cultural transition and upheaval, are theorising these moments of dramatic change: dispersed inhabitants of the former Yugoslavia; Palestinians living in a 'permanent temporariness' in refugee camps in Lebanon; and Soha Bechara, a member of the Lebanese National Resistance/Lebanese Resistance Front, exiled in Paris. The 'interstitial', as working metaphor, represents an underlying thread in Salloum's articulation of an accumulative archive, an indefinite epistemology drawing distinct parallels with Hall's concept of archiving as a 'practice which both has its limits and its disciplines yet has no definitive sense of origin, boundary or termination' (2001: 91). Most forceful is Salloum's video interview with Bechara – an ex-detainee of the infamous Al Khyam detention centre in south Lebanon – in her Paris room, epitomising the intersubjective encounter between self and other. She responds in Arabic to the halting French of Salloum's questions; the dialogue is intense, with the tightly cropped shot of Bechara staring out to camera, to filmmaker, to viewer. Critics may well question the nature of the 'dialogue', given the blockage in linguistic communication, yet it can be argued that what is being produced here is a mode of knowledge expressed by Bechara and later acknowledged by Salloum in the course of his ongoing installation work. As Fabian writes:

> Sense and knowledge must not be confused. Sense or meaning can be brought along; they affirm and support – most of the time ideas or values already held … The term knowledge, unless it is taken as a synonym for projection, should be reserved for insights and understandings that the knower does not already possess and that, when they occur, change the knower. (2001: 161)

Ethnographic knowledge is thus not merely produced through 'recognition', in the sense of one party granting it to another, or indeed through the 'politics of recognition', synonymous with discourses of multiculturalism, but rather entails 'exchanges that have startling, upsetting, sometimes profoundly disturbing consequences for all participants' (2001: 175). Significant here is Fabian's analysis of 'memory' as a communicative, transitive device bringing 'self and other' to a place where they 'remember the present', thereby pulled into a 'mutual recognition' built on knowledge which 'changes the knower' and simultaneously 'reconstitutes his or her identity' (2001: 177).

The productive tension between a 'politics of recognition' and a 'mutual recognition' based on provocative knowledge exchange is further evident in the work of Graeme Rodgers and Andrea Spitz, and Lawrence Taylor and Maeve Hickey, in longitudinal ethnographic fieldwork produced through still photography and video. Here, the 'border' features as a concrete site marking transnational familial alliances, processes of interconnection and infranational dislocation, explored in Rodgers and Spitz's notion of 'social relatedness' between refugees and their families displaced across the Mozambique/South Africa border, alongside Taylor and Hickey's immersion in migrant youth culture on the US/Mexico border.

In 'Video Messaging in Contexts of Forced Migration: "Amplifying" Social Relatedness across the Mozambique/South Africa Border', the collaboration between cultural anthropologist Rodgers and documentary filmmaker Spitz engages with the performance of an 'interacting doubleness of epistemology' (Taussig 1987: 196), symptomatic of a complex trans-border social economy. The project underwent a series of methodological transformations, from audio 'messages' that provided for the documentation and transmission of cross-border relationships, to the deliberate introduction of video messaging that enabled people to 'see' and present reciprocal stories about life in the border environment, to a more formalised, staged, arguably risky, documentary project for South African television (*Voices Across the Fence*, 2002). Acutely aware of these methodological and by association ethical turns, in particular the implications of moving to a larger documentary crew and the subsequent limitations imposed when documentary 'direction' threatens to empty out the richness of the ethnographic encounter in the pursuit of a televisual programming logic, Rodgers and Spitz risk 'translating' this visual fieldwork in order to reach a broader audience. The narrative structure underpinning the video messages moves by way of a dual logic, one sustained by the pragmatics of staging and filming the performances of subjects on either side of the border and the other by a postproduction ethics, dramatising emotionally-charged dialogues across the border's spatial divide. The 'intimate proximity' between speakers is constructed through continuous playback of material to respective subjects and related communities of actors. The choreography of cross-border exchanges builds momentum and has its own internal pro-filmic tension and filmic drama, amplifying the 'transnational dynamics, culture and gender politics of life on this border zone'.

'By providing access to adjacent countries and cultures, borders are places not only of transition but also of translation and transgression (Naficy 2001: 240). Printed on the gallery wall at the aforementioned 'Migration and Location' conference, Naficy's words acted as backdrop to the *Tunnel Kids* installation, a visual ethnography by cultural anthropologist Taylor and collaborator/photographer Hickey, working with young Mexican migrant street children in and around the tunnels linking the twin cities of Nogales, Mexico and Nogales, USA. Drawing on material from *Tunnel Kids* (2001), which narrated the everyday lives of a gang called El Barrio Libre, the installation combined portrait photographs taken by Hickey with Hi-8 footage shot by Taylor – the camera operating as a 'fieldwork tool' rather than a central mediating agent. The rawness of the footage, its uneven quality and serendipitous capture of fleeting moments and interactions on both sides of the border is striking. As Taylor suggests, the cavernous and eerie subterranean space of the tunnel symbolised, for members of El Barrio Libre, '"*su tierra*" in the Mexican sense; a home territory; an identity'. Projected on the opposite gallery wall was footage depicting Taylor travelling with a US Immigration Patrol Agent. Clearly edited, and therefore shaped by 'buried stylistic signals' (Vaughan 1999: 62), it places the viewer alongside the anthropologist as he angles his camera to embody the sightline of US Immigration's ongoing 'surveillance' of the border fence. For Taylor, to understand the border is to engage with both sides, 'scene of a complex and shifting political economy'. 'Picturing the Tunnel Kids' sketches a transient, unpredictable terrain wherein migrant teenagers are cast as key characters in a drama punctuated by photographic portraits which, like Jordan's images, are 'co-productions'.

In Alan Grossman and Áine O'Brien's chapter, an interview transcript of conversations with various members of the production team behind the seven-hour documentary television series *The New Americans* (2004), attention is drawn to collective expressions of transmigration and the material and cultural tensions sustaining both the disintegration and reunification of the extended family. Comparative practices of cultural 'bifocality' (Rouse 2002: 163) are meticulously documented over a three-year period, during which new modes of citizenship constitute the focal point of a transnational documentary production. For Rosella Ragazzi, ethnographic film fieldwork in France and Ireland highlights the complex re-negotiation of family life in the 'host' country, viewed through the perspective of the migrant child. In this context, the migrant family and the domestic home function as both site of and vehicle for cultural refuge, protecting former childhood identities in the performance of embodied cultural memory.

The longitudinal documentary *The New Americans* produced by Kartemquin Films, Chicago is a transnational collaboration between five film crews, documenting the stories of immigrant families to the US from their homelands in Nigeria, India, Palestine, the Dominican Republic and Mexico. Grossman and O'Brien's decision to interview the series producers, editors and story directors stemmed partly from what they perceived to be an unexpected and innovative dimension of this televisual production: a persistent anthropological gaze coupled with a dramatic documentary narrative structure, in which transnational migrant families are portrayed as constructing a social process or field, enacted across geographical, political, communal and cultural borders (Glick-Schiller *et al.* 1992). Border-crossing is represented throughout as a collective ritual with contradictory implications for those who occupy diverse positions within circuits of migration. In the Flores family, for example, Ventura (the mother), decides to transplant the family (which has already migrated from Cueramaro, Mexico) from Garden City, Kansas to California to be with her extended family, arguably initiating a 'step-down in the migration cycle'; the backbreaking work of seasonal fieldwork in California stands in stark contrast to what her children could hope to achieve in the Kansas multilingual educational system. *The New Americans* realises Kartemquin's commitment to 'cinematic social inquiry', described by executive producer Gordon Quinn as 'the day-to-day observation of human behaviour and social interaction, the accretion of detail over time', combined with the desire to dramatise a story and reach a wider audience. Interviews with the production team foreground questions surrounding the logistical contingencies and research agendas/strategies shaping preproduction: the collaborative nature of film work with migrant communities; communication with executive producers who have a vision of a collective yet integrated narrative structure (sometimes at odds with individual filmmakers' viewpoints); and the equally taxing ethical demands of editing a multi-perspectival account with all of the possible re-translations entailed.

In 'Migrant Children and the Performance of Memory: Film Fieldwork', Ragazzi addresses the 'double bind' facing young children forced to choose between family allegiances and the demands of a host country. Through comparative participant observational fieldwork in Paris and Dublin, Ragazzi opens up a space 'surrounding' the camera, rather than having the camera 'search' for the event, thus enabling migrant children to tell their own stories. The children's physical journey from one space to another tends to be over-emphasised at the expense of a psychic journey shaped by memory and fantasy; Ragazzi advocates an approach that can hear, see and feel these complex motivations. For the young Chinese girl, Mang Mang, language acquisition in the Paris classroom is acutely bound up with a desire to resist acculturation and retain a fragile sense of cultural identity, and a contrary wish to move towards a new language and culture. Ragazzi documents these subtle moments and silent resistances through long uninterrupted film sequences, constructing a filmic biography of accumulative fragments and mirroring Mang Mang's transitional emotions. The camera style shifts in Dublin, when Ragazzi focuses on a young, recently arrived Algerian migrant, Tahar, who leads the visual anthropologist out of the classroom into the family home. Tahar's biography is embedded in a cluster of diasporic subject positions, entanglements linking layers of intergenerational memory and co-relational expression, seen in various sequences: his grandmother talking about her involvement in the Algerian War of Independence; the observance of family prayers at Ramadan; the family listening to 'Idir's song', a sequence marked by the intimate gaze back to camera, acknowledging the transcultural intricacies underpinning the politics and poetics of a filmic intersubjectivity.

For Harry Browne and Chinedu Onyejelem, the ritual of 'hearing' offers a way to engage with an emergent multiracial public sphere in Ireland and in so doing, initiate a radio aesthetic which will hopefully provoke a form of '*deep listening* … to work toward what might be called agile listening … attuning our ears to listen again to the multiple layers of meaning potentially embedded in the same sound' (Bull & Back 2003: 3). In a radically dissimilar transcultural context and use of medium, David Coplan and Gei Zantzinger are attracted to 'poetic cartograph[ies]' (Feld 2003: 227), creating a cinematic narration of performance of Lesotho mine and factory workers in southern Africa. In both these projects the 'voice is evidence, embodied as experiential authority, performed to the exterior or interior as a subjectivity made public, mirrored in hearing as public made subjective' (2003: 226–7).

Radio has historically encouraged public dialogue in Ireland, producing an audio landscape through which to 'speak' and participate, facilitating expressions previously censored and repressed. Yet in 'Textualising Radio Practice: Sounding Out a Changing Ireland' journalists Browne and Onyejelem argue that the concept of 'voice' is highly contested, given the 'persistently monocultural broadcasting environment' in which immigrant perspectives are all too often tokenised via uncritical celebrations of diversity. *Home from Home* (a combined book and radio work-in-progress) is an attempt to break through this media hegemony. The essentialist concept of 'voice' is rendered problematic, providing a central methodological framework through which to construct a 'life story' documentary structured through a form of biography locating knowledge in the dialectic between individual subjects and social systems. In a sound-based medium such as radio, the temptation has always been to paint an acoustic narrative anchoring social relations in the form of backdrop environments and effects. Browne and Onyejelem's method is to produce a highly-edited sound tape made up of 'what people say' rather than how they say it; their methodology involves piecing words together, with different subject positions brushing against each other and little manipulation in the form of discursive packaging.

In 'Iconology: Exploring the DVD in Southern African Migrant Culture Research', cultural anthropologist Coplan and ethnomusicologist Zantzinger provide a critical engagement with the history of a documentary project as it has evolved across film, photography and presently DVD. *Songs of the Adventurers* (1986) is an ethnographic film engaging with the oral folk performances of (male) Basotho migrant workers in Lesotho, as well as women migrants performing their own sets of stories. Shot on 16mm, the film is part expository, part performative documentary, with an emphasis on translating Coplan's notion of 'metapoetics'. The spatial and temporal images in *difela* poetry move in a circuitous fashion, reflecting the economic migrant's journey from Lesotho to South Africa in a translation of the capitalist infrastructure of the mines – the cables, ore buckets, explosives – into poetic metaphors enacted through the performative gestures of *difela* poets. Turning to the potential of the DVD format two decades later, Zantzinger argues for a move away from voice-over narration, seen in the earlier film, toward a less mediated aesthetic experience for the viewer. Still very much a work-in-progress (presented here as a five-minute sequence), the attempt to translate the extensive film fieldwork into DVD format aims to reconfigure the opaque, submerged ethno-aesthetic in the form of a horizontal (multi-perspectival) narrative, documenting the layers of historical and cultural sedimentation shaping *difela* performance.

The sequential arrangement of the book's chapters does not represent an attempt on our behalf to privilege a particular location, disciplinary focus or media format. Rather, we hope that the cumulative effect of the eleven chapters and their cross-referenced content on the DVD-ROM exemplify the scope and potential of audiovisual practice-based scholarship as a vital, necessary and expanding mode of engagement with migration in its multidimensionality.

Notes

1   Two similarly oriented arts and media practice initiatives were developed in the UK in 2003: 'Field Work: Reports from the Fields of Visual Culture', Victoria Miro Gallery, London, and 'Backup of Field-works: Dialogues between Art and Anthropology' symposium, Tate Modern, London.

2   G. Mirdal and L. Ryynänen-Karjalainen (2004) *Migration and Transcultural Identities (European Science Foundation Standing Committee for the Humanities Forward Look Report 2)*. Available at <http://www.esf.org/publication/184/ICICE.pdf> [Accessed 15 August, 2006].

3   Available at <http://www.ahrb.ac.uk/apply/research/sfi/ahrcsi/diasporas_migration_identities.asp> [Accessed 25 August 2006]. See the important corpus of scholarship by Russell (1999), Marks (2000) and Naficy (2001) for an excellent discussion of the cinematic production of diasporic, exilic, transnational and intercultural identities.

4   *Silent Song* (UK, 2000, 15 min.). Screened at numerous international documentary and cinema and migration film festivals, among others: Turkish Film Festival, London (2000); Arab Mediterranean Film Festival, Edinburgh (2001); UK Refugee Week, Edinburgh (2001); and Taiwan Ethnographic Film Festival, Taipei (2003).

5   These concerns formed a focal point for discussion in a panel we convened titled 'Re-framing Migration through the Prism of Practice-Based Research', Visible Evidence XI Documentary Conference (2003), School of Cultural Studies, University of the West of England. See Hess & Zimmerman (1997; 1999) for compelling discussion of the need to situate documentary practice within a transnationalised cultural economy and digital imaginary.

6   For discussion of the flexible dimensions of citizenship within the logic of transnationalism and related international discourses on human rights, see Sassen (1996) and Ong (1999).

7   See Mirzoeff (2000), King & Wood (2001), Ginsburg *et al.* (2002) and Shohat & Stam (2003) for readings of diasporic visual cultures, media and migration, an anthropology of the media, and the development of a transnational media studies, respectively.

8   This new media practice research economy is further evident in the inauguration of journals foregrounding interdisciplinary questions of theory and practice, for example, the *Journal of Media Practice* and *Visual Studies*. Furthermore, practice-based research is supported and recognised by the Arts and Humanities Research Council (UK) for evaluation under the Research Assessment Exercise (RAE, 2008); relatedly, see the AHRC-funded 'AVPhD: Supporting Doctoral Work in Audio-Visual Practice Research' initiative (www.avphd.gold.ac.uk/about.php), in addition to PARIP – Practice as Research in Performance media (www.bris.ac.uk/parip/introduction.htm).

9   For notable exceptions to this trend, see Martin Rieser and Andrea Zapp's (2002) combined text and DVD-ROM publication on new narrative forms in hypertext, multimedia, interactive broadcast and screen media, together with *Screenworks* (2007), a DVD published in association with the *Journal of Media Practice*, featuring practice-based work in Communication, Media and Cultural Studies, Art and Design, Performing Arts and related fields. For both further discussion and examples in the emerging area of ethnographic/anthropological hypermedia in teaching, learning and academic publishing, see Coover (2003), Pink *et al.* (2002; 2004) and Pink (2006).

10 See also Ginsburg (1998); Ruby (2000); Grimshaw (2001). Referencing Banks & Morphy (1997), Taylor cautions against the uncritical embrace of the pictorial or visual turn in anthropological enquiry, inclined towards the substitution of an 'anthropology *of* the visual for a *visual* anthropology, when in actual fact, the two can very well co-exist, with their respective practices and principles, side by side' (1998: 536).

11 For a useful identification and differentiation of 'transmigration' scenarios and transnational linkages in the context of historical approaches and implementations of multicultural policies in Europe, see Grillo (2001). See Faist (2000) for a discussion of context-specific strategies enacted by transnational migrants.

12 For an ethnographic perspective of a 'grounded globalisation' approach, see Burawoy *et al.* (2000).

13 See MacÉinrí (2003) and Ruhs (2005) for a detailed account of labour immigration flows and policies in Ireland.

14 *Here To Stay* (2006, Ireland, 72 mins) was first screened in the Stranger Than Fiction Documentary

Film Festival, Irish Film Institute, Dublin (September, 2006). Part 2, titled *Between Promise and Unrest* (2008), foregrounds the political agency of a Dublin-based Filipina domestic worker previously a housekeeper in Malaysia, who is one of a growing constituency of Filipinas employed in Irish homes, prone to isolation and vulnerable to the restrictions of the temporary 'work permit'. The film portrays the labour conditions, socio-economic effects of remittance payments to her family in Babatgnon, Philippines, alongside the subject's participation in a 'Domestic Workers Forum' facilitated by a national, rights-based migration NGO. The protagonist's mobility and multiple-situated subject position epitomises the now established feminisation of migration flows (Castles & Miller 1998; Momsen 1999; Willis & Yeoh 2000; Kofman *et al.* 2000), gendered circuits of migration in which transnational motherhood (Hondagneu-Sotelo & Avila 1997) has become an emerging norm in the sending-countries (mostly South), complemented by the breakdown of intergenerational care in the receiving context (predominantly North).

Bibliography

Anzaldúa, G. (1987) *Borderlands/La frontera: The New Mestiza*. San Francisco: Spinsters/Aunt Lute.

Appadurai, A. (2000) 'Grassroots Globalization and the Research Imagination', *Public Culture*, 12 (1): 1–19.

Banks, M. and H. Morphy (eds) (1997) *Rethinking Visual Anthropology*. New Haven: Yale University Press.

Bailey, D. and S. Boyce (2001) '"The Living Archive" Papers', *Third Text*, Spring: 87–8.

Banks, M. (2001) *Visual Methods in Social Research*. London: Sage.

Barber, P. G. (2000) Agency in Phillipine Women's Labour Migration and Provisional Diaspora, *Women's Studies International Forum*, 23(4): 399–411.

Basch, L., N. Glick Schiller and C. Szanton-Blanc (eds) (1994) *Nations Unbound: Transnational Projects, Postcolonial Predicaments, and Deterritorialized Nation-States*. New York: Gordon and Breech.

Bhabha, H. (1994) *The Location of Culture*. London: Routledge.

Bloch, E. (1962) *Heritage of Our Times*. Berkeley: University of California Press. Trans. N. and S. Plaice.

Bourdieu, P. (1977) *Outline of a Theory of Practice*. Cambridge: Cambridge University Press.

_____ (1990) *The Logic of Practice*. Stanford: Stanford University Press.

Brettell, C. and J. Hollifield (eds) (2000) *Migration Theory: Talking Across Disciplines*. London: Routledge.

Buchan, J. (2000) 'Planning for Change: Developing a Policy Framework for Nursing Labour Markets', *International Nursing Review*, 47(4): 199–206.

Bull, M. and L. Back (eds) (2003) *The Auditory Culture Reader*. Oxford: Berg.

Burawoy, M., A. Burton, A. A. Ferguson and K. J Fox (2000) *Global Ethnography: Forces, Connections, and Imaginations in a Postmodern World*. Berkeley: University of California Press.

Caglar, A. (2001) 'Constraining Metaphors and the Transnationalisation of Spaces in Berlin', *Journal of Ethnic and Migration Studies*, 27(4): 601–13.

Castles, S. (2001) 'Studying Social Transformation', *International Political Science Review*, 22(1): 13–32.

_____ (2002) 'Migration and Community Formation under Conditions of Globalization', *International Migration Review*, 36(4): 1143–68.

Castles, S. and M. Miller (1998) *The Age of Migration: International Population Movements in the Modern World*. New York: Palgrave Macmillan.

Clifford, J. (1992) 'Traveling Cultures', in L. Grossberg., C. Nelson. and P. Treichler (eds) *Cultural Studies*.

New York: Routledge.

_____ (2003) *On the Edges of Anthropology*. Chicago: Prickly Paradigm Press.

_____ (1997) *Routes: Travel and Translation in the Late Twentieth Century*. Cambridge: Harvard University Press.

Coover, R. (2003) *Cultures in Webs: Working in Hypermedia with the Documentary Image*. Cambridge: Eastgate.

Emmison, M. and P. Smith (eds) (2000) *Researching the Visual*. London: Sage.

Fabian, J. (1983) *Time and the Other: How Anthropology Makes Its Object*. New York: Columbia University Press.

_____ (2001) *Anthropology With an Attitude: Critical Essays*. Stanford: Stanford University Press.

Faist, T. (2000) *The Volume and Dynamics of International Migration and Transnational Social Spaces*. Oxford: Oxford University Press.

Feld, S. (2003) 'A Rainforest Acoustemology', in M. Bull and L. Back (eds) *The Auditory Culture Reader*. Oxford: Berg.

Feldman, A. (1991) *Formations of Violence: The Narrative of the Body and Political Terror in Northern Ireland*. Chicago: University of Chicago Press.

Foster, H. (1996) *The Return of the Real*. Cambridge, MA: MIT Press.

Ginsburg, F. (1998) 'Institutionalizing the Unruly: Charting a Future for Visual Anthropology', *Ethnos*, 63(2): 173–201.

Ginsburg, F., L. Abu-Lughod and B. Larkin (eds) (2002) *Media Worlds: Anthropology on New Terrain*. Berkeley: University of California Press.

Glick Schiller, N., L. Basch and C. Blanc-Szanton (eds) (1992) *Towards a Transnational Perspective on Migration*. New York: New York Academy of Sciences.

Grillo, R. (2001) 'Transnational Migration and Multiculturalism in Europe'. *Transnational Communities Programme Working Paper Series*, WPTC-01-08.

Grimshaw, A. (2001) *The Ethnographer's Eye: Ways of Seeing in Anthropology*. Cambridge: Cambridge University Press.

_____ (2002) 'Eyeing the Field: New Horizons for Visual Anthropology', *Journal of Media Practice*, 3(1): 2–15.

Grossman, A. and A. O'Brien (2006) 'Kurdish Lyrical Protest: The Terrain of Migration', *Journal of Ethnic and Migration Studies*, 32(2): 271–89.

Guarnizo, L. (1997) 'The Emergence of a Transnational Social Formation and the Mirage of Return Migration of Dominican Tranmigrants', *Identities*, 4(2): 281–322.

Guarnizo, L. and M. Smith (1998) 'The Locations of Transnationalism', in M. Smith and L. Guarnizo (eds) *Transnationalism From Below*. New Brunswick: Transaction Press.

Hall, S. (2001) 'Constituting an Archive', *Third Text*, Spring: 89–92.

Harper, D. (2005) 'What's New Visually?', in N. Denzin and Y. Lincoln (eds) *The Sage Handbook of Qualitative Research* (third edition). London: Sage.

Henley, P. (2000) 'Ethnographic Film: Technology, Practice and Anthropological Theory', *Visual Anthropology*, 13 (3): 207–26.

Hess, J. and P. Zimmerman (1997) 'Transnational Documentaries: A Manifesto', *Afterimage*, 24(4): 10–14.

_____ (1999) 'Transnational Digital Imaginaries', *Wide Angle*, 21(1): 149–67.

Highmore, B. (2002) *The Everyday Life Reader*. London: Routledge.

Hondagneu-Sotelo, P. and E. Avila (1997) '"I'm Here, but I'm There": The Meanings of Latina Transnational Motherhood', *Gender and Society*, 11(5): 548–71.

IOM *World Migration 2005: Costs and Benefits of International Migration*. Available at <http://www.iom.int/iomwebsite/Publication/ServletSearchPublication?event=detail&id=4171> [Accessed 25 August 2005].

Kearney, M. (1995) 'The Local and the Global: The Anthropology of Globalization and Transnationalism', *Annual Review of Anthropology*, 24: 547–65.

King, R. and N. Wood (eds) (2001) *Media and Migration: Constructions of Mobility and Difference*. London: Routledge.

Kofman, E., A. Phizacklea, P. Raghuram and R. Sales (2000) *Gender and International Migration in Europe: Employment, Welfare and Politics*. London: Routledge

Kracauer, S. (1969) *History: The Last Things Before the Last*. Oxford: Oxford University Press.

MacDougall, D. (1998) *Transcultural Cinema*. Princeton: Princeton University Press.

——— (2001) 'Renewing Ethnographic Film: Is Digital Video Changing the Genre?', *Anthropology Today*, 17(3): 15–21.

——— (2006) *The Corporeal Image: Film, Ethnography, and the Senses*. Princeton: Princeton University Press.

MacÉinrí, P. (2003) *Labour Migration into Ireland*. Dublin: Immigration Council of Ireland.

Manalansan IV, Martin F. (2003) *Global Divas: Filipino Gay Men in the Diaspora*. Durham: Duke University Press.

Marcus, G. (1995) 'Ethnography in/of the World System: The Emergence of Multi-Sited Ethnography', *Annual Review of Anthropology*, 24: 95–117.

——— (1998) *Ethnography Through Thick and Thin*. Princeton: Princeton University Press.

Marks, L. (2000) *The Skin of the Film: Intercultural Cinema, Embodiment, and the Senses*. Durham: Duke University Press.

Mirzoeff, N. (ed.) (2000) *Diaspora and Visual Culture: Representing Africans and Jews*. London: Routledge.

Mitchell, W. J. T. (2005) 'There are No Visual Media', *Journal of Visual Culture*, 4(2): 257–66.

Momsen, J. (ed.) (1999) *Gender, Migration and Domestic Service*. London: Routledge.

Moorehead, C. (2006) *Human Cargo: A Journey Among Refugees*. London: Vintage.

Naficy, H. (2001) *Accented Cinema: Exilic and Diasporic Filmmaking*. Princeton: Princeton University Press.

Ong, A. (1999) *Flexible Citizenship: The Cultural Logics of Transnationality*. Durham: Duke University Press.

Papastergiadis, N. (2000) *The Turbulence of Migration*. London: Polity Press.

Pink, S. (2001) *Doing Visual Ethnography*. London: Sage.

——— (2006) *The Future of Visual Anthropology: Engaging the Senses*. London: Routledge.

Pink, S., L. Kürti and A. Afonso (eds) (2002) *Visual Teaching, Virtual Learning: Anthropology and Pedagogy in Europe*, a Special Issue of *Anthropology in Action*.

——— (2004) *Working Images: Visual Research and Representation in Ethnography*. London: Routledge.

Portelli, A. (1998) 'What Makes Oral History Different?', in R. Perks and A. Thompson (eds) *The Oral History Reader*. London: Routledge.

Portes, A. (1998) 'Globalisation from Below: The Rise of Transnational Communities', *Transnational Communities Programme Working Paper Series*, WPTC-98-01.

Prosser, J. (ed.) (1998) *Image-Based Research: A Sourcebook for Qualitative Researchers*. London: Routledge.

Reiser, M. and A. Zapp (eds) (2002) *New Screen Media: Cinema/Art/Narrative*. London: British Film Institute.

Renov, M. (1999) *Collecting Visible Evidence*. Minnesota: Minnesota University Press.

Rogoff, I. (1998) 'Studying Visual Culture', in N. Mirzoeff (ed.) *The Visual Culture Reader*. London: Routledge.

_____ (2004) 'The Where of Now', in J. Morgan and G. Muir (eds) *Time Zones: Recent Film and Video*. London: Tate.

Rose, G. (2001) *Visual Methodologies*. Sage: London.

Rouse, R. (2002) 'Mexican Migration and the Social Space of Postmodernism', in J. Xavier-Inda and R. Rosaldo (eds) *The Anthropology of Globalization: A Reader*. Oxford: Blackwell.

Ruby, J. (2000) *Picturing Culture: Explorations of Film and Anthropology*. Chicago: University of Chicago Press.

Ruhs, M. (2005) *Managing the Immigration and Employment of Non-EU Nationals in Ireland*. Studies in Public Policy No. 19, Dublin. The Policy Institute, Trinity College Dublin.

Russell, C. (1999) *Experimental Ethnography: The Work of Film in the Age of Video*. Durham, NC: Duke University Press.

Sassen, S. (1996) *Losing Control? Sovereignty in an Age of Globalization*. New York: Columbia University Press.

Sekula, A. (1999 [1984]) *Dismantling Modernism, Reinventing Documentary (Notes on the Politics of Representation)*, in *Dismal Science Photo Works 1972-1996*. University Galleries of Illinois State University.

Shohat, E. and R. Stam (eds) (2003) *Multiculturalism, Postcoloniality, and Transnational Media*. New Brunswick: Rutgers University Press.

Seremetakis, C. N. (ed.) (1994a) *The Senses Still: Perception and Memory as Material Culture in Modernity*. Boulder: Westview Press.

_____ (1994b) 'The Memory of the Senses: Historical Perception, Commensal Exchange, and Modernity', in V. Taylor (ed.) *Visualising Theory: Selected Essays From V.A.R. 1990–1994*. New York: Routledge.

Smith, M. P. and L. E. Guarnizo (eds) (1998) *Transnationalism from Below*. New Brunswick: Transaction Press.

Stoller, P. (1997) *Sensuous Scholarship*. Philadelphia: University of Pennsylvania Press.

Taussig, M. (1987) *Shamanism, Colonialism and the Wild Man: A Study in Terror and Healing*. Chicago: University of Chicago Press.

_____ (1993) *Mimesis and Alterity: A Particular History of the Senses*. New York: Routledge

Taylor, L. (ed.) (1994) 'Visualizing Theory Foreword', in *Visualizing Theory: Selected Essays From V.A.R. 1990–1994*. New York: Routledge.

_____ (1996) 'Iconophobia: How Anthropology Lost it at the Movies', *Transition*, 69: 64–88.

_____ (1998) 'Visual Anthropology is Dead, Long Live Visual Anthropology', *American Anthropologist*, 100(2): 534–7.

Thurlow, C. (2006) 'Transcultural Communication: A Treatise on Trans'. Available at <http://faculty.washington.edu/thurlow/research/transculturalcommunication> [Accessed 31 May, 2006].

Vaughan, D. (1999) *For Documentary: Twelve Essays*. Berkeley: University of California Press.

Vertovec, S. (2004) 'Trends and Impacts of Migrant Transnationalism', *Centre on Migration, Policy and Society Working Paper Series*, WP-04-03.

Weber, C. (2000) 'Brecht's Concept of Gestus and the American Performance Tradition', in C. Martin and H. Bial (eds), *Brecht Sourcebook*. London: Routledge.

Willis, K. and B. Yeoh (eds) (2000) *Gender and Migration*. Cheltenham: Edward Elgar.

VIDEO MESSAGING IN CONTEXTS OF FORCED MIGRATION: 'AMPLIFYING' SOCIAL RELATEDNESS ACROSS THE MOZAMBIQUE/SOUTH AFRICA BORDER

Graeme Rodgers and Andrea Spitz

INTRODUCTION

High-quality digital video technology is becoming more accessible, affordable and 'user-friendly' to a larger public market. This new potential appears to be finding particular resonance amongst migrant and diaspora communities, who are increasingly incorporating video into their strategies for confronting the everyday stresses and challenges of geographical separation. The documentary series entitled *The Last Peasants* (2003) shows how Romanian migrants used 'home videos' to maintain a social presence in their home areas in rural Romania whilst they engaged in risky and often unprecedented attempts to extend their livelihoods beyond the village and into the urban centres of western Europe.[1] Similarly, Ann-Belinda Steen Preis (1997) has shown how Sri Lankan Tamil refugees in Denmark exchanged home videos with relatives in Sri Lanka and used these to generate a social presence through the recognition and performance of physical absence. Researchers and filmmakers have begun to recognise the potential use of video as a tool to try to elicit further the experience of exile. In Mai Masri's documentary video, *Children of Shatila* (1998), Palestinian refugee children were given video cameras to record their own experiences of daily life in Beirut. In all cases, video emerges as a powerful format for revealing the personal, social and cultural implications of the forms of separation and displacement that are becoming so characteristic of a globalised world.

This chapter examines the deliberate introduction of video messaging between Mozambicans settled across the Mozambique/South Africa border, in the areas of Massingir and Timbavati respectively. We used video not simply to document or represent these relationships, but to provoke their expression in a form that could be accessed, observed and analysed. Video therefore emerged as a tool for 'amplifying' disrupted social relationships. Expressions of social relatedness, which emerged through the intrusion of our video messaging service, constituted 'data' that was analysed anthropologically as well as 'footage' for a television documentary entitled *Voices Across the Fence* (2002).[2] At every point in the process, the participants were aware of the broader aims of the project and were willing to participate, even knowing that their messages might be broadcast on television.

The chapter is structured as follows. The section immediately below describes and reflects on the process of video messaging. In comparing two 'rounds' of collecting and screening video messages we describe how a 'leaner', less intrusive approach yielded more expressive, spontaneous and passionate messages. After outlining our process we proceed into a more detailed exploration of the social implications of this technique through selected case studies – 'characters' within the documentary film. Finally, we discuss the more general potential of this technique as a response to forced migration, both as a 'research tool' for improving our understanding of the phenomenon of forced migration and as a 'development tool' for structuring and informing positive developmental interventions. Using video to explore the responses of Mozambican refugees from war to the ongoing transnational relationships into which they were thrust produces, particularly in the post-war context, information in a form that is, we argue, not only palatable to policy makers and development organisations, but also demanding of more locally appropriate official responses to the issue of transnational migration in the African context.

VIDEO DYNAMICS: REFLECTIONS ON THE MESSAGING PROCESS

A collaborative effort between a filmmaker and an anthropologist, the video messaging technique that we describe here developed as a joint product of our somewhat diverse interests. Over a number of years, Andy Spitz had experimented with film as a 'tool for development', mainly in the environmental impact assessment (EIA) arena. Her work examined how video could both document the opinions and concerns of affected communities, 'specialists' and government authorities, and bring these together on the same platform, with equal weighting, for decision-makers.[3] In addition, Andy's primary focus was on making the highly technical information usually contained in voluminous EIA reports accessible to illiterate and semi-literate communities affected by these developments, so that their participation in the process would be an informed one and not participation in name only. Andy's approach to filmmaking highlights the presence of the camera in a gentle yet self-conscious way, acknowledging the presence and impact of the filmmaker without distracting from the focus of the film.

Over the same period, Graeme Rodgers had conducted fairly localised anthropological research amongst Mozambican refugees in South Africa, largely using the techniques of conventional participant observation. Fieldwork on both sides of the border led him to appreciate the importance of transnational relationships in sustaining the everyday lives, both of refugees and of their relatives living in their villages of origin. To get some sense of the nature and significance of these everyday cross-border relationships, he spent the latter part of his research transporting audio messages between families. This unplanned research strategy was improvised in the field and undertaken using a small portable cassette recorder with a built-in microphone. In discussing Graeme's research and experiences we decided to take this messaging approach one technological step further and introduce video messages that would enable people to see each other and present aspects of themselves, their environments and social lives to relatives on the other side of the border. We were also interested in documenting these relationships visually and then subjecting the message content and presentation, as well as participants' responses, to an anthropological analysis that highlighted the extent to which everyday practice shaped the border environment.

We collected footage for *Voices Across the Fence* over two separate trips, in 2000 and 2001. Each trip involved arranging and then recording video messages in the Timbavati area; 'dumping' these on to VHS and organising them for screening in Mozambique; embarking on the twelve-hour journey to the Massingir area; tracking down and screening messages to recipients in various villages located across the district; arranging and recording responses; returning to Timbavati and screening responses; and finally discussing the issues and process with the Mozambicans who participated in the project. At all stages the process was supplemented by interviews and numerous informal discussions with participants. This was done to clarify relationships and collect more background on the issues that were raised in the messages.

The first trip in 2000 was highly experimental and done on an excruciatingly slim budget, put together from leftover research funding and our own resources. The 'crew' included Andy, Graeme and Freddy Mathabela. Freddy had worked with Andy on a documentary film, *Environments of Post Modernity* (1994), as a 'fixer', using his intimate knowledge of people and relationships in the community to facilitate access to traditional healers, poachers, conservationists and community leaders. He had also worked closely with Graeme during the late 1990s, conducting research in the villages and refugee settlements on which we focused. Graeme's previous research presence in Timbavati and Massingir was important in facilitating our entry to the residents who were familiar with the practice of sending messages through him and were eager for the opportunity to have their messages sent through video. This familiarity meant we could record people's messages in their own home environments with relative ease. It also meant that screening the messages in Massingir would be made easier as we would generally know the exact villages, homesteads and families to visit.

Our equipment included one small digital video camera (Canon XL1) with tripod and sound equipment, a standard television set and videocassette recorder. To ensure that we could recharge camera batteries at a sufficient rate, we also hired a petrol generator from a local funeral parlour, which needed constant provoking to get it into action. As a backup source of power we also took a static inverter along – a device that steps up the voltage of a car battery from 12 volts to 220 volts, enabling the use of some lower-powered electrical devices. We also collected various other items along the way, such as a large plastic sheet that was useful in shading the television during daylight screenings when visibility was otherwise difficult.

As well as directing, Andy operated the camera and controlled sound levels. She shot using available light and mostly 'hand-held'. The effect of this was to produce footage with a 'gritty' feel that constantly reminded the viewer of the presence of the camera. Graeme and Freddy, who had no previous experience of the equipment or the filmmaking process, doubled up as boom operators. Their inexperience is evident occasionally when the microphone 'dips into shot', or when the sound fades mysteriously, as the boom follows the gaze of the camera rather than the source of the sound. 'Message senders' were given little by way of direction. They generally positioned themselves where they wished and 'structured' the messages themselves. Prior to recording, the crew knew little of the content of the messages or the manner in which they would be performed. On some occasions, message senders would walk off unexpectedly, for example to show off their homesteads to their relatives on the other side of the border. A hand-held camera was rather more apt to respond effectively on such occasions. On one occasion, a young man in a refugee settlement produced a pistol unexpectedly in the middle of sending a message and waved it about as he emphasised to his family in Mozambique his ability to protect himself from the dangers of '*Jhoni*'.[4] On our return in 2001 we were told that this man had been killed in a motor accident. Our agreed approach on this first shoot was, as far as possible, to allow the environment to dictate the pace and focus of what we captured, in line with

Graeme's more general 'participant observation' approach. The result was sound and footage of varying quality with content rich in spontaneity and integrity.

Messages were filmed on mini-DV tapes and then transferred directly from the camera on to VHS, using the video recorder. For playback convenience we collated the messages according to individual or family recipients and broad village or settlement areas in which the recipients lived. The VHS tapes, used for screening purposes, were played through the video recorder that was linked up to the television. Although we could have played the messages directly from the camera, we wanted the camera to remain available to record people's responses to the messages. It was also more convenient to locate the correct messages quickly on a VHS tape, by simply using the counter on the video recorder. The 'rawness' of our approach to both the shooting and the screening of the first round of messages was a function of our experimental attitude as well as our commitment to preserving the spontaneity of the messages. A small crew, simple and relatively unobtrusive equipment, and a short 'start-up' time from arrival to recording or screening meant that messages could be collected and screened with a minimum of fuss. This relationship between the simplicity of our process and the spontaneity, passion and dramatic expression of the messages was noticeably evident when we compare the dynamics of the first and second trips.

The second trip took place in 2001 – about a year after the first. In the interim, Andy had used the footage from the first trip to secure a commission for a half-hour documentary from a South African television station.[5] This trip was undertaken on a marginally better budget and with a broadcast quality documentary film as a clear objective.[6] Our crew expanded to include Eran Tahor and Sean Moloi, a professional director of photography and sound recordist respectively. Extra crew and an explicit concern over the quality of images collected meant extra equipment. Eran used a rather imposing Sony 500 camera for recording the message-making process and capturing images for inclusion into descriptive scenes in the film, whilst Andy continued to use her smaller Canon XL1 to record the messages. To work in variable light conditions we used a 400-watt light that required a constantly running generator to keep it powered. To improve sound quality we used a sound mixer, two radio microphones and a directional microphone, this time operated by a professional sound person. In addition to collecting video messages, we also had to concentrate on collecting 'cut aways' and interviews, which would be necessary to edit our footage into a coherent film. Concern over the quality of the footage collected meant that some messages had to be 're-shot', for example when light conditions deteriorated or when the sound was contaminated by a distracting noise. Some messages were therefore repeated and only recorded to completion on a second or third 'take'.

Amongst the crew, different roles and responsibilities, experiences, relationships to the local environment and personalities, combined with tough working conditions, meant that interpersonal tension was inevitable during the shoot. Eran, for example, had a lot of experience in shooting fictional work in highly-controlled environments and an eye for composition and light that brought out the textures of the refugee environment with an aesthetic finesse. However, his highly specialised role in the team made him less open to an appreciation of Graeme's broader and ongoing ethnographic project, out of which the film had grown, and of the sensitivity and complexity of the relationships that sustained the project. While Andy was as sensitive to the broader project as Graeme, she had to balance this against the need to produce sufficient and appropriate material for a 'final product' and was also responsible for keeping a diverse crew happy under uncomfortable conditions. Aware of the importance of his role as a cultural and linguistic intermediary between the crew and the participants in the project, Freddy's naturally enthusiastic personality led him constantly to push the crew to pick up the pace of their work and capture as much of the social context as possible. It was only after the event that the crew was able to recall with amusement Freddy waking us all before first light to begin filming the morning after a gruelling sixteen-hour day of travelling. Sean's quiet professionalism and rather more relaxed personality helped balance the pace at which we conducted the ten-day shoot.

Although an arguably higher percentage of 'usable' footage was collected on the second trip, those of us who were on both trips (Andy, Graeme and Freddy) all felt that, in general, the messages from the first trip seemed more animated and pressing. It is difficult to know exactly why this was the case; factors such as the novelty of the process and the pent-up urgency to send information may have contributed. However, our expanded crew and our focus on producing a documentary film, as opposed to simply collecting messages, certainly had an effect. The larger, more imposing crew directed the focus away from the content and performance of the message to the production of an image of it. Unlike the first trip, message-senders were connected to radio microphones, positioned in front of backgrounds that were not necessarily their choice and generally given greater direction in the delivery of the message, in order to sustain the quality of the recording.

Over the two trips we gathered and screened over 120 messages in total. The length of messages ranged from a few seconds to over 30 minutes. Most messages involved extending greetings to individuals and families on the other side of the border and presenting news relating to births, deaths, employment and other family matters. In some cases messages highlighted disputes over cattle, land, bridewealth and roles and responsibilities within families settled across the border. In some cases, as shown below, the matters raised and debated in the messages were considered by the participants to be extremely serious. Some messages were presented in rather a cryptic fashion, suggesting that the message senders were able to decide how they wanted to use this new medium to their best advantage. These messages gave little by way of background to an outside viewer and were therefore screened to recipients, but generally not considered for the final film. Responses to the messages were diverse and ranged from cold and formal, to highly emotional. Large crowds of villagers, often not closely related to the recipient families and individuals, sometimes turned up, their interest apparently sustained by a combination of curiosity and entertainment aroused by the novelty of the medium.

The documentary was commissioned as a 24-minute programme. We therefore needed to be highly selective in what we took from the more than thirty hours of footage. A deciding factor in choosing the 'characters' on which we focused was that they should have participated in both rounds of filming. This would allow an audience a greater depth of understanding even if the messages were mere glimpses of life captured at the times of filming. We also selected stories that highlighted what we identified as relatively 'universal' themes to which viewers from a broad range of backgrounds would be able to relate. After presenting some brief background to the social and historical contexts of Timbavati and Massingir, the remainder of this chapter focuses on these characters and their stories.

BACKGROUND TO *VOICES ACROSS THE FENCE*: MASSINGIR AND TIMBAVATI

The dramatis personae in *Voices Across the Fence* hailed from socially connected sites on both sides of the Mozambique/South Africa border. Most of the participants in South Africa lived in a refugee settlement on the periphery of Timbavati village. This informal refugee settlement developed from the late 1980s onwards, after people arrived in large numbers seeking refuge from war and drought. Most walked the 120 kilometres across the vast and dangerous Kruger National Park,[7] from remote rural parts of the Massingir district of Mozambique. Whilst South Africa's apartheid government refused to recognise the Mozambicans as international refugees, some self-governing 'homeland' authorities (mainly village chiefs) permitted refugees to settle informally on the peripheries of rural villages (see Rodgers 1996).

The members of the South African 'host community' in Timbavati amongst whom the refugees settled were also mainly Tsonga-speaking. Most were descendants of refugees who had fled various waves of political turmoil that had defined the political landscape in nineteenth-century Mozambique. As well as language, many refugees and hosts shared the same surnames and clan identities, and consequently associated senses of emplacement and traditional belonging in Mozambique. Some Mozambicans and South Africans could even trace discernible kinship links. Mozambicans who crossed into South Africa in the 1980s were therefore incorporated not simply as international refugees but as 'relatives' (*maxaka*) who had sought refuge more recently than the local host communities. The remote and underdeveloped parts of Mozambique from which the refugees originated stood out in sharp contrast to what both refugees and hosts experienced as the 'modernity' (*xilungu*) of rural life in South Africa (see Rodgers 2002).

The Timbavati area comprises a number of large, densely settled and interconnected villages around the town of Acornhoek. The infrastructure of Acornhoek, a bustling commercial centre, includes a railway station, a large training hospital and a police station. Settlement patterns were shaped by the policies of apartheid (see de Wet 1995). In the 1960s residents were involuntarily relocated from scattered settlements into denser residential areas, ostensibly to promote more efficient and sustainable land-use practices. The effect, however, was that most people lost land and local peasant production was almost totally destroyed (Niehaus 2001). Fieldwork conducted in the 1990s revealed that very few residents had access to land beyond their residential stands. A shortage of grazing land and rampant stock theft meant that few kept substantial herds of cattle or goats. Most households survived on combinations of migrant remittances, old age pensions, local employment and entrepreneurial opportunities and household-based agriculture and gardening.

In contrast to the hustle and bustle of the Timbavati area, the district of Massingir appeared as 'on the margins' and 'out of the way'. A dam, begun by the Portuguese colonial regime and not completed in the post-independence era, and a tarred road, built to connect the dam to the agricultural centre of Chokwe, comprised the district's only major infrastructure. Colonial development in Massingir seemed limited by its natural environment and location; it was too dry, sandy and remote to elicit significant levels of colonial interest. A weak colonial presence produced relations premised on violent forms of exploitation, typically of land, labour and women. Following independence, an administrative centre located close to the dam wall was the social and economic focal point of the district. It sustained a small market (selling chiefly South African goods) that was becoming increasingly encased by a peri-urban periphery, as more people moved to the district centre in search of economic opportunities. This marginal characteristic of Massingir was exacerbated by the war. Scattered villages and homesteads that characterised the countryside were effectively depopulated and destroyed during the war, permitting nature to reclaim its own (to paraphrase the narratives of many Massingir residents).

Tension between the modernity (*xilungu*) of South Africa (*Jhoni*) and the traditionalism (*xintu*) of Mozambique emerged as a central narrative in the refugees' struggles to confront their dynamic post-war environment. Most people seemed unable to abandon one side of the border for the other and, through a range of practices and relationships, straddled their livelihoods and identities across the borderlands. The video, and the research from which it emerged, highlighted this tension in the lives of the Mozambicans, not as a pragmatic hurdle that needed to somehow be overcome, but as an historically entrenched and integral aspect of social life in this part of the world. For Mozambicans in Massingir and Timbavati, South Africa and Mozambique stood alongside each other as 'not merely a dualized but an interacting doubleness of epistemology, two universes apart, each requiring the other, each demolishing the other' (Taussig 1987: 196).

CENTRAL CHARACTERS: PERFORMANCE AND CONTEXT

The central characters of *Voices Across the Fence* included two elderly men exchanging light-hearted banter across the border, a woman – stranded in South Africa by her husband – appealing to relatives in Mozambique for assistance to return, and a dying man cursing his neglectful relatives in the South African refugee settlements. None of these could be described as typical scenarios or as representative of broader patterns of behaviour or social exchange. They did, however, reveal something of the nature of these complex transnational social relationships in a way that rendered them intelligible within the framework of a documentary and accessible to anthropological analysis.

The possibilities offered by the use of video did not necessarily coincide with predicaments in the lives of those being filmed; rather, we captured snippets of people's lives at moments that were arbitrary to them. These snippets were further whittled down to fit into the format, time limits and storyline of a documentary video. Despite the limited and haphazard conditions of their production, video messages opened an important 'window' into the lives of a few Mozambican refugees struggling to negotiate the post-war environment and revealed something of the nature of their predicaments. Each of the following case studies summarises the essence of a few message encounters, considers how these were portrayed in *Voices Across the Fence* and reflects critically on some of the more detailed lifeworlds that were both suggested and partially masked by the video messages.

Case study 1: Philemon, Omar and the Power of Tradition

Philemon was an elderly man who lived in Timbavati refugee settlement with his two wives and some of his children and grandchildren. The family originated from an area called Nyangweni, in the Massingir district of Mozambique. Philemon's father, Nambretti, was buried in the area and his grave was still discernible (an important symbolic marker of belonging). During the tumultuous political processes of the nineteenth century, his grandfather, Mswazi, had exerted the most important influence over the area, entrenching the claim of the Mongoe clan over this 'country' (*tiko*). Even in the poverty-stricken context of a refugee settlement, Philemon Mongoe stood as a powerful symbol of tradition.

Prior to the 1970s, Philemon worked frequently as a migrant worker in the South African mines. Like most men of his generation, going to *Jhoni* (Johannesburg) was part of an important rite of passage into manhood. Apart from being a symbolic assertion of strength and independence, migrant labour also provided men with the means to marry (through bridewealth exchanges) and establish their own homesteads (*muti*). Philemon knew the gold fields of the Free State and the urban metropolis of Johannesburg intimately. From his rickety plastic chair under a large wild fig tree in Timbavati he frequently recalled, in the many interviews we held with him, the layout of Johannesburg as the city must have appeared in the 1950s and 1960s.

Back in Mozambique Philemon was, in his own words, a 'chief'. Following the achievement of independence from Portuguese colonial rule in 1975, the residents of Nyangweni were relocated from their scattered settlements into the 'communal village' (*aldeas communal*) of Xivovo, in accordance with the post-independence Frelimo government's pursuit of a policy of agrarian development governed by socialist principles. Despite the unpopularity of this initiative, the residents of Nyangweni complied, as was the case across most of Gaza Province (see Roesch 1992). Life was uncomfortable in Xivovo. The village was far away from a reliable water supply, residents felt constrained by their new and unfamiliar settlement arrangements and the promised government support was deflected by an encroaching war that was to destroy and depopulate the rural countryside. In 1985, Xivovo was attacked and destroyed by Renamo (then an anti-communist movement, later a conservative political party). Philemon fled to South Africa, a place he knew well. He was one of the earlier Mozambicans to settle in Timbavati, which was why he was able to rebuild his homestead around the large wild fig tree, the shade of which gave highly enviable comfort from the searing summer heat. Omar Ndlovu, Philemon's brother-in-law, who also lived in Nyamgweni and Xivovo, fled to Massingir town, where a government military unit that had been deployed to protect the Massingir dam from sabotage also offered some protection to the local population.

The next time that Philemon and Omar saw one another was almost fifteen years later, on our video monitor. Over the years they had kept in touch in a rather basic way through information passed along by migrants, refugees and returnees who traversed the border landscape. In response to the new opportunities to communicate with each other with a degree of eloquence guaranteed by technology, the two men resorted to light-hearted nostalgia and banter. These sets of exchanges made clear Philemon's sense of longing and his commitment to return to Mozambique and Omar's encouragement and support.

Voices Across the Fence highlighted the endurance of Philemon and Omar's relationship over highly disrupted experiences of time, space and everyday life as two old men talking about elephants. It conveys footage of Philemon expressing concern over rumours that elephants were taking over his ancestral territory of Nyangweni. Omar responds by urging him to return, to protect his place from elephants. Rosia, Philemon's sister and

Omar's wife, joined in the discussion at one point, suggesting that the elephants would disappear if Philemon were to return. The two men also showed off their homesteads to each other. Philemon stressed that they were not sitting idly in South Africa – they were making children to replace the one's killed by Renamo. Omar showed off an impressive herd of cattle that he was re-establishing in the wake of the war, no doubt knowing that his brother-in-law was unlikely to be able to do the same from the South African side. [DVD REF 1: VIDEO]

The light-hearted display of nostalgia and fantasy conveyed through *Voices Across the Fence* conceals a tactical use of humour and its performance in the contexts created by our video messaging service. Philemon was elderly, sickly, almost completely dependent on his employed sons for support and therefore unlikely to ever return to Mozambique. The security of his everyday life depended strongly on his ability to wield the authority of tradition within the modern environs of South Africa. As the bearer of traditional authority, he needed to assert his vital links to the ancestors, the source of good fortune and collective well-being. But his position as the traditional head of the homestead was at odds with his economic dependence on his sons, a constant reminder of his being out of place.

Omar Ndlovu was in a similarly ambiguous position. As one who remained in Mozambique during the war, he was responsible for looking after the interests of his relatives in their absence. Although still depopulated after the war, Nyangweni was where Omar occasionally hunted, collected medicinal herbs and once tried to plant a crop of maize – which, as it turned out, was destroyed by elephants. In the post-war era, contest over access to land was common in Mozambique and 'tradition' (*xintu*) was an important basis upon which to claim authority and entitlement.[8] Omar's presence and authority over the land was intimately entwined in his complex relationship with senior men from the Mongoe clan, such as Philemon. By pleading for Philemon to return and light-heartedly elaborating on the importance of that return (through messages that were up to 30 minutes in length), Omar was reconstituting the ideological framework of 'tradition', upon which he depended so strongly.

The Philemon/Omar sequences in the film highlight the rather general themes of friendship, humour and a sense of belonging to place and community. Despite our commitment to letting the material 'speak for itself', these themes were emphasised deliberately in the editing process of *Voices Across the Fence*, precisely because we regarded them as being more accessible to a broader television audience. Within the 26 minutes we had to 'play with', we could not accommodate the full complexity of this relationship, as situated within the cultural and social environments of Timbavati and Massingir. Though we consciously sought to explore and highlight the particularity of exile in this context, through highly personal cross-border narratives that were as uncontrolled and unprovoked by us as possible, much of this 'depth' ended up being 'edited out' in the interest of accessing a broader audience. Some of the material, although interesting from an anthropological perspective, did not 'fit into' a film, either because the quality of the visual image was not high enough or because the content of the narrative was too convoluted or confusing for an outside audience to access quickly enough. Unlike more conventional anthropological analyses that have words and time to explore these processes in depth, we quite literally did not have the 'space' for too much anthropological detail in the final cut of the film.

Case study 2: Rauletta, Majavula and the Betrayal

Whilst walking through Timbavati settlement arranging our messaging schedule, we were approached by Rauletta Malungane, who asked us if she could send a message to Mozambique. As she had not participated in Graeme's research, we had no background information on her against which to interpret the video messages. We therefore agreed though with some reluctance, because we knew that we would have a full schedule. Later, we discovered that Rauletta was a recently-arrived 'younger mother'[9] of Lizi Nyathi, who was a well-established participant in our project. The following day, when the sun was high and the contrast and shadows were strong, making filming against back-light difficult, we arrived to record Rauletta's message. Rauletta stood in front of her one-roomed, mud-brick house, wearing a delicately threadbare blouse, with her young daughter at her side. Andy positioned the camera directly in front of her – 'hand-held' to save time and on the assumption that this 'footage' was unlikely to make it into the 'final cut' of the documentary that was still a vague possibility in our minds at that stage. Attempts to shoot the previous messages from a tripod had proved difficult as some message senders moved around spontaneously, as they generated their unrehearsed messages. When everyone was ready, Freddy shouted 'action!' as he was becoming inclined to do. Rauletta stood motionless. We waited a few seconds for her to begin and only when Freddy prompted her in Tsonga to proceed, she began. After a brief pause she launched into a song, which she had composed to express the problems that she was experiencing in South Africa. Between haunting melodic repetitions of 'I have hardship' ('ni mashangoa'), Rauletta summarised her complex and dire predicament. She alluded to the difficulty of life in Timbavati and spoke of how her husband, Majavula, had abandoned her in South Africa, in favour of another woman, with whom he had returned to Mozambique. [DVD REF 2: VIDEO]

Despite some rather vague and localised references to 'civics'[10] and headmen, Rauletta's performance was so strong, desperate, visually engaging and universally touching that we used it in the opening message sequence in *Voices Across the Fence*. A more coherent sense of her predicament began to emerge once she had finished singing and, almost without taking a breath, launched into a desperate cry for help from Mozambique. (As footage for *Voices Across the Fence*, this segment was too long, too detailed and too backlit to make it into the final cut.) Addressing her husband, Rauletta proclaimed:

You Majavula, your in-laws are saying that at their home you think there are no men … I am strongly requesting, in this month [she spits on the ground], before this spit dries, Anika must be back. Anika has taken my place and you don't love me anymore. Please tell me but please look after my children. I am left only with this child but I will send her with people with cars and I, the person whom you do not love, will stay here … So don't throw me away. I have my father and I can go to Maduzana to stay at the family, instead of you throwing me away. In this country they kill people. I am dead! I am dead! [starts unbuttoning her blouse] Your child Marta is still alive [referring to the by now terrified little girl standing next to her] but look at me! I am getting thin because I am worried. I will die [ripping her blouse open]. I don't know what will kill me but I will die. You are staying there [in

Mozambique] sitting comfortably, eating well – good food. Meanwhile, regarding myself, sometimes they chase me and I run away and stay in the bush.

Majavula's 'in-laws', referred to by Rauletta, were actually the husband and in-laws of Anika, his new 'wife', whom he had taken to Mozambique. Anika, as it turned out, was a married South African woman who was apprenticed to Majavula as a traditional healer. Majavula had taken Anika with him to Mozambique shortly after Rauletta had arrived in South Africa. In their attempt to get her back, Anika's family had threatened to harm Rauletta, hence the involvement of the headmen and the 'civics'. To Anika, the 'wife' whom Majavula had 'stolen', Rauletta emphasised:

> You Anika! You Anika!! [angrily] Anika, look after my children after you have married into that house. I am not trying to stop your marriage. I have already spoken to you and urged you to return to Phalaborwa to say goodbye to your family. Then you can go back to Mozambique. I won't have a problem. Even if I remain in *Jhoni* I have no problem. After they arrived here … if there were no civic or *tinduna* (village headmen) I don't know what would have happened to me…

At the end of the message Rauletta had become so worked up that she yelled at her daughter for being too terrified to send a message of her own to her father.

Rauletta's message provoked a highly emotional response from her relatives in Massingir, especially Majavula's first wife, who responded with a series of strong supportive messages, and Rauletta's older children, who were understandably upset by their mother's performance and frequent references to death. [DVD REF 3: VIDEO] Majavula and Anika, however, were not in the village when we arrived and therefore did not see the message. However, enough people in the village did see the message to ensure that he would have been informed in detail.

Soon after completing this round of messages, we were surprised to hear from people in Timbavati that Rauletta had returned to Mozambique shortly after the screening of her message. When we conducted the second round of video messaging just over a year later, she was still in Mozambique. We arrived at her home unannounced at 11p.m. and she welcomed us, immediately setting about clearing a space alongside a cattle byre in front of her home for us to set up camp. We told her of the messages we had brought from Timbavati and settled in for the night. Barely five hours later, at first light, our exhausted cameraman was woken and told that Rauletta was ploughing a patch of garden nearby and should be filmed. Her determined and forceful effort at driving the yoked cattle forward, the single-bladed plough churning the soil, stood out in sharp contrast to the quivering image of desperation that she conveyed a year earlier. [DVD REF 4: VIDEO]

Reflecting on the impact of her earlier video message, Rauletta was adamant that it played an important role in her being able to return to Mozambique. From her home in Massingir, she sent the following in a video message to Lizi Nyathi, her co-wife's daughter in Timbavati:

> I thank the TV people who have arrived here. Even for the first time, when they brought my message here. The day that I arrived here at home, it was full of people

who had come to see the sufferer. The people came like they were coming to a funeral … So it was me who was suffering in the country of [Timbavati]. I was caught by my husband.

The social consequences of Rauletta's betrayal extended far beyond her personal predicament. Video messaging could not obviously capture the full extent of the case but gave a unique 'window', particularly into the transnational dynamics, culture and gender politics of life on this border zone.

Case study 3: Nyankwavi, Death and Family

When we left Timbavati with video messages for Massingir in 2000, we were warned that Nyankwavi might already be dead by the time we arrived. As a senior patriarch of a large family in Massingir, and an in-law of Philemon Mongoe, Graeme and Freddy had come to know Nyankwavi through their previous anthropological research. His steady decline in health over a number of years had reached the point where his relatives in South Africa were no longer certain if he was alive or dead.

Although the severity of Nyankwavi's condition was known, the messages sent to his homestead in Massingir from his sister's homestead in Timbavati were uncomfortably jovial. Jane Nyathi, Nyankwavi's niece, boasted unashamedly about the beautiful house she lived in, the commercially-produced food she ate and the wonderful life she was living. Her brother, Kwaar, who was roaring drunk on the day we recorded his message to his relatives in Massingir, expressed a similar sentiment. After shoving a beer bottle in front of the camera to prove that he was drunk on bottled lager rather than home-brewed beer, he produced a mobile phone, suggesting that his relatives would not be familiar with such a sophisticated device and taunting them with their backwardness. [**DVD REF 5: VIDEO**] The enthusiasm generated by the messages culminated in the whole family coming together and, following the lead of a young boy, erupting into repeated renderings of 'God is a good God, yeah' (in English) to a modern, distinctively South African 'kwaito' beat.

The message was received in shocked and angry silence by Nyankwavi's family in Massingir. Nyankwavi was still alive and had been carried out of his house to watch the greetings from family on the other side. He was placed lying down on the floor in front of the television set, a thin blanket covering his withering limbs. While the messages were still playing Nyankwavi started to gasp out his response. He was angry and bitter. The camera, which was filming general responses to the screening, focused on him and the microphone was brought in close to isolate his soft voice from the sound coming out of the television in front of him. He criticised his relatives with embittered vulgarity and suggested that following his death they would suffer for their socially neglectful 'modern' lifestyle in South Africa and – which was not necessarily obvious to a cultural outsider – that his spirit would plague them. [**DVD REF 6: VIDEO**] Such a suggestion was taken very seriously in the Timbavati/Massingir context. Realising this, the video messaging team felt some concern over the ethics and impact of being the 'bearers' of such bad news. In the end we decided to show the message that essentially conveyed a curse. Numerous discussions afterwards with Nyankwavi's family in Timbavati led us to the conclusion that, despite the seriousness of the content, people still appreciated seeing Nyankwavi and hearing his words and did not feel that the video aggravated the problem.

We heard later that Nyankwavi died in 2000, shortly after our filming of his message. Kwaar, the drunken nephew who had provoked so much anger from Nyankwavi, was motivated to travel to Massingir and pay his respects to the immediate family. Subsequent messages suggest that this was intended to alleviate some of the tensions between the two groups of relatives, but some bitterness was still expressed by Nyankwavi's son and daughter, Robert and Joyce Ngoveni, in the next round of messages. [DVD REF 7: VIDEO]

As in the other cases, *Voices Across the Fence* was unable to explore the full significance of this set of interactions within the constraints of a half-hour documentary film. The film could not really go further than to convey the tension created by what seemed to be a series of inappropriately light and selfish responses to the death of an old man. For the purposes of anthropological analysis, it does, however, highlight the power of the spirits of the dead in a world that had, in many ways, been turned upside down.

CONCLUSION: THE POTENTIALS AND PITFALLS OF VIDEO MESSAGING

In a social context where the transnational flow of information was curtailed by geography, poverty and illiteracy, the appearance, however briefly, of our video messaging project both recorded and affected the lives of those who became involved. Some of the characters in the film participated willingly and actively, while others were implicated without their knowledge or consent, as in the case of the ever-absent Majavula, Rauletta's husband. Our professional identites as 'filmmaker' and 'anthropologist', and more particularly our possession of passports and access to resources, enabled us to cross the border with an ease that the participants could only envy. Our movements, and our video cameras, not only highlighted but were also dependent on their 'discomforts of localized existence' (Bauman 1998: 2). Thus, despite the way in which we intended to use video, our relationships remained, to some extent, colonial in character.

Darcus Howe, a well-known British-based filmmaker and social critic who assisted in developing *Voices Across the Fence* at the start of the television commissioning process, was highly critical of the concept. He maintained that it was inevitably exploitative, voyeuristic and akin to 'opening other people's mail'. The charge of voyeurism needs to be considered carefully. To what extent would people have 'opened up' if they had not been so desperate to make use of the 'window of opportunity' that our 'message service' represented? Numerous subsequent visits to Timbavati suggest that people were less concerned with the voyeuristic dimension than one might expect. Perhaps it was because there was very little about their lives that they reserved as private. In this part of the world, secrecy and solitude may be interpreted as signs of witchcraft, jealousy and other forms of social mischief (see Niehaus 2001). Among the Mozambicans, where literacy rates were low, the production and consumption of letters was often a highly public group effort. The public form of the information that we transported back and fore across the border was therefore not at odds with established local practices.

Despite our control over collecting, transporting and broadcasting these images, the participants in the project were never completely subjected to the power of the 'gaze' of the camera lens. As writers such as Ernest Goffman (1961) and Michel Foucault (1986) have noted in contexts characterised by even more extreme power relations, resistance is always possible. Although neither framed nor necessarily experienced as *resistance*, 'coded' and overtly convoluted messages were 'packaged' in such a way as to make them inaccessible to the outsider and therefore impractical as footage for a television programme. Such silences, absences and insinuations, finding expression through people's engagement with the video messaging process, may nevertheless be highly revealing of the nature of social relationships. The most obvious example of the 're-appropriation' of the film footage was Rauletta. Her reflections, a year after her dramatic plea for help, suggest that she was conscious of the impact that her message would have in her village in Mozambique. She anticipated that the novelty of our video message screening would attract relatively large numbers of curious villagers (which it did) and she made efficient use of this audience to highlight her desperation to return to Mozambique. As her relatives' responses and her prompt return demonstrate, it worked. This testifies to the agency of the participants in the project. It demonstrates clearly that they did not simply use video to represent themselves to the other side but incorporated their performances in front of the camera into their tactics and strategies of everyday life (see de Certeau 19

Andrea Sabbadini notes that 'to a large extent, film speaks the language of the unconscious' (2003: 2). The ability of people to see their relatives on the other side of the border also meant that the rest of the frame could be packed with symbolic reference, gestures and clues. These were sometimes flaunted in front of the camera, such as Omar's display of his traditional power and Jane's boasting of the 'modern' life she enjoyed in the refugee settlement in South Africa. In other cases, such symbols and codes were communicated inadvertently and noticed by the audience. Some of the commentary from audiences suggested that their focus was, at least partly, on the background to the message-senders. Such multiple meanings were something over which we – and to some extent the message senders themselves – had limited control.

As a collaborative experiment between anthropologist and filmmaker, much of the overlap in our respective approaches lay in the ease with which we accepted a certain loss of control over our efforts to make sense of the social worlds on which we focused. Familiar to anthropologists, who generally accept cultural, linguistic and geographical disorientation as part of their fieldwork experience, it also characterises a particular approach to filmmaking, adopted by Andy and summed up by Hugh Brody:

> Loss of control in the creative process is just what delivers the wonder of film. One of the central experiences in filmmaking, unlike other arts, is the loss of control: but the loss, if you are lucky or those involved are skilful enough, turns out to be gain. Selection of the key moments from an infinity of possible moments is the route to coherence and, if you are a little wise and very fortunate, to some insights and glimpses of truth. (Cited in Sabbadini 2003: 239)

The evolution of *Voices Across the Fence* from an anthropological field study to a documentary film suggests that the imposition of video into the everyday lives of migrants and refugees comprised an effective, though not unproblematic, tool for eliciting the social meanings of their movement. But despite the local tensions that were unveiled and provoked by the intervention of video, and our inability and unwillingness to control every outcome of the process, this visual experiment highlights important possibilities for video and other digital media as a 'tool' for promoting the restoration of lives that have been thrown into disarray by war and other social disruptions. The refinement of such an intervention may contribute positively towards expanding the notion of post-war reconstruction beyond a fairly narrow focus on infrastructure and livelihood restoration and recognise, in some tangible way, the existential importance of restoring social relationships in the wake of war. We do not claim to have achieved that to any great degree through our brief encounters with video messaging on the Mozambique/South Africa borderland, but merely suggest it as a methodological possibility for future research work on forced migration.

Notes

1   Broadcast on BBC Channel 4 on 9, 16 and 23 March 2002.
2   The film was commissioned by eTV, a South African television station and was broadcast in 2002. It was also screened at the following film festivals in 2002 and 2003: Encounters International Documentary Film Festival, Cape Town and Johannesburg, South Africa; Durban International Film Festival, Durban, South Africa; 13th Festival of African Cinema, Milan, Italy; 10th International Women's Film Festival, Turin, Italy; Festival of Dhow, Zanzibar, Tanzania; Africa in the Picture, Amsterdam, Netherlands; and 1st Human Rights International Film Festival of Spain.
3   See *Crossing Over* (1995), *Tigen Environmental Impact Assessment Video* (1998) and *Ga-Pila Resettlement Video* (1998).
4   *Jhoni* translates literally as Johannesburg, but in this context refers to South Africa in general. The notion of *Jhoni* encapsulates complex historical images of modernity.
5   *Voices Across the Fence* was developed through the Encounters Documentary Film Laboratory, which aimed to develop first-time documentary filmmakers. The laboratory was part of the Encounters International Documentary Film Festival established by Nodi Murphy and Steven Markovitz.
6   We had a total of £3,000 for the shoot and £5,000 for postproduction.
7   A large, depopulated and fenced-off wildlife conservation area that defines much of South Africa's border with Mozambique.
8   See Sidaway (1991), West & Myers (1992; 1996) and Myers (1994) on conflicts over land in Mozambique in the early 1990s.
9   A wife of her father who was younger than and junior to her mother.
10 Local community organisations.

Bibliography

Bauman, Z. (1998) *Globalization: The Human Consequences*. Cambridge: Polity Press.
de Certeau, M. (1984) *The Practice of Everyday Life*. Berkeley: University of California Press.
de Wet, C. (1995) *Moving Together Drifting Apart: Betterment Planning and Villagisation in a South African Homeland*. Johannesburg: Witwatersrand University Press.
Foucault, M (1986) 'Space, Power and Knowledge', in P. Rabinow (ed.) *The Foucault Reader*. London:

Penguin.

Goffman, E. (1961) *Asylums: Essays on the Social Situation of Mental Patients and Other Patients*. New York: Anchor Books.

Myers, G. W. (1994) 'Competitive Rights, Competitive Claims: Land Access in Post-War Mozambique', *Journal of Southern African Studies*, 20(4): 603–32.

Niehaus, I. (2001) *Witchcraft, Power and Politics: Exploring the Occult in the South African Lowveld*. London: Pluto Press.

Preis, A. (1997) 'Capsized Identities and Contracted Belonging Among Sri Lankan Tamil Refugees', in K. F. Olwig and K. Hastrup (eds) *Siting Culture: The Shifting Anthropological Object*. London: Routledge.

Rodgers, G. E. (1996) 'Place to Suffer: An Anthropological Study of Aid to Mozambican Refugees in a South African Settlement'. Unpublished MA dissertation, University of the Witwatersrand.

_____ (2002) 'When Refugees Don't Go Home: Post-War Mozambican Settlement Across the Border with South Africa'. Unpublished PhD dissertation, University of the Witwatersrand.

Roesch, O. (1992) 'Renamo and the Peasantry in Mozambique – A View from Gaza Province', *Canadian Journal of African Studies*, 26(3): 462–84.

Sabbadini, A. (2003) 'Introduction', in A. Sabbadini (ed.) *The Couch and the Silver Screen: Psychoanalytic Reflections on European Cinema*. New York: Brunner-Routledge.

Sidaway, J. D. (1991) 'Contested Terrain: Transformation and Continuity of the Territorial Organisation in Post-Independence Mozambique', *Tijdschrift voor Economische en Sociale Geografie*, 82(5): 367–76.

Taussig, M. (1987) *Shamanism, Colonialism and the Wild Man: A Study in Terror and Healing*. Chicago: University of Chicago Press.

West, H. G. and G. W. Myers (1992) 'Local-Level Political Legitimacy and Security of Land Tenure in Mozambqiue'. Unpublished report, Land Tenure Center, University of Wisconsin-Madison.

_____ (1996) 'A Piece of Land in a Land of Piece? State Farm Divestiture in Mozambique', *Journal of Modern African Studies*, 34(1): 27–51.

Filmography

Children of Shatila (1998), Mai Masri. Nour Productions, 50 mins.

Crossing Over (1995), Andrea Spitz. Left-Eye Productions, 28 mins.

Environments of Post Modernity (1994), Andrea Spitz. Left-Eye Productions, 34 mins.

Ga-Pila Resettlement Video (1998), Andrea Spitz. Left-Eye Productions, 20 mins.

The Last Peasants (2002), Angus Macqueen. October Films, 138 mins.

Tigen Environmental Impact Assessment Video (1998), Andrea Spitz. Left-Eye Productions, 20 mins.

Voices Across the Fence (2002), Andrea Spitz. Left-Eye Productions and Quintet Productions, 24 mins.

HISTORY READ BACKWARD: MEMORY, MIGRATION AND THE PHOTOGRAPHIC ARCHIVE

Roberta McGrath

> Photographic archives can and should be subjects of social study in their own right. While academic studies of museums, grand expositions and other repositories of 'heritage' have boomed in recent years, visual archives have been curiously ignored.
> – Marcus Banks (2001: 103–4)

> Indeed, history begins at Home.
> – Meir Wigoder (2001: 19)

> History is Past Politics and Politics Present History.
> – Herbert Baxter Adams (cited in Smith 1998: 110)

PART I: THE PAST IN THE PRESENT

I begin with a series of interrelated questions and reflections. In what ways might visual archival research constitute a form of creative practice in itself? When working in the photographic archive, what are we producing? What, indeed, is the nature of this mode of production? Where are the boundary lines between archival object and its accompanying re-presentation? What is the 'object of study' in archival photographic research and how and in what diverse forms can it be narrated?

In recent years disciplines across the social sciences have reshaped, if not challenged, the manner in which the visual arts are studied, particularly within art history, visual, cultural and media studies. Given this transdiciplinary dialogue surrounding the status of the 'visual' and 'visuality', is it possible to further utilise methodological approaches inherent in creative practice to redirect the epistemological axis between theory and practice, so that practice is in productive dialogue with theory and not the other accepted way round? For writers such as Roland Barthes, genuine interdisciplinarity 'is not about confronting already constituted disciplines (none of which, in fact, is willing to let itself go)', but 'consists in creating a new object that belongs to no one' (cited in Clifford 1986: 1). The concept and research practice of transdisciplinarity has a kinship with modernist techniques and strategies of representation, since it is a methodological approach that can simultaneously acknowledge connections across disciplines while pinpointing distinctions within them (Marcus 1994). Montage allows for re-arrangements and re-alignments; it enables us to shift images around and to produce differing sequences that can be spliced together.

The methodological approach throughout this chapter draws upon visual techniques of montage as a compelling strategy, engaging with photographic content in multi-layered archival formations. Montage, it must be said, is not a jigsaw where there is only one predetermined arrangement. But, crucially, neither are the arrangements entirely arbitrary. In montage the pieces never resolve into one image on a single, smooth surface; rather it produces a different and disjunctive image. Montage employs the fragment as its theory. Such an approach has an affinity with photography as a quintessentially modern visual technology. Photographs, too, are fragments, uprooted and disembedded from time and place and they belong to no one. Montage is, in an important sense, a theory of relationships. 'When making films', Alexander Kluge says, 'I am always confronted with the problem that whatever I see does not actually contain these relationships' (1981: 218). Relationships, like histories and identities, are not there to be discovered; they have to be made.

How, then, can we think with and theorise through photographs? And what is it we see with words? The work that I present here is part of a wider documentary archival project in which I imaginatively trace historical parallels and differences between past and contemporary Scottish narratives of migrancy. In this chapter I want to raise some questions about the nature of vision and historical memory in relation to present understandings of migration. I attempt to develop a methodology that will allow me to work *between* archival spaces and *across* historical time. My approach could be called interdisciplinary 'circumstantial activism' (Marcus 1999: 17), bringing into dialogue images and texts, film and photography, letters and public reports from different registers, from other times and places.

Although the archive must not, indeed cannot, be dispensed with, it is not, crucially, a source of an absolute, incontestable truth. Archives are intrinsically incomplete; they contain only the remnants, feint *traces* of material lives that are then fashioned by historians into narratives that are, necessarily, 'pictures' of the past produced in the present. Following Robert Coles, I take 'documentary work' to be 'the place where imagination encounters and tries to come to terms with reality' (1992: 267). This chapter is an argument against institutionalised vision and for more imaginative, politicised *and* passionate visual fields.

What follows is provisional and partial. It is the outcome of exploration and experimentation by a subject interested in shifting locations in both a personal and a political sense. I attempt to render the sensual (embodied), material (political and economic) and symbolic (cultural) aspects of historical research as inseparable. The trajectory I trace is deliberate in its order; I begin with historical research as embodied process. Images and texts only come to life in the interplay of personal memory and public history. Moreover, while 'we tend to think of history in the long term, history is, in fact, a very sudden thing' (Roth 2001: 86). As I show below, it is as sudden as walking through a door.

THE SMELL OF THE REAL

In the summer of 2002 I stepped over the threshold of the Mitchell Library, Glasgow.[1] This rather grand public library is now home to the archives of Glasgow City Council. The old part of the building, built in the nineteenth century, has marble-clad walls, gold paintwork, polished chequerboard floors and Doric columns. It displays a certain civic pride more reminiscent of the state buildings of the old eastern bloc than of Britain. A concierge sits at a desk as one enters; attendants are uniformed in city council livery; the water in the toilets is scalding hot. As I walked through the door for the first time in more

FIGURE 1: INTERIOR OF THE MITCHELL LIBRARY, GLASGOW

than twenty years, I was overwhelmed by a pungent smell, a heady mix of Jeyes disinfectant and lavender polish. This was, is, the smell of sanitary improvement and civic pride with which I grew up.

The journey to the council archives located on the top floor of the modern extension is labyrinthine. (I'll come back to the length of string later.) One walks through long corridors, round sharp corners, until one reaches a lift that ascends to the top floor. Here one steps out on to an Axminster-carpeted hallway of red swirls.

Only in Glasgow, I found myself thinking, would you find not a water dispenser but a soft drinks machine outside a manuscript room; moreover, it offered not the usual Coca-

FIGURES 2 AND 3: INTERIOR OF THE MITCHELL LIBRARY, GLASGOW

FIGURE 4: INTERIOR OF THE MITCHELL LIBRARY, GLASGOW

Cola but Scotland's national soft drink, Irn-Bru, meant to symbolise the industrial strength of Scotland (and her people), hard as tempered steel. The 'Bru', as the slogan says, is 'made from girders', hence its bright orange colour: rust. (There is of course a very literal irony here given the destruction of Scotland's steel industry.)

If all this seemed unsettling, nothing could have prepared me for what lay behind the archive doors. The place was in chaos and had the appearance of having been recently burgled. Papers were strewn everywhere, plans, maps and books piled up, desks overflowing and the paper equivalent of rust: dust. This was the space not of civic pride but of civic disintegration.[2] There were no call slips; one merely wrote down what one wanted to look at on a scrap of paper – of which there was an abundance – and handed it to the librarian. The computerised catalogue was erratic and probably devised in the days when Atari was at the forefront of computer technology. After some time I ordered photographs, ledgers, pamphlets and then I waited … and waited. Several hours passed. Eventually, someone who appeared to be an odd job man, as dishevelled as the archives themselves, delivered the boxes. There was soot in them and this seemed symbolic. As he walked away I noticed a length of coarse string (the kind used for tying potato sacks – his safeguard in the labyrinth perhaps) hanging out of his back pocket. For some reason Kafka came to mind.

As it happened, I had plenty of time to let my mind wander and when I had got over my irritation I realised that here was tangible, material evidence that if history is made, it is also unmade, and this is not a tidy or clean process. Efficient order conceals and represses random disorder, the terrible jumble of papers, pictures, objects that make up any archive. I was reminded that history is quite literally a dirty business and that the imposition of logic on history is, as Joan Scott says, 'a fantasy' (2001: 289). Carolyn Steedman reminds us that archives are not only 'made from selected and carefully chosen documentation from the past' but also from what she calls 'mad fragmentations' that no one intended to preserve (2001: 78). Moreover, much is lost; archives are spaces of historical absence as much as of presence, a warehousing or stockpiling of 'fragments that are formed around a nothing' (Kracauer 1993: 431). This describes well the ways in which images are culled from around the world, assembled in the archive as a repository that holds 'in effigy the last elements of a nature alienated from meaning' (Kracauer 1969: 435).

It was this experience that made me acutely aware of the sensory dimensions of conducting research as C. Nadia Serematakis asks: 'What happens to the senses when theories haul meaning from social institutions to material artefacts and then back again as if the dense and embodied communication between persons and things were only a quick exchange between surfaces?' (1994: 134). The human body is not a surface (as my experience showed), but permeable skin penetrated by sounds, smells, memories that are sharp and diffuse, histories public and private. Thought is made not only of words, but also of flesh and blood. It is this sense of the density of embodied research that I want to preserve in looking at these images. Photographs and letters are handled and touched and sniffed, not just looked at. All experience is an embodied encounter with an object: images smell, they conjure sounds, resonate with poignant meanings that penetrate and may even overwhelm the body – they are not only about sight. These sensory qualities are downplayed in what Allen Feldman has called the 'symbolic evisceration' of the researcher's body (cited in Stoller 1997: 82). In the Glasgow archive, however, I experienced a kind of sensory overload for which I was quite unprepared. I was forced to have second thoughts and mixed feelings. I both 'lost the place' (or, as they would say in Glasgow, 'the heid' [head]) and simultaneously found a radically different space in which to think with my body.

My experience was overwhelming, unmanageable, indeed frightening. I was not in control of my research material; instead, it possessed me. This particular archive was quite unlike most archives, which are dedicated to reassuring the researcher that their materials are clean, deodorised, neatly filed, placed in transparent envelopes and methodically accessible in an air-conditioned environment. The researcher is usually relieved of the burden of his or her own bodily presence, in order to focus upon disembodied documentation, but here I was made all too aware of both my own body and those of others. Archives

FIGURES 5 AND 6: INTERIOR OF THE NATIONAL LIBRARY OF SCOTLAND, EDINBURGH

are spaces where textual volume dominates and the body of the researcher, small and insignificant against the vast weight of history and mountains of paper, virtually disappears. Doors are usually large and heavy and staircases wide, which intensifies the impression.

In the National Library of Scotland the door handles are thistles, and every time I cross that threshold, I literally have to grasp *that* particular nettle.

The truth is that we make history with our bodies, not just our minds. This is a reciprocal process: taking meaning *from* and giving historical meaning *to*. Moreover, here I was confronted with 'the wreckage of the inadmissible' (Feldman 1994: 104): the semiotic and historical fall-out, the stuff from which history is made. As Paul Stoller has suggested, history in many non-Western cultures is 'not a subject or text to be mastered, but a force that consumes the body of those who speak it' (1997: xvi). This acknowledges the power of history and memory to awaken and transform the body, as indeed it did my own, and consequently, as I argue, the power of the senses to transform our understanding of what history is.

THE TOUCH OF THE REAL

In Siegfried Kracauer's work, *History: The Last Things Before the Last*, metaphors of alienation and exile, of being a stranger, recur; the historian is 'a stranger to the world evoked by the sources, he is faced with the task of penetrating its outward appearances, so that he may learn to understand the world from within' (1969: 84). For Kracauer, as for Walter Benjamin, tactile contact – pressing close to the object in order to experience its power – is crucial. For both writers the historian must 'really want to get a *feel* for it and not only aim at verifying his initial hypothesis and hunches with its aid' (ibid.; emphasis added). To this end he advocates 'an active passivity', a waiting for 'what the picture may, or may not, want to tell him' (ibid.). Michael Taussig calls this 'tactile' or 'yielding knowing' (1993: 25). This is a reversal of the usual relationship between subjects and their objects, a kind of exploration of the 'unrealised possibilities' that are stored in any image (Raymond Williams cited in Gallagher & Greenblatt 2000: 60). Both Taussig and Kracauer acknowledge the power of the image-object over the observer-subject, the power to touch the viewer in some way even if its voice is muffled or vision no longer clear. The 'pictures', photographs and films literally move us, transport us (Gallagher & Greenblatt 2000; Bruno 2002).

A minute and a half of silent, grainy, black-and-white Gaumont newsreel (*c.*1924) does exactly this. It tracks the embarkation of a group of emigrants from the Outer Hebridean islands St Kilda and Barra to Canada, using photographs and film footage in order to montage together a 'moving story'. Transport, in both its literal and metaphoric sense, is employed here. The opening sequence is shot from a plane. Our eyes seem to brush over a bleak landscape, as if borne on the wind. We swoop down, bird-like, over crofts that are about to be abandoned and cut to a still image of two women followed by a single child and then to a photograph of boys beside a much older form of transport, a cart. This format of still/moving images continues. The photographs act as punctuation marks, full-stops. Cut to the ship and passengers on deck with a banner that reads: 'We've got jobs in Canada. We don't want the dole.' These are the only words in a mutely eloquent film. We see women and children boarding the ship. The gangway is no more than a rough, steep plank and the film closes with three moving, fluid sequences: the view from the pier as the boat casts off and begins to edge away; the view from the stern deck as the ship pulls further away while passengers wave hats in the air; and finally the view from the shore as the ship carries off its cargo. This last shot is the longest take in the film as the distance grows and an unbridgeable, irretrievable gulf opens up. We know that soon the ship will disappear over the horizon as it travels towards a future that is unknown. The film ends abruptly and we, the observers, are left on the brink.

As Kracauer reminds us, citing Leo Strauss, the historian too 'embarks on a journey whose end is hidden from him'. Cast adrift at sea, 'he is not likely to return to the shores of his time as exactly the same man who departed from them' (Strauss cited in Kracauer 1969: 91). He or she is changed in the process and, like the passengers aboard, will not retain his sovereign identity. Kracauer adds: 'incidentally, he is not likely either to return to his point of departure' (ibid.). In this sense, the past is another country to which the historian travels without any guarantee of what he or she will find. Vision 'captivates' us not only because it is a journey towards external things, but also because, as my archival research demonstrates, 'it is a *return* to a reality of origin, which is perceived at a distance from the shore of some other place' (de Certeau 1983: 26). This is the nature of any intellectual itinerary.

It is this uncanny sense of a melancholy, haunted place that I am left with at the end of the newsreel film – a sense of heaviness, a burden of silence and stillness. This footage has its echoes in other images, both earlier and later. A photograph of the late nineteenth century [DVD REF 1: PHOTO] is obviously set up, melodramatically posed to show that crofters, including women and children, were not only forcibly evicted from their homesteads but had their homes simultaneously demolished, so that any possibility of return was destroyed. In this image, what was once a home is no more than a pile of rubble. Read alongside an image from the 1940s – a different context but a similar location – another narrative emerges. [DVD REF 2: PHOTO] Here, the youngest son is being sent off proudly and it is a cause for celebration. This random family snap only becomes comprehensible in the context of earlier and later pictures that frame the ambivalent meanings of migration. In a story taken from a newspaper of the 1950s, [DVD REF 3: PHOTO] the woman's anxious gaze as she contemplates her family's future is revealing, as is the gap that opens up in a view taken from the deck of the ship. [DVD REF 4: PHOTO] By that time, emigrants had to travel to the major ports; ships no longer came to them. [DVD REF 5: PHOTO] Cast adrift at sea, these photographs and the newsreel film are merely points of departure to unknown destinations. They are 'unhomed' images (Rogoff 2000: 7).

HISTORY, MEMORY, ARCHIVE

Like the archive, 'memory is organized not only according to chronology, but also to chains of association which cut across time' (Laplanche & Pontalis 1973: 247). 'Memory does not pay attention to dates; it skips years or stretches temporal distance' (Kracauer 1993: 425). While photographs 'fix' a particular moment, lived experience itself is anything but fixed (Gabriel 1999: 78). Memory, like the photograph, cuts up and compartmentalises the past and both are 'put away haphazardly without regard to the temporal and spatial compartments that are experientially contiguous to it' (Cohen 1979: 194). It is this sense of contingency that was 'brought home' to me as I crossed the threshold of the Glasgow archive. In that moment it was as if kaleidoscopic fragments of long-forgotten sensory knowledge fell into place.

Photographs and films are themselves fragments that only come to life in the 'interplay' of personal memory and public history. What is 'narrated and unnarrated inadvertently reveals the extent to which everyday experience is organized around the reproduction of inattention, and therefore the extent to which a good deal of historical experience is relegated to forgetfulness' (Serematakis 1994: 20). Archives are places of historical selection, forgetting as much as remembering, and history is neither linear nor about continuity. Indeed, narrative is a way of resolving this problem; as Scott argues, it is always fantasised, 'impos[ing] sequential order on otherwise chaotic and contingent occurrences' (2001: 288–9). As Benjamin suggests, history is arranged *post hoc* (and, we might say, *ad hoc*) into various constellations. Thus, 'the present becomes intelligible as it is aligned with a past moment with which it has a secret affinity' (Benjamin cited in Durham-Peters 1999a: 3).

Archival images, letters, pamphlets and ledgers are, in Meir Wigoder's words, 'orphaned' (2001: 4). They belong to no one and wait to be claimed. History, he considers, does, indeed begin at home and he describes the archive as a melancholy, haunted place where documents lie jumbled, images abandoned. But, crucially, it is also the place where we can find 'a new order that enables reality to be examined critically through the use of film montage, the photographic collage, and through adopting a (surrealistic) approach that estranges reality' (ibid.). These images and documents should, and must, be claimed less as a 'record of what has already been thought' (although I would substitute 'seen' in place of 'thought') and more as 'what can yet be envisioned' (Dudley Andrew cited in Marks 2000: 26). Understood as subjunctive images they might provide resources of hope (Williams 1983).

I look into the archive in order to move beyond its confines; I gaze at the photograph in order to understand how what took place 'there, then' lives on, albeit selectively, in the 'here and now' (Barthes 1977: 44). This is also to ask about the kind of pasts we want to bring into the present and, therefore, about the different futures we might imagine. Photographs and films are material forms of collective cultural memory, and as Jacques Le Goff suggests, collective memory is the 'one of the great sites of developed and developing societies, of dominated and dominating classes, all of them struggling for power or life, for survival and advancement' (1992: 97). History as 'collective memory is not an inert and passive thing but a field of activity in which past events are selected, reconstructed, maintained, modified and endowed with political meaning' (Said 2000: 185). The construction of such histories is absolutely fundamental to the democratisation of social memory. Ethical, political and cultural questions lie at the decentred heart of contemporary debates in visual culture as it endeavours to envision things differently. Vision is always in the realm of the senses, while history, I argue, begins at home; both are embodied, lived. As Serematakis says, 'the senses are the bearers and record-keepers of involuntary and pervasive *material* experience, and therefore potential sources of alternative memory and temporality' (1994: 20; emphasis added). For Kracauer, 'once vision becomes an institution clouds of dust gather about it, blurring its contours and contents' (1969: 7).

PART II: THE PRESENT IN THE PAST

While looking at the photographs, I was taken beyond the confines of the archive out into Glasgow as it is now. The archive is a kind of microcosm of the city, just as the city is in microcosm the embodiment of the processes of globalisation. Modern cities are 'sites for the concrete operations of the economy' (Sassen 2000: 141). As Saskia Sassen suggests, globalisation 'is not only constituted in terms of capital and the new international corporate culture (international finance, telecommunication, information flows), but also in terms of *people* and *noncorporate cultures*' (2000: 143; emphasis added). Sassen's economic, social and feminist analysis demonstrates the correspondence between 'great concentrations of corporate power and large concentrations of *others*' (ibid.; emphasis added). This is a history of the present that can be traced through archival research. The city is, and always has been, a strategic terrain, a contested space. In a cultural parallel, Laura Marks argues for the centrality of the visual in tracing the paths of global capital 'rematerializing and re-embodying the global movements that transnational capital seeks to render virtual' (2000: 9). These authors refuse the specious distinction between the 'economic' and the 'political' and emphasise that migrants are, and have always been, 'refugees fleeing the wasteland that has been created by the economic equivalent of a scorched earth strategy' (Walden Bello cited in Lipsitz 1999: 193).

It is salutary to remind ourselves that by the start of World War II, 85 per cent of the world was colonised in one form or another (Mirzoeff 1998: 282). Globalisation emerges phoenix-like from the ashes of imperialism and colonialism. Its roots lie in the nineteenth-century shift from country to city and from homeland to colony. The city, as a microcosm of a growing global economic disparity, has its other both in the country and in other countries. Migration, both locally and globally, is then a question of the economic and political history of modernisation. At the level of the economic, statisticians were 'already acquainted with the general laws determining emigration, one of the principal being the difficulty of procuring *the means of subsistence*' (Levasseur 1885: 77; emphasis added). However, Emile Levasseur continued, 'there are other special influences at work in inducing so enormous an exodus. The most powerful of those is unquestionably *liberty*' (ibid.). As Karl Marx describes it: '"great masses of men are suddenly and forcibly torn from their means of subsistence and are hurled on to the labour market as free, unprotected and rightless proletarians" – free, but only in the sense that they lost their own means of production and subsistence and free, but of necessity required, to sell their sole remaining possession, their labour power, on the market' (Marx cited in Cohen 1996: xi).

Photographs record the conditions in which these uprooted proletarians were housed: the bedroom with its romanticised picture of sailing ships above the bed [DVD REF 6: PHOTO]; the makeshift bundle of blankets in a dark cellar [DVD REF 7: PHOTO]; the picture of the mother sitting before an unlit, filthy range, so malnourished herself that she is unable to feed her child [DVD REF 8: PHOTO]; the same woman in a clean but soulless room at the Council Milk Depot with a child whose belly is distended, his eyes fixed with the vacant stare of malnutrition [DVD REF 9: PHOTO]; a woman and baby from a series of portraits of mothers and babies, orphans and abandoned children. [DVD REF 10: PHOTO]

Such images are a reminder of the past in the present, since we need now, as then, to resist the 'liberal assumption of the congruence of capitalism, democracy and freedom' (Lowe & Lloyd 1992: 1). Despite a nominal equality in law and the endless talk about the international economy and the 'free' movement of goods, capital and communications, the movement of people is increasingly heavily regulated. Corporations, the loyal heirs of imperialism and colonialism, are able to decide for themselves 'their investment site, production site, tax site and residence site and to play these off against one another' (Beck 2000: 4); as investment capital roves around developing countries in search of ever-cheaper labour and production costs, workers are forced to move to developed countries in search of employment they no longer have at home. The rights of refugees and asylum seekers to citizenship, however, are increasingly withheld; vilified and pauperised, they are forced into illegality.

In 2003 the entire European Union received approximately 3 per cent of the world's refugees; Britain was eighth in this league. Emotive phrases such as 'swamping' or 'excessive spending' appeared regularly in the press, as if increase in numbers or capital expenditure was the problem. It is not; the question is one of racism. For it is hard to accept that some 200,000 immigrants to Britain could swamp a population of 60 million, while government spending on all aspects of immigration accounted for only 0.425 per cent of the overall budget (see Martin 2003). Prime Minister Tony Blair announced that he would 'derail the asylum legal aid gravy train' (Wren 2003) and David Blunkett, then home secretary, 'came out' over immigration; 'coming out' had a sinister meaning in this context because, ironically, at precisely the same moment as the right to civil partnerships was extended to lesbians and homosexuals (crucial voters in the forthcoming general election), the right to family life, enshrined in European human rights legislation, was being taken away from refugees and asylum seekers.

In the United Kingdom new legislation reduced legal aid fees for initial application for asylum and removed the right of appeal from the appellant body to an appeal tribunal; the right of *appeal* has been replaced by an internal review *procedure* giving unprecedented power to the Appeals and Immigration President. These changes, coupled with the curtailment of the period within which an appeal can be made, have eroded basic human rights and heavily restricted the access of non-citizens to courts. Moreover, electronic tagging has been proposed for those whose applications are rejected, 'as an alternative to secure removal centres', as has off-shore 'processing centres' outside the European Union that would ensure that 'illegitimate' refugees never reach Britain's shores (Travis 2003). State benefits have already been withheld from failed asylum seekers, while their children could be removed and taken into care. David Blunkett claimed that this was a mark of equality that dealt with these parents in the same way 'as any others who put their families at risk' (Press Association 2003). Unsurprisingly, politics has increasingly become re-nationalised, as globalisation de-nationalises economics. Ulrich Beck suggests that it is 'an irony of history that the very losers of globalization will in future have to pay for everything – from the welfare state to a functioning democracy – while the winners of globalization post dream profits and steal away from their responsibility for a future democracy' (2000: 6). There is a history to these changes in law; that history is located not only in the council's written records, but also in the photographs strewn across and stored in its archives.

Between 1846 and 1853, at the height of the Irish Famine, Rev. Bernard Tracy recorded that 'no fewer than 46, 882 persons were removed from Scotland to Ireland' (1863: 10). In 1849, Glasgow's Medical Officer of Health, Dr Strang, reflected on rising mortality rates and the need to check Irish immigration at both ends:

> In Glasgow, as well as Edinburgh, there is of late a gradually increasing rate of mortal-ity which may be fairly attributed to the increase of Irish immigration and its con-comitant misery, destitution and pauperism. To check this growing evil, productive not only of increased deaths, but of fearfully increased pecuniary burdens among our city populations, is absolutely necessary, otherwise Glasgow will become a City of paupers and of the plague. No time must now be lost to ward off from all the great towns in England and Scotland, and particularly from Liverpool and Glasgow, the scourge of wandering and famishing Irish; and the only apparently effective mode of doing so, in the present state of matters, is to apply remedial measures to Ireland itself, to check, in fact, the evil at its source, to oblige that country to find employ-ment for its own people, or bread for those who cannot be employed; and if Ireland, in its present condition, be not able to meet that requisite of all countries – which is not to be credited – then would it be better for England and Scotland to contribute something out of the general Treasury to keep Irish paupers at home, rather than to extend their baleful influence over the, as yet, less degraded population of the British Isles. (1848/49: 215)

Such measures were introduced in the law of parochial settlement. In order to qualify for poor relief, 'residents' had to have lived in the same parish for five years, a requirement as impossible for migrants then as it is now. Tracy commented that this was

> a law that would almost appear to have been framed with the intention of securing to Scotland the Irishman's labour as long as he was able to toil and then throwing him back upon Ireland to be supported in his old age ... these victims of unparalleled, though legalized cruelty, were mercilessly shipped off in cargoes, like cattle infected with plague, and inhumanly cast ashore here and there on the Irish coast ... There they wandered about houseless and friendless in a land of famine, perhaps a hundred miles from their native spot (if it could be said that many were born in Ireland at all). (1863: 8, 10)

In the National Archives of Scotland is lodged a letter written by one emigrant, John Colquhoun, written in November 1841 and addressed to his mother. [DVD REF 11: PHOTO; PDF] Colquhoun has travelled from Paisley to Liverpool to embark for Canada which, at £4, roughly a quarter of the price of a ticket to Australia, was one of the cheapest destinations for emigrants in the mid-nineteenth century. The evening before his depar-ture, he composes his missive 'at the midnight hour'. 'The letter', as Steedman puts it, 'is a part of the body that is detachable: torn from the very depths of the subject' (2001: 74). Colquhoun's letter is marked by a certain violence, by fluids, blood and tears, written by a body that is in dissimulation. He is 'brocken [sic] hearted, tears falling', at leaving behind wife, mother, sister, children. We wonder what such letters did to the bodies of those that received them as well as to those who wrote. Colquhoun agonises about having taken too many blankets, leaving his wife short, and begs his mother to 'spare a pair or so my heart bleeds for her'. He ends poignantly: 'I may never see any of you again … I *hope* for the best but who can tell?'

It is we who can, and indeed must, tell. The National Archives of Scotland print this letter in their guide to resources on migration but they do not reproduce other letters written by Colquhoun. These tell a different, more ambivalent and more familiar story that does not fit so well with a nationalist mythology of emigration. Within a few months nostalgia for what has been lost has been replaced by self-aggrandisement and a tougher, more optimistic sense of undreamed-of possibilities: 'Perhaps I am speaking rather big, but I realy [sic] believe that I will do something bright yet I am greatly changed for the better it relay [sic] had a great effect to be so far and so long from home. There are thousands of ways of obtaining a livelihood [sic] here – I do not know if you yourself might be induced to risk a trip across the Atlantic Mother – if not I do not think we will see each other again.' [DVD REF 12: PHOTO; PDF] A couple of years later, he is doing even better and has risen to the rank of manager, overseeing women hand-sewing shawls. (It was the collapse of the market for the Paisley shawls on which the entire economy of Paisley rested that forced Colquhoun to leave his hometown and migrate in search of work.) By the time his last letter is penned he has changed the spelling of his name to the simpler Calhoun and states bluntly: 'I have no desire to return home'. [DVD REF 13: PHOTO; PDF] This is a common story of migration that oscillates between, as Hamid Naficy puts it, 'dysphoria and euphoria' (1999: 26). What is clear, however, is that there is no going back.

Colquhoun's story reflects in part the economic and political history of modern migration, but also its cultural history, in which the representation of others has played a central role. It has been, and increasingly is, a question of the grossly unequal allocation of symbolic as much as of economic resources that force some to live 'through the identities ascribed to them by others, rather than through the identities they might choose for themselves' (Morley 2001: 427). What we learn from these orphaned images, letters and ledgers is that they belong to no one, but wait to be claimed: less a record of what has already been seen and more a signpost that points to what has still to be envisaged or done. These photographs of people, places, things, are a means, not an end. They are spaces through which we can begin to think about ourselves, others and the world that we now inhabit. Archival excavation is a staging post on the way to creating new stories; by dismantling dominant histories, we might also learn to make history anew. For writers like Kracauer, history is not simply the past; like journeying, it 'is also the realm of contingencies, of new beginnings' (1969: 31).

Photography and film, as these images show, have an ignoble history as a technology of ethnographic domination and control, whether imperial, colonial, racial or sexual. They are, however, equally forms of counter-memory, a means of creating 'a sensory and collective horizon for people trying to live a life in the interstices of modernity' (Kracauer 1997: xxxiv). Kracauer argued against the view of photography and cinema as simply or only instrumental. While 'photographability' had, even by the 1920s, 'become the condition under which reality is constituted and perceived', both media still offered their 'share of exhilarating and liberatory impulses' (1997: xvii; xxvi) because of their unique ability to picture 'transient material life, life at its most ephemeral' (1997: xlix; 19). For writers like Kracauer, photography and cinema equally provide the possibility of 'an alternative public sphere' (1997: xxxiv). I want to preserve this idea because it is still relevant to the present. The global culture in which we now live is predominantly a visual and aural culture. Our eyes and ears have been, and are, shaped by powerful corporations and there is growing evidence that 'the psychic world', as Richard Kearney puts it 'is as colonized as the physical world by the image industry' (1988: 1). Yet, as Kracauer argues, it is much too simplistic to suggest that this is all that happens, or can happen.

Our task will be 'to find the forms of language, visual, verbal, that will allow for the connections between cultures – of affiliation, recognition, antagonism – without dissipating the voices in which they clash' (Rose 1996: 149). Jacqueline Rose suggests that the solution will not be pluralism: 'The rhetoric of pluralism can be a way of concealing the depths of our conflicts. It can also be a way of promoting them' (ibid.). For writers like Rose, there can be no way of understanding political (and here I include cultural) identities 'without letting fantasy into the frame … fantasy, far from being the antagonist of public, social being plays a central, constitutive role in the modern world of states and nations' (1996: 4).

In a contemporary analysis of culture and communication, John Durham-Peters suggests that we 'should eschew the project of assigning everyone a homeland in the world of representations … and instead join the project of attacking the inequitable allocation of the opportunity to dream and follow dreams … [We should] move from a hermeneutics of suspicion to a pragmatics of justice … the only antidote to insulting fantasies is the right of reply' (1999b: 37–8). Arguing against censorship and a cultural asceticism, he suggests that we need 'a public sphere, not a smashing of images … a conflict of representations, not a purity of depictions' (ibid.). Such a vision, or voice, will not be univocal; it will necessarily be imperfect. It will be about the power of the unconscious fantasy as much as about conscious reason. It will also have to be an act of imagination rather than a simple return to realism (although realism has not yet had its day).

Cultural experimentation, however, need not be at odds with politics or ethics. Ella Shohat and Robert Stam usefully remind us that 'images are representations not only in the mimetic sense, but also in the *political* sense' (1994: 180; emphasis added). The photograph's frame thus 'marks a *provisional* limit; its content points beyond that frame, referring to a multitude of real-life phenomena which cannot possibly be encompassed in their entirety' (Kracauer 1969: 58; emphasis added). The question then might be how to expand the parameters of the frames we have and really perceive them as merely provisional in order to produce a different picture. Deconstruction, as Jacques Derrida suggested, 'must neither reframe nor dream of the pure and simple absence of the frame' (cited in Carroll 1987: 131). Deconstructive analysis can and indeed must now be brought together with material realities. Modernity, whether late, post or liquid, is still wrestling to find answers to the question with which it arrived: 'how to deal with the people' (Chow 1995: 14). In essence the crisis of modernity provides an opportunity to re-think and re-evaluate not only what modernity is, but what it might be. This necessarily entails a re-thinking of questions of political representation and cultural identity. As I have argued elsewhere (McGrath 1990; 1993), representation is a question of human rights. Visual cultural studies has a key role to play here.

For writers such as Durham-Peters, the problem of communication (and this must include visual communication) is therefore less a question of semantics, more one of politics and ethics: the demands of morality and justice. He suggests: 'we should be less worried about how signs arouse divergent meanings than the conditions that keep us attending to our neighbours and other beings different from us' (1999a: 268–9). A politics of cultural theory urges us to think beyond either 'transcendental sameness' or 'the most dehumanizing exile and estrangement, an otherness in which the humanity of the other cannot be recognized' (Levin 1993: 18). Narratives of either total homogenisation or absolute otherness are unsatisfactory.

PART III: THE PAST AND THE PRESENT IN THE FUTURE

How then do we move from what is to what ought to be? This is a task of transformation and a question of ethics. It is a question of the relationship of freedom and obligation. Ewa Ziarek terms this 'an ethos of becoming and an ethos of alterity' which is necessary in order to develop a 'non-appropriative relation to the other' (2001: 2). Similarly, Stoller defines lived experience as 'one's implication in the life of others' (1992: 215). It is we ourselves who must be responsible and accountable, in the present, here and now. Moreover, this is a responsibility to those with whom one wishes to communicate and the historian, according to Alain Corbin, 'must strive, at the very least, to identify what it is that conditions the frontier between the spoken and the unspoken' (1996: 190) or, in the context of the visual, between the seen and the unseen. Vision and voice must be given to those archives and claimed by those subjects who have until recently remained below the threshold of vision. This means rummaging through documents and images in long-forgotten presses; re-arranging temporal sequences and making connections across various registers. In the end, as Zygmunt Bauman puts it, 'the chance of human togetherness, depends on the rights of the stranger, not on the question of who – the State or tribe – is entitled to decide who strangers are' (1997: 57). Bauman draws upon writers such as Emmanuel Lévinas who constantly remind us that 'with the other our accounts are never settled' (1993: 125). For Lévinas, 'the humanity of the human is not to be found in knowledge, but in ethics. More important than epistemology: ethics is the demand for morality and justice' (Cohen 2001: 5).

Politics (and this includes cultural politics), does not, in itself, give meaning. It 'creates or refuses conditions of possibility' (Luce Giard cited in de Certeau 1997: xiv). Creating such conditions, as well as refusing others, is crucial in the present political climate of new patriarchies and racisms. The task of a new visual cultural studies is to 'redefine both what it *is* to see and what *there is* to see' (Latour 1986: 10). Looking is always an act that involves subjects and objects; seeing is historical and political, social and cultural. We need to keep looking, while bearing in mind that vision is embodied; it is always in the realm of the senses and therefore our ways of seeing must be linked to our ways of being, because 'the final arbiter in any philosophy is not how we think, but what we do' (Hacking 1983: 31).

We consume the products and values of our society through our eyes and ears, but this is not all we do. Arjun Appadurai contends that the view that 'the mechanical acts of reproduction largely reprimed ordinary people for work is far too simple ... there is growing evidence that the consumption of mass media throughout the world often provokes resistance, irony, selectivity and, in general, *agency*' (1996: 7; emphasis added). How then do we produce other subjunctive images? These will emerge from the space between how we are written by culture and how we want to write, transform and re-make our culture. Images and texts, and other ways of observing, listening and reading and writing about them, are places in which we can explore the past in order to enable a different future to come into being.

In an age of accelerated transition, of rapidly shifting identities and horizons, incompatible ideas have to be kept alive in a spirit of hope. I would argue that this is what imaginative theories and images do. Imagination, generally seen as something childish, is often underestimated. Political imagination is about the power to transform, to conjure up, to evoke, to provide spaces in and through which we can begin to think not only about ourselves, our own subjectivities, but about the complex material and conceptual worlds we inhabit and share with others. As Stoller suggests, 'the key to doing research in complex transnational spaces devolves less from methods, multidisciplinary teams or theoretical frameworks – although these are, of course important – than from the supplements of the imagination' (1999: 703). These are the spaces in which we all now live, where 'difference is encountered in the adjoining neighbourhood (and) the familiar turns up at the end of the earth' (Clifford 1988: 14). Rose suggests: 'In terms of the future, our link to the past must be broken experientially by reversing our methodological practices. Such reversal would foster ethnographies of intimacy, not distance; of stories, not models; of possibilities, not stabilities; and of contingent understandings, not detachable conclusions' (1990: 6). If we are to create a vital, visual cultural studies in which all has not already been said, or perhaps more importantly done, then it is here that we must begin. As I have tried to show, history is past politics, and politics present history. The history of migration does indeed begin at home, in the here and now, in our bodies as much as in our minds.

Notes

1   Photographs in this chapter are included by kind permission of the following: Mitchell Library, Glasgow, Trustees of the National Library of Scotland, Trustees of the National Museums of Scotland and Robin Gillanders.

2   Here there is an absence; I have no photographs. By the time I returned the place had been cleaned up and later still the council archives were removed to a lower floor.

Bibliography

Appadurai, A. (1996) *Modernity at Large: Cultural Dimensions of Globalization*. Minneapolis: University of Minnesota Press.

Banks, M. (2001) *Visual Methods in Social Research*. London: Sage.

Barthes, R. (1977) 'The Death of the Author', in *Image, Music, Text*. New York: Hill and Wang.

Bauman, Z. (1997) 'The Making and the Unmaking of Strangers', in P. Werbner and T. Modood (eds) *Debat-*

ing Cultural Hybridity: Multi-cultural Identities and the Politics of Anti-racism. London: Zed Books.

Beck, U. (2000) *What is Globalization?* Cambridge: Polity Press.

Bruno, G. (2002) *Atlas of Emotion*. London: Verso.

Carroll, D. (1987) *Paraesthetics: Foucault, Lyotard, Derrida*. London and New York: Methuen.

Chow, R. (1995) *Primitive Passions*. New York: Columbia University Press.

Clifford, J. (1986) 'Partial Truths', in J. Clifford and G. E. Marcus (eds) *Writing Culture: The Poetics and Politics of Ethnography*. Berkeley: University of California Press.

_____ (1988) *The Predicament of Culture*. Harvard: Harvard University Press.

Cohen, K. (1979) *Film and Fiction: The Dynamics of an Exchange*. New Haven: Yale University Press.

Cohen, R. (ed.) (1996) *The Sociology of Migration*. Cheltenham: Elgar Press.

Cohen, R. A. (2001) *Ethics, Exegesis and Philosophy: Interpretation after Lévinas*. Cambridge: Cambridge University Press.

Coles, R. (1992) *Doing Documentary Work*. Oxford: Oxford University Press.

Corbin, A. (1996) *The Foul and the Fragrant*. London: Papermac.

de Certeau, M. (1983) 'The Madness of Vision', *Enclitic*, 7(1): 24–31.

_____ (1997) *Culture in the Plural*. Minnesota: Minnesota University Press.

Durham-Peters, J. (1999a) *Speaking into the Air: A History of the Idea of Communication*. Chicago: Chicago University Press.

_____ (1999b) 'Exile, Nomadism and Diaspora: The Stakes of Mobility in the Western Canon', in H. Naficy (ed) *Home, Exile, Homeland: Film Media and the Politics of Space*. London and New York: Routledge.

Feldman, A. (1994) *Formations of Violence: The Narrative of the Body and Political Terror in Northern Ireland*. Chicago: University of Chicago Press.

Gabriel, T. (1999) 'The Intolerable Gift: Residues and Traces of a Journey', in H. Naficy (ed.) *Home, Exile, Homeland: Film Media and the Politics of Space*. London and New York: Routledge.

Gallagher, C. and S. Greenblatt (2000) *Practicing New Historicism*. Chicago: Chicago University Press.

Geertz, C. (2001) *Available Light: Anthropological Reflections on Philosophical Topics*. Chichester: Princeton University Press.

Hacking, I. (1983) *Representing and Intervening*. Cambridge: Cambridge University Press.

Kearney, R. (1988) *The Wake of the Imagination: Ideas of Creativity in Western Culture*. London: Hutchinson.

Kluge, A. (1981) 'On Film and the Public Sphere', *New German Critique*, 24/25(Fall/Winter): 206–20.

Kracauer, S. (1969) *History: The Last Things Before the Last*. Oxford: Oxford University Press.

_____ (1993) 'Photography', *Critical Inquiry*, 19(3): 421–36.

_____ (1997) *Theory of Film*. Chichester: Princeton University Press.

Laplanche, J. and J. Pontalis (1973) *The Language of Psychoanalysis*. London: Hogarth Press.

Latour, B. (1986) 'Visualisation and Cognition', *Knowledge and Society: Studies in the Sociology of Culture Past and Present*, 6: 1–40.

Le Goff, J. (1992) *History and Memory*. New York: Columbia University Press.

Levasseur, E. (1885) 'Emigration in the Nineteenth Century', *Journal of the Royal Statistical Society*, 48: 63–81.

Levin, D. M. (ed.) (1993) *Modernity and the Hegemony of Vision*. Berkeley: University of California Press.

Lévinas, E. (1993) *Outside the Subject*. London: Athlone Press.

Lipsitz, G. (1999) 'Home is Where the Hatred is: Work, Music and the Transnational Community', in H. Naficy (ed.) *Home, Exile, Homeland: Film, Media and the Politics of Space*. London and New York: Routledge.

Lowe, L. and D. Lloyd (eds) (1992) *The Politics of Culture in the Shadow of Capital*. Durham: Duke University Press.

Marcus, G. E. (1994) 'The Modernist Sensibility in Recent Ethnographic Writing and the Cinematic Metaphor of Montage', in L. Yalor (ed.) *Visualizing Theory: Selected Essays from V.A.R. 1990–1994*. London: Routledge.

_____ (ed.) (1999) *Critical Anthropology Now*. Santa Fé: School of American Research Press.

Marks, L. U. (2000) *The Skin of the Film: Intercultural Cinema, Embodiment and the Senses*. Durham: Duke University Press.

Martin, G. (2003) Letter, *Guardian*, 26 November.

McGrath, R. (1990) 'Dangerous Liaisons: Health, Disease and Representation', in T. Boffin and S. Gupta (eds) *Ecstatic Antibodies*. London: Rivers Oram.

_____ (1993) 'Deviance and Difference: The Representation of HIV and AIDS', in V. Harwood, D. Oswell, K. Parkinson and A. Ward (eds.) *Pleasure Principles*. London: Lawrence and Wishart.

Mirzoeff, N. (ed.) (1998) *The Visual Culture Reader*. London and New York: Routledge.

Morley, D. (2001) 'Belonging', *European Journal of Cultural Studies*, 4(4): 425–48.

Naficy, H. (1999) 'Framing Exile: From Homeland to Homepage', in H. Naficy (ed.) *Home, Exile, Homeland: Film, Media and the Politics of Space*. London and New York: Routledge.

Press Association (2003) 'Electronic Tagging Plan for Asylum Seekers', *Guardian*, November 27.

Rogoff, I. (2000) *Terra Infirma: Geography's Visual Culture*. London and New York: Routledge.

Rose, D. (1990) *Living the Ethnographic Life*. London: Sage.

Rose, J. (1996) *States of Fantasy*. Oxford: Clarendon Press.

Roth, P. (2001) *The Human Stain*. London: Vintage.

Said E. (2000) 'Invention, Memory, and Place', *Critical Inquiry*, 26(2): 175–92.

Sassen, S. (2000) *Cities in a World Economy*. London: Sage.

Scott, J. (2001) 'Fantasy Echo: History and the Construction of Identity', *Critical Inquiry*, 27(2): 284–304.

Seremetakis, C. N. (1994) 'Implications', in C. N. Seremetakis (ed.) *The Senses Still*. Boulder: Westview Press.

Shohat, E. and Stam, R. (1994) *Unthinking Eurocentrism*. London and New York: Routledge.

Smith, B. (1998) *The Gender of History: Men, Women and Historical Place*. Harvard: Harvard University Press.

Steedman, C. (2001) *Dust*. Manchester: Manchester University Press.

Stoller, P. (1992) *The Cinematic Griot: The Ethnography of Jean Rouch*. Chicago: Chicago University Press.

_____ (1997) *Sensuous Scholarship*. Philadelphia: University of Pennsylvania Press.

_____ (1999) 'Back to the Ethnographic Future'. *Journal of Contemporary Ethnography*, 28(6): 698–704.

Strang, Dr (1848/49) 'Report to Glasgow City Council on the Contribution of the Irish to Mortality in Glasgow', Glasgow Council Minutes, A2/1/5/24.

Taussig, M. (1993) *Mimesis and Alterity: A Particular History of the Senses*. London: Routledge.

Tracy, B. (1863) *Our Poor Law and our Poor or, the Poor Law of Scotland as affecting Irishmen and Catholics. A Lecture by Rev. Bernard Tracy*. Glasgow: Margey, Tracy and Walsh.

Travis, A. (2003) 'Nowhere to Go', *Guardian*, May 9.

Wigoder, M. (2001) 'History Begins at Home: Photography and Memory in the Writings of Siegfried Kracauer and Roland Barthes', *History and Memory*, 13(1): 19–59.

Williams, R. (1985) *Towards 2000*. London: Chatto and Windus.

Wren, M. (2003) Letter, *Guardian*, 26 November.

Ziarek, E. P. (2001) *An Ethics of Dissensus: Postmodernity, Feminism and the Politics of Radical Democracy*. Stanford: Stanford University Press.

IMAGING THE UNIMAGINABLE: *DISPUTED TERRITORY*
Anthony Haughey

PROJECT BACKGROUND

Disputed Territory (1999–2004) is a combined photographic and video-practice artwork project investigating the continuing conflict over territory, rights and ownership of land in Europe and the subsequent displacement and disappearance of communities in the aftermath of conflict. Culminating in photographic exhibitions, art books, installations, video and sound artefacts, *Disputed Territory* utilises diverse media formats in its effort to document post-conflict landscapes. What follows is a series of reflective commentaries looking back to when the work was first conceptualised in 1999, tracking the fieldwork and methodological detours that emerged along the way, in addition to analyses of critical debates on the nature of the photographic image and its complex relationship to the 'real'; finally I pose a series of questions as I look forward to and anticipate the possible methodological problems associated with the translation of accumulated research material into an exhibit in Wolverhampton Art Gallery (2007).

At the end of 2002, according to the estimates of the United States Committee for Refugees and Immigrants (USCR) the former Yugoslavia hosted the largest population of refugees in Europe (USCR 2004). Ten years of inter-ethnic conflict had led to internal displacement and forced migration within the international community. Although the central discussion throughout this chapter is focused on the challenges of representing the aftermath of conflict through practice-based research methodologies, it also engages with the displacement and forced migration that have followed the cessation of violence. The chapter, like the project, questions historical and emerging art and media discourses and explores the process and dynamics of working within a practice-based research framework.

From the outset, I anticipated the end point of this research to be an artefact, for which the traditional and temporary place of its public dissemination would be an art gallery or museum. There is, however, always a distance between what is presented to an audience on a museum wall or in a book and the experience of the viewer; as the research progressed I adopted a more experimental approach, potentially undermining established ways of encountering visual media. In producing *Disputed Territory* and the installation *Resolution* that forms part of it, the question of where and how the viewer should encounter the completed work was therefore a key consideration. Was it possible to embed the viewer within the completed artefact, in an environment simulating the original fieldwork locations?

The situation changed when in 2004 Wolverhampton Art Gallery expressed an interest in acquiring the *Resolution* installation for its permanent collection. This was not the outcome I had envisaged as it raised new, indeed potentially complex if not troubling, questions as to how the installation should be contextualised and interpreted within a museum environment, while remaining critically connected to the world outside. The research process, incorporating human rights interviews with survivors of the Bosnia and Kosovo conflicts articulated within experimental audio-visual presentations, had come to an unforeseen conclusion; its journey – through foregrounding and thinking about research methodologies to fieldwork, critical reflection and analysis, to the collation of visual media material and the public dissemination of the results in a series of experimental installations – was to end in a final definitive installation archived in a prominent gallery collection.

PHOTOGRAPHIC FIELDWORK

In 'Diaries and Fieldnotes in the Research Process' (2001), Darren Newbury advocates the use of fieldwork notes, diaries and logbooks as a critical component of art practice. He argues for a symbiotic relationship between theoretical concepts and field observations in which subjective and objective modes of conducting research become part of an inter-subjective paradigm. Following field methods used by Leonard Schatzman and Anselm Strauss (1973), Newbury outlines a logbook division into three sections: observational, theoretical and methodological notes. Fieldwork notes direct and continually inform the research process, and the recording tactics, according to Newbury, provide the researcher with an 'on-going, developmental dialogue'. Working with this fieldwork model in *Disputed Territory*, I documented everyday events in Ireland, Bosnia and Kosovo through the use of logbooks and visual media experimentation, alongside collaboration with specialist practitioners, social scientists, biotechnology researchers, conflict resolution agencies and NGOs.[1]

The use of photography and digital video provides a fast and efficient way of documenting unfolding phenomena and events. The legibility and legitimacy of such representations, however, is subject to a series of questions, negotiations and ethical responsibilities. In this respect, documentary photography has undergone rigorous scrutiny within realist and poststructuralist discourses over the last thirty years. The photographer Walker Evans acknowledged photography's subjective positioning as early as 1964, when he referred to his own photographic style as a form of 'lyric documentary' (see Tormey 2003). As Sarah Pink comments, subjectivity is a complex relationship between author, subject and viewer:

> A reflexive approach to analysis should concentrate on how the content of visual images is the result of the specific context of their production and on the diversity of ways that video and photographs are interpreted. Photographs and video may be treated as realist representations of the reality of fieldwork contexts as ethnographers understand them (as in the 'realist' tradition in documentary photography). But they are always representations of the subjective standpoints of the image producer and other viewers including informants. (2001: 117)

Critical debates within photographic discourse continue to be centred upon the photograph's relationship to reality. In the case of chemical photography, C. S. Peirce posits this relationship as 'indexical' in that the indexical sign points towards the event or situation it is recording (see Green & Lowry 2003: 48), described further by Susan Sontag as a 'trace, something directly stencilled off the real, like a footprint or a death mask' (1977: 154). The photograph has also been subjected to scrutiny for its capacity to 'gesture' beyond its immediate 'evidential force'. In this context David Green and Joanna Lowry situate the photographic image as a 'performative gesture' and see 'the very act of photography as a kind of performative gesture which points to an event in the world, as a form of designation that draws reality into the image field' (2003: 48) – not as a 'truthful' record of an event but 'question[ing] and draw[ing] our attention to the ways in which notions of the real are discursively produced' (2003: 58).

This debate about the limitations and the potential of the photographic 'real' has long preoccupied critics, with Walter Benjamin referring to Bertolt Brecht when he calls for a radical realism: 'less than ever does a simple *reproduction of reality* express something about reality' (1980: 213). Instead, Benjamin argues for something artificial to be constructed in order to mediate/document the 'real' to the viewer. Similarly, Allan Sekula argues for complex formulations of the 'real' or the reproduction of the 'real' through the photographic image and the necessity of documenting 'concrete social formation[s]' (1999: 122). Artists working toward this end, according to Sekula, 'may or may not produce images that are theatrical and overtly contrived, they may or may not present texts that read like fiction. Social truth is something other than a matter of convincing style' (ibid.) For Sekula, 'social truth' emerges in the intersubjective dialogue with the viewer, whereby lived concrete events are mediated through a photographic practice, conscious of the limitations of a simple-minded indexicality yet unwilling to let go of photography's ability to witness, document and translate the intricate and detailed realities, the often banal horrors of everyday life.

It is fair to say that the debate concerning photography's relationship to the 'real' is at best contradictory, with critics making contrary, often competing statements about photography's epistemological status. Take Sontag, for example, who vociferously points to the weaknesses of photographic representations of war and horror and how repeated exposure to such images desensitise the viewer; images therefore 'corrupt' and 'anesthetise' (1977: 21). In *Body Horror, Photojournalism, Catastrophe and War* (1998), John Taylor contradicts Sontag's arguments, arguing that on balance it is more important to view images of horror than to risk forgetting them. We may well live in a 'scopic regime', where global conflicts invade our living rooms daily, but as Taylor has commented, there are real bodies and real pain beyond the media representations. He invokes John Keane's definition of public controversy and the public sphere:

> Public spheres have four effects: they help keep alive memories of times when terrible things were done to people; they heighten awareness of current cruelty; they canvass and circulate judgements about whether violence is justified; they encourage people to find remedies for savagery. (1998: 4)

Taylor argues that the absence of images of horror in society can mislead viewers by

> drawing them away from recognizing significant crimes: through no obvious fault of their own, these people simply do not know. On the other hand, the presence of imagery and reports means that forgetting about them or refusing to see them is a deliberate choice, a conscious act of citizenship. (1998: 195)

Sontag re-evaluated her critique of conflict photographs in *Regarding the Pain of Others* (2003), noting that it is the medium specificity of television and news reporting that generates a passive response from the viewer. As an alternative, she argues that it is precisely how and where we encounter these images that dictates our response: 'An image is drained of its force by the way it is used, where and how often it is seen' (2003: 94). She also notes that the diversity of ways in which a photograph is encountered affects its impact; originating as a photojournalistic account in the pages of a newspaper or magazine, it can end up advertising commercial products. Art practitioners are not immune to this blurring of boundaries either; the supposed undermining of conventional subject/viewer relationships and commercial distribution systems associated with art practices can very quickly revert to product endorsement.

There is in all these accounts, despite their apparent differences, an acknowledgement of the role and function of the viewer/spectator or indeed what Green and Lowry cite above as the 'performative gesture' of the photograph, its ability to 'draw reality into the image field', a field that can only be accessed through an active or dialectical mode of 'looking'. Roland Barthes has long argued for this reflective approach to photographic representation of conflict, critically considering the discursive position of the viewer. In 'The Scandal of Horror Photography' from 1969 he reviews an exhibition of conflict photographs at the Orsay Gallery in Paris, noting that most of the pictures have no effect on him. He suggests that the photographers have 'over-elaborated' the horror, arguing, for example, that a photograph of a group of soldiers juxtaposed with another photograph of human skulls makes us conscious of the photographer's attempt to make the image signify 'horror'. This prevents the viewer from self-consciously analysing the event represented: 'We are each time violently dispossessed of our own freedom to judge the fact: another has groaned for us, thought for us, judged for us; the photographer has left us nothing – save only the right to intellectual acquiescence' (1999: 32). He refers to straight photographs: 'the naturalness of these pictures forces the spectator to interrogate them violently' (1999: 34). He is clearly more interested in the question of affect than in the essence of photographic truth and suggests that 'straight photography leads you to the scandal of horror, not to horror itself' (ibid.).

PHOTOGRAPHING CONFLICT

War has been a major subject for photographers since the invention of photography in 1839 and Roger Fenton carried his apparatus to the front line in the Crimean War (1854–56). As the official war photographer, he was under strict instructions from the British War Office not to portray the dead or injured and consequently most of his photographs were staged and featured heroic uniformed officers and groups of soldiers preparing cannon for battle. However, one photograph, 'The Valley of the Shadow of Death', goes beyond the sanitised version of war he was sent to capture: six hundred British soldiers, ambushed and killed by Russians near Balaklava and famously depicted in Tennyson's poem, 'The Charge of the Light Brigade'. Fenton's photograph did not show bodies strewn across the battlefield; instead, he inferred death by focusing upon hundreds of cannonballs scattered throughout the valley. He asks the viewer to work with the image, but more importantly

FIGURE 1: SHOTGUN CARTRIDGES, ARMAGH/LOUTH BORDER. 1998

for my argument here, the image assumes a level of active, forceful spectatorship; much like Barthes, somewhat ironically, calling on the spectator 'to interrogate violently'.

Conceived as a longitudinal project, *Disputed Territory* has evolved alongside critical reviews, which have served as meta-dialogue informing the work, allowing me to be more reflective (often with hindsight) about the relationship between fieldwork, the 'constructedness' of the image and the impact on the viewer. For example, Anne McNeill (2000), writing in the exhibition catalogue *Warning Shots*, compares Fenton's photograph to one from the *Disputed Territory* series, where the foreground is emphasised, revealing thousands of red, white and blue shotgun cartridges. [DVD REF 1: PHOTO]

This image could be read as an artist's intervention, as in land art when an object is artificially constructed or the topography of the landscape changed by mechanical or other means, but in *Disputed Territory* there is no such physical construction of objects. It reflects rather a process of long-term observation, a kind of archaeological mining, where my aim was to uncover tensions beneath the surface appearance of the contested terrain between the North and South of Ireland, while reflecting upon historical, political and emerging discourses within the specificity of this geographical location.

Mirroring Green and Lowry (2003), McNeill argues that 'landscape can be made to perform; be altered and (re)presented for and by the camera' (2000: 12). She acknowledges the subjective position of the author; this is not simply a recording of what is in front of the camera lens, it is a re-framing of collective memory/history to encourage a critical dialogue with the viewer. Similarly Justin Carville's writing informs my research process when he comments on some early images from *Disputed Territory* and the difficulty of representing contested territories in locations such as Northern Ireland in his *Re-Negotiated Territory: The Politics of Place, Space and Landscape in Irish Photography* (2001). He argues for oppositional strategies to engage with the viewer in order to undermine predominant media images of Northern Ireland and suggests that by reconsidering visual methodologies it is possible to present 'multiple and contested narratives' for the viewer. For Carville, it is the necessary documentation of 'the allegory of the everyday [which] incorporates the use of everyday objects, banal and frequently arbitrary fragments, [a strategy employed] to rescue those histories and narratives of subaltern groups that are in danger of disappearing under the weight of traditional and totalizing images' (2001: 7). And here the 'traditional and totalizing' images are of course the repetitive, cliché-worn images of news reporting. Echoing Benjamin, Barthes, Sontag, Sekula and Green and Lowry, Carville acknowledges the intersubjective interpretation of images: 'The image as allegory is in need of completion by the viewer' (ibid.).

Documenting conflict or post-conflict landscapes remains, however, a difficult and challenging process for the photographer. Historically it has proved problematic yet it is even more so today, with the somewhat discredited tradition of the photojournalist (now often embedded) and the failure of media technology to 'capture' the complexities of modern warfare. Complicating this further is the emergence of a new orthodoxy of the gallery-oriented image, influenced by a neo-modernist aesthetic and clearly at odds with the 'committed' reportage method. As Sekula comments, there is currently a glut of images circulating the globe which 'appear' to be immersed within the politics of representation:

> The genre has simultaneously contributed much to spectacle, to retinal excitation, to voyeurism, to terror, envy and nostalgia and only a little to the critical understanding of the social world … A truly social documentary will frame the crime, the trial, the system of justice and its official myths (1999: 122).

What Sekula calls for is a mode of discursive documentation, framing the 'event' in its historical, lived and official context. No easy task given the messiness of most conflicts, the intractable nature of 'evidence' and the politics of silence that emerges in the aftermath of conflict. How then can documentary photography adequately address such intricacies? Can it claim to 'document' phenomena and events which have multiple and contradictory spatio-temporal frames of reference? For whom is this post-conflict landscape being documented and to what end? If I expanded my fieldwork to include other media formats and methodologies – including video installation and sound – would this necessarily solve the problem of exoticising conflict, of rendering complex social realities abstract in the hallowed and white halls of the art gallery? These were just some of the questions I carried with me as I began the section of *Disputed Territory* that was situated in the Balkans. I was faced with an event which had already passed into memory/history (since the conflict, albeit, officially ended in 1995), and had been hyper-represented in the press, yet I knew the experience of ten years of war was etched into the psyche of Bosnian, Croatian and Serbian citizens.[2] I was in many ways the quintessential figure imagined by David Campany, the photographer who represents events long after they occurred, documenting 'the trace of a *trace of* the event' (2003: 124):

> Turn[ing] up late, wander[ing] through the places where things have happened totting up the effects of the world's activity. This is a kind of photograph that foregoes the representation of events in progress and so cedes them to other media. As a result it is quite different from the spontaneous snapshot and has a different relation to memory and to history (ibid.).

CONFLICT: BOSNIA AND KOSOVO

In 1995 the Dayton Accord signalled the official cessation of violence in Bosnia, but four years later the landscape was still 'scarred' with obvious relics of conflict. I was interested in signs, often invisible on the surface, which 'gestured' to underlying questions connected to history and memory. Close observation of landscape can reveal reminders of struggle and spaces of reflexive mediation, as Jan-Erik Lundström suggests:

> Imaging the landscape is a particularly incisive and charged practice within contemporary visual culture, where landscape is a contested space, a cultural, historical and political variable, defined by human action and imagination. Visual representations of landscape are instrumental not only as ways of exploring meaning or reflecting collective knowledge, but also as paths towards identity, self-recognition and transformation. (2002)

In one image the viewer is directed towards a large area of grey ash in an open field. [DVD REF 2: PHOTO] Weeds have started to emerge from the ashes and visible within the remnants of the fire are thousands of rusting metal objects: lever arch files used to collate and index information. Why were the files burned? Was it to remove evidence of citizenship? Reports during the conflict in the former Yugoslavia suggested that, in addition to widespread slaughter or forced removal across 'national' boundaries, ethnic groups were in many cases erased from state records, their passports and identity papers taken away at gunpoint, while churches (Orthodox and Catholic) and mosques were destroyed in a blatant attempt to wipe out historical and cultural traces of specific ethnic identities. But the destruction of official records is not always an aggressive act; it can be a defensive strategy or an act of defiance, intended to protect the identity of prominent citizens, politicians, activists and others who influence and lead communities under attack. Meaning is never fixed; it is contingent and shifts with the passage of time, and here the immediate 'evidential' force of the photograph is transcended by an avoidance of images normally associated with war, encouraging a quieter, reflective 'reading'.

FIGURE 2: DESTROYED FILES, SARAJEVO, 1999

Photographic 'evidence' has played a significant role in the aftermath of the Kosovo conflict. Serbian military carried cameras into the conflict zone and produced snapshots (war trophies) of each other following attacks on ethnic Albanian villages.[3] Photographs were reportedly recovered from Serbian homes in the Pejë/Peć area in Kosovo by members of the Kosovo Liberation Army following the ceasefire and subsequently handed over to Human Rights Watch researchers, who used them during interviews with survivors to identify alleged perpetrators of war crimes (see Abrahams *et al.* 2001: 131–78). There are historical precedents for battlefield photographs of this kind: soldiers posed next to destroyed military hardware and killed or injured combatants during World War II.

During August 1999 I conducted fieldwork in the city of Pejë/Peć, seat of the Orthodox patriarch and strongly associated historically with Serbian identity. The majority ethnic Albanian population there had been forced into exile, an estimated 90 per cent of them having been expelled across the border into refugee camps in neighbouring Albania and Macedonia in the first week of the conflict. On 24 March 1999 NATO intervened, bombing Serbian positions and pushing the Serbian military out of Kosovo. By the end of August 1999, an estimated 235,000 Serb civilians and other minorities either left with the military convoys or were subsequently intimidated into leaving by extremist ethnic

Albanian groups and are currently displaced within Serbia and Montenegro (Amnesty International 2003). The majority of ethnic Serb refugees continue to live outside Kosovo, unable to return to their homes for fear of recrimination. Ethnic Serbs and other minorities such as the Roma who remained in Kosovo after June 1999 live in fear within enclaves, unable to travel freely without KFOR protection. Ethnic Albanians returned from exile in June 1999 to find their homes, schools, mosques and businesses destroyed. According to UNHCR figures, 250,000 people were still internally displaced in Kosovo at the end of 2000.

As Serbian troops retreated from Kosovo, international non-governmental organisations (NGOs) moved in and began to re-construct houses before the onset of winter. GOAL, an Irish NGO, was also anxious to ensure that the education of returning refugee children did not suffer and embarked on a school reconstruction programme with financial support from the Irish public. One project was based in Vaso Pashe Primary School, Pejë/Peć, which had been used as a barracks and defensive position by Serbian forces between February and June 1999. During my research visit I found several 'damaged' official photographs of groups of schoolchildren buried under debris in the corner of a classroom. Several had been torn to pieces but one was still intact.

On closer inspection of this 6 x 4 inch, black-and-white photograph, I saw that the face of every child in the group had been scratched out, a practice reminiscent of the Soviet Union in the Stalinist era, when the faces of prominent political figures were erased from photographs and history. [DVD REF 3: PHOTO]

The headmaster of Vaso Pashe Primary School had taken the original photograph in 1973. He had photographed the graduation class every year for as long as he could remember and it had been a rite of passage for these ethnic Albanian children. In 1973

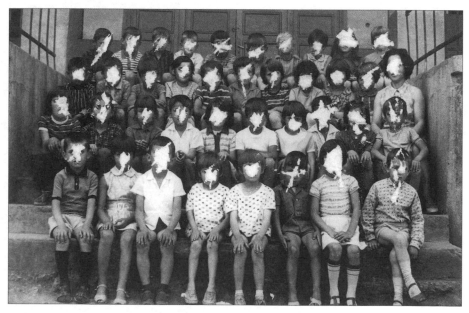

FIGURE 3: FOUND PHOTOGRAPH, KOSOVO SCHOOLCHILDREN, PEJË/PEĆ

Kosovo had been part of the Federal Republic of Yugoslavia, a country with a Communist regime, although it had been expelled from the Soviet-led eastern bloc in 1948. Between 1974 and 1989 Kosovo had enjoyed a period of autonomy within Yugoslavia and ethnic Albanians had a measure of cultural freedom. For 26 years the photograph of the school-children lay undisturbed in the classroom. Then, in 1999, Serbian military forces had occupied the school.

On my return to Ireland I archived this photograph, but almost two years later I came across it in my studio and was struck by its significance. In September 2001 I returned to Kosovo and revisited the repaired Vaso Pashe Primary School, where I showed the damaged photograph to the headmaster and teachers; during the discussion that followed, the historical and symbolic resonance of this violated photograph emerged. The teachers circulated copies within the Pejë/Peć community and accessed school records that had escaped the attention of Serbian forces in an attempt to reveal the identity and fate of each of the pupils. Several days later I received an incomplete register of the identified schoolchildren. Ten years old in 1973, they would have been about 36 during the conflict in Kosovo and by 2001 many would probably be parents with children much the same age as they had been when they were photographed. The research indicated that most of them had survived the conflict, although many had been displaced and were living in other parts of Europe. A silence surrounded several in the group, whose whereabouts and identity could not be confirmed.

For an artist, the re-reading of an archive is not only an academic exercise; it can also be a societal intervention, where historical narratives are ruptured and re-contextualised, generating an emerging critical and contested site of re-interpretation. Stuart Hall argues for a 'living archive' (2001: 90), extracting and elucidating past histories and hidden information for critical attention; re-reading the archive in this way may be considered transformative. I subsequently used this photograph (with the school's permission) and produced an intervention where the photograph was re-contextualised and re-circulated in *An Leabhar Mór/The Great Book of Gaelic* (Maclean & Dorgan 2002), a collaboration between artists and writers in Ireland and Scotland who were invited to respond to the theme of migration. The photograph was titled 'Class of 73' and a list of names and current whereabouts was printed beneath it, with additional references to war and displacement. Where a member of the group could not be identified the text read 'fate and identity unknown'.

In February 2004 the same photograph (without text) was copied onto a slide and projected life-size into the courtyard of the Centre Culturel Irlandais in Paris, where the exhibition/installation *Disputed Territory/Resolution* opened to the public. [DVD REF 4: PHOTO] The centre, an art gallery and residential building, had formerly been a seventeenth-century seminary known as the Irish College and was later used by the US army at the end of World War II as a haven for war refugees. The projected photograph was juxtaposed against the architecture and historicity of the institution, encouraging a dialectic re-reading of the image. Also installed within the courtyard and pinned to trees around the garden was a series of enlarged ink-jet passport photographs of ethnic Albanian women, a poignant reminder of the plight of this group of refugees who had their passports confiscated at gunpoint as they left their villages or at border crossings; many were also forced to leave without their sons and husbands.

FIGURE 4: PROJECTION, 'CLASS OF 73', PEJË/PEĆ, KOSOVO

FIGURE 5: ETHNIC ALBANIAN REFUGEE

IMAGING THE UNIMAGINABLE   63

Thousands of ethnic Albanian citizens entered refugee camps without any identity documents, rendering them stateless. However, passport photographs were produced by Izmai Luta, a Macedonian commercial photographer, who had, it is estimated, photographed 26,879 Kosovar Albanians by June 1999 in a humanitarian gesture which was also the symbolic restoration of a stolen identity; more importantly, refugees with an identity document combined with an IRC Green Card could avail themselves of UNHCR services (Dalrymple 1999: 5–9).

In 1995, during the height of the Bosnian conflict, Srebrenica's civilian population lived under the protection of United Nations Security Council Resolution 819, which established the world's first UN Safe Area, protected by Dutch UN troops (Dutchbat). 'Safe areas' were supposed to obviate the need for citizens to seek refuge in other countries, effectively negating the international community's responsibility to intervene and stop inter-ethnic conflict or to offer asylum in their respective countries. On 10 July 1995 two-thirds of Srebrenica's population of 40,000 fled to the Dutch base at Potocari, several kilometres from the centre of the town, to escape the onslaught of Serbian troops under the command of General Mladic. Despite assurances from the Dutch UN commander that the population would be protected, the Serbs quickly took control at Potocari. Reportedly assisted by Dutchbat soldiers, they separated the men and boys from the women. It is estimated that, in one week, over seven thousand mostly Muslim men and boys 'disappeared'. It was widely reported and corroborated by eye-witness accounts that the 'disappeared' had been removed from Potocari and systematically murdered.[4] A report published in April 2002 into the Srebrenica massacre, the worst atrocity in Europe since the Holocaust, led to the resignation of the Dutch government. Recovery of the victims of the massacre has proved to be problematic. Tampering with graves has complicated efforts to bring prosecutions at the War Crimes Tribunal in The Hague and also means that relatives may never find the remains of dead family members. The former battery plant in Potocari, where the Dutch UN forces were stationed and the Srebrenica atrocity occurred, has become a memorial to the victims of genocide in Bosnia; a section of the site is now a burial ground for the recovered and identified remains of the missing.

POST-CONFLICT

In the aftermath of conflict it is possible to observe history under construction. Visual media can contribute to knowledge and understanding of past events and keep alive the memories of those who lost their lives. Taylor argues that 'memory is not simply a trick or faculty of the mind without obligation … The act of remembrance is also the payment of a debt owed to the dead; failure to bear witness may be even more unendurable than the act of recollection' (1999: 298). In September 2002 I visited a facility of the International Commission on Missing Persons (ICMP), a non-political organisation in northeast Bosnia. It was set up to support the recovery and identification of victims exhumed from mass graves all over Bosnia and Kosovo and is supported by the Podrinje Identification Project (PIP), which concentrates on the recovery of persons missing following the fall of Srebrenica and the systematic murder of Muslim citizens in July 1995. My experience of immersion within the ICMP facility and my interviews with key personnel were documented, collated and critically analysed for subsequent media representation.

The ICMP is endeavouring to bring closure to grieving families and friends who live in hope of being reunited with a registered missing person following a decade of conflict in the Balkans. Its main co-ordination centre is located at Mejdan-Bosna Srebrene, a former sports stadium in Tuzla in northeast Bosnia. Located at the edge of the town is another ICMP facility, a morgue which contains the remains of thousands of massacre victims exhumed from sites in Bosnia and Kosovo. It is believed that, in many cases, the remains are those of victims of the Srebrenica massacre. The ICMP has been developing a DNA-testing system since the beginning of 2000 and proposes, using recently developed technologies, to identify 90 per cent of massacre victims over eight to ten years. 'Using traditional identification methods', states Adnan Rizvic, director of the project, 'the process would take eighty to ninety years'.[5] DNA profiles from blood samples of family members who survived the conflict are compared to profiles from exhumed bodies. A match between a sample in the blood reference database and an exhumed body is a 'strong indication' of an individual's identity. There are family outreach centres for collecting blood samples in Tuzla, Sarajevo, Mostar, Sanski Most and Banja Luka. There are also mobile teams that collect samples from all over Bosnia-Herzegovina. 'Most of the staff have worked for a long time with the ICMP', Rizvic noted, 'and are trained on how to approach people (relatives) and how to take blood samples'. During this process a series of questions is asked about the visual appearance of the missing persons, the clothes they were wearing, and their personal belongings such as jewellery or a cigarette case. There will also be questions about physical characteristics such as height, distinguishing body characteristics or former bone fractures. When the information is gathered a file is opened and data transferred to a computer database.

The Podrinje Identification Project (PIP) supports the DNA sampling project, as well as carrying out more traditional forensic work, such as identifying bodies by means of old injuries and clothes. Small bone samples are also taken, bar-coded for anonymity (to prevent tampering) and sent to a laboratory in Sarajevo, where the DNA is extracted. DNA results from the blood and bone samples are returned to the ICMP in Tuzla, where matches are co-ordinated. The DNA programme had its first successful match on 16 November 2001 and by the end of December 2003 the number had risen to 5,727. The number of missing individuals represented by blood samples amounted to 22,827 according to an IMCP quarterly report in 2003.[6] The ICMP estimate that 'around 100,000 blood samples need to be collected in order to identify all of the missing in the region'.[7]

Rizvic claims that the DNA identification project is completely objective and scientific but, as Nedim Durakovic, case manager of the PIP points out, 'a positive DNA match is only the beginning of the process; clothing and personal belongings recovered from exhumed remains must be cross-referenced for conclusive identification by family members'. 'This', Durakovic claims, 'also empowers family members to be in control of the final positive identification. Local personnel are trained to do this work.' Rizvic explains that 'the most important aspect of this job is not the pay cheque, but the commitment of each member of the team to get results as efficiently and quickly as possible'. The project relies on international funding, of which the largest contributor is the USA, closely followed by the Netherlands. The ICMP's DNA-profiling software technology (designed by Bosnian researchers) has subsequently been used to help identify victims from the terrorist attack on the World Trade Center in New York and was offered to teams recovering remains in mass graves in Iraq.

The real horror of the aftermath of genocide is contained within the morgue, a former warehouse located at the edge of the town of Tuzla. Walking into it is truly harrowing: row upon row of unidentified human remains stacked six-high on stainless steel mortuary trays, currently identifiable for administrative purposes only by a bar code or number hand-written in marker pen on the surface of plastic refuge sacks. Lost individual identities await DNA analysis to begin the lengthy and difficult process of recovery, which will lead to the dignity of burial in a marked grave and allow the grieving process to begin.

RESOLUTION:[8] THE PERSISTENCE OF EVIDENCE AND TESTIMONY

During my fieldwork in the ICMP facility I produced a series of photographs and digital video footage. In one of the video sequences the viewer is confronted with the forensic examination of clothing following the exhumation of human remains discovered in mass graves. [DVD REF 5: VIDEO] A continuous cycle of searching, cataloguing and cross-referencing is repeated daily until the identification process is complete. In the digital video sequence the camera is locked down and focused on the floor. The viewer is denied a direct view of the forensic technician searching through the detritus of human life, looking for clues that may identify a registered 'missing person'. As the sequence slowly unfolds bullet holes can be seen in clothing. On the floor there is a steady accumulation of dust, which has fallen from clothing and forensic bags. The technician walks out of the frame and returns with a brush; carefully, he sweeps the dust to one side of the room, but is never quite out of sight. He returns to the mortuary to collect further bags and the cycle repeats, with further forensic examination of the recovered clothing of other individuals. Later, during editing, the sequence is looped to emphasise the continuity and endless cycle of searching. What is represented in this video sequence is not only the aftermath of the Balkan war, but also a wider historical reference to conflict and to the Sisyphean task of recovering the identities of individuals who have disappeared, erased from state records and kept alive only in the memories of family and friends.

Human Rights Watch researchers have gathered evidence and eyewitness accounts of wide-scale human rights abuses following the cessation of hostilities in the Balkans and survivors' narratives describing acts of extreme barbarism have been collated. It is clearly important that these testimonies are recorded, not only to give justice to the victims of genocide but also to bear witness so that future generations will know the history of one of Europe's darkest moments. Primo Levi (1988), recalling the horror of the Nazi camps and the pleasure the SS guards took in telling their victims that their experiences would not be remembered, was aware of the threat that the oppressors would attempt to control history by erasing memory. I collated testimony from survivors' accounts in the Human Rights Watch archives and directly from informants in fieldwork locations in Bosnia and Kosovo; many of the survivors and NGOs I spoke to insisted, as Levi did, 'the world should know what happened here'. Gendered survivors' stories were narrated and recorded bilingually (Serbo-Croat and English) by a man and a woman (names withheld), former residents of Sarajevo who had been evacuated during the siege of 1992 and were currently living in Ireland. A further recording was produced in (American) English, evoking a nuanced international dimension – the 'CNN effect'. The three recordings were subsequently edited together and the resulting bilingual audio track contains the accounts of survivors; sixteen minutes long, it is looped to allow for co-ordination with other elements of the *Resolution* installation. The opening sequence is relayed to the listener without translation, acknowledging the integrity of the original location and source. [DVD REF 6: AUDIO] The recorded testimonies document acts of great courage, as well as instances when a split-second decision meant the difference between life and death. Human Rights Watch researcher Fred Abrahams recorded the testimony of an ethnic Albanian man on 16 July 1999:

> They cursed Albanians and then they set the house on fire. They broke a window and lit the stuffing from a mattress and put it over the bodies. I pushed the bodies aside and got out. I decided it was better to kill me than to be burned alive, so I jumped out of the window. I went one hundred metres and hid. (Abrahams *et al.* 2001: 152) [DVD REF 7: AUDIO]

And so in May 2003, *Resolution*, the culmination of the fieldwork cited above, was opened in White's Cold Store, Dundalk, Co. Louth, Ireland. The material was translated into an experimental, site-specific, audio-visual installation, where the architecture, temperature, smells and sounds within this space referenced a material manifestation of the original fieldwork location, the ICMP facility in Tuzla, Bosnia. There was no interference with day-to-day arrangements at White's, which continued to function as a cold-storage facility. The installation was constructed to replicate a series of critical interventions undertaken throughout the field work, and was thus integrated into the very fabric of the building. Borrowing from Stoller's argument concerning the limitations of a purely 'visual' knowledge, I was interested in staging the research material so that it reflected the diverse realities shaping this post-conflict landscape. As he writes: 'it is especially important to incorporate into the ethnographic works the sensuous body – its smells, tastes, textures, and sensations' (1997: xv). *Resolution* attempts to place the viewer somatically closer to the experience of the subject, encouraging an intense reflective and critical engagement, while simultaneously acknowledging the audience as an integral part of the work.

On entering the storage facility, the viewer was confronted by a 1:1 scale projection. [DVD REF 8: PHOTO] The projected image was a representation of the morgue facility in Tuzla, the scale of this projection mirroring the original fieldwork location. The viewer interrupted the projection by walking through a light beam, momentarily casting a shadow on to the image, an implicit acknowledgement of the viewer's role in constructing meaning from the installation. The viewer then walked into the main meat-preparation area, [DVD REF 9: PHOTO] where previously recorded survivors' testimonies from Bosnia and Kosovo were relayed bilingually in a continuous sound loop. [DVD REF 10: AUDIO] This was combined with references to DNA analysis, outlined above, and the forensic apparatus used in the recovery of human remains during fieldwork in Bosnia and Kosovo. The DVD video sequence was installed at one end of the meat-preparation area and projected from the entrance of a walk-in refrigerator on to the opposite wall; the viewer could choose to stand at the entrance or walk inside to observe video footage. [DVD REF 11: PHOTO]

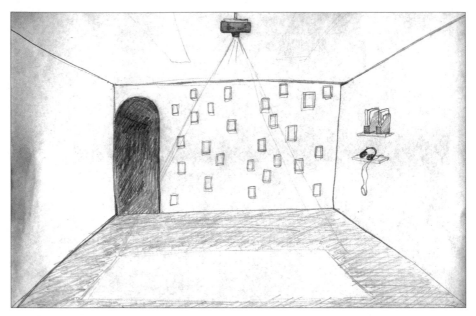

FIGURE 6: WOLVERHAMPTON INSTALLATION DRAWING

At the beginning of this chapter I mentioned that the installation *Resolution* was to be placed in the permanent collection of Wolverhampton Art Gallery. This involved lengthy negotiations with gallery staff and visits to the gallery to discuss with curators how it should be installed, contextualised and 'read' alongside the existing collection. While in Wolverhampton I used a digital camera to map the proposed exhibition space visually and subsequently produced an installation drawing for further discussion.

Resolution opened to the public following the refurbishment of the existing galleries in early 2007. The installation contains interactive elements, which enable the viewer to handle and read files relating to recent events and to reports following the cessation of conflict in the Balkans, including references to The Hague War Crimes Tribunal. 'Class of 73', described earlier in this chapter, is included in the exhibition *Children in Conflict* at the Wolverhampton Art Gallery, autumn 2007.

Notes

1   Originally concerned with conflict in Ireland, the project later extended its scope to include Bosnia and Kosovo, the main focus of this chapter.
2   For an account of the Balkan conflict, see Milosevic (1991), Silber & Little (1996), Glenny (2001) and Abrahams et al. (2001).
3   See <http://www.guardianunlimited.co.uk/gall/0,8542,514609,00.html> [Accessed 1 April 2005].
4   See <http://www.pbs.org/wnet/cryfromthegrave> [Accessed 31 March 2005].
5   Interview with Adnan Rizvic, Head of the International Centre for Missing Persons Identification Coordination Program, Tuzla, N.E. Bosnia (8 September 2002).

Interview with Nedim Durakovic, case manager of The Podrinje Identification Project, Tuzla, N.E. Bosnia (9 September 2002).

6   See International Commission on Missing Persons Quarterly Report (October–December 2003). Available at <http://www.ic-mp.org/home.php?act=actupd> [Accessed 12 April 2005].

7   See International Commission on Missing Persons Activity Update (May-August 2002). Available at <http://www.ic-mp.org/home.php?act=actupd> [Accessed 12 April 2005].

8   There is a certain ambiguity to the title of this installation. It refers to the resolution, through scientific research, of the question of the identity of missing persons, but it also has a political dimension, evoking the UN resolutions pertaining to the conflict in the Balkans.

Bibliography

Abrahams, F., G. Peress and E. Stover (2001) *A Village Destroyed May 14 1999: War Crimes in Kosovo*. Human Rights Center, Berkeley: University of California Press.

Amnesty International (2003) '*Serbia and Montenegro (Kosovo/Kosova) 'Prisoners in our own homes': Amnesty International's Concerns for the Human Rights of Minorities in Kosovo/Kosova*'. Available at <http://web.amnesty.org/library/index/engeur700102003> [Accessed 12 April 2005].

Barthes, R. (1982) *Camera Lucida*. London: Jonathan Cape.

_____ (1999 [1969]) 'The Scandal of Horror Photography', in D. Brittain (ed.) *Creative Camera: 30 Years of Writing*. Manchester: Manchester University Press.

Benjamin, W. (1980 [1931]) 'A Short History of Photography', in A. Trachtenberg (ed.) *Classic Essays on Photography*. New Haven: Leete's Island Books.

Campany, D. (2003) *Safety in Numbness: Some Remarks on Problems of Late Photography*, in D. Green (ed.) *Where is the Photograph?* Brighton: Photoworks/Photoforum.

Carville, J. (2001) 'Re-Negotiated Territory: The Politics of Place, Space and Landscape in Irish Photography', *Afterimage*, 28, July/August.

Dalrymple, J. (1999) 'The Faces in the Crowd', *Independent on Sunday*, 6 June.

Glenny, M. (2001) *The Balkans 1904–1999: Nationalism, War and the Great Powers*. London: Penguin.

Green, D. and J. Lowry (2003) 'From Presence to the Performative: Rethinking Photographic Indexicality', in D. Green (ed.) *Where is the Photograph?* Brighton: Photoworks/Photoforum.

Hall, S. (2001) 'Constituting an Archive', *Third Text*, Spring: 89–92.

Levi, P. (1988) *The Drowned and the Saved*. London: Abacus.

Lundström J. E. (2002) Press release for exhibition, *The Politics of Place*. BildMuseet, Umea, Sweden (10 Feb–28 April).

Maclean, M. and T. Dorgan (eds) (2002) *An Leabhar Mór/The Great Book of Gaelic*. Edinburgh: Canongate.

McNeill, A. (2000) *The Squalid and the Sublime*, in the Exhibition Catalogue *Warning Shots*: Royal Armouries Museum Leeds.

Milosevic, M. (1991) 'The War that is Tearing us Apart. The Protest of the Serbian Academics'. *Vreme News Digest Agency*, 9. (November 25).

Newbury, D. (2001) '*Diaries and Fieldnotes in the Research Process*'. Available at <http://www.biad.uce.ac.uk/research/rti/riadm/issue1/abstract.htm> [Accessed 8 April 2005].

Pink, S. (2001) *Doing Ethnography: Images, Media and Representation in Research*. London: Sage.

Schatzman, L. and A. Strauss (1973) *Field Research: Strategies for a Natural Sociology*. Englewood Cliffs:

Prentice-Hall.

Sekula, A. (1999 [1984]) 'Dismantling Modernism, Reinventing Documentary (Notes on the Politics of Representation)', in *Dismal Science Photo Works 1972–1996*. University Galleries of Illinois State University.

Silber, L. and A. Little (1996) *The Death Of Yugoslavia*. London: Penguin.

Sontag, S. (1977) *On Photography*. London: Penguin.

_____ (2003) *Regarding the Pain of Others*. London: Hamish Hamilton.

Stoller, P. (1997), *Sensuous Scholarship*. Philadelphia: University of Pennsylvania Press.

Taylor, J. (1998) *Body Horror, Photojournalism, Catastrophe and War*. Manchester: Manchester University Press.

_____ (1999 [1998]) 'Shock Photos', in D. Brittain (ed.) *Creative Camera: 30 Years of Writing*. Manchester: Manchester University Press.

Tormey, J. (2003) 'Walker Evans' Counter Aesthetic', *Afterimage*, 31, July/August. Available at <http://find-articles.com/p/articles/mi_m2479/is_1_31/ai_113683511> [Accessed 8 April 2005].

USCR (2004) *World Refugee Survey 2003 Country Report, Yugoslavia*. Available at <http://www.refugees.org/countryreports.aspx?subm=&ssm=&cid=189> [Accessed 12 April 2005].

ICONOLOGY: EXPLORING THE DVD IN SOUTHERN AFRICAN MIGRANT CULTURE RESEARCH

David Coplan and Gei Zantzinger

Between 1984 and 1986 anthropologist David Coplan and ethnomusicologist Gei Zantzinger created a cinematic narration of the folk performances of Lesotho migrant workers in southern Africa, entitled *Songs of the Adventurers* (1986).[1] The title is as close as to the sense of the Sesotho[2] name for the poetic song style on which the project was focused, *difela tsa ditsamaya-naha*, literally, 'songs of those-who-travel-the-country'. David Coplan's research into the history, ethnography and performance culture of Basotho 'peasantarians' (1994: 104) continued, and additional still photographs and footage from both the original and subsequent field tours have been worked into the body of the film. Gei Zantzinger, who has never lost his fascination with Sesotho ethno-aesthetics and historically emergent forms of cultural practice and self-narration, has sought ways to use the hours of fascinating primary footage on allied domains of Sesotho performance that he had not been able to include in the 48-minute documentary. So when DVD technology appeared it seemed most suitable to this end. Zantzinger has been designing ways of reworking the film so as to make both the original cut and lengthy sequences of additional footage available as a single, integrated work for those who might wish to see or use it for educational and research purposes.

Before discussing how the possibilities of DVD are employed to enhance and transform *Songs of the Adventurers*, we provide an account of the genesis and history of the project, as well as some insight into the implications of the space in time between the original ethnographic research and film project and the current DVD re-production. Over the past twenty years we have ourselves come to feel like adventurers, and the film our song. *Ho tseba naha ke ho hata mohlaba* ('To know the world one must walk the country') say the Basotho. Let us then sing some parts of our adventurous song, each in his own voice, like *difela* poets answering one another at a session.

DAVID COPLAN...

The cinematic dimension of the project was conceived in April 1984, when I was holed up in Lesotho, a black country that colonial history had deposited like Jonah in the belly of the white-ruled leviathan of South Africa; Lesotho is the only independent state in the world completely surrounded by another. How this came to be is a story both heroic and tragic in the classic dramatical sense; it is also a story of African cattlemen deprived of their fields and herds and forced instead to labour in the bowels of the earth as part of a system of racial capitalist production which, while rapidly transforming, survives to this day. The Basotho of King Moshweshwe I's emerging nation were migrating south to work in the Cape Colony from the beginning of the 1820s. By the 1860s, despite a heroic defence against a stream of local, imperial and colonial invaders, they were on the verge of defeat and dispossession by the settlers of the neighbouring Republic of the Orange Free State. Fearing Afrikaner expansionism, the British high commissioner stepped in and annexed 'Basutoland' as one of the Cape's native reserves. Still fearing national extinction, the Basotho aristocracy sent their followers to Kimberley, where Cecil Rhodes happily sold them the best firearms available as the price of their labour in the diggings.

On the more than 200-mile walk to the diamond fields, groups of young migrants used the resources of Sesotho song and spoken art to beguile the time, boost their courage and seek a common understanding of the changes in Basotho life of which they were both the subjects and the instruments. In time, they created *sefela* (*difela* is the plural form), a partly narrative, partly lyrical genre of sung poetry. The importance of Kimberley in the emergence of the *sefela* genre is reflected in contemporary poets' references to the immoral, diamond-rush atmosphere of the city's early years:

> *You know, I speak of Kimberley;*
> *I speak of Sodom...*

When the Cape ordered all natives in their dominions to disarm, the Basotho refused to surrender their rifles and in the 'Gun War' of 1880–81 shot up and expelled the Cape cavalry. Basutoland became a direct protectorate of the British crown. The basis for the eventual political independence of Lesotho was set, but the economic die was also cast. Confined to the largely uncultivable mountainous remnant of their former domain, Basotho flocked to the mine compounds of Johannesburg after gold was discovered there in 1886. They also held their own as cereal farmers and stockmen until colonial underdevelopment and the Great Depression turned Lesotho from a granary to a labour reserve (Murray 1980). By the mid-1980s there were more than 125,000 Basotho migrants employed in the gold, diamond, platinum and coal mines of South Africa. Mine migration involved over half of Lesotho's male population of working age and earned more than half of the country's gross domestic product. Basotho women either remained behind, dependent on mine wage remittances to feed their children or, legally and illegally, followed their men out of the harsh poverty of Lesotho to the mine shantytowns and urban black locations across the border. It was this world of work and wandering, of roots and routes (Clifford 1997) that the songs of the adventurers – male and female – poeticised, reflected upon and celebrated.

The word *sefela* ordinarily refers to Christian hymns; the first collection of Sesotho hymns, published in the mid-nineteenth century, was called *Difela tsa Sione*, the 'Hymns of Zion' (see Adams 1974: 137). The term was, however, loaned to rather than borrowed from the missionaries. R.I.M. Moletsane (1982: 2) suggests that *sefela* originally referred to the self-praises recited as solo passages within the choral songs performed by initiates upon their graduation. If so, then conceptual linkages can be established that relate the performance contexts and expressive purposes of *difela tsa ditsamaya-naha* to the praise poetry of proud new initiates. Questioned about the linkage that might have led the missionaries to identify Sesotho hymnody with initiates' praises, informants referred to the intense emotionality of hymns, choral and praise passages, and migrants' sung poetry. All of these they described as 'cries from the heart,' emphasising the importance of feeling in the expressive impact of oral texts. *Difela* represent a kind of expressive realisation of the imaginative projection of experience in initiation songs and praises through the aesthetic construction of a man's actual experience at the mines.

My mission in Lesotho was to research these songs within the broader, intertextual performance culture of these Basotho migrant mine workers and working women. South Africa's mineral wealth was, after all, expended in significant measure on the securocratic apparatus required to oppress black workers such as the Basotho who, lacking other options, left their homes and risked their lives to extract it from the entrails of the earth. As foreign blacks on mine contract permits and speaking only Sesotho they had, in the early 1980s, little place in the public discourse of protest. Yet the politics and consciousness emergent from four generations of lived experience could be found inscribed in their live performative genres. In a tour to Lesotho six years previously I had 'discovered' such a genre: *difela*. These songs provided a remarkable poetic of a particular 'structure of feeling' (Williams 1977): Basotho experience in South Africa's 'primitive accumulation' by means of racial capitalism over the previous century. In their performance, those with the requisite cultural knowledge and inclination might hear the history of South Africa's black mineworkers in their own aural literary voices.

Four months into the tour Gei Zantzinger, who had been responsible for my first tour to South Africa in 1975, arrived on an exploratory visit. His antennae for potential projects finely tuned, Zantzinger asked me what I was doing in such a 'woebegone backwater'. 'Listening to the voices of the publicly voiceless', I explained. While researching the social history of black music and theatre – later published as *In Township Tonight!* (1985) – in Johannesburg, during the Soweto Uprising of 1977, I had been ceremoniously tossed out of South Africa. I spent 1978 in Botswana, Lesotho, Swaziland and London and it was in Lesotho, the most unusual of the African 'Front Line States' opposed to South Africa, that I had found the most evocative and revealing forms of 'grass roots' performance culture. These ironic songs were workers' culture, expressing an articulation of experience with broad social forces and expressions of ideology, of authoritative genres and metaphors, with what Mikhail Bakhtin calls 'the common people's creative culture of laughter' (1981: 20). As a form, *difela* provided the Basotho workers (and me) with a means 'to represent the embedding of richly described local cultural worlds in larger impersonal systems of political economy' (Marcus & Fischer 1986: 77). Speaking no English and only just beginning to unionise, these workers were never allowed any form of self-expression in the state-controlled media. Yet they, as much as anyone, represented the suffering of the dispossessed in that mineral-based economy and produced the wealth with which South Africa paid apartheid's price-tag. So there I was, living amid the eroded, rocky slopes in dust or mud (depending on the season), paleo-technic audio cassette recorder, notebooks and still camera in hand, excavating not simply the African Voice but its artistic genres, qualities and values.

To bring the sparkling auriterary[3] facets of these gems out of the ground of Sesotho into the refracted light of cross-cultural appreciation, I employed an *ad hoc* seven-stage process to produce readable texts in English that, while hardly unmediated, appeared to me defensible as the best one could do. This method began by finding musical poets of reputation; one artist or *aficionado* would recommend others, often volunteering to take me and my assistant, Seakhi Santho, to abodes in remote villages or hidden peri-urban warrens otherwise impossible to locate. At outdoor sorghum beer bars, in tiny courtyards or sitting rooms of breeze block and corrugated iron, the migrant *dikheleke* ('eloquent ones') recorded their long poetic songs before a motionlessly attentive audience of comrades, family and neighbours. [DVD REF 1: VIDEO] The presence, quite often, of more than one *chanteur* gave the occasion a competitive spirit. Male performers, for the most part, eschewed the arena of the unlicensed taverns where female barmaids held court, singing their hearts out about the Mosotho working-woman's lot in shorter, strophic songs, to the accompaniment of a piano accordion and twenty-gallon tar-can drum. While male customers might rise to sing in like manner in riposte or support, the masters of migrants' 'adventurers' songs' (*difela tsa ditsamaya-naha*) required a quiet ambience and not the boisterous cacophony of the crowded speakeasies.

After recording the performances, we conducted detailed interviews on the subject of artistic biography. Then we went back to our own near-unfurnished digs to transcribe the tapes into notebooks in Sesotho and back again to the artist and, with any luck, a coterie of knowledgeable associates, for a line-by-line correction and exegesis of the Sesotho text. Many poets found this process unsettling, as the texts were composed semi-improvisationally with an emphasis on unbroken musical rhythm rather than textual logic; they were not used to having their performances laid out on a page for the purposes of literary autopsy. The results were not only fascinating but damned entertaining: a window into an expressively virtual world of Basotho experience. Nor were they self-evidently about the mines, but rather employed a vast range of metaphoric images self-consciously and meta-poetically displaying the artists' 'eloquent knowledge' (Coplan 1987) of *Sesotho*, a word that encompasses both the language and the culture of the Basotho. The next stage required a preliminary, rough translation of the transcriptions into English, Seakhi's not quite adequate English partnering my totally inadequate Sesotho. Then on to other commentators with a richer knowledge of the Sesotho of the migrants and eventually a final English version, in which literal correspondence was explicitly sacrificed in order not to lose the poetry in translation.

These were the texts I sent to Zantzinger. I thought that he might fail to see anything attractively cinematic about this genre of performance, given the restrained declamatory style of the male singers, and the almost motionless concentration of his auditors. Then again, there were the female *chanteuses*, who had the barroom backdrop, the insouciantly sensual dancing and the accordion-and-drum accompaniment to offer. But Gei and his crew – camera wizard and professor of film studies Thomas Ott, field-producer Lynne Gulezian and grip Mark Binder – were fascinated by the rich esotericism of the texts and intrigued by my collection of photographs. Perhaps most important to Zantzinger was the presence on the ground of a veteran performance ethnographer – myself – who could provide the kind of reflective insight into these forms of expressive practice that his own meticulous style of documentary representation demanded. The productive value of the brief time available for the team to shoot original footage in the field could be maximised by the use of ethnographic expertise and materials already acquired in my previous six months of research. I knew who the most promising performers were, where they performed and what their performances were all about from almost every angle (cinematic pun intended). I also had Seakhi Santho, whose professional dedication and tough, tireless persistence were the perfect qualities for the pursuit and capture of the wily, hard-case mineworkers and barflies who were our creative quarry. So down to wintry-brown Lesotho they came, that gang of four, and set up camp in a borrowed house on the campus of the National University of Lesotho, where electricity was in reliable supply.

As we mulled over my recorded song texts together, the discussion returned repeatedly to the question of how to represent a culturally esoteric, intensely verbal art form in the cinematic medium. What was involved was the translation not only of *Sesotho* – as a totality of language and culture – into clear, evocative English, but also of word-music into a rhythmic montage of narrative, visual images. It seemed evident that the narrative quality of the songs must be the basis for this kind of inter-sense modality (Merriam 1964: 94–101). Naturalistic audio-visual sequences would provide T. S. Eliot's 'objective correlatives' of the imaginative landscapes painted in poetic song. While there was little in the performances themselves to appeal to eye or ear (unusual for Africa, but the Basotho are a nation of alpine troglodytes at heart), the texts are intensely visual both in the images they evoke and in the vivid, concrete metaphors and synecdoches they invent to embody existential experiences and identities. The quintessential elaboration of this compositional process is metapoetics: the staking of a claim to artistic stature through the figurative self-representation of one's power to conjure with words. Here is the singer Majara Majara, performing an extended trope of praise for his own powers as a poet:

I am already running long distances:
I (recite) as long as the cable pulling orebuckets around the scotch-winch.
I refuse (to empty) into the collecting drum,
Even back down to the diggings still full.
These mine compounds, I've long worked them…
What do I say to you, gamblers? [4]
I am a dog's stomach; I don't get cooked,
I am skin with lice; I am not worn
I am a nest of mites; I am not entered.
I'm like a charge that remained in the oreface (unexploded),
Look, that stopped the drillboy from working;
Drillboy, I slashed his head,
Drillguide, I slashed his hand,
It's then the drillguide started to scold:
You, charge-setter; you, timber-boy,
Shut off the water, so you stop the steam;
These cables have burned us;
Men's blood is mixed with the stones…

In the first part, Majara uses cables, ore buckets and other mining machinery as a meta-poetic metaphor for his own ability to extemporise in *sefela* performance. Then he inserts a burst of characteristic migrant irascibility and toughness, comparing himself to infested clothing and shelter and to inedible animals, for a travelling man and a champion poet is not to be used or digested by others. Shifting into high gear, he uses the theme of a frequent workplace oversight, leaving an unexploded charge in a drill hole, as a metaphor for his own explosive poetic powers. But he returns to his first metaphor to do the real damage, slashing and burning the miners with the long (-winded) cables of a performance now too hot for other poets to handle. Hardly ever, I think, has the power of performance been figured in speech more potent.

The documentary must, like the *difela* songs, have story structure and portray movement not just in time but, like the working lives of the migrant poets (male and female), also in space. From herd boy and homestead girl to border town to train to mine shaft, labour compound and shanty tavern; from cool, Elysian sunny mountain pasture 2,000 metres up to sweltering, dark, hellish ore face 2,000 metres down. Of course the *difela* almost never followed the temporal sequence from youth to adulthood, or the spatial one from rural peasant to veteran mine hand in anything like a straight narrative line. Occupations, experiences and identities rather circled back on one another and the iconic mode of transport, the smoky, cinder-spewing engines of the South African railways, became metaphors for the inveterate singing travellers, the mine migrant poets themselves. So ultimately the team could fix upon how the film should be structured, the montage assembled, the songs portrayed. Its narration must parallel, as nearly possible, the form and progress of a migrant's song itself: a *sefela* in celluloid, shooting through the landscape like the train that (in historical memory)[5] took the workers to the mines:

> It is the horse of our distant forefathers,
> It was tamed by the Boers, in times of old.
> You know, there when young men feared to ride,
> I rode it, I, Child of Rakhali.
> When that train moved it performed miracles:
> It began to do amazing feats,
> Rail spikes popped, joints jumped up and down.
> You know, at the sidings it passed in a hurry,
> Well it took notice of no one...
> When it leaves here, it will run fast, yes the train,
> It showed it was ridden by a wandering-man.
> When it left, it went wandering,
> It went wandering as if it had stolen (something) away,
> It coughed as if it might spit,
> It murmured as if it would speak
> The train rattled like the dying chief Makhaola...
> You know a poor Boer was running, his cap twisted sideways
> A lion was running, its colours (hide) turned inside out
> You know when it came to the other side.
> Tikoe[town of Virginia] the European place (mines)
> I was saying these whitethorn trees would spear it.
> Whitethorns, the train pierced the spear-sharp whitethorns.
> A bushman's ghost jumped from the culvert
> With our own eyes we saw it;
> The ghost of the Bushman was dreadful.
> Girls herding there headed for the train to stop it;
> It did not even wait.
> They insulted it, saying, 'You (ass)hole Boers' train,

Do you know where you are filing to?'
A madman with iron legs, hyena, it rocked side to side.
You listen, my fathers,
My friends, I feel I want to praise a train.
You say a train does not know (appreciate) it?
You come to me, Rakhali's child;
I may reveal for you things about the train...
It saw Francolins (birds) hopping quickly,
It saw sheep grazing,
It took fright at a hyena and lost the rails...
Why should I speak this way, my fathers, my parents,
My heart is in pain...

How might this cinematic mode of parallel performance be composed? The larger narrative frame would consist of the archetypal journey, from village path to trunk road to border recruitment centre to South African mine compound and tavern and back again, but of course by the circuitous routes of song. The montage of experience would be portrayed through the filming of incidents and images from the lived environment of the performers, illustrating visually the flights of verbal imagination in their mind's eye. Angling for the right sets and sequences of images would not be exactly like shooting fish in a barrel, but like this sentence it would provide a wealth of mixed metaphors and not a little slapstick fun. In a number of instances this strategy more than rewarded itself, providing an 'understanding' of *difela* that surpassed verbal explanation.

One morning we ventured into the high central mountain plateaux to get a sense of the visual resources of the area. Soon the weather turned dark, extremely cold and rainy. As Gei tip-toed the Landcruiser over the rutted, muddy mountain road, we fell into silent awe and amazement as we turned a bend and saw an expanse of freshly-fallen snow covering the slopes of the surrounding bowl of dark peaks and the tawny grass of the fields below. Thomas got out, breath steaming in the thin air, and shot a breathtaking 360-degree pan in the frozen alpine quiet. Later we took close-ups and long shots of the upper reaches of the Phutiatsana ('little antelope') river, where ice had crystallised around its edges. The result, edited together, is in the film, 'narrated' by the voice of actor Welcome Msomi reciting from *difela* by Mphafu Mofolo and Rabonne Mariti. I think something has actually been found, rather than lost, in translation. [DVD REF 2: VIDEO]

One morning our film truck laboured up the windy track to the high village of Ha-Shale. 'Look', I shouted to Thomas as I gazed across the winter pastures at a small clump of herd boys and cattle stirring up dust in the distance, 'bulls fighting!' We had been in search of an appropriate visual sequence to portray a passage from a dramatic *sefela* by Makeka Lihojane:

Hear the noise in that village!
Boys are shouting the alarm,
As they see the bulls go on fighting;
Khodlibe contends with Terebere,
They fight mightily towards the house...

'Let's go!' confirmed Thomas, already snatching his camera. Awkwardly swinging our gear about our necks and arms, Thomas and I set off full-tilt across the fields, desperate to arrive at the distant scene before one of the bulls sent the other packing. Bounding over the clods, I realised that breaking an ankle in an unseen hole or, worse, doing irreparable harm to our expensive and, in the short term, irreplaceable equipment was the most likely outcome of my enthusiasm. By some miracle we both arrived panting and unscathed among the herd boys, cattle and children gathered to watch the contest. While Thomas set about attempting to capture the action, I explained to the stout lads in charge of the animals who we were, where we had appeared from and what we wanted to do. 'Cool', they answered, anticipating some token of our appreciation. The great, snorting beasts grunted and strained their horns against one another until, in a final great flurry of hooves and dust, one emerged the victor. Except for that final moment, during which he had been filming the enraptured spectators, Thomas captured all the action.

In *Songs of the Adventurers* Ben Levin, accompanied by Makeka's passage, cleverly edited this scene for maximum effect; the whole thing would have been considerably easier if we had had today's compact DVD recording technology. The episode reflects another strategy, initially unforeseen, that ultimately elevated the film's montage of word and image nearer the level and quality of the *difela* we were trying to evoke. This was to open the film with the necessary omniscient narration of factual context, and then slowly to abandon the documentary voice and text (both mine) in favour of the voices/texts of the poets. While this might sacrifice a certain amount of explanation and understanding, we decided it was worth it if it meant that in the end the film would not mean, but be. *Difela*, after all, are not something that the Basotho simply know, but something that they do. So too would a cinematic *sefela* be to us.

In the later sequences of the film, ethnographic and didactic voice-over fades away to nothing, and scenes are narrated by *difela* texts, either recited by the mellifluous voice of Welcome Msomi, or subtitled when the pace of text and image are slow enough to allow the editor to get the titles on-screen for long enough and then off-screen quickly enough: a tricky problem indeed, given the pace of *sefela* performance. As Gei explains:

> Welcome's narration worked well, but the subtitles were the problem. Sometimes you had to cut out chunks of the poem, so the subtitles could keep up. Film is a compromise, but with DVD not so much – you have more space. In *Songs of the Adventurers* we only subtitled parts of the performance. In other cases we cut parts of the recitation but gave a complete subtitled transcription. The body language, the physicality of the recitation was sometimes important, so I would use Welcome so they could hear the performance and attend to the image. At other times I thought the words were more important. DVD can be done anyway you like: words, image, sound, altogether, or all separate.

Another technique employed to good effect in order to allow performers to run their course was the inter-cutting of still photographs and scenes on film into the moving montage. [DVD REF 1: VIDEO] While Zantzinger has never been entirely satisfied with the way these look, they do facilitate concentration on the verbal flow of the poetic text while the visual remains focused on a solitary image. Other 'solitary images' that did not function well and had to be left on the cutting-room floor were talking-head interviews with performers conducted during shooting. Perhaps the failure on these occasions can be laid at my door, although I had enjoyed dozens of animated, enlightening interviews with performers when accompanied only by my assistant, a small cassette recorder and a notebook. Possibly it was the film crew, with their outlandish vehicle bristling with finicky gear that intimidated or irritated our Basotho friends. In those days a single reel only allowed them eleven minutes of shooting, and I do recall how impatient they became when shooting had to be interrupted while technical problems were solved or cameras unloaded and reloaded.

Liason with the performers and 'extras' was a job for Seakhi and myself, and although the rewards could be worth every danger, tricky situations were the order of almost every day. The filming of *difela* and men's *indhlamo* dance performances outside a particularly rough unlicensed tavern in Thibella, an old, decaying neighbourhood in central Maseru, will surely remain a vivid memory for everyone in the crew. Although the denizens of this drinking hole were obliging enough, one of the more inebriated onlookers, who had lived for a while in Johannesburg, insisted on accompanying the central performers on a plastic melodeon. At the end of the difficult day, Seakhi and I were sent to change some large notes into smaller denominations to pay the performers and extras. Arriving at a local bar and bottle store, Seakhi asked whether we might not watch the last half of an important South African football match on television. The match over, we obtained our change and returned to the scene of the filming, only to find our Sesotho-less crew backed-up against the film truck, besieged by a rather more than impatient crowd of thirsty actors. 'Show them the money!' shouted Gei, too nervous to enquire where we had been all that time. We did, to the excitement of the crowd and the ultimate satisfaction of everyone – except our friend on the melodeon, who stubbornly demanded a ride in the film truck. Our hearts sank, but rather than delay our departure, we stretched him out in the back of the Landcruiser. We set off to a chorus of cheery goodbyes from our actors, the melodeon trailing random notes in our wake. A hundred metres down the street I shouted to Gei to stop the truck, and with an immensely satisfying sense of finality, Thomas, Mark, Seakhi and I opened the back and heaved our saloon hep-cat and his melodeon out.

Women performers, usually more understanding of and patient with the cinematic process, are of two kinds; while their roles and order of appearance reflect the ethnographic process rather more closely than the cinematic, the filmmakers made a virtue of necessity in the effectiveness with which they are featured. One type of female performer is the *letuela* diviner-medicine-dancer, accompanied by the singing and clapping of randomly assembled members of the community and by the small *moropa* drum, played by a female acolyte. It is a peculiarity of the Basotho that only women play 'traditional' hand drums. Such mediums appear on three separate occasions in the film, to considerable dramatic effect. The second category of performer is the female counterpart of the male song poets, 'women of eloquence' as one might, by extension, call them. My attention had only just been drawn to these artists when the film crew arrived and therefore they do not feature as central performers in their own right until the last part of the film. Yet it may seem to the viewer that we were cleverly saving the best for last, as when they appear centre stage they take over the screen and the viewers' attention with virtuosic command.

This is how it happened: I had a friend locally, Simon Motolo, who had some experience as a studio musician backing the Basotho migrants' accordion and drum bands on bass guitar when they recorded cassettes in South Africa. Motolo's aunt ran a raucous informal shebeen (tavern) in a backstreet in the border town of Hlotse. This barroom employed several of the most renowned young 'women of eloquence' we were ever to encounter in Lesotho. When we asked their permission to film them performing for customers, they flashed broad grins and took off, only to return an hour later made up and dressed to kill (the audience). Thomas, determined as always to shoot only under natural lighting, gave me stern but futile instructions to keep the door and small windows clear of curious onlookers. The accordion and tar-can drum band struck up a solemn but swinging Sesotho rhythm and three ladies held forth in turn, brandishing the men's heavy *melamu* fighting sticks, their hearts of gold glinting through their lyrical texts, delivered in the impassioned, penetrating, full-throated cadences of the Sesotho *famo* ('flared nostrils' – and skirts) tavern dance songs. The packed audience sat or stood transfixed until the last poetess had retired, and then jumped to their feet as the band switched into a lively local urban 'jive' rhythm. Forming a circle, the dancers revolved around the floor, in spectral silhouettes traced in rays of external light, improvising words and steps as the pure fun of playing to the camera took hold of them. The scene is the climax to *Songs of the Adventurers*, carrying on through the credits, the footage screened as shot, almost unedited. [DVD REF 3: VIDEO]

The positioning of male and female performers in relation to these song forms is a fascinating and revealing arena of contestation around social personhood and artistic status. Such positioning is always in the process of renegotiation. In 1984, during my first period of research in Lesotho, I discovered that the songs sung by female brewers and barflies to the accompaniment of piano accordion and drum in the back-street beer bars bore a strong generic relationship to the men's *sefela*. Women too, it appeared, could be 'eloquent ones'. Why did I take so long to follow through? A conspiracy of silence and the witting and unwitting misconceptions of my assistants, key informants and myself about the place of women and their forms of self-expression in Basotho migrant society had blinded me to the potency of women's arts of words. Though I had often dropped in at shebeens in search of *sefela* singers in a mood to hold forth, the male singers refused to perform there, saying the raucous, noisy atmosphere was not conducive to serious extemporiation or listening. Unlike shebeen songs, *difela* are not performed to instrumental accompaniment. Now we were going back to the bars to hear the women. I explained to a male visitor that we were 'studying women [oral] poets'. He gave me a look of concern. There were, he stated categorically, no women poets; women were 'singers', a less authoritative and prestigious category of wordsmith. I could have mentioned the well-known praise poet chieftainess 'MaMpho Chopo and the outstanding published poetry of Mrs B. M. Khaketla, but I didn't. Back at the shebeens, I enquired if women had their own genre; what were shebeen songs called? They didn't have a name; just *dipina tsa Basotho* ('Basotho songs').

I wasn't really surprised. In rural life there are few occasions for a woman to express herself directly to a mixed audience. Before the pervasiveness of male migrancy made this untenable, a Basotho woman (like a child) was not allowed to speak on her own behalf or to give testimony at the chief's court or public assembly (except of course for the chief, who was quite often a woman!). If she sought to express explicit disapproval in the presence of authority, she affected a stony, sullen silence that spoke more powerfully (and more safely) than angry words. In conversation a married woman was forbidden to use the personal names or even words whose sound resembled the names of her senior male affines, using instead *hlonepho* ('respect'), the vocabulary of avoidance. Ironically, women used *hlonepho* as a form of verbal competition (Kunene 1958: 162), testing one another's knowledge and cleverness in the elaboration of 'restricted synonyms' that could at once avoid an in-law's name and praise or skewer him by veiled metaphor. Another episode in the gender politics of Sesotho, I thought; men withholding authority from women's words by denying women's most formidable genre a name.

But the reality was far more complex and dialogic: I had forgotten that song is the one medium where Basotho women enjoy poetic licence, and can gain through performative eloquence a degree of personal authority otherwise denied them. Study of shebeen performance revealed that the personal compositions of women were as intentionally artful, as reflective and critical, and as persuasive and cathartic as the *difela* of their men. It is precisely for this reason that shebeen songs have no generic name. Socialised to avoid direct public criticism of men, Basotho women have no interest in identifying and thus singling out for condemnation a genre in which their most serious complaints are publicly, evocatively and viscerally expressed: 'These are just songs, Father David.' On close listening I was more than tempted simply to call them women's *difela*, but I could get no Mosotho to call them that unless I reverted to that fieldwork favourite, 'leading the ethnographic witness'. Just songs they may be, but that did not stop male customers from jumping up to sing angry ripostes when stung by women's lyrical barbs, nor did it stop the women from pushing a man back down when they were in no mood to be interrupted. The tavern is a public domain where, as the proverb says, 'woman is chief', providing a rare public forum for women's discourse on problems that are unacknowledged in other contexts. And, as reflected in their songs, the truth is that though they may not face the immediate threats of injury and death in the mines or the violence of the mine compounds, women's lot under the migratory labour system is on a continuing basis more fraught with insecurity, dependence and hardship than that of their men. The women of eloquence sustain themselves and their companions in affliction with songs of innocence and experience (Gunner 1979); in which their misfortunes are lamented but their care for true friends and lovers never dies:

> *Mr Kapa 'Muso, my husband, he comes on his own account.*
> *They slander me as a prostitute,*
> *I am not a prostitute; I narrate the causes (of my circumstances):*
> *At my home, girls,*
> *At home eating is difficult;*
> *Yes! I am a prostitute.*
> *My father looked away to the kraal,*
> *My mother looked away, deep inside the hut;*
> *But why? (because) I am a prostitute*
> *I still think I shall go wandering;*
> *You have left me wandering about, little girl of Lioling!*

(Teyateyaneng, a border town)
You will not see me married;
(yet) I get married (fall in love) daily,
Daily my heart is long (hopeful),
You will never see me surly.

GEI ZANTZINGER...

If, as phantom South African novelist Dugmore Boetie put it in the title to his novel, *Familiarity is the Kingdom of the Lost* (1984),[6] then the film crew was indeed lost in Lesotho, where what little was familiar was elaborated in unfamiliar ways. Ethnographic direction came from David Coplan and his Sancho Panza, Seakhi Santho, but ultimately we strange filmmakers in a strange land had to trust in ourselves. I had inherited from an older and less reflexive tradition the notion that the camera was something of which one should be ashamed, that the impression of actuality could only be preserved within the carefully constructed reality of documentary film by excluding all technical processes, technicians and creative interventions from the visual frame. Many times I had to shout at Coplan, engrossed in cajoling the Basotho to stand where and do what we needed, 'White man in the shot!' to get him off screen. Now that ethnography is held to inscribe the consciousness of ethnographers as much as that of their subjects (Clifford & Marcus 1986), success in persuading sceptical audiences of even the possibility of authenticity and honesty in documentary representation becomes maddeningly elusive. Audiences can never be adequately appraised of what was feasible in particular conditions and it is easy to query why and by whom certain material was selected or de-selected. Furthermore, compared to written ethnography's dialogue between the lone ethnographer and his/her subjects, film requires an astonishing range of inputs from diverse contributors (most of whom are *not* working as a team and cannot interact) and directions as it moves through its various stages of production; any of these collaborators can derail the progression from conceptualisation to realisation.

The concatenated assemblage of production steps and processes, not unlike if less spontaneous than the rhythmic verbal *bricolage* of a migrant's *sefela*, makes it extremely difficult to construct a descriptive and analytic portrait that also directly evokes the art form and engages the irremediably distanced American or European audience in its performance. How can documentary convey the interior world of meanings expressed in and framed by Sesotho texts to an audience, even a Basotho one, let alone illuminate the aesthetic and social contexts of their complex personalistic as well as cultural form? In any language, written or oral poetry – so compact and distilled, complex in formal expression and semantic allusion – requires considerable study. Linguistic transmutations allow for multiple interpretation, while in oral-performative traditions aesthetic enjoyment of a song-poem depends partly upon the simultaneous apprehension of multiple metaphors, references and meanings. This complexity makes difficulties for translators working on cinematic treatments and striving to arrive at fitting interpretations.

That said, it seemed unfortunate that the aural literary genius of the Basotho migrant poets should remain inaccessible to audiences who spoke no Sesotho but were nevertheless appreciative of poetic song. The efforts, however imperfect and open to criticism, of David Coplan and Seakhi Santho to transpose Sesotho *difela* songs into English, gave me and my crew something to work upon. When we saw in their written versions of the texts not only the challenges but the potential rewards of bringing this genre of poetic song and its unsung heroes to the screen, it seemed, in both senses of the word, worth our best shots. The complexities of the linguistic situation cannot be wholly blamed for video's limitations in faithfully representing this performance art. Film production technique can be seen as an artefact of the professional experience, reigning paradigms and cultural frameworks of those who manipulate the technology that gives sensory form to performance; it is the quality of their identification with the performers that enables the process to enhance rather than misrepresent the final product.

The final editing process was carried out in the manner of an ascetic as well as an aesthetic retreat. Responsibility for the final product was mine and I rented an old farm in Chester County, Pennsylvania, where every weekend I conspired with the editor, Professor Ben Levin of Temple University's Film Studies Department. Levin's interventions were entirely aesthetic. I would talk for hours about Lesotho, to give him some sense of what he was looking at, and then go away. He would work on it and ask me afterwards if he had realised my somewhat inchoate vision of the world I sought to evoke. I would explain why I thought he had or had not. Levin's genius lay in his unerring ability to portray the spirit of a sequence, no matter how many times we re-worked his edited version. He was interested in the challenge of transforming something very aural into something cinematic, something violently particular and strange into something humanly familiar and cross-culturally intelligible, making the window of cinema as translucent as possible. That was what I was trying to do in making the film: to see what might result from an attempt at the kind of cultural translation that lies at the heart of the impossible enterprise of visual anthropology. Whatever one's intentions, films of this sort are always in some ways a failure, but this doesn't mean one shouldn't work uncompromisingly to make them better: *finished products*, not discussion pieces, works-in-progress or *productivités*.

The necessity of working within strict time limits constrains the filmmakers, shaping in part the parameters of the final product. The US Public Broadcasting Service, an important potential purchaser and exhibitor of films like ours, requires that they remain within the standard 'TV Hour' of 58 minutes. While film festivals and conferences provide alternative venues for screening and distribution, it is researchers, teachers and students in institutional settings and the educated non-specialist viewing public who comprise our most important audiences. Making film for such audiences leads necessarily to a compression of ethnographic data, and since all such data is unfamiliar and possibly unintelligible to them, the degree and kind of information they will ultimately find comprehensible is unpredictable. During the editing process, we constructed a series of scenes that we felt would be concise and comprehensible at the level to which they were directed, only to discover that aspects of meaning we had thought to convey were misconstrued or simply missed. Even Richard Bauman, the distinguished folklorist and ethno-linguist, suggested that the *difela* performances in *Songs of the Adventurers* were frustratingly opaque. As the film entered general circulation and we received feedback from a range of viewers, the realisation dawned that some topic areas and aspects of montage presented were not faithfully communicated.

The filmmakers' own familiarity with the material and the implicit, experiential understandings of those who have 'been there' may have been part of the problem. So filmmakers may assume that a carefully designed series of 'logically' juxtaposed shots in a montage will play for the viewer as they do for themselves; often they do not. This is the fundamental contextual dilemma of documentary filmmaking: how much information and awareness does the viewer already possess, and how much does the film need to supply? The pressure to condense information into the time allowed is ever present.

This problem is evident at certain points in *Songs of the Adventurers*, where we attempt to suggest the unity of spiritual and physical aspects of healing in Lesotho. [DVD REF 4: VIDEO] I well remember the hours we spent trying to edit the material into a sequence that was economical in time yet brought all the important points into focus. In the first two and a half minutes of the segment the viewer is exposed to nine shots and hears five/ six narration sections (Coplan), two voice-over translation sections (Welcome Msomi), three untranslated bits of poetry in Sesotho (Kanono Nthako) and at least three miscellaneous sound takes, such as the voices of the herbalist and the bone thrower. The narration, though in English, is dense with information that concerns unfamiliar concepts. The translated recitation speaks for itself; have we heard poetry like this before? The word 'wonderful' in its most fundamental sense is apt.

Fast forward – two decades on: over the years I had retained my friendship and working relationship with David Coplan, my curious fondness for *Songs of the Adventurers* and a fervent desire to refashion the problematic aspects of the montage, all of which made the film a favoured candidate for re-production in DVD format. DVD would, we hoped, remedy the kinds of problems I perceived in *Songs of the Adventurers* by providing viewers with essential information presented in self-standing modules that would make the body of the film comprehensible. This additional footage and text would not simply supply context that was originally lacking, but enhance viewers' understanding and experience of local frames of cultural practice and ideology.

The DVD functions not as new technology for recording in the field, but as a medium for postproduction. It has a huge capacity, ranging from 4.7 to 17 gigabytes, on which one can archive anything that can be digitised: video, audio, still pictures, multi-media, documents, files, games. There is room for tributary explorations, behind-the-scenes filmmaking processes: trailers, still photos, scripts, previously deleted scenes, alternate endings. Viewers can, for example, switch seamlessly between different camera angles of the same scene, making them the editors of these sequences. The possibilities for documenting cultural performance, where simultaneous actions, reactions and perspectives can be linked together and chosen by 'design', bypassing the constraints of traditional editing schemes, greatly expanded our horizons.

DVD also provides multiple, integrated options for audio, such as a commentary track on its own discrete channel, where filmmakers and content experts talk viewers through the film as they watch, or a channel that provides only the music and natural sound environment, enabling viewers to choose more- or less-mediated presentation. A performance could be heard in its original language on one track, and in a voice-over translation on another. Yet another could provide the filmmaker's commentary, explaining the various logistical or contextual aspects that had to be considered in filming the scene, offering built-in reflexivity. The DVD subtitle function provides another range of creative options, with up to 32 tracks that can be turned on, off or combined at will. Text is text, so only the technical imagination limits the approaches that can be applied to documentary work beyond basic subtitling: captions, trivia, points of interest, alternate translations, ethnographic exegesis, what you will.

The interactive aspect of DVD is foregrounded through the use of remote control buttons, menu choices and icons that appear at any time during playback of the film. The viewer can choose to watch the film in its original, linear form or branch to another content stream of relevant ancillary material. Older films, like *Songs of the Adventurers*, can be remade and updated, preserving the original version but also enhancing it with commentary, additional support materials and relevant postscripts. A single disk provides for the presentation of the material in a number of dynamic contexts, from simple exposition to complex layering of translations, interpretations and representations of the cinematic process, the collaborative production of knowledge and the ethnographic terrain.

I travelled to South Africa to work on the new tracks with Coplan, who had written more than 24 pages of new narration relating to out-takes from the original film and to the new video footage and still photographs taken during his years of subsequent research. The editor was Michael Bailey, whose understanding of the technical, editorial and expressive possibilities of DVD technology is unsurpassed, but whose view of the subject matter places him in the role of audience. Among the most significant topics we identified for DVD format amplification were the colonial and post-colonial political economy of Lesotho, labour migrancy and life on the land, the Sesotho domain of illness and healing and *difela* songs in inter-textual and aesthetic relationship to Sesotho performance genres.

From the outset, we sought to highlight *sefela* performance as a mode of self-production and reproduction in response to processes of identity dissolution experienced at the mines. *Sefela* accesses Sesotho's totalising concept of healing – practices that include herbalism, trance-dancing and divination – as a key domain of self-representation. Despite the extended and multi-faceted presentation of these figurative parallels in *Songs of the Adventurers*, it appeared in retrospect that viewers found this central strand of narrative opaque. The DVD re-working of the film enabled us to provide adequate background and context so that viewers outside the literally charmed circle of Basotho migrant society might comprehend something of the senses in which 'conjuring with words' can advance a comprehensive project of social and spiritual as well as individual and physical healing.

Basotho artistic activity is so intimately associated with such spiritual and social aspects of life that their inscription in *difela* cannot be too strongly emphasised. The domain – should we use the older notion of the 'art'? – of medicine is inseparable from the religious, moral and social connections that Western aliopathic bio-medicine has severed. In performative terms, we might simply note that when a master singer holds forth in *difela*, quiet prevails and universal attention is riveted upon the performer. Something of great value is being delivered, and even small children pay close attention. What kind of programme could be devised to prepare non-Basotho viewers for so many unfamiliar references and manifestations? The point of view of Sesotho medicine does not proceed from a theory of germs and subsequent infection, or from trauma and its results. Disease and death are not caused by those unsentient vectors alone, but by others who wish misfortune upon a victim. We spent considerable time filming the various sorts of healers that many Basotho would customarily consult.

Our revised treatment of this key domain of healing illustrates the relationship between the original film and the DVD re-working of *Songs of the Adventurers*. In the film the famous '*sefela* doctor', Kanono Nthako, recounts his miraculous descent from heaven and subsequent birth, and his restorative capacity to conjure with words. [DVD REF 4: VIDEO] The alternate stream of the DVD begins with a shot of a trance-dance diviner (*lethuela*) in her traditional costume dancing on a street in Mafeteng. In the next shot we see the curb-side herbalist who appears in the mainstream *Songs of the Adventurers*, describing to us the names and the healing properties of various herbs, all widely available throughout southern Africa, and used not only by Basotho but by other neighbouring peoples well. In the film, the herbalist's voice is lowered as the voice-over English translation is delivered; on the DVD, he is heard at full volume, with English subtitles. Since his description of the plants is much shorter than our explanations, we have to freeze the frame to allow the viewer time to read his words. The DVD also allows his Sesotho to be fully comprehensible to those who speak it.

A close-up reveals the ankle rattles of a trance/dance healer dance-divining in the remote mountain village of Ha-Shale. Another *letuela* joins her in the dance, accompanied by the vigorous singing of the village children. A drum keeps the solid, hypnotic beat of the trance dance music. In another scene, we filmed two other diviners. One of our assistants, Joe, had an arthritic condition which we asked the healers to treat. One of them dealt with Joe's problem by going into trance while dancing, while the other worked by taking a snuff of magical properties and 'seeing' the solution to the problem. Although they had never met before, both their diagnoses were correct, to the obvious surprise of our assistant! This considerable length of footage taken from out-takes allowed time for brief voice-overs. During the interaction between Joe and the healer, we see her taking snuff and working herself up into an emotional state, close to tears.

The narration runs over the healing sequence into a shot of the Full African Gospel Church of God at Mautse shrine in the Free State. The footage from the shrine was shot on ordinary palmcorder VHS by David Coplan during his research in 2002. After the night shots of this church, we provide a sequence showing the ordination of a traditional healer-diviner through the ritual submersion of a rooster and finally the initiate herself into the sacred pool. The sequence ends with Kanono Nthako reciting his *sefela* while villagers sit or stand, listening in rapt attention. Clearly something of great value is being communicated. Throughout the sequence, images of persons and performances, together with text, are woven into the narration. The effect should be not only to make the visuals pertaining to healing more accessible, but to illuminate for viewers the mutual reference of musical-poetic and medical domains in Sesotho. [DVD REF 5: VIDEO]

DVD production goes far beyond rectifying problems in the original film format. It represents a new instructional medium for performance and film studies, allowing viewers and pedagogues to delve quickly and as deeply as they wish into any of the domains documented in the work. As *Songs of the Adventurers* illustrates, the potential for adding subsequent research material to films from an earlier date is enormous. With the techno-opulence of DVD, we move on to new planes of possibility. In our attempt to capture performance, we are only just beginning our film-faring on such high seize. Cast anchor and click the remote.

Notes

1   *Songs of the Adventurers*, produced and directed by Gei Zantzinger.
2   Sesotho, like all southern Bantu languages, uses a system of noun classes inflected by prefixes for singular and plural. So the root -sotho is inflected as Mosotho, one sotho person, Basotho, two or more sotho people, Lesotho, the land of the Basotho, Sesotho, the language and culture of the Basotho, and so on. Further, the Lesotho orthography for Sesotho differs from that used in South Africa. For convenience we are using the South African Sesotho spelling conventions.
3   Admittedly this is not a word, but an adjectival inflection of the noun form I have invented to describe this complex of musical poetic forms, *auriture* (see Coplan 1994: 8–10).
4   It is customary for *difela* to be performed competitively, with each contestant 'putting his money where his mouth is' by betting on his prowess and against his rivals, who are here addressed as 'gamblers'.
5   Today migrants no longer ride the trains, but take taxis, cars and buses to the mines.
6   Although the author of the novel *Familarity is the Kingdom of the Lost*, nobody has met Dugmore Boetie, or otherwise clarified his true identity.

Bibliography

Adams, C. (1974) 'Ethnography of Basotho Evaluative Expression in the Cognitive Domain *Lipapali* (Games)'. Unpublished PhD dissertation, Indiana University.

Bakhtin, M. M. (1981) *The Dialogic Imagination: Four Essays by M. M. Bakhtin,* ed. M. Holquist, trans C. Emerson and M. Holquist. Austin: Texas University Press.

Boetie, D. (1984) *Familiarity is the Kingdom of the Lost*, ed. B. Simon. Johannesburg: Arena.

Clifford, J. (1997) *Routes: Travel and Translation in the Late Twentieth Century*. Cambridge: Harvard University Press.

Clifford, J. and Marcus G. E. (eds) (1986) *Writing Culture: The Poetics and Politics of Ethnography*. Berkeley: University of California Press.

Coplan, D. (1985) *In Township Tonight! South Africa's Black City Music and Theatre*. New York and London: Longman.

_____ (1987) 'Eloquent Knowledge: Lesotho Migrants' Songs and the Anthropology of Experience', *American Ethnologist*, 14(3): 413–33.

_____ (1994) *In the Time of Cannibals: The Word Music of South Africa's Basotho Migrants*. Chicago: Chicago University Press.

Gunner, E. (1979) 'Songs of Innocence and Experience: Women as Composers and Performers of Izibongo, Zulu Praise Poetry', *Research in African Literatures*, 10(2): 239–67.

Kunene, D. (1958) 'Notes On Hlonepha Among the Southern Sotho', *African Studies*, 17(3): 159–82.

Marcus, G. E. and M. Fischer (1986) *Anthropology as Cultural Critique*. Chicago: University of Chicago Press.

Merriam, A. (1964) *The Anthropology of Music*. Evanston: Northwestern University Press.

Moletsane, R. I. M. (1982) 'A Literary Appreciation and Analysis of Collected and Documented Basotho Miners' Poetry'. Unpublished MA dissertation, Orange Free State University.

Murray, C. (1980) 'From Granary to Labour Reserve: An Economic History of Lesotho', *South African Labour Bulletin*, 6(4): 3–20.

Williams, R. (1977) *Marxism and Literature*. London: Oxford University Press.

TELEVISUALISING TRANSNATIONAL MIGRATION:
THE NEW AMERICANS
Alan Grossman and Áine O'Brien

I

The title of this book [*The New Americans*] and the documentary series upon which it reflects proclaims that something is fundamentally different about our most recent wave of immigration … The racial and ethnic identity of the United States is – once again – being remade. The 2000 Census counts some 28 million first-generation immigrants among us. This is the highest number in history – often pointed out by anti-immigrant lobbyists – but it is not the highest percentage of the foreign-born in relation to the overall population. In 1907, that ratio was 14 percent; today, it is 10 percent.

Yet there is the pervasive notion that something is occurring that has never occurred before, or that more is at stake than ever before. And there is a crucial distinction to be made between the current wave and the ones that preceded it. As late as the 1950s, two-thirds of immigration to the US originated in Europe. By the 1980s, more than 80 percent came from Latin America and Asia. As at every other historical juncture, when we receive a new batch of strangers, there is a reaction, a kind of political gasp that says: *We no longer recognize ourselves*. This is the mythical 'middle American' speaking.

– Ruben Martinez (2004: 17–18)

We follow an Indian couple to Silicon Valley through the dot-com boom and bust. A Mexican meatpacker struggles to reunite his family in rural Kansas. Two families of Nigerian refugees … escape government persecution. Two Los Angeles Dodgers prospects follow their big dreams of escaping the barrios of the Dominican Republic. A Palestinian woman … marries into a new life in Chicago.

– Kartemquin Films[1]

The series prologue to the first two-hour episode of the seven-hour documentary miniseries *The New Americans*, as screened in the Stranger Than Fiction Documentary Film Festival (Dublin, 2003),[2] comprises a montage of immigrant subjects interwoven with a cacophonous medley of accented voices. Our immediate reaction to this unexpected use of an established televisual convention, although impressively facilitating a polyvocal perspective for the viewer is, however, one of surprise, if not disappointment. This feeling diminishes rapidly, ruptured emphatically in the film's opening sequence by the sound of a tribal call and response ritual carried over tracking shots, transporting viewers into the interior landscape of a refugee camp in the west African Republic of Benin, and the subsequent introduction to the first of five immigrant stories in the series – the Ogoni family of Israel and Ngozi Nwidor, prior to their departure to the United States. [DVD REF 1: VIDEO] Steve James, co-executive producer and co-editor of *The New Americans* is seated in the

FIGURE 1: THE NEW AMERICANS PRODUCTION TEAM, KARTEMQUIN FILMS, CHICAGO

audience, invited to the festival to introduce and screen his most recent film *Stevie* (2003), and teach a documentary master-class, supported by Screen Training Ireland. Exiting the theatre, we reflect on how the extraordinary scale and transnational collaborative components of the production, specificity of immigrant subjects/families, locations and varied film crews, collectively provide a compelling and challenging subject for possible address in the book/DVD-ROM project that was to become this publication, linking questions of migration with documentary practice.

Our meeting over breakfast the following day in a central Dublin hotel was brief and purposeful. Steve responded favourably to our proposal of an extended interview format, suggesting the most beneficial, indeed egalitarian, way to engage with the production and thematic concerns of the seven-hour film would be to speak directly with the series producer and directors/producers of the stories, together with his Chicago-based colleagues at Kartemquin Films, including his co-executive producer of the series, Gordon Quinn, who was also co-director of the Palestinian story with Jerry Blumenthal. Given the impracticality and the impersonal nature of long-distance e-mail interviews with so many members of *The New Americans* production team, we happily accepted Steve's invitation to visit Kartemquin in early January 2004, months prior to the film's inaugural three-part television screening on PBS (29–31 March).[3] Following on from Chicago we travelled to New York to interview Susana Aiken and Carlos Aparicio, directors of the Dominican Republic segment. Due to time and budgetary constraints, it was not possible to meet with the directors/producers of the Mexican and Indian stories, Renee Tajima-Peña and Indu Krishnan respectively; however, we did receive from them detailed written responses to our questions, which are incorporated selectively, and hopefully seamlessly, in the transcript that follows, as well as appearing in pdf format on the DVD-ROM. The same can be said for the contribution of series producer Gita Saedi. Further integrated into this mosaic transcript – divided into four sections, ranging from the film's preproduction to postproduction considerations – is the inclusion of previously published reflection (here italicised), designed to provide a meta-commentary where relevant. Thematic subjects discussed include among others: the history and production concerns of Kartemquin Films; storytelling and the dramatic aesthetic in documentary filmmaking; outreach campaigns and the politics of public television documentary funding; the salience of family relations in the context of transnational migration; and the ethics of collaboration in documentary postproduction. In myriad ways the chapter's textual assemblage and synthesis of interview material, video clips, pdf files and interview audio extracts mirrors the very demanding and time-consuming process of independent documentary film editing; the resulting narrative account is similarly partial and necessarily condensed, by no means representing an exhaustive account of the interview research materials generated.[4]

II

To call Kartemquin Films only a production company would be to understate its impact on the critical societal issues it addresses as well as the documentary art form it has shaped. Indeed, Kartemquin envisions the documentary 'as a vehicle to deepen our understanding of society through everyday human drama'.
    – MacArthur Award for Creative and Effective Institutions (2007)[5]

Áine O'Brien: As executive producers of *The New Americans*, could we begin by asking you to sketch the film's preproduction background, dating back to its inception as a Kartemquin Films project on transnational migration.

Steve James: Well, I remember very clearly when the idea for the film first came to me. I was doing a final editing pass on *Hoop Dreams* (1993) after the film had played at the Sundance festival and had been bought for distribution and theatrical release in 1994. At that time there was much talk about the cost of immigrants on the airwaves – of closing the border with Mexico. Pat Buchanan was running for the presidency and expressing provocative thoughts on the subject. So too was then-governor Pete Wilson seeking re-election with his immigrant-bashing campaign. These debates and discussion led to the 1996 Welfare Reform Act that put in place very restrictive measures regarding immigrants. I was also at that time travelling far more extensively than usual because of *Hoop Dreams* and I'm somebody who enjoys talking to cabbies to and from airports. Most of them I met in the big cities were immigrants, who were often willing to share with me their extraordinary and dramatic stories. I quickly realised that I had yet to meet an immigrant whose life story was anything but compelling.

Alan Grossman: Incidentally, we came in with a Sudanese man.

James: Exactly. So there we were completing *Hoop Dreams*, which is essentially a film about the American Dream seen through the eyes of inner-city African-American teenagers and it just occurred to me how fascinating it would be to look at America and issues of race through the eyes of immigrants. When I eventually shared the idea with Gordon a good while later in 1995, early 1996, I wasn't particularly informed about issues surrounding immigration. What I knew was mostly anecdotal, my knowledge sketchy and neither did I have any close friends who were immigrants. *I didn't know how I felt about undocumented workers crossing the border and getting jobs in America … I thought taking on a job like this would be an interesting way to figure that out* (James cited in Rosen 2004: 8). I guess my instincts as a filmmaker told me that that there was a really great story to be told.

Gordon Quinn: I like Steve's cab-driver's story because when he first mentioned the idea for the series, something really resonated with me, since it was a very genuine interest on his behalf. The question he was raising was very much a sincere expression of curiosity: 'Who are these people? Who are these people in the fullest sense of their humanity?' Asking such questions is always a good place to begin to start thinking about a film project. Interestingly, a similar kind of question arose from the outset in relation to *Hoop Dreams* when these two very tall guys (Steve James and Fred Marx) walked into Kartemquin, wanting to do a film about inner-city Chicago high-school kids dreaming of becoming NBA stars. *One of the longest-running documentary companies in the country, Kartemquin has always been a home to young, ambitious filmmakers, providing equipment, expertise and encouragement* (Terry 1996: 98). I remember thinking, well, Kartemquin does have a political background in filmmaking and that as white filmmakers we were informed about issues in the black community. That said, what was distinctive about Steve and Fred was the fact that they were passionate about basketball. That was their common ground with the teenagers. So for me what resonated was precisely this kind of human quality inherent in Steve's curiosity about immigrants.

Also, another aspect I recollect from my discussion with Steve was the fact that when Kartemquin made a series of labour films (*Taylor Chain 1: A Story in a Union Local* (1980); *Taylor Chain 11: A Story of Collective Bargaining* (1984)), we did actually research and study early twentieth-century immigration into America – particularly the Irish and eastern Europeans, the people who came over to work in the steel mills, and we saw what happened to these immigrants and their offspring in later generations. One of the things I'm able to say on the subject of immigration when addressing students in universities or wherever in response to when, for example, a white student happens to raise concerns about America, about their own dominant white culture, is this: 'You, who are in the class of Irish or Italian descent, your ancestors weren't considered white when they first came to America, they were considered dirty, foreign, or Catholic, not part of the dominant culture. There was absolutely no way that your ancestors were going to fit in.' This was the stereotype of immigrants who came to America at that time. So with hindsight, since the issue of immigration is so thick in the air right now in America,[6] both Steve and myself intuited that it made a lot of sense strategically to grapple with a film about immigrants, that this topic would be important for what was going to happen in America over the next decades – little did we appreciate just how important when we actually started. If you're going to address an issue such as immigration in the context of globalisation, you have to have an appreciation of immigrants as complicated and contradictory human beings, a sensitivity arguably lacking in much public political discussion in America on the subject.

James: From the get-go, I should add, we never thought of ourselves as re-inventing the wheel in how we wanted to do the series. We were quite clear though that it had to be distinctive, that we didn't just want to find one immigrant story to tell. Had we opted for a single story, we would never have been able to get at what was really at the heart of the series, which was to try and reckon with the multidimensionality of the immigrant and refugee experience in contemporary America – in other words, seeing America through their eyes. No one story alone could accommodate this reach, so we thought in terms of multiple stories that we would interweave together and narrate over a long period of time, each of which would ideally begin in country of origin. [DVD REF 2: AUDIO] This kind of approach was fairly rare then, but is becoming more common now. Unlike Gordon, I haven't seen nearly enough films about immigration, but I think it's fair to say that they fall generally into two categories. One being a broad historical survey, providing a great deal of information combining archival material, photographic and moving image, alongside the views of experts. The other category has been a very intimate treatment of migration, for example, the filmmaker's individual or family story.

Grossman: Steve, could you say more on your use of the word 'story'? We'll want to return to this subject later with yourself and David Simpson as co-editors of the series. In a preliminary way, what for you is story in relation to documentary film?

James: I've always, and I think this is true for Kartemquin too, been fascinated with the idea of telling people's stories. For me the idea for a film starts with a story, it's often someone else's story that I hear, somebody struggling or working towards a goal – the classic stuff of drama. Like most documentary filmmakers, when I first fell in love with film, it was with dramatic film, because that's what you're exposed to from an early age. So what has always interested me are not issue-based films with social questions in mind, but rather films in which one is witness over a period of time to the unfolding drama of people's everyday lives, as in the case of *Hoop Dreams* and more recently, *Stevie*. By and large the Kartemquin approach I heartily adopted is this notion that we are less interested in what experts have to say on the topic and more attentive to what the people who are actually going through the experience think and feel, whether working-class kids in an ethnic neighbourhood, immigrants or refugees. We've found time and time again that by following people closely over long periods that they themselves have much to say on various social issues as eloquently and as thoughtfully, to our mind more so, than academics and political experts on the subject. Kartemquin's body of work, I would say, certainly those films I've been involved with, is non-polemical. Now that is not to suggest that these films are non-political and don't make a progressive statement, that they don't have a point of view. They do, with considerable complexity and contradiction. This is something I value and I know Gordon does too.

Quinn: I think the question here is an important one and it's certainly an area that has evolved in our various films over the years.[7] Almost all filmmakers, whether dramatic or documentary filmmakers, would say that it's all about the story, in one way or another, but the question 'what is the story and what kind of story are you telling' is something that really does change. If, for example, you look at our early *vérité* films like *Home for*

Life (1967) about old age or the *Taylor Chain* films mentioned earlier, which are pure *cinema vérité*, everything is in strict chronological order as it happened; even within any given scene we were cautious not to shift things about in order to make it work. I think one vital point we learned in doing *Hoop Dreams*, and this is very much something that Steve brought to Kartemquin, is the value of borrowing storytelling elements from narrative film. Emerging out of this purist *vérité* background we've come to learn that the rules and conventions are there to be broken; you need, however, to know what they are while having an appreciation of your roots. It's important to realise that there are a multiplicity of ways of telling any particular story and no one particular approach is more valid than another. This whole question is something we've been working through during the past 15 years or so – what lines do you cross and which ones not?

James: It's a slippery issue in any kind of documentary filmmaking, though especially in Kartemquin's approach which is to go out and collect a great deal of material across different locations and situations. We don't go out and simply shoot at random – we do so with a focused idea as to what we're interested in but don't allow that focus to prohibit us from letting the story unfold in whatever direction. That is the whole appeal of this kind of filmmaking; we come back with an enormous amount of material that can be shaped in any number of dramatic ways, shaped pretty much to say whatever we want it to say.

Quinn: The most exciting building block for us in terms of narrative development, dating back to our early more ethnographic/anthropological films like *Home for Life* and *Thumbs Down* (1968) and continuing into the present, is the day-to-day observation of human behaviour and social interaction, the accretion of detail over time, which is such a different process to doing oral history films – here, you sit someone down and say tell me your story, it's driven by language and sure, we've done projects like that. We never, I should stress, try to be invisible and neither would we claim invisibility; rather, in our films we attempt to create some kind of convention in which the relationship of the filmmaker to the subject is conveyed in both subtle and explicit ways – the end product, I would argue, always falls back on the integrity of the filmmaker. It's not as if we adhere to some kind of magic formula, certainly in our early days we used to talk at length about this and I'm told this issue still comes up in film classes today. In Kartemquin's 'cinematic social inquiry'[8] days we talked about story, but what we were often doing, in an ethnographic or anthropological way, was trying to edit things down, shaping them, trying to get to the core, to figure out what in essence was happening in a given scene. I think in some sense the ability to stand back and look at the larger picture, at the larger dramatic structure of the documentary is what we're doing now, which certainly makes our work more amenable to a televisual audience. But, you know, it's not just a question of seeking a broader audience. For us, it's an ongoing artistic struggle to find new ways of telling a coherent story – if we don't evolve, then there's always the danger of becoming static.

James: As my father would say, 'when you're green you grow, when you're ripe, you get rotten'. Why should the documentary format concede dramatic aesthetics to fiction film? For makers of documentary such as myself and others, there's a strong feeling that we should have at our creative disposal as many tools as possible in dramatising people's everyday lives. Of course there are critics and academic writers who begrudge this development in documentary film.[9]

Quinn: One final thought about our approach to storytelling that to my mind links into your question yesterday as to why we chose to focus exclusively on stories of legal, or as you put it, documented migration. In the making of *Home for Life*, we set out to locate the best possible home for the aged in Chicago, not the worst. Why? Because if you want to get at the dynamics of social structures in society through the work of any given institution, if you choose to represent incompetent and corrupt professionals, then the audience response to the film will often be to remove these people from office. Essentially, you're out to expose a snake pit and that's not part of the tradition of Kartemquin filmmaking. If, however, you identify competent and well-intentioned professionals working in an institution trying to provide the best possible practice, then as filmmakers we can begin to impact on and reveal larger social structures at work. The link here to our choice of legal immigrants in *The New Americans* is this. I think one of the overriding perceptions in America is that most immigrants arriving in this country are undocumented, illegal, and so often when people talk about immigrants, there seems to be this unspoken assumption that they are illegal. It's always stories of undocumented immigration in the news, which fuel and drive public debate. So as a form of intervention if you like, we felt we had to counter this trend by concentrating on the majority of immigrants who enter this country legally and who are engaged by various institutions and immigrant advocacy organisations doing their very best to shape national immigration policy.

III

> Independent Television Service (ITVS) has found that broadcast alone is not enough to ensure that a social-issue television programme achieves its potential impact – or even reaches the audience for which it is intended.[10]

O'Brien: You've begun to identify the imagined audience for the film. In order to make this question of audience more concrete and having looked at the PBS companion website[11] to the series back in Dublin, could you outline, in terms of development and funding, the relationship between the civic engagement campaign or outreach project and the film itself? Were the two conceived as integrated parts from the very beginning?

Quinn: Very early on we knew it was vitally important that the film would speak to those communities represented in it and to the wider immigrant community. So from the outset, some two years before production commenced, we got involved with our outreach partners, whose main focus is working with public television stations, encouraging them to work with their local constituencies and organisations with a view to creating outreach activities prior to and well beyond broadcast. There were, however, some frustrations along the way. For example, we wanted the film to be accessible to immigrant communities in the various languages spoken in the film. A huge part of our outreach campaign did a lot of research work in the area of presenting materials multilingually, reflecting the languages represented in the film. Sadly, this component never got funded, which was very disappointing.

James: The breakthrough for me in knowing that the project could really be something of value to immigrant communities was when we presented what for Kartemquin was an unusually long 24-minute demo used as a fundraising device at conferences and in meetings with immigrants, refugees and members of numerous organisations working on their behalf. A substantial component of these events was made up of professional immigrants working in the field who were very responsive to the demo. I remember feeling completely energised by their response and thinking, 'yeah, this is something that can speak to those audiences' because we were telling human stories full of complexity, humour and contradiction. They understood that we weren't trying to portray immigrants in symbolic ways. We also had the experience of showing the demo to non-immigrant activists. They were equally engaged, but far more reverent about what they saw.

Grossman: What did the demo consist of?

James: It was material from the first year distilled down greatly and represented the Ogoni, Palestinian and Dominican Republic stories. The Indian story, while underway at the time wasn't developed sufficiently and Anjan, its central character, had yet to come to America. The Mexican story about the Flores family, directed by Renee Tajima-Peña, was later added on. She had been working on this story independently. [DVD REF 3: PDF]

Quinn: In the course of talking about the project to immigrants, ESL teachers and immigrant-serving organisations, we hooked into a group called 'Grant Makers Concerned with Immigrants and Refugees', where for three years in a row we were the entertainment, screening the demo and presenting ideas about the film. I recall an experience I had with Gita that surprised both of us in its intensity of feeling. In one of the later meetings, after we had shown the demo and other clips, presented materials, introduced the objectives of the outreach programme, identified possible publication materials to be made available to them and discussed pre-screens leading up to the broadcast, in short, the various facets of the project, the audience was just stunned, tearful, not willing to talk about our agenda at all. What they really wanted to talk about was what they had seen in the footage, what many of them had experienced – the incredible pain, shock, loss and dislocation that immigrants go through, the grieving process and what they'd left behind. Immigrants arrive in America and we're quick to say to them we have this and that programme for you, present a whole range of opportunities before them, which they're then asked to sign up for. My point is that we forget their experiences and so this meeting for me represented a very sobering moment because while I had seen glimpses of it in our work, it all too easily disappeared and here we were reminded of the reality for immigrants so powerfully.

O'Brien: At what point did you receive initial funding for the film and outreach campaign?

James: The foundation funding for the film and outreach programme didn't really gather momentum until 1997 when we got funding in place initially from the John D. and

Catherine T. MacArthur Foundation, and then subsequently from the Corporation for Public Broadcasting (CPB) and PBS. Between them we raised approximately a million dollars, which is a lot of money. Yet, for the kind of series we were proposing at that time it amounted to approximately a third of our projected budget. Kartemquin had a track record with MacArthur at that point because of *Hoop Dreams* and other projects, so there was an already established relationship of trust between us. They provided funding up-front which was straightforward. Yet when it came to public television even though CPB and PBS had awarded us the grant, they were not going to release the money until we had raised at least 75 per cent of the total funding of the budget for the series. This forced us to scale back the budget and project to telling three stories although ideally we had five in mind. We put it to them at the time that if successful in raising further funding from other sources, we would then want to expand the film to our original plan. So we asked them to release the money in order to get started. Had we insisted on the five stories from the outset and waited for the money to come in perhaps we would still be sitting here today waiting to begin the production. This is the way the system works in America with public television funding – it's a dance that American documentary filmmakers have to do. Funders are fearful of being burned, very conservative about awarding money and then releasing it to filmmakers, which at the time made a project like ours impossible without certain compromises in place.

Quinn: To be honest, when we started both Steve and I thought, well, immigration was very much in the public eye, we were coming off the success of *Hoop Dreams*, we had a terrific film project, a dynamite demo that we knew was really moving people's hearts, and so therefore it wouldn't be too difficult to raise the outstanding budget. We were actually dismayed at how difficult this task became. In fact we never raised the total amount of our budget, which was reduced over and over again during the course of the production. Had the MacArthur Foundation and ITVS not bailed us out then we might never have finished the film.[12]

James: Our problems surrounding funding had less to do with the demo, since those who turned the film down thought it was a terrific project. The struggle with funding had to do, in large part, with the reality of the funding of documentaries in this country. In the foundation world funding has diminished to a significant degree and there are only a handful of major foundations that still fund media projects. MacArthur is the exception. Given the size of our project, we had to cobble together a lot of small grants.

Quinn: There were foundations that fund major television documentaries with whom we entered into long conversations over the years, all the while encouraging us to think that that funding would be forthcoming. When it never materialised, we were all a bit shocked. I certainly was.

James: I think one explanation for that and drawing on our experience in making *Stevie* was that some of these foundations that Gordon is referring to had issues with our approach to filmmaking. It's much easier for them to fund something that's more straight-forward in terms of style, using experts and commentary and so on. Kartemquin's more intimate approach posed questions to them about our exploitation of people, putting their personal lives up on the screen.

Grossman: Could we move on to the content and funding aspects of the outreach component of the series? The perspective of series producer Gita Saedi would be a good starting point.

Gita Saedi: Throughout the process myself, Gordon and Steve were all thrilled and involved with how expansive the campaign got as we kept picking up partners. It's any filmmakers' goal to reach the widest audience possible, and with a seven-hour series having an outreach campaign as wide-ranging as ours is a wonderful thing. In its incubation stages, we drove the conversation with partners to create something clear and potentially real. Once the partners all came on board and we mediated their roles both shared and specific, the outreach truly took on a life of its own. There were growing pains with the union of outreach partners, but like siblings, they learned how to work together and make their collaboration help their own campaign that much stronger. Both guiding and then assisting our partners to create the wide-reaching initiative was enjoyable, necessary and extremely successful.

Quinn: We started off working with Active Voice, one of our outreach partners, putting together a series of 20–60-minute video modules excerpted from the series and associated discussion guides.[13] Leslie helped on this.

Leslie Simmer: As part of my postproduction supervisory role at Kartemquin and after Gita had moved away from Chicago and I had been part of an editing team on the Dominican Republic and Ogoni stories, I helped with the content development of three modules with Active Voice for multiple use in the workplace and schools and by community organisations. The three modules were 'Supporting Families' – helping teachers and other professionals meet the needs of immigrant families; the second was 'Finding Community' – opportunities for immigrant civic participation, which is designed especially for service producers and policymakers in identifying ways to engage new immigrants in public life. The third, 'Building Bridges', is designed for community work, for deepening an understanding between long-term residents and new immigrants. Gordon has actually used these modules in college classes.

Quinn: Later ITVS came on board with funding and services support once production was underway *recognizing that The New Americans could be a footprint program in their mission of reaching underrepresented communities* (Creekmore 2004). ITVS has a very developed outreach division and they're also doing the community engagement campaign website for the series.[14] So a huge outreach campaign has been established in conjunction with the film, much of which has been funded independently from the series itself.

James: One of our frustrations and something we were constantly up against was the fact that there were organisations interested only in funding the outreach programme and not the media. For example, the Annie E. Casey Foundation gave us a substantial grant for the production in addition to separate grants towards outreach extensions they were supporting. The MacArthur foundation did that with Active Voice too. We had to therefore navigate back and forth between chasing production funding on one hand, and funding for the outreach project, on the other. Not easy. While there were competing interests at play, moving between the two invariably uncovered further leads to pursue. Fortunately, there were no major mishaps along the way.

I think it's important to note a fundamental shift here for American documentary filmmakers. Increasingly it's hard to get your project funded unless you have an outreach programme in place. That places yet another burden on the shoulders of independent filmmakers trying to get their work done. One good result coming out of this is the necessary skill that filmmakers are forced to learn in terms of being wily and enterprising, finding new ways to get their films made. There was a time when outreach concerns never mattered or, if they did, it was something you thought about only after the film was completed. More and more funding bodies have now realised that it's insufficient to invest huge sums of money into a production for the sole purpose of a single television broadcast. They now ask questions about outreach; they may not support it directly, some will as I said, but they want to know about the film's utility beyond the broadcast itself.

Saedi: Best intentions aside, to receive foundation support, your film inevitably needs to be more than just a film. This reality was our impetus to get together an initial proposal.

Quinn: Foundations want to be in a position to gauge the film's social impact. Fair enough. For us at Kartemquin, the concept of outreach has never been problematic; it's what we've always done at a micro level though not necessarily at the level of national broadcast television. It's an integral part of our roots dating back to the 1970s when we operated as a collective.[15] Many of Kartemquin's films, for example, have toured cities with special screenings organised in schools and in collaboration with community organisations. So as this development increasingly becomes the norm, well, we're there, that's how we do things and as questions of outreach became increasingly important for potential funders, it was just a matter of toning down our more politicised language. Through working with Active Voice during the past five years or so I've become quite educated about how documentaries can be used to shape policy.

O'Brien: A compelling feature of *The New Americans*, particularly from our European vantage point, is given that it has been shot for prime-time viewing and so in effect has a popular appeal attached to it, the various online and outreach stands of the broadcast add up to something extremely ambitious that arguably isn't present elsewhere.

James: No, not on American television.

O'Brien: Nor on European television in the sense that a broadcast film wouldn't necessarily be connected to an outreach project on the scale of *The New Americans*.

Quinn: What's right for Kartemquin to be doing at this moment in time is to reach a broad American audience with powerful emotional material supported by outreach components designed to create maximum social impact. 'The New Americans outreach effort in many ways represents the best in public broadcasting's desire to not only reach but engage audiences', says Maria Alavarez Stroud, executive director of the National Center for Outreach. 'By taking the national broadcast and giving it legs through public television outreach, it ensures that the issues raised on air are actively addressed locally' (Creekmore 2004). The more confrontational agitprop kind of filmmaking is still alive, for example in the form of indymedia, but in many ways Kartemquin did that twenty-five years ago. Now it is the turn of much younger filmmakers and online activists stylistically experimenting in different and exciting ways, organising events and using the internet as a political platform for their work; for example, MoveOn.org, has this contest right now for anti-Bush campaign spots designed to be shown on the internet and there is all sorts of documentary material getting up on satellite television. I pick it up on Free Speech TV and LinkTV, so the broadcast mix is radically changing all the time.

James: This kind of work though is never screened in theatres and doesn't appear on public television.

Quinn: Sure. But then, neither was our early work.

James: Because of the recent explosion of awareness of documentaries in recent years, I think there is this tendency to consider whatever is seen in theatres, on public television, on HBO, as comprising *the* world of documentary filmmaking.

Quinn: But that's just *one* field of documentary, right?

IV

Migrant life places a tremendous strain on family relations. The ceaseless movement over and over the horizon to the next town, the next state, the next country, across rivers and oceans, is stressful enough, as are the long separations between parents and children. Another toll is the disintegration of extended family. The social fabric of Old World societies is made up of the complex network of relations the nuclear family has with the greater family of aunts, uncles, cousins, in-laws. Collective identity based on the geographic proximity of intimate relations – in the village, you may be within walking distance of most of your extended family – starts to crumble as one after another relation takes to the road.

It is one of the terrible ironies of the global era that many migrants undertake their journeys with the goal of providing a better life for their families, yet the separations that result often can work against that very goal. What happens when Dad leaves for the States, saying he'll be back in six months, and three years later his presence in the village is only manifest a couple of times a month by a disembodied voice on a long-distance line, or, perhaps, every once in a great while, a VHS videotape greeting? (Martínez 2004: 99)

Grossman: *The New Americans* accomplishes the difficult task of rendering visible the transmigration of subjects within the intersecting contingencies of globalisation, class, gender, family and community in both country of origin and destination. What's so compelling in the series and something observed closely over time is the extent to which economic pressures on the individual migrant threaten the collapse of family and communal values, generating tension within and between family members. We're wondering whether the series producer and the directors/producers of the stories anticipated in advance the collective role of families in shaping migration patterns and whether this influenced production decisions made in the field, necessitating the cultivation of relationships with various members of migrant families and indeed the wider community. Gita, could we begin with yourself and then move on to responses from the various crews to our illustrative pre-selection of clips across five family stories in the series?

Saedi: I was certainly aware of the fraught dynamics you describe in families living both in the homeland and the new land. How we shaped our filming around this is a little too related to chance for any identifiable strategy to be discussed. I would say, however, that one main crux of the film was to get to know these individuals in their countries of departure before they would come to be labelled 'immigrant' or defined as outsiders. By introducing the audience to the families of these immigrants-to-be, by humanising the long lost family and communities, the financial ties and woes make more sense. Had we not introduced the viewer to the six adorable Flores children in the Mexican story, or the priceless mother of Israel [Nwidor] in the Ogoni segment, then when the financial hardships arose the idea of 'just not helping' would possibly spring to mind. Knowing who they were helping in the country of origin and why they had to, makes it all the more real and important. Also, through knowing and following them for so long, we therefore had access to these intimate moments and stories.

O'Brien: In the Indian story, Indu, family tensions surrounding the decision to migrate are enacted powerfully through the ideologically fraught relationship between Bangalore-based computer programmer Anjan Bacchu and his father, who opposes his son's desire to exchange *the Silicon Valley of India for the real Silicon Valley* (Martinez 2004: 198). This relationship comes to a head in the culmination of a sequence prior to his departure in which Anjan is lectured by his father on the meaning of genuine 'freedom'. [DVD REF 4: VIDEO]

Indu Krishnan: I was very interested in exploring the economic tensions that a family would experience, especially in the case of someone like Anjan. From the very first interview when he talked about conflict with his father over his spending habits, I became hooked. [DVD REF 5: PDF] His father, M.A. Bacchu, was a labour leader and devout Gandhian who had been let go for his union activities and so I had the strong impression that money was going to be an area of contention, especially given that Anjan was so liberally throwing it around. That said, I think that Anjan's wanting to come to the US was more than just earning buckets of money, since he was already doing that in India. I think it was very important for him to prove himself here – almost a matter of prestige for him. But I am sure he was hesitant to voice it openly, especially given his father's dim view of

America. And so when asked his reasons for coming to the US, he often said it was to gain knowledge, expand his horizons, couching it in such terms to avoid possible confrontation with his father.

Regarding the 'freedom' conversation you highlighted, I think his father felt strongly that the 'brain drain' was an aspect of the neo-colonial domination of India by countries like the US who were depleting the reserves of highly-skilled talent in India which had been nurtured at the expense of the common man. *Anjan would become one of the 240,000 Indians [nearly half of the country's newly graduated engineers and scientists] who left the motherland between 2000 and 2002 ... It is perhaps the greatest emigration in India's history* (Martinez 2004: 188). But like Gandhi, being somewhat feudal in his personal relationships, he firmly believed in maintaining a somewhat patriarchal pecking order. While Anjan was very affected by his father's politics, the US nevertheless represented for him freedom at the level of the individual – the freedom to do this and that and be his own person away from the overbearing influence of his father. I found this father/son conflict interesting because I believe it is deeply-rooted in the Indian middle-class mindset, especially those caught up in the Gandhian ethos; I wonder how many viewers were able to make sense of this?

O'Brien: The other source of immigrant family strain in the Indian story, fuelled by economic imperatives, is Anjan's relationship with his newly-wedded wife Harshini Radhakrishnan, a computer instructor from Mysore whom he met through a computer-aided marriage bureau and who subsequently joins him in California. We were struck by the fact that Anjan does not immediately tell Harshini about being laid off from his job at 2Wire. Were the film crew then in a position of knowing what was happening to him, yet Harshini wasn't. If so, did this present any ethical dilemmas?

Krishnan: At the time of Anjan's redundancy we had been following him around for over three years. We actually interviewed him for the film some two weeks after he and Harshini met in late 1998. So in a sense, I had become a close friend and perhaps because I had lived in the US for many years, he felt I was more tuned in to the way things worked here and, therefore, would be sympathetic to his situation. But yes, I too found it odd that he hadn't been able to tell Harshini about his redundancy and even asked him why. To which he replied they would argue if she knew; she wouldn't be supportive and would just plain freak out with all the uncertainty. So not wanting to put Harshini through all that he felt the lesser evil was to keep the news away from her as long as he could. But I think the decision to use it in the film was to signal the tensions that had crept into their relationship, tensions that may have played out very differently had they been back in India, and tensions that were part and parcel of their experience as highly-skilled immigrants working in the United States.

O'Brien: A striking illustration of this tension in their relationship is the compelling *vérité* sequence in a shopping mall when after buying a pair of sneakers Anjan expresses the desire to eat french fries and sets about persuading Harshini to join him. She, however, resists. This encounter is preceded by Anjan's reflection on his struggle to negotiate family and career, conflicting material and spiritual values. [DVD REF 6: VIDEO] A further powerful sequence is towards the end of the Indian story, when Anjan is left absolutely alone at San Francisco airport having said farewell to Harshini who is returning to India. He speaks of being 'lost' – he is, as he says, without his 'compass'.

Krishnan: In some respects Harshini had far more quickly internalised American values than Anjan who remained locked in internal combat over his 'Indianness' and its erosion in the US. Regarding the airport scene, his sense of rootlessness does seem to reflect what is quintessentially the postmodern condition; his career, the work he does, the mobile workforce he belongs to and communicates with in faceless chat-rooms and alias-ridden bulletin boards has in some sense deterritorialised him. What is touching about his predicament is that when he is dealt the last final blow and is forced to be separated from that last source of identity – his wife and child – he has no one left to be his 'compass' and is forced to refer back only to himself. In his worldview this moment, when he has chosen to trade in family and country in pursuit of a chimerical career, represents a low point in his life. Ironically, and in contrast, the Mexican [Flores] family, although imploding from all the internal and external tensions, manages to reunite and remain together.

Grossman: In the film's depiction of Mexican economic migrant Pedro Flores and his family, we are collective witness to numerous intergenerational separations, departures and homecomings, characteristic of the Mexican labour migration journey, which *is not an end unto itself, but rather a means to lift the family out of poverty in the only way the migrants know how: crossing the Rio Grande and staking a claim on the future* (Martinez 2004: 150). Having obtained the right to legal residency in the US, a process he initiated seven years previously following thirteen years of peripatetic low-paid manual labour in the field, Pedro is currently employed in a meatpacking plant in Garden City, Kansas. The Flores family is finally about to be reunited in Kansas, pending Pedro's ability to secure visas for the seven other family members via an upcoming immigration interview at the American Consulate in Ciudad Juárez, located just across the border from El Paso, Texas. [DVD REF 7: PDF] Two intergenerational departure sequences involving Pedro's eight-year-old son 'Pedrito' and his wife Ventura, illustrate simply and dramatically the process of upheaval from school, family, land and community in their hometown of Cueramaro, Guanajuato. [DVD REF 8: VIDEO]

O'Brien: Renee, building on Alan's comment, in the Mexican story, to my mind more so than any other in the series, the question of gender and its entanglement with circuits of migration is most forcefully highlighted, together with pressures placed on the extended family unit. I want to ask you in particular about Ventura's role and agency in that her transition from being a single parent in rural Cueramaro, holding the family together in Pedro's absence, to Garden City, Kansas is quite dramatic. In Kansas, she spends much of her time in the home, appears bored and unhappy even though her children have gained enormously. She then makes the decision to take the children out of the school system in Kansas where Nora, the eldest daughter, has the opportunity to finish high school, with a view to relocating to Mecca, California to reunite with her sister and five children, where the Flores family knowingly will have to endure backbreaking work in the heat of Mecca's greenhouse nurseries and picking fields (as one subject comments this is virtually a 'step-down in the migration cycle). Ventura's catalytic decision is arguably extreme, yet at the same time, understandable. Here we see the dialectic of family migration with full force. [DVD REF 9: VIDEO]

Renee Tajima-Peña: I think Vangie and I, because of our respective backgrounds and work in our communities, were hyper aware of the effect of mobility, globalisation and immigration on families. (See my written response to your question on selection of Pedro Flores which I link to questions of family reunification). [DVD REF 10: PDF] Ventura was really interesting to me. The conventional wisdom and 'marketing' of the American Dream, so to speak, is that the US offers educational opportunity, and therefore class mobility. For Ventura, that meant physical and psychic mobility, and thus, the possibility of further separation within the family. Pedro and Nora opposed the move from Kansas to California, because they would lose both job and educational opportunities. Meatpacking is dangerous, relatively low-paid work, but offers higher pay in a region with a relatively low cost of living, compared to fieldwork in California. The schools are better in Kansas, and Garden City in particular has tried hard to serve the needs of immigrant working families. Also because it's such a small community, there isn't the 'white flight' out of public schools as in metropolitan areas, or what we have here in California. The Flores kids went to school with other immigrant kids, but with native English speakers, so they were exposed to English in a way they are not in the highly segregated community of Mecca.

It's interesting that my husband, who grew up in a migrant farm-worker family, was really disappointed and somewhat angry when he heard the family was moving to Mecca and forgoing the opportunities afforded them in Kansas. In our definition of success, the kids would learn English, go to college, get a good job, and get out of south-west Kansas. But the mobility that has pushed almost all of his brothers away from the poverty-stricken Rio Grande Valley is also the greatest source of sorrow for the family. They are scattered, adrift from the anchor of home and each other. I think Ventura feared the same thing for her children and her family – the essential condition of American modernity is this mobility and the alienation from home. Furthermore, when a child crosses the border from one class to another, there is another kind of potential alienation from their family.[16]

Grossman: At this point, we'd like to shift discussion to the production of the Ogoni story, to the selection of the refugee families of Israel and Ngozi Nwidor and Barine Wiwa-Lawani, sister of writer and activist Ken Saro-Wiwa executed by Sani Abacha's military regime in Nigeria. [DVD REF 11: AUDIO] [DVD REF 12: PDF] They have finally secured political asylum in the United States having resided for more than two years in a Benin refugee camp. Steve, as somebody who was on camera for some of the location shoots in both Nigeria and Chicago, alongside your co-directorial role of the segment with Gita, and as co-executive producer of the series from the outset, to what extent did you anticipate the impact of economic pressures on the refugee family unit in Chicago? For example, the everyday difficulties surrounding separation from their extended family and native community in Ogoniland on the Niger Delta, alongside the demands and expectations of success bestowed on the Nwidors as representatives of the Ogoni exiled from their family and community.

James: Across the various stories there were a number of surprises. We did anticipate in advance that for some of the immigrants and refugees such as Israel and Ngozi who came with next to nothing, their lack of financial resources would always be a daily struggle, affecting their individual wellbeing and the kinds of jobs that they would have to end up doing, despite being very educated, Israel in particular. He had a degree in petrochemical engineering, which was worthless in the US. I think what surprised us though was that this economic struggle alongside having to deal with unforeseen daily demands took less of a toll on their marriage than the demands and expectations of family back home who were reliant on them. [DVD REF 13: VIDEO] It was an eye-opening experience to see how on one occasion when filming them calling home they were arguing with relatives on the phone about how much money to send back. Israel spoke about how the family just wanted the remittance money to be sent and that he couldn't get himself to tell them how the money was earned, the low prestige of the jobs they were forced to take. So, the impact of economic imperatives reverberates not only on the immediate family but down the immigrant family line – this was certainly apparent in their case, which I found to be quite revealing. *'Today, when you leave here [refugee camp] and enter that bus and go to the airport, be determined and ready to work', says Israel's pastor. Israel listens intently with his head bowed. 'If you don't succeed, the Ogoni have failed because your success is your family's success, it is your village's success, it is the success of the Ogoni. If you fail, it is an Ogoni failure, we have all failed'* (Martinez 2004: 73).

Grossman: Each was earning $7 an hour, doing steward and housekeeping jobs in hotels.

James: That's right. Sadly it's still true today. I met up with them a few weeks ago at Barine's birthday party and they're still juggling jobs, working split day and night shifts because they can't afford a baby-sitter. In the other immigrant stories of the series, there were further surprises and developments, Take Anjan for example. Here was somebody who was relatively well off whose reasons for coming to the US had little to do with real economic need. In a similar way that the Dominican Republic ballplayers José Garcia and Ricardo Rodríguez wanted to play in the major leagues of US baseball, Anjan wanted to play in the big leagues of Silicon Valley. When he arrives and it's the dot-com boom, all is well. Harshini comes too, we see them shopping for a car, clothes, gadgets, on vacation. They have a nice apartment and their life and relationship is comfortable. Yet when the dot-com bust hits you see the toll it begins to take on them individually and on their marriage. In the series as a whole I would say that the stresses and strains on the families are sometimes economic and other times not – an example being the Palestinian story where the tensions are less economic and more political in the relationship between Naima Saddeh and Hatem Abudayyeh.

Grossman: Staying with the Ogoni story, I want to ask you about the memorable 'video letter' exchange between Israel, Nogozi and their extended families back in Ogoniland. Could you contextualise this sequence? How did it materialise? [DVD REF 14: VIDEO]

James: This is a very emotional sequence in the story. Let me answer your question by referencing to begin with the bilingual Spanish/English film *Balseros* ('Cuban Rafters', 2002) that Gordon mentioned yesterday in our conversation about documentaries we looked at on the subject of immigration. Essentially the film dates back to 1994 when a Spanish crew of telejournalists filmed and interviewed Cubans attempting to reach the US on homemade rafts. Many drowned en route, hundreds turned back, and some were picked up by the Coast Guard and held for a year or so in a temporary refugee camp in Guantánamo Bay. The film crew gained access to the camp, following the flight of the rafters as they waited for their immigration status to be sorted out. Seven years later, the crew reconnects with these same subjects to discover the outcome of their new lives in different cities across the country. What's interesting is that throughout the film the directors deploy the tactic of facilitating video letters between the rafters and their families back in Cuba and in so doing, very much become a vital link between the two – something that we happened to do only once in the Nigerian story.

Israel and Ngozi could not afford a return trip back home to pay their respects to Ken Saro-Wiwa whose remains were removed from a mass grave for burial in a tomb. This also would have an opportunity to reunite with their family whom they hadn't seen for several years. So we suggested videotaping them – at the time they were having difficulties in reaching the family by phone – and then showing the video letter to the family, which they wanted us to do. This is an example, really, of a completely orchestrated moment in the series, something that never would have happened without the presence of the filmmakers. We made an assumption, rightly or wrongly, that viewers would guess from the way it was shot that the film crew engineered this exchange. Whether you know this to be the case or not doesn't detract from what this sequence powerfully conveys; that the two families on either side of the screen miss each other profoundly, that intimate dialogue occurs between screens and that while photographs, letters and email are still sent home, video contact has become very common. *In today's migrant world, VHS or digital video is increasingly the preferred 'virtual epistolary form'* (Martinez 2004: 93). So observing the dialogue unfold and interaction between screens and people separated by thousands of miles was quite a revelation.

Grossman: The disembodied modes of communication and material exchange depicting transnational Ogoni family relations are arguably in marked contrast to the Dominican Republic story in which we are exposed to some of the visible benefits of remittance payments sent home by baseball players Ricardo Rodríguez and José García, alongside recurring face-to-face contact and pressures imposed on them by their respective mothers in the Caribbean to succeed in the US major leagues. Susana [Aiken] and Carlos [Aparicio], unlike other immigrant family living arrangements in the series, what's interesting is that Ricardo and José take up residency in Great Falls, Montana with their adopted 'houseparents' Ole and Marie Mackey, an elderly Catholic couple, while playing for the Dodgers in the minor leagues. Here begins a fascinating account of intricate transcultural relationships, including a trip undertaken by the Mackey's to Ricardo's family in the Dominican Republic and significantly, a rape allegation by a white woman in Great Falls against Dominican player Ramon Martínez. [DVD REF 15: VIDEO] As Spanish immigrants and co-directors of the story living in New York, what was your response to these 'house-parent' families, to relations between your two key subjects and the wider community in this small northern town? [DVD REF 16: AUDIO]

Carlos Aparicio: First, I want to say something about Lala and María, the mothers of José and Ricardo. They play a huge role, policing them at all times and occasionally slapping them if need be even though José and Ricardo are these 18-year-old giants. Why? Because the mothers project the dreams and ambitions of the entire family onto their sons, giving them the responsibility of extricating the family from its state of poverty. So when asked about what they would do with any money earned, the first response from both of them would always be 'to buy a house for my mother'. In relation to their adopted parents, I want to say how shocked, how pleasantly surprised I was in meeting them – yes, I went to Montana with a lot of prejudice and preconceived ideas and then, to my amazement, discovered this very progressive Catholic community who are somehow connected to ideas about liberation theology in central America. What the relationships between the host families and the Dominican players revealed was that the film Susana and I were making was not strictly about immigration and sport; the material we were getting opened out, like every human story in documentary, to the quality of relationships between people, which always has the ability to attack prejudice of one sort or another. So many of the prejudices that I took with me to Great Falls, about the kind of people and community I expected to encounter, about this particular geographical area in the US, were very much shattered when I met and came to know people like Ole and Marie and saw at first hand the quality of interaction between the Dominican players and members of the community.

For example, you see Ricardo and José being lovingly received into the congregation of the Mackeys' church, invited to sing in the choir. *The presence of Ricardo, José and their Caribbean cohort in Great Falls might be unusual, but it's no longer a unique migrant experience in the US. The 2000 Census provided ample evidence of a dramatic demographic shift. In the course of a decade, immigrants from Latin America, Africa and Asia spread out from the traditional portals of major cities and into the American heartland* (Martinez 2004: 130). What was enriching for me was that every time we explored questions of racism, their experience as 'black' kids in a white town, 99 per cent of the time they responded positively – they were in fact widely accepted by most of the community. Interestingly, there was some conflict at a later stage when José became the boyfriend of a Mormon girl and things got slightly out of hand because the Mackeys thought that this was a ploy on behalf of the Mormons to take away their 'son' and somehow make money out of him. It's important to remember that the presence of the Dodgers in this small town gives it some kind of status and respectability and the Dominican players coming into the town get caught up in the local mix of religious politics.

Grossman: How in fact are the players assigned to particular families? Is this an existing arrangement between the Dodgers and the community?

Susana Aiken: Yes, and unsurprisingly it's mediated through the church – the Dodgers are very intelligent in this regard. One aspect I find totally compelling in the material we shot is the extraordinary presence and contribution of Ole and Marie. They for me symbolise the white American person who has a total longing to embrace others different to them in skin colour, language or whatever, but haven't had the opportunity to do so or in reality would never have the chance of embracing a non-white person in America. So they openly accept the opportunity of taking these 'black' Dominican players into their home despite the fact, culturally speaking, that the Dominicans don't see themselves as black. What particularly struck me when I accompanied Carlos on the second shoot to Great Falls was this sheer abundance of physical affection, the sensuality displayed between these two attractive non-white players and their adopted white working-class hosts whose social conventions are quite defined in terms of how you relate physically to others, when and how you touch. Suddenly these 'black' Dominican men come into their homes and you witness this incredible alchemy between them, hugging one another at every opportunity. The downside or negative dimension of this open expression of sensuality resulted in the rape incident involving Ramon [see section V, below], which really tore the community apart. The allegation by a white woman of being ravished by a black man is so ingrained in race relations in this country.

O'Brien: In relation to the Palestinian story, the three of you have spoken about your respective roles, discussed issues surrounding gender, access and the timing of the production just prior to the outbreak of the second intifada. [DVD REF 17: AUDIO] Compared to the other family stories, the Palestinian segment stands out in terms of its camera style and ethnographic approach, reminding me of the dominant aesthetic in Michel Khleifi's fiction film *Wedding in Galilee* (1987), which is an intimate and allegorical portrait of a Palestinian village under Israeli occupation in which the politics of place is accessed through everyday relations and a wedding ritual. I'm particularly thinking of material shot in the West Bank village of El Jib, home to the tightly-knit Saadeh family and the period immediately prior to Naima Saadeh's emotive departure to Chicago, where she will join her American-born Palestinian future husband, Hatem Abudayayah. [DVD REF 18: VIDEO] In your representation of the migrant journey undertaken by Naima, the individual immigrant as an integral part of a collective, be it family, community, or in this case and most significantly, the specificity of location allied to political struggle, is marked emphatically.

Jerry Blumenthal: As a crew I think we certainly set out to establish and develop a keen sense of place, situating Naima, her siblings and mother Um Mujahid in a landscape that has very much shaped their moral and geographical universe. We expected to do so from the outset and were attentive to the significance of place throughout the film work given the Israeli/Palestinian conflict, which of course is so much about ownership of the land. One example here was filming Jihad, Naima's brother, who was imprisoned during the intifida, actually replacing windows for a living in an Israeli settlement nearby – something he found extremely distasteful for what it represented. The Chicago end of the story has an obvious sense of place built into, for example, their new home in the basement of Hatem's family, but not as much as we would have liked. [DVD REF 19: VIDEO]

Quinn: I think that it's no accident that sense of place in the story is most tangible for viewers in and around El Jib because here, in this world, the people, the look and feel of the village, her mother's house, collectively have a great deal of material and symbolic meaning to Naima. In stark contrast, when she arrives in Chicago, 'our' city, Naima didn't appear to respond to and wasn't interested in our pedestrian questions about what she thought about the city; it was if she wasn't there which was so radically different to how we experienced her in El Jib. *Chicago is in the realm of the imaginary; only El Jib is real for Naima. Her body lives in the village and the village lives in her body* (Martinez 2004: 27).

Blumenthal: I recall how on one occasion in Chicago we were driving in the car with Naima on the way to her first job interview at a battered women's shelter – we were very excited. I was at the wheel, Gordon had the camera and Naima was wired sitting at the back. We tried in vain to ask her all sorts of questions, but she just sat there quietly, gazing out the window, blanking us out.

Quinn: We definitely wanted the politics to emerge out of our filmic construction of place, which is why I spoke earlier about the absence of maps and their importance in the context of Occupation. [DVD REF 17: AUDIO] It was very frustrating because I felt we've got this village and this extraordinary family, and the potential was there, but we just weren't able to actualise it, of going straight from their feelings and emotions of living in this particular place, to the actual maps that people argue over in terms of the politics.

Grossman: The invocation of place, it seems to me, is not so much established in and throughout El Jib and its surrounding area, which arguably is an incidental landscape to the story. Rather, the real sense of place conveyed in the footage was the domestic setting, the Saadeh family home and the intricacy of relationships within. It very much felt as if the crew had taken up residency in the family home.

Fenell Doremus: Well, we did! [collectively voiced]. We were living with the family. We spent most of our time in the home, so much so that at some point we were thinking that we had to film outdoors and asked Naima to give us a guided tour of the village, of specific places that were important to her. It was fascinating to see her get dressed up for this occasion, much like a television newscaster, looking very slick in her black jacket and white shirt, black pants, heels and make-up. What emerged though from this tour was that not a great deal had much meaning for her in the village, because female members of the family didn't simply just wander around freely in the village, hanging out at the coffee shop – it's a strict Muslim village. The women stay at home and if they do go out, then it's to their neighbours, socialising in the kitchen or in the courtyard. So, apart from some interesting voice-over we ended up using very little visual material from this outing.

Quinn: I would say we have enough material that is not in the film itself to make a complete feature on the domestic life of the Saadeh family. We shot tons because we were fascinated by it; they used to have to drag me away from filming somebody cooking or doing the laundry. There was something incredibly appealing about the ethos of this family home. With a great deal of affection we used to refer to it as a certain kind of domestic idiocy. Why are we filming this?

Grossman: What you're describing is possibly a function of your Jewish American subject position, entangled as you are whether you like it or not, in having to take a particular view of the Israeli/Palestinian conflict. The Palestinian story presents itself as your first opportunity to film on the West Bank and so, when actually confronted with the reality and novelty of the Saadeh domestic arena, are you arguably susceptible to exoticising the family environment?

Quinn: Yes, a good point and I think there is some truth to that. Yet I would also want to say that we all felt this way … that we were working with a rather exceptional family. Although we did spend some time with other families, relatives of the Saadeh family, there was something extremely appealing about Um Mujahid's family, how this wise and wonderful widowed woman who had also lost a son in an Israeli prison managed to raise seven children and somehow keep things ticking over in a patriarchal society.

Blumenthal: It's not just that it was appealing, but also particularly rich, intimate and physically expressive at the level of domestic familial relations between mother, son and daughters; for example, the scene where Naima and her sister are going through Jihad's letters, which he smuggled out of prison. To have stayed in this house, in this atmosphere and not get incredible material would suggest there was something dramatically wrong with you as a filmmaker. I also want to make the point, and this was something we always talked about during filming, that the material we were shooting, showing the humanity of the family against the everyday politics of the situation, carried the potential to subvert stereotypes viewers have in the West about Palestinians.

Quinn: Yet even from a pro-Palestinian angle in the West there remain powerful stereotypes. What we were really striving for was to demonstrate the levels of complexity in these people. Yes, they live under Occupation, but as a people they are just as contradictory and complicated as any other.

O'Brien: An illustration perhaps of what you're describing in terms of competing and complex subject positions is an illuminating discussion on the night of Naima's college graduation party before her departure. The men, including Hatem and Jihad, gather upstairs on the rooftop courtyard and in the heat of this political conversation Jihad, his credentials as a veteran resistance fighter respected by all, speaks openly, indeed provocatively, about his feelings towards Palestine. [DVD REF 20: VIDEO] The other interesting aspect of this sequence is its orchestration, since the conversation doesn't appear to occur spontaneously.

Quinn: There are two things to say about this particular sequence. To begin with, it is heavily condensed and in fact is an intercut, creating the impression that the discussion occurs on the night of Naima's celebration, which it did not. So it was edited out of sequence in terms of space and time, something we would tend not to have done in our earlier work. Secondly, it was Hatem who alerted us in advance to these kinds of political discussions between himself and cousins whenever he was visiting El Jib. In fact they had a similar conversation the night before which we missed for some reason and so here was another opportunity to film, which Hatem instigated. Once it started we just shot for three hours.

Doremus: It even ended seamlessly, probably at that point where we were getting tired. They said, that's enough and wrapped things up.

Blumenthal: It really had its own engine. Hatem didn't have to play the role of leading the conversation and sparking the others. All of them were totally clued into the issues at stake and were clear about their positions.

Doremus: Though I do think there were fresh issues being debated and that they weren't faking it.

Blumenthal: Having gone through it once before you would think that when asked to re-group, they would simply go through the motions, acting out their positions. Yet the issues they were discussing were so real, so immediate and so much a part of their lives. Take Jihad's comments for example. He was absolutely furious with those who took the position that you have to stay and fight because he felt that he had done his fair share, served his country and was now ready to leave.

Grossman: I want to ask about how you managed to film and follow closely a group conversation in Arabic, assuming the three of you don't speak the language. The issue here also opens out to the important question of translation in the production context of developing relationships with Naima and her family.

Blumental: That's an interesting question.

Quinn: In Kartemquin we are fortunate to have this person Jim Morrissette who you should speak to about this sequence. He is otherwise known as the 'Dean of Chicago video', who we consulted with regarding the technological aspects of simultaneous translation. He is a technical wizard, also a cameraman with an engineering background. We knew from the outset we would have a potential problem understanding what our subjects were saying, since none of us spoke Arabic although crucially we did work with a translator [Siham Rashid] who became an essential part of our crew. [DVD REF 21: AUDIO]

Blumenthal: The Palestinian story in general and that particular discussion would have been extremely difficult and messy had we not figured out in advance how we were going to do the simultaneous translation so we did all kinds of tests – we had to get it right and fortunately it worked smoothly.

Jim Morrissette: It was really Gordon's brilliant idea to come up with the question of whether it would be possible to do simultaneous translation using the equipment we had. My goal was to get the simultaneous translator's audio on to the sound track directly with the original footage, so that you would always know where you were, as opposed to the original idea of recording the translation on a separate audio recorder. This would be fine for making typed transcripts but to synchronise it with the film would be the hard part for people like us who don't speak Arabic. So I simply devised a way whereby the translator could go into a separate audio track with a wireless microphone and feed a headset so that the camera operator could hear what the translation was while he or she was shooting. On the opposite sound track then was the actual synchronised sound of the original language, Arabic, and because digital has essentially total isolation between the two tracks of audio we could load both tracks into the editing system, edit using the scratch track and then pull the scratch track out once we put down our subtitles.

V

> *The New Americans* was definitely the largest in-house project that Kartemquin has done to date. We did all the logging, editing, colour correction and sound mix entirely in-house in order to save money. We purchased two DV-Avid systems for editing. I fought hard for the Avids because I knew that if we were to edit the old-fashioned way – loading material into the computer at low resolution and then returning later to recapture and locate all the pieces – we would not have had the time or the money. The Avids allowed us to load everything in at full resolution, all one thousand hours of footage, which remained in the machines throughout the whole postproduction phase, which lasted approximately two years. Having two machines enabled Steve [James] and David [Simpson] to edit simultaneously...
> – Jim Morrissette, Kartemquin Films Technical Supervisor [**DVD REF 22: PDF**]

O'Brien: In this final session we want to focus the discussion on selective aspects of the postproduction phase of the series. In particular, the collaborative editorial division of labour, beginning with the reception of the material from the directors/producers of the stories, the conversations and negotiations surrounding its content and form in the final cut, since it was your role and responsibility, Steve and David [Simpson] as series editors and Leslie too as postproduction supervisor to transform the one thousand hours of material into a seven-hour documentary television series. Moving on from that, we have more specific questions about decisions shaping the method and structure of the edit given the film's comparative and integrated televisual narrative logic, which draws on *vérité* material, in addition to the inclusion of the voice of a male narrator throughout. In contrast to stand-alone documentaries, interweaving stories, in this case migrant narratives, always carries the danger, does it not, that the comparative juxtaposition of subjects creates a potential imbalance in that one subject is viewed as doing better than another. So, how then to avoid the trap as editors of inserting value judgements in this regard? Steve, in addition to your position as series co-editor you were of course also editing material from your co-produced Nigerian segment, so there are further points of tension to explore here. [**DVD REF 23: AUDIO**]

James: The other dimension to consider, which we spoke about in Dublin, is the creative process not only between David and me as a team of editors, but between us and the producers of the stories, the filmmakers themselves who subjected their cinematic impulses to the greater good of the film. As one of them commented, 'they handed their babies over to us'. In the Ogoni story, for example, and this is my own personal view, I'm happy with the way it plays in the series; people identify with Israel, feel for him and what he's going through. Yet had this been a stand-alone film about the two Ogoni families, how different they are, how one struggles more than the other, then much more of the material we shot would have been used to make the story significantly stronger as a feature-length piece. So it would be interesting to ask the other filmmakers whether they think their story would have been stronger alone rather than interwoven into a series. I suspect they'll probably tell you that they can appreciate the gestalt form of the series, but there's a part of them that wishes they could have made the film as a stand-alone. I happen to think that there's something really terrific about all these integrated stories as part of one long series as opposed to a bunch of stand-alones. Ultimately it will make the series more successful, for both viewers and the press.

David Simpson: It's a case of the whole being greater than the sum of its parts.

James: Since we're documentary filmmakers who value real honesty and the contradictions in the work we do, I would urge you to speak to the story producers on the issues you raised. I would like them to feel comfortable in voicing their opinions – I don't want to speak for them. I do though want to stress the point that we all came through this process with our respect for each other intact. We're excited about what has been accomplished and hopeful that the series is going to achieve everything we want it to do. Sure, it's been tricky at times, but ultimately a positive experience. We were aware in advance that the editing process was going to be tough – we even spoke about this openly in a group meeting saying 'a point would come in time when you will have to hand your baby over and no matter how much time we will have given you, it was never going to be enough'.

O'Brien: We'll certainly convey your openness to critique and reflection to the other directors. Could we begin with your respective roles when the material started coming into Kartemquin?

James: I had very little to do with Kartemquin's organisation of the massive influx of material. It was really Leslie and Gita who managed this from the outset.

Simmer: We were getting the material in several years before the in-house editing actually began. The story producers submitted rough cuts of their work which varied in length, anything up to three hundred hours in the case of the Ogoni story, for example. They also provided some translated transcripts, but not enough, and it was Gita who organised the transcription in Kartemquin, using a huge and impressive voluntary army of interns. So there was a mechanism in place before the editing got started and David began with the Palestinian story.

Simpson: This was the only case in which I began working with the footage of a story and not the rough cut itself, mainly because a large chunk of the Palestinian story was based here in Chicago and I was ready and available for work. The directing-producing teams did most of the initial editing, giving the material some shape.

James: So David operated initially as the primary editor of the Palestinian story before putting on the hat of series editor that followed. Jerry then stepped in to continue editing the Palestinian story because we didn't have the luxury of time to go through the story as the two of us had to begin the process of series editing. Gita as series producer did something similar on the Ogoni story, initially editing in an attempt to get our arms around the three hundred Ogoni hours, since I wasn't available for a period of time as I was finishing editing *Stevie*. [DVD REF 24: PDF]

Simpson: At the beginning of the series edit each story was considered separately and we weren't overly concerned with interweaving the segments. In the back of our minds we were aware of resonances between the stories, thematic connections; for example, between Hatem and Naima and Israel and Ngozi's circumstances. So from the start, our editorial concerns were not necessarily shaped by how intersecting points of interest could be joined up; instead we were searching for the content and strength of the material in each of the stories.

James: What happened was, we organised a meeting in Kartemquin where all the filmmakers came together for a discussion about the process we were about to start in terms of series editing, which was very productive. At that point not all of them had completed their own editing of the segments; there was though enough material in each of the stories to engage with. The idea behind the meeting was initially for everybody to give each other feedback on the individual cutting of the stories, but more importantly to get all the filmmakers in the same room, talking about thematic points relevant to immigration that they wanted raised in the series. We then reflected on these issues as we moved into and through the editing process. I actually roughed out an outline of the entire series for the meeting based on what we had received and what I knew had been shot. If you were to look at the outline now compared to the film today, there is little resemblance. So it was really an attempt to dive into the individual stories and begin the process of structuring the series around the interweaving of stories. [DVD REF 25: AUDIO]

O'Brien: In our discussion with Steve and David on the subject of editing the series, Steve reflected on a remark by one of the story producers that you the directors had 'handed your babies over' to himself and David. We understand that you had done some initial editing of material shot prior to sending it on to Steve and David and that a collective directorial meeting was held at Kartemquin. How did you respond to relinquishing editorial control of your material? During the course of the lengthy series edit, were there any points of tension/debate in your communication with Steve and David? Were they responsive to suggestions on your behalf? [DVD REF 26: PDF] [DVD REF 27: PDF]

Aiken: As Spanish immigrants critical of US immigration policy and having done various migration projects during the past eighteen years, it was very exciting for us to get involved with a group of Americans [Kartemquin] whose work we knew and respected. But there were a number of real difficulties beginning with the fact that unlike the other directors we never got to choose the story ourselves – José and Ricardo were picked in advance by the previous director who we subsequently replaced some six to eight weeks into the production. When we came on board the Dodgers were already on their way to the US and we didn't get to do the background work on the film – looking at the social and political conditions of where the two came from in the Dominican Republic. So coming late into the production meant that we were handicapped in terms of time and budget, that we had to use and rework material that we never shot and wasn't compatible with our style of filmmaking.

Aparicio: The other big challenge for us was that we were asked to explore immigration through baseball, a sport most Americans love, lending a positive and bright side to the series. [DVD REF 28: PDF] This particular focus was going to be the selling point of the series, at least that's the impression we got from Steve early on. Unfortunately the story we inherited was locked into the dynamic of coming to the US to make it big, or not make it at all. All of this was a totally new experience for us, as was the fact that we were tied into a group of filmmakers with an executive production structure above our heads, something we hadn't known before as independent filmmakers. We both feel there wasn't enough dialogue with Steve in the cutting of the film. We were very worried, and said so to Steve, that the Dominican story would be seen as a moral or ideological celebration of Ricardo's success in contrast to the failure of José to establish himself as a professional player; two different characters pitted against each other, their destinies linked to an American Protestant work ethic. [DVD REF 15: VIDEO] What for me is absent in the story, something we would have wanted to emphasise, is that Ricardo's success is really an exception to the rule. What in reality happens to José is a far more accurate measurement of the bigger picture, of the experience of the majority of players, who arrive in this country, dreaming of becoming a millionaire, but return to the Dominican Republic defeated and ashamed because they couldn't make it. Or they stay on illegally, and here in New York we have a huge Dominican community. If you talk to them, you learn that most of them had been involved in the baseball world at some point or another but are now working in a little bodega. They are the losers. To realistically explain why somebody like José didn't make it, we would have had to do an in-depth exploration of the politics inside the Dodgers.

Grossman: Yet present in the Dominican story and at work throughout the series is an implicit critique of 'Americanness', of certain values and of a civilising discourse imposed on these new migrant subjects. A forceful illustration of this was a combination of scenes in the Dodgers training camp in the Dominican Republic where Ricardo, José and the other recruits undergo an 'Americanisation' training in acceptable forms of public social conduct. We saw this as quite brutalising. [DVD REF 29: VIDEO]

Aiken: I'm happy to hear that because we were frustrated that we couldn't actually devote a significant part of the film to exposing the farming techniques of these camps which are run like a military academy whereby the kids are picked up young and in some cases deformed physically for life. Instead of shooting guns, they hit balls. After you train for four years non-stop from the age of sixteen to be a pitcher, if you're then released, one arm could well be half a foot longer than the other, you've had no academic education, which means unemployment and the family's impossible dream effectively over. We did touch on some of these issues, but it wasn't really the intended focus of the film. [DVD REF 30: AUDIO]

Aparicio: The most difficult aspect of the production for us was that at certain points there were very crucial events unfolding, for example, the Ramon story, which we wanted to tackle in greater depth, but couldn't. The funding wasn't available from Kartemquin.

Aiken: This was also because Kartemquin, especially Gita and Steve, didn't really appreciate how important the story was in the community. Ramon wasn't a central character and so the rape allegation and everything surrounding it was seen as a side story. Gita did do a fine job as series producer, but she was also a master of resistance. What was happening with Ramon happened to coincide with a six-month period in which funding for the series was frozen. [DVD REF 31: PDF] We pushed and pushed and did lose precious weeks and finally had to be quite forceful in our communication with Steve, who I don't think really made himself available to us. He was probably overwhelmed and had his own deadlines. This absence of sustained communication was definitely the weakest and worst part of the process.

Aparicio: We did have a couple of tough conversations with Steve where I would call saying 'filmmaker to filmmaker, surely there must be a few thousand dollars somewhere in the production budget for an emergency'. Kartemquin didn't want to tell us how and what we should do, but the problem was that they were so preoccupied with the overall funding for the project at this time and we, on the other hand, with developing Ramon's story, which we thought extremely important.

Aiken: The Ramon incident should really be the dramatic climax to our story in the series in which these Dominican players are militarised and indoctrinated in the training camps, from how to eat to how to treat white women. They're then brought to the US, given the best possible training and in the end, whether they like or not, are still seen as black and threatening. That's the reality check and an essential part of our story. Steve at the time was most likely thinking, well, we have this material and more, including action from the minor leagues and relationships with the house-parents. That was enough for him, but he wasn't living the story as we were. As of now, we still don't know how Ramon features in the final cut. We've seen pieces here and there and I'm certain it won't be central.

O'Brien: We have viewed the series in its entirety and what happened to Ramon does come out in the end.

Aiken: The story is there, but in order to do justice to it we would have really needed to immerse ourselves in that community, shoot for weeks rather than days, dig ourselves in, do many more interviews and follow people around. Essentially, bring to the surface the legacy of Harper Lee's novel *To Kill a Mockingbird* (1960). [DVD REF 32: PDF]

O'Brien: Could we move the discussion along by examining the role, gender and accent of the narrator in the series – a question directed at the entire production team. Was the inclusion of voice-over designed to accommodate the demands of a televisual audience? Or was it used more as a device to draw the viewer in by the very accent of the narrator, given the fundamental significance of accent to the project?

James: In that meeting with the directors I spoke of earlier, the question of the series narrator was first raised. The discussion – it was civil, it wasn't nasty – turned into an interesting debate about 'accent'. Hardly surprising, because assembled in the room were a group of people most of whom were immigrants or first-generation immigrant filmmakers. I recall arguing that ultimately if the *The New Americans* couldn't be narrated by an immigrant voice, if we didn't commit ourselves to this, then what series could? Some agreed with my suggestion, but quickly raised questions about whose voice should it be, which led to further discussion that maybe after all it shouldn't be an immigrant voice, because deciding on a particular voice or accent as it turned out, was far too complicated. In fact, in the early stages of the edit, David, myself and Leslie too, were working with three different voices as scratch narrations. The narration question was thrown out quite provocatively at the end of this meeting and I remember writing a memo a week later, re-opening the matter and there was a lot of communication back and forth between the directors. David, you certainly had strong views on the subject.

Simpson: The narration was always going to be a difficult issue, essentially because the film draws heavily on the voices of immigrants as they speak in *vérité* appearance. The film's narration is for the most part utilitarian – it carries information and is not about personal musings. It certainly is not first-person narration or 'voice of God' narration; I think of it more as the voice of the filmmaker or of the filmmakers who are looking at this particular group of people and narrating a set of stories. My own view at the time was ideally to use an accented voice that never pretended to be that of an immigrant. It was a real struggle to find the right voice, one that had to be non-identifiable in terms of its heritage, while at the same time conveying an authentic quality and clear enunciation.

James: I wanted a little more, not exactly what David is saying. The voice of the narrator had to sound like an immigrant – the straight narration wouldn't have worked with false emotion or soulfulness when it was basically serving a utilitarian purpose. I remember telling Ismail [Bashey], the series narrator who we eventually worked with and who Leslie helped to locate via one of the immigrant civic organisations here in Chicago, that we wanted him to speak with conviction, from a certain depth of experience.

Simmer: We immediately identified this quality about him when we first met; it wasn't necessarily his accent that persuaded us, but the quiet ability in his voice that made you want to listen. Ismail himself is an amalgam of different cultures, originally from an Islamic family in India who's also lived in the Middle East and for a long time in the US. So I think these various influences come together in his voice.

Saedi: Since we wanted the strongest voice to be that of the immigrants we were following and because we also needed cohesion for the film to work, I think the choice made was the right one. I was always fighting for the voice of an immigrant, definitely not an American one. Our directing team and principal subjects were immigrants and non-immigrants alike; if you fused all our voices together I'd imagine you'd get a product of the same vein as the series narrator.

Aiken: There was some serious debate in the meeting about the narrator. It seemed early on that Steve was going to narrate the series. At least this was a possibility.

Aparicio: As he did in *Hoop Dreams* and *Stevie* and we were familiar with this particular style of narration. Susana and I discussed this and were very concerned that his voice and what it represents should not carry the series. Others jumped in too, particularly Indu and Renee. It was really Renee who most openly and persuasively spoke out against the use of Steve's voice, arguing it would be synonymous with a dominant white male perspective on PBS.

Tajima-Peña: Throughout editing the Flores family story, I could never 'hear' a third-person narrator in my head. When you put together a documentary it is necessary that you hear and know the voice of its narrator. The voice is the starting point, the embodiment for the story itself. Every time I tried to imagine a third-person narrator, I'd feel like I was listening to an ethnographic educational film about the aboriginals. I think Vangie and Johanna felt the same way. So we tried to assemble the story with Nora's voice. She was the central emotional force in the film; for us, she was the person who changed and emerged in the story. Nora was a transitional figure on the immigration stage. Old enough to be tied to Mexico, young enough to be transformed by America. I think if we had more time to edit, we could have really made it work with Nora. But of course, it never was going to work in the context of the series, which was intercut with a single narrator's voice. But that's the process we had to go through to understand the shape of the story, and give it a point of view. I think I would have preferred a woman's voice, but probably because I'm a woman and directors all in some ways consider themselves gods, so of course you want to remake the world on film in your own image. As a director I have to hear and see the story through someone else's lens. The most difficult thing about editing this piece was that I didn't know whose perspective and voice that would be. I could only imagine it through my own voice, or what made the most intuitive cinematic sense to me – that of Nora. I did, however, feel strongly that a male voice with an American accent would have been a disaster. The fly-on-the-wall, *cinema vérité* style we all used is particularly vulnerable to that anthropological/ethnographic, outsider's voyeurism; and an American male voice could have tipped all our good intentions over the edge. I liked the final narrator's voice – he had an insider's quality due to the accent.

Krishnan: I initially felt that I could find no internal justification to suggest a South Asian-accented male voice as the point-of-view of the series except for an aesthetic one. I didn't see anything wrong with using a compassionate Anglo-accented male voice, fully aware of the historical burdens that point of view suggests; especially since the series had been shaped through a process which had centralised the edit, imposing a consistency on its look and feel, which in the end very much had the Kartemquin imprint.

Notes

1   Kartemquin Films. Available at <http://www.kartemquin.com/films/index.html> [Accessed 20 April 2005].

2   Irish Film Institute, 2–5 October 2003.

3   For a selection of US press reviews following the PBS screening, see <http://www.bbc.co.uk/bbcfour/

documentaries/storyville/new-americans_reviews.pdf> [Accessed 18 April 2004]. BBC Two, *Storyville*, screened the series in five episodes between 26–29 October 2005.

4   Online interviews to date with the producers of *The New Americans* typically include accounts by James, Quinn and Saedi. See, for example, the PBS Independent Lens 'Producers' Q & A'. Available at <http://www.pbs.org/independentlens/newamericans/theseries_producers.html> [Accessed 18 April 2005]; and BBC4 (*Storyville*) 'Filmmakers Interview'. Available at <http://www.bbc.co.uk/bbcfour/documentaries/storyville/new-americans-interviews.shtml > [Accessed 18 April 2005].

5   See John D. and Catherine T. MacArthur Foundation. Available at <http://www.macfound.org/site/c.lkLXJ8MQKrH/b.855229/k.CC2B/Home.htm> [Accessed 10 June 2007].

6   Several days after this conversation, and illustrative of the prevailing immigration debate in the United States, President George W. Bush urged Congress to pass his controversial plan to give illegal immigrant workers, most of whom are Hispanic, temporary legal status. The debate surrounding undocumented (illegal) immigrants has since developed to a level of intensity no doubt unanticipated by the filmmakers; the McCain-Kennedy Immigration Reform Bill (2005) proposed that an estimated 10–12 million illegal immigrants in the United States should obtain legal jobs and eventual citizenship. The debate about immigration reform continues. With the near defeat of the bipartisan Senate immigration bill on the Senate floor at the beginning of June 2007, the Immigration Reform Bill is up for reconsideration, having been brought back to life in what is called a 'Grand Bargain' compromise, with the aim of achieving workable legislation within a year.

7   For an in-depth discussion with Gordon Quinn on the subject of story and storytelling in the context of documentary production, see Centre for Social Media (November 2003) 'Gordon Quinn and *The New Americans*'. Available at <http://www.centreforsocialmedia.org/res_filmmakersspeak.html> [Accessed 26 January 2005].

8   For an elaboration of cinematic social inquiry as both a methodological research tool and medium of communication, see Temaner & Quinn (1974).

9   Patricia Zimmerman, for example, discussing American independent documentary production, critiques its 'homology to narrative film in its deployment of characters in whom larger social and political structures are condensed' (2000: 11). She views this practice as a problematic celebration of exceptional individuals at the expense of a more discursive analysis of national/social/political agendas and governmental structures.

10   Independent Television Service (2003) *Outreach*. Available at <http://www.itvs.org/outreach> [Accessed 31 December 2003].

11   See Public Service Broadcasting (PBS) (2003) *New Americans*. Available at <http://www.pbs.org/independentlens/newamericans> [Accessed 31 December 2003].

12   See Zimmerman (2000) for a rich and detailed history of the systematic conservative attack on the programming of independent documentary within public broadcasting in the US and the subsequent defunding of public television documentaries from the mid-1980s onward, with the discontinuation of WNET's Independent Documentary Fund in 1984, in addition to a restructuring (privatisation) of internal production infrastructures within PBS and the Corporation for Public Broadcasting.

13   See Active Voice (2005) *The New Americans*. Available at <http://www.activevoice.net/new_americans.html> [Accessed 26 January 2005].

14   For a comprehensive guide to the goals, audiences and resources of *The New Americans* community engagement campaign, see ITVS (2005) Available at <http://www.itvs.org/outreach/newamericans/index.html> [Accessed 26 January 2005].

15   For an interview with members of the Kartemquin collective, see Lesage (1975).

16   Embedded in DVD-ROM chapter reference n. 25 is an account by Steve James and David Simpson of their concerns surrounding the editorial depiction of Ventura's decision.

Bibliography

Centre for Social Media (November 2003) *Gordon Quinn and 'The New Americans'*. Available from: <http://www.centreforsocialmedia.org/res_filmmakersspeak.html> [Accessed 26 January 2005].

Creekmore, T. (2004) 'Engaging Communities: *The New Americans* Outreach Campaign Hits the Mark'. Available at <www.beyondthebox.org/vol.22/BTBWS042html> [Accessed 26 January 2005].

Graff, K. (2002) 'The Truth Seekers', *Chicago Social*, October, 116–17.

Lesage, J. (1975) 'Filming for the City: An Interview with the Kartemquin Collective', *Cineaste*, 7(1): 26–30.

Lee, H. (1960) *To Kill a Mockingbird*. Philadelphia: J. B. Lippencott.

Martínez, R. (2004) *The New Americans*. New York: The New Press.

Rosen, S. (2004) 'Immigrant Song', *International Documentary*, 4: 8–10.

Temaner, G. and G. Quinn (1974) 'Cinematic Social Inquiry', in P. Hockings (ed.) *Principles of Visual Anthropology*. Paris: Mouton.

Terry, C. (1996) 'Kartemquin: A Different Kind of Dream Factory', *American Cinematographer*, April, 98–101.

Zimmerman, P. (2000) *States of Emergency: Documentaries, Wars, Democracies*. Minneapolis: University of Minnesota Press.

Filmography

American Dream (1991), Barbara Kopple. Buena Vista Home Video, 98 mins.

Balseros (2002), Carles Bosch and Josep M. Domenech. Seventh Art Releasing, 120 mins.

Best Hotel on Skid Row, The (1990), Christine Choy and Renee Tajima-Peña. HBO, 48 mins.

Home for Life (1967), Gordon Quinn and Gerald Temaner. Kartemquin Films, 80 mins.

Hoop Dreams (1993), Steve James. Kartemquin Films, 170 mins.

Labor Women (2003), Renee Tajima-Peña and Asia Women United. 30 mins.

My America (...or Honk If You Love Buddha) (1997), Christine Choy and Renee Tajima-Peña. National Asian-American Telecommunications Association, 85 mins.

My Journey Home (2004), Renee Tajima-Peña and Lourdes Pontillo. PBS, 120 mins.

New Americans, The (2004), Kartemquin Films, 411 mins.

Stevie (2003), Steve James. Kartequin Films, 140 mins.

Taylor Chain 1: A Story in a Union Local (1980). Kartemquin Films, 3 mins.

Taylor Chain 11: A Story of Collective Bargaining (1984), Jerry Blumenthal. Kartemquin Films, 30 mins.

Thumbs Down (1968), Gordon Quinn and Gerald Temaner. Kartemquin Films, 102 mins.

Wedding in Galilee (1987), Michel Khleifi. Lasa Films, 113 mins.

Who Killed Vincent Chin? (1988), Renee Tajima and Christine Roy. Film News Now Foundation, 87 mins.

PICTURING THE TUNNEL KIDS
Lawrence Taylor

FIGURE 1: VERO (LA FANTA)

'You take that bitch out of my picture!'

La Fanta gestured toward the photo with an angry thrust of her chin, her hands occupied in holding her squirming new baby, Mayra [DVD REF 1: PHOTO]. A beautiful and fiery sixteen-year-old who might better have been nicknamed for a drink stronger than a brand of orange soda, La Fanta's unflinching stare was directed at one of the series of framed photographs that adorned the otherwise spare walls of the day shelter. Most were single, full-length, black-and-white portraits of the shelter's 'clients' – the gang members of El Barrio Libre, the notorious tunnel kids of Nogales, on the US/Mexico border. The object of her fury was the photo framed along with her own, that of her sometime friend, La Flor. Apparently they were no longer getting along. Just one of a number of 'unintended consequences' of our continuing fieldwork/relationship with this volatile community of adolescents, La Fanta's comment reminded me of the complexity of the photographic dimension of our interaction with the kids. This chapter is a reflection on that field experience, and on the nature of the interaction of photographer, anthropologist and field subjects, from the anthropologist's point of view.

BACKGROUND

The US/Mexico border is the scene of a complex and shifting political economy where huge volumes of legal and illegal goods flow, helped or hindered by the various agencies of both states. The illegal traffic is the most important economically: billions in drugs and millions of undocumented immigrants going north, billions in profits and remittances going south. Naturally, this kind of wealth attracts entrepreneurs of every stripe: the drug cartels, people smugglers known as coyotes or *polleros*, and even – close to the bottom of the food chain – gangs of teenagers, like the members of El Barrio Libre. [DVD REF 2: PHOTO]

If they are, in a limited and tragic sense, entrepreneurs, these adolescents are of course also migrants themselves. Like many other developing countries, Mexico has been subject to its own massive internal migration, mainly from impoverished rural regions to the larger urban sprawls, particularly Mexico City. Migrants have also flocked to northern and especially border cities that offer employment in foreign-owned *maquiladoras* (assembly plants) facilitated by NAFTA (North American Free Trade Agreement) and a relatively prosperous local economy. For many of these migrants this is the second 'dislocation'; they, or their parents, have already left rural communities for the slums of cities and towns like Guadalajara or Guaymas and have then, in desperation and hope, moved once again, to the burgeoning shack-town *colonias* of Juarez, Tijuana or Nogales. Life in these *colonias* is difficult (there is often no reliable source of water or sanitation) and dangerous (with stash houses for both drugs and would-be emigrants watched by heavily-armed men). While many do attempt to raise families in stable homes, they are surrounded by a dynamically unpredictable world. In the *colonias* of cities like Nogales, neighbours and neighbourhoods change rapidly. People leave and more people arrive. It is a liminal space best summed up by one of its residents: *'Nogales, no es un rancho, es un corral!'* The tunnel kids, alone or with their families, were part of this movement to the border towns, and were among the most liminal inhabitants of this ambiguous space. And if some adults struggled to find a meaningful 'place' for themselves – economically, socially and psychologically – in the seething colonias, the tunnel kids, as their name implies, discovered and created an identifying place for themselves underground.

The tunnels in question are two cavernous concrete passages that run perpendicular to and beneath the border, connecting Nogales, Mexico with its 'non-identical twin' just across the line in the US: Nogales, Arizona. [**DVD REF 3: VIDEO**] They were constructed many decades ago in order to channel the summer floods out of poorly drained Nogales, Mexico into a wash and river on the US side. When, in the early 1990s, US enforcement was increased above ground, drugs and migrants began to move below, via the drainage tunnels. Street kids, who had themselves migrated to the border from various parts of Mexico, found each other in the abandoned rail cars, vacant lots and confiscated drug-lord

FIGURE 2: TUNNEL ENTRANCE

houses of Nogales and formed a gang – El Barrio Libre – that began to exploit this new and lucrative niche, mainly through guiding and robbing migrants. But the tunnel was, so we discovered, far more than a 'work place' to these kids. However transient, ephemeral and ultimately doomed to fail them, the tunnel was their place: *'su tierra'* in the Mexican sense; a home territory; an identity. 'Where is your *barrio* (gang/neighbourhood)?' El Boston asked his friends in the course of an astounding interview (see below). Each and every one answered, *'En el Túnel'*.

Photographer/collaborator Maeve Hickey and I first met these adolescents in a kind of 'half-way house,' called Mi Nueva Casa, financed and managed from the US side but located just over the border in Mexico. This day shelter had been founded with the intention of providing meals and school lessons for the kids, thus luring them out of the tunnel. While as many as a dozen or so of them were happy to avail themselves regularly of whatever was on offer in the shelter, they saw no reason to give up the tunnel, the many attractions of which are explored in our book, *Tunnel Kids*:

> For them [the kids] the Casa was one element in a delicate adjustment to a world formed and manipulated by forces well beyond their control, if not beyond their ken. The brutal edge of those forces was typically manifest in the guise of men with guns: representatives of the US and Mexican states or the criminal forces of drug and immigrant runners. All were there to protect the interests of free trade – a movement of electronic parts, grapes, drugs, or labor from Mexico into the United States. That movement was answered by a flow of money going the opposite direction in the forms of 'legitimate' profits from Maquiladoras, 'illegitimate' profits from contraband, and emigrant remittances. This 'exchange' was based in disparities and inequalities that were not about to disappear. Moreover, this world of powerful actors was, to make matters worse, unpredictable. Drug cartels and their local associates were subject to reorganization and realignment, and agents of the Mexican state might seem as volatile. US enforcement of anti-drug or immigrant control laws was also somewhat quixotic, subject to sudden bursts of legislation, movement of manpower, increases in technology. Among the representatives of this shifting if powerful world, the tunnel kids found enemies and untrustworthy friends, and they attempted to put together lives, families, and 'clans' in the face of all that. The result was a powerfully imagined but loosely structured band, without the formal rituals or hierarchy typical of many street gangs. (Taylor & Hickey 2001: 133–4)

Mi Nueva Casa provided us with a 'way in' to their world. We began volunteering at the shelter, trying to help in various ways, and it was only after we had begun spending time with the kids that the idea for the book arose. I recall showing El Boston and some of the other kids a copy of another of Maeve's and my collaborative books, *The Road to Mexico* (1997) and suggesting that we could write a book about their lives that would include images of them. They seemed interested. By that time, Maeve was already taking photographs of the kids, and so the idea for a combination of portraits and written narrative took shape, a book that we hoped might engage with the border through the kids, whose everyday existence was shaped significantly by living on and under *la linea*. We also wanted to present a human portrait of these kids who, while certainly not angels, were widely misunderstood and misrepresented.

After a period of several weeks hanging out with them at the shelter, we were able to follow them on, and below, the streets of Nogales, and continued to do so during fieldwork lasting more than nine months and spread over three summers (1996–98), together with return visits in the ensuing years:

The noon skies turned midnight black and cracked open, roaring with lightening. The summer monsoons had come at last to this southwestern desert. We just made it onto the bus, three of the younger kids and I, but the windows would not close, and the weather followed us in. First came the sheets of rain – soaking stoic adults and ecstatic children – then the hail, like silver bullets from some army of drunken outlaws, bouncing off the green vinyl seats and into our laps. David and Gordito rushed from window to window, pointing with delight. Outside, water was everywhere, cascading down the steep hillsides from rooftop to rooftop, roaring through the avenidas, turning parking lots into ponds. We made it back to Mi Nueva Casa by the border, where it had already stopped raining. The streets down there were far less flooded, but the water was still on its way down the hills, as I discovered twenty minutes later when I tried to walk the few hundred yards to the border gate. The roads were gone, replaced by raging rapids three feet deep, black with muck and heaving sticks and plastic jugs onto my legs as I staggered from one pole or building site to the next. I waded through a final swirling eddy, where a young woman clasping an infant to her breast balanced uncertainly on a battered shopping cart. Past the turnstile into the United States, I climbed the higher streets of Nogales, Arizona, where I had left my car. Safely on my way north toward Tubac, I remembered the tunnel and tried to imagine what the rains brought to it. I heard the story the next day from Chito, who, along with many others, had been too far inside the silent gloom to hear the thunder.

'We were deep inside, in the tunnel they call "Los Vampiros" – the one that goes through Buenos Aires. All of a sudden we heard noise, and some people came running; they had been crossing to the other side. There were about fifteen. And then we heard a wave behind them. They shouted, "Here comes the water!"' Chito undulated his arms to imitate the flood waves.

'And the next thing I knew, firemen, police and *la migra* (Border Patrol) started coming, and they grabbed us and pulled us up. There were many in the water, and many people were on the other side. The migra took only a few friends and put them in a room, so I ran for the border.' (Taylor and Hickey 2001: ix–x)

COLLABORATION

My collaboration with photographer Maeve Hickey had begun with an earlier project that eventually produced *The Road to Mexico* (1997). When we began working together we agreed not to 'illustrate' one another, and evolved a fieldwork modus operandi. Though we sometimes arrived at a particular location together, Maeve would wander off and take photos of the things that struck her and I would inevitably engage somebody in conversation. This method was, in fact, reflected in the actual form of the book. The chapters each present a series of encounters with people and place, and, together, offer parallel narratives of the road: one in photographs and the other in words. On a more subtle level, however, that experience of both field research and book production certainly had a profound impact on my way of thinking and working. Already likely to define myself as a writer who does anthropology as the other way round, the collaborative experience certainly pushed me further in the artistic direction. Working with an artist represented a kind of licence, an opportunity that I found enabling and liberating.

This sense of what I was doing carried over into what might have otherwise been a more typical ethnographic project in *Tunnel Kids*, a book perhaps better described as a story narrated by an anthropologist than an ethnography in the traditional academic mode. In the writing, I was trying not only to talk about the world, sometimes in an analytic way, if subtly, but also to capture, as an artist or novelist would, the texture and quality of everyday life:

> Soon we were on the road again, heading farther south. As we approached the edge of the city, the vista widened, and newly plowed, wide dirt roads led into industrial parks with dozens of huge, hanger-like structures. 'Maquiladoras', Boston said. 'There are many of them.' In fact, there were nearly one hundred by then, assembly plants that formed the core of the new industry dominating every big Mexican border town and a fair few some distance into the interior.
>
> 'There, turn left', Boston told me, and we jolted over the railroad tracks that, like the main road there, traveled from south to north, from the rest of Mexico to the border. We sailed through a knot of cars nudging one another in a triple dirt-road intersection and began to climb slowly out of the narrow valley floor of the city and up increasingly provisional and crumbling roads into the colonias that housed the great majority of Nogalenses.
>
> 'Here is Solidaridad. I know those people there', Jesús said, nodding toward a knot of young men, women, and dust-smeared, lively children chatting by a large white plastic pipe jutting out of a dirt hillside. Behind them were a ditch road and a line of houses, each assembled out of available materials – particle board, plywood, cardboard, even sheets of plastic – fastened together and topped by roofs of yet more uncertain construction, considering the sudden winds and rains of the summer storms. The sheets of tar paper or tin were weighted down by concrete blocks or large stones – or, in one fascinating case, by all the metal belongings of the family, including several bicycles and a wheelbarrow. (2001: 27)

I wanted to give the reader a sense not only of what was going on and why people were doing what they were doing, but also to engage his/her imagination and thereby convey some sense of what it is like to find oneself in such a place, doing this strange work of living alongside a group of migrant kids who have been shaped by forces and conditions so different to what most readers know. For me, this is not only better writing, but better anthropology. Our knowledge of the other is, after all, always mediated. Somebody is always out there on the edge of whatever world they are attempting to understand, actually meeting people, talking with them and trying to make sense of their lives, and attempting to convey what they are doing and why. I tried to give both an emotional and conceptual sense of this research experience, with all its attendant frailties. I hoped as well that this lived sense of the anthropologist 'being there' would not be an end in itself, but rather offer a bridge for the reader over which to travel on the more demanding imaginative journey into the lived world of the kids. In this way working with an artist led me to a more creative engagement with 'writing culture' (Clifford and Marcus 1986) and I was increasingly aware of the kids themselves as artists performing identities crucial to their survival:

> Juán Manuel and Marco Antonio had arrived, the new kids on the block, and had to be shown the line that separated them from the tribe and the clan. It was an opportunity for Boston and his friends to perform their identity, but it was also an opportunity for instruction: this is how to dress and behave they were saying; learn it, and you have passed over the first hurdle in becoming one of us. Of course, the demonstrated distance and disdain made the outsider want to belong. (Taylor and Hickey 2001: 69)

If collaboration made me aware of the similarities between writing and photography, it also engendered reflection on the differences, in both process and product. In terms of the first, while the writer notes and records, the way those observations and reactions become words involves choices that are made and unmade, changed and changed again. The photographer will, of course, discard or save, and alter images in the development process, but if the picture is not 'taken' to begin with, no amount of alteration will do.

Comparing a descriptive passage with a photograph, one also notes the different senses of time in the two forms. There is the photographic moment, that perishable second, characteristic of the captured image that makes one conscious of time and its passage as such. There is also in the photo, as in life and unlike in the written passage, a simultaneous depiction and possible reception of objects, emotions and events. There is something immediate and emphatic about literally seeing everything at once in a photograph. In the portraits of the kids, for example, both within and between the images, one feels the layers of doubt and aggressiveness at play. You therefore not only sense their forceful presence, but their vulnerabilities and ambiguities on the surface of the image.

VIDEO

My own interaction with the kids was in a sense mediated by a Hi-8 video camera, though not perhaps in the most usual way and not immediately. I am neither a filmmaker nor a photographer and had only recently begun to use a video camera as a fieldwork tool, where it had proved an improvement over an ordinary tape recorder. I could record the words of many of my informants while taking pictures that were less often of them than of what they were talking about. The small LCD screen was particularly useful in this context as it allowed me to hold the camera in my lap if seated, or at waist-level if standing or walking, thus avoiding having it take centre stage as object, disrupting face-to-face contact. This may seem a simple and obvious point, but in terms of the mechanics of fieldwork as interaction it was absolutely crucial. There was no question of hiding the camera, but rather of simply relocating it in the triad, if you will. Crucially, I did not show up first with the video camera, and certainly did not present myself as a 'filmmaker' or use the camera to establish a position of authority. Rather, we already knew these kids for many weeks before the video camera came into play and I introduced it more or less as a toy and tool that we could share in our various excursions. As it would turn out, Flor, Boston and Jesús actually took possession of the camera most of the time. On occasions, Flor would pretend she was a reporter, poking the video camera into kids' faces, urging them to respond to her questions.

In the beginning, though, I was hesitant to bring the video camera into the shelter. Frankly, I was afraid of adding to the already great social distance of class, age and ethnicity that seemed to yawn between the kids and myself. However, I remembered that whenever and wherever in the world I had been spotted using the video camera by children of all ages they had been tremendously interested, and most particularly in the possibility of filming themselves and watching what had just been filmed on the little screen. I had, for example, established excited communication with a group of children playing in a Turkish street by letting a ten-year-old film his playmates. Within minutes he and his friends were leading me through their street and even into their astonished mothers' kitchens. So I wondered if the tunnel kids might respond in a similar manner and risked bringing the camera in one day and asking a couple of the boys with whom I had already established a conversational relationship whether they might be interested in using it to 'make a film'. They showed some interest and it was not long after that I found occasion to film them:

A few days later it was raining again, and this time I took my car through the low streets of Nogales, Sonora. Afraid of more floods, I tore out of the house and tiptoed across the swirling, stinking pond that had in twenty minutes filled Avenida Fenochio, climbed into my car, and plowed a wake through Calle Capillo, driving north a few hundred yards to the border. But it was just an average summer afternoon rain, enough to send a few inches of brown water flowing through the border streets. Safely across on the drier Arizona roads, I thought of Chito and the others, and pulled up to the US end of the tunnel, where it opens up into the concrete embankments of the the Nogales Wash, just past Church's Chicken on Grand Avenue.

Leaning over the guardrail, I looked down into the opening – the scene of Chito's rescue a few days earlier. Chocolate water about a foot and a half deep was rushing through the large rectangular opening, just big enough for a car to drive through. I saw a sneaker flash in the gloom, then the pale smiling face of Chito 'of the flood'. The others were there, too: El Boston, La Fanta, Jesús, El Negro, La Negra, Humberto, Gilberto, and two little boys of about eleven and eight whom I did not yet know. They came grinning into the daylight, flashing Barrio Libre gang signs, and pushing a soccer ball through the churning rapids. They formed a circle in the open tunnel and began to knee, head and throw the ball around – laughing and falling into the water. They were like any group of exuberant teenagers enjoying a summer rain. 'Lorenzo', they shouted up to me, 'No tiene el video?' – 'Don't you have the video?' I obliged, taking a film of their water sports that they would often ask to see in the coming months (2001: x–xi).

The next day I brought the camera to the shelter:

El Boston was blasé. It was a nearly normal morning.

'You have the video again', he noted over his breakfast, looking at the camera on the table.

'You filmed us in the tunnel yesterday. Are we going to make a film?'

'We could make a video about all of you here in Mi Nueva Casa', I suggested. 'We could go around Nogales and film whatever you think is important. We could start with the interviews.'

Boston turned serious. 'I could do that; Soy el reportero!'

'Maybe you could write down some suggestions to ask all of your friends here', I suggested.

He agreed immediately, and I handed him a piece of paper and a pen. Boston bent to his task. Nose inches from the paper, he scribbled without looking up for half an hour or more. He handed me the completed sheet, a list of numbered, neatly scribbled questions, but then took them back before I could read them.

'They are not in the right order. I will recopy them.' Finally, Boston handed me his reworked list of forty-four questions…

Reading through the questions, I was stunned by their number and surprised by their direction. They began as you might expect: 'What's your name? Where are you from?' But the subsequent questions sought nothing more on the distant past of family and tierra (homeland), turning rather to where and how the kids lived and who they were now – in and under the streets of Nogales. Boston wanted to explore the life of Barrio Libre. The markers of that life, of that identity, were clear in the questions: fights, drugs, and clothes. Most of all, he wanted to know how long and how deep was their sense of belonging in that fellowship.

But then, somewhere in the middle of the list, Boston's focus switched. Subtly, his questions began to suggest a certain ambivalence: he wanted to press his friends to defend their life and even to think about the future.

Have you ever been bored by your barrio?
    Why?
Have you thought about changing your way of being?
If you were king of this world, would you like there to be cholos?
    Why?
Are you happy as you are?
    Why?

The intent seemed almost subversive – and from Boston, the most cholo of cholos. Further down the list, he returned to the life of the barrio, but in a more reflective and even critical way that might encourage his friends to think about how they had been changed, and not always for the better, since joining the gang. That same mood seemed to continue with questions that linked the present with the future: questions about girlfriends and boyfriends and about the possibility of marriage.

'Very interesting', I said. 'Do you want to ask them something more about the future at the end? Like where they hope to be, say, ten years from now?' Boston liked the idea, but tempered the 'hope'. He wrote, 'Dentro de diez años mas adelante, que cres que pase contigo?' – 'In another ten years, what do you believe will be happening with you?'

Those were Boston's questions. I was evidently impressed, and he was proud, but all business.

'Let's go in the schoolroom', he told me. 'I will interview everyone, and 'you can film it with the video camera.'

'Juán', he announced to one of his friends, 'come with us; you're first.' (2001: 6–9)

I had begun with only a hope that the camera might open up access to their points of view on various issues. Yet when Boston remarked that he wanted to be a reporter and ask questions, I thought, 'that's interesting, let's see what he comes up with'. I had not expected the TV Newsperson studio interview to be the model, but on reflection I could see the logic of it. The kids were avid consumers of all kinds of video production – everything from classic Mexican films to Kung Fu to hip-hop music videos. But it was only in the TV news interview that the camera itself appeared and the interaction between filmmaker and subject was visible. There was, therefore, a familiar model of the act, and El Boston was going to be the reporter in that sense. I then took the further step of asking him to write the questions down, thereby both taking control of a situation and simultaneously allowing something to happen – a 'conversation' if you will. I am confident in saying that if I had not asked him to write the questions, they would not have developed as interestingly as they did in a number of respects. Thinking about the questions and writing them gave Boston an air of seriousness that was astounding to watch. It became a hugely significant project for him once he began, making him feel important. There was something very real and tangible about the task. This interaction, mediated by the video camera, was typical of the sort of opportunistic, open-ended, 'conversational' field method that established my relationship with the kids and generated the 'ethnographic knowledge' embodied in the resulting text.

In addition to all that emerged in the course of these interviews, the process served to create an especially reflective state of mind in El Boston and, perhaps, affected his relationship with me. He began to see himself as a mediatory figure, at once performing and exploring the ambiguities and ambivalence of his world and his situation in it; a guide and interpreter of that world to me. I should say that the intensity of our relationship produced both sorrow and frustration when months later El Boston was sent to a US federal prison on assault charges. By the time that had happened I had grown especially close to the extended 'family' of kids of which Boston was a member. At the centre of this tiny clan was a sixteen-year-old girl named La Flor, her baby, Davidcito and her current boyfriend (Boston's closest friend), Jesús.

Unlike Boston, La Flor was not especially communicative, but she had developed a very affectionate relation with Maeve. Now Maeve's manner of interacting with the kids was unshaped by any anthropological goal, but rather a product, I think, of her maternal and human concern for the kids, as well as her artist's eye for their beauty and potential creativity. The girls who hung out at the Casa were soon at ease with her. La Flor, whose own mother had left her at an early age, was particularly drawn to Maeve, and through that relationship, as well as mine with Boston and Jesús, she grew sufficiently comfortable with me to suggest that she should use the video camera, once again taking on the familiar '*reportera*' role.

FIGURE 4: LA FLOR AND DAVIDCITO

But La Flor, who spoke little as a rule, hadn't Boston's interest in or patience for the carefully constructed interview. Her forte was rather the impromptu interrogation. During one of our typical outings, she and I were sitting in the front seat of my car, with Jesús and the baby in the back alongside another pal, Guanatos, and a girlfriend he had only met the night before. We were rattling over a dirt road, taking an uncharacteristic trip through the rural outskirts of the city, seeking the cool shade of a park one of them knew to be out there. Jesús mentioned that he was familiar with such settings having spent some time years ago at his uncle's little ranch. La Flor, perhaps unfamiliar with this aspect of her boyfriend's past, grabbed the video camera, and pointing it over the seat at Jesús, began to interview him, very much in the voice of a news magazine reporter, about his knowledge of and pleasure in such rural locations. Everyone was highly amused, but interestingly Jesús himself took on a rather serious, subdued demeanour, reminiscing with some emotion and pride in response to La Flor's questions.

At another point, La Flor and Guanatos came to me together, suggesting a filmic tour of Nogales – to 'important places'. [**DVD REF 4: PHOTO**] Another revelatory trip ensued, in which they took turns leading Maeve and me to places where they had slept since arriving in the city. And so it went on. Over the months of two long, hot summers, the video camera was nothing like a constant active presence. I would bring it along wherever we went, but leave it in the case. It was usually one or more of the kids who suggested taking it out, more or less as a game they occasionally enjoyed playing. On the other hand, the 'game', although playful, once begun was nearly always an opportunity for real reflection and exploration of self and others.

There was one rather surprising case of such exploration with Chuy, a boy of thirteen rendered nearly blind by a reaction to penicillin. [**DVD REF 5: PHOTO**] He saw only by tilting his head back and scoping the world through the narrow slits left between lids that adhered to his eyes. I had not thought Chuy would be interested in the video camera and even tried to avoid using it with the other kids in his presence, fearing that he might be frustrated and jealous (as he frequently was) if others were enjoying it in front of him. But one day Chuy showed up at my side asking to operate the camera. When I showed him the LCD screen, he immediately plastered it up against his tilted face and was apparently able to see things he otherwise could not. He ran about the room, euphoric at this newfound augmentation of his world, filming the other kids one after another.

In all these cases, so far from increasing any distance between the kids and myself, the camera rather acted to bring us all closer together, and to let me see and understand – at least to some degree – through their eyes:

> We all sat on the wall over the tunnel entrance, and looking down into it, I thought of one last thing I could ask them. 'Could you make a map of the tunnels?' I asked.
>
> 'Of course', Guanatos said, so I took a few blank pages from a notebook and taped them together to make a long sheet. Guanatos took it from me and spread it on the sidewalk, grasping the pen I gave him and squinting back and forth between the world around us and the blank paper. He began to draw. As he did, Chito and Jesús leaned over his shoulders, adding names and correcting lines. All the others watched with fascination as the map took shape before our eyes. There was the border, here ran the dry tunnel, here the wet one. All the while, below us men went in and out of the actual tunnel to use it as a lavatory. Flor filmed the whole event, and the little kids scrambled around us, watching the boys do the map and craning for a look at the camera. Passers-by on the street looked at us with some amazement: 'Who can that gringo be in the midst of that crowd of street kids and the toothless crone of thirty-five, and what was the dark chola filming?' (2001: 147–8)

PHOTOGRAPHS

Maeve was not the first person to bring cameras into the lives of the tunnel kids. Mexico has a long and rich history of photography, itself resonating with an even broader and deeper reservoir of powerful images in artistic and popular culture. Even the poorest Mexican families – like those of the tunnel kids – are likely to have at least two kinds of photographs in their possession: simple pictures of family members, posed or candid, and pictures of those same people on important occasions. Such photographs are 'used' in the household, picturing present and absent members in a definitive or memory-provoking way. But they can also be taken to and left at shrines, thus bringing the person pictured into direct, probably healing, contact with the sacred figure, actually 'there' by way of a two- or three-dimensional image. This kind of practice is not extraordinary or limited to the especially devout, but rather commonplace. Any local, regional or national shrine of Our Lady or any of the saints will be littered with curling Polaroids of the visitors and their families. As a consequence of this traffic in images, there is something very home-like about many Mexican shrines, and there is equally something shrine-like about the display of family photos, often near overtly religious objects and images, in many Mexican homes. This sense of the photographic image, along with other senses available through the popular media, influenced, I think, the way the kids acted before and behind the camera as well as the way they saw and used the photographs so produced.

I opened this chapter with the story of Fanta's angry response to seeing her photograph framed along with that of La Flor in Maeve's portrait gallery. Although Maeve had also been taking candid photos of the kids and their world, she had been particularly drawn to the idea of portraiture, a form in which she had an artistic interest and, happily enough, one that was highly valued by the kids themselves. Before she took any of the portraits included here (and in *Tunnel Kids*), she gave lessons in photography to those of the kids who were interested. About half a dozen or so managed to show up at the shelter for at least a few of the scheduled weekly lessons, where they learned to operate everything from a Polaroid to a fully manual Pentax. When it came to the latter, only the most perspicacious managed the technical intricacies, but all were very interested in the act of taking pictures and generally wanted to take pictures of one another. When Maeve began taking portraits, they followed her lead, imitating her manner of setting up a shot and taking it. From the outset, many found the process of picture-taking riveting and all were extraordinarily interested in the products.

For her own portraits, Maeve had selected a courtyard doorway behind the shelter as an unchanging background, bearing in mind the very limited spatial and temporal possibilities. When a kid showed up who had not yet been photographed, several of the others would literally leap up at the opportunity, shepherding the 'new victim' to the proper spot while Maeve got tripod and camera ready. [DVD REF 6: PHOTO] After that, it was up to the subject to pose in any way s/he chose. While nearly all the kids seemed very much to enjoy posing – only one, an eccentric clown in many ways, always laughingly refused – they took the occasion seriously, taking wonderfully varying positions and expressions. Many took the opportunity to make their 'gang signs', each different enough to be a personal as well as a collective signature:

> Maeve was also trying to help make Mi Nueva Casa more like a home by covering its walls with a series of portraits of the kids. Flor and Chito decided they would help her. They took their own photos and acted as her assistants, handling equipment, directing subjects, discussing the virtues of black and white over color. 'Next victim', Chito would shout into the house and then bring another kid out into the sun-drenched courtyard. 'You must stand here', he told each one. 'That's where we all stand.' And so they would. Each one would strike his or her own pose, some looking like they always did, but others becoming suddenly 'other' – posing, pretending, revealing – proud, hopeful, frightened, distant. (2001: 64)

When Maeve brought a pile of prints back to the shelter, there would be an excited huddle over the table as each kid found him/herself and held up the portrait with pride, while the others made the obligatory comments: 'You're so ugly, man!' The prints were 'valuable', so much so that when the first batch was re-gathered after being inspected in this manner, we noticed Jesús' picture had somehow disappeared.

With justifiable pride, Maeve felt that she had turned the shelter into a home, not through furniture – the usual method – but by creating a family album. She was right, but the 'family' so represented was perhaps not exactly the one we had in mind, as the following incident made evident. Not every kid served in the shelter was a tunnel kid from El Barrio Libre; occasionally, others would turn up at the door looking for food and companionship. So it was one morning when two boys, Juan Manuel and Marco Antonio, were found waiting at the door at opening time. They were new arrivals on the streets of Nogales, having spent only a few scary and hungry nights crouching in alleys and glass-strewn lots. As they told us, they had heard on the street that there were meals and help to be had at Mi Nueva Casa. Anxious to make these two shy and frightened boys feel welcome, Maeve invited them outside for portraits. El Boston quickly strolled over to her and, in a stage whisper, told her that she needn't bother, as they were not 'of Barrio Libre'. As far as he was concerned, 'the family' was the Barrio, and did not include any waif who happened to blow in off the street. Thus the kids came to exercise a proprietary right over their own collective representation, using the photographs to define who was and who was not part of the gang, and, of course, to define the house as 'theirs'. After all, you wouldn't hang portraits of strangers in your home, would you? The photographs thus captured the space in which they hung and came as well to enjoy a temporal function as representations of family history, just as they might in any household. Veteran gang members might be provoked to nostalgia by portraits of vanished friends – 'he's in prison now … on the other side'. New members could be taught who was who, and might themselves aspire to have their likeness hung along with the others, probably flashing a 'B' or 'L' with elegantly turned fingers.

As for La Fanta's fury over the photo of herself and La Flor, they had in fact been friends, but had fallen out over a debt. If the collective unity of the gang could thus be 'pictured' by the portrait gallery, then the social proximity implied by the shared frame could apparently prove uncomfortable in a situation of conflict. Not an intended consequence of the portrait gallery Maeve had been assembling on the shelter's walls, but certainly an indication that it was taken seriously as 'representation':

> The kids, especially Chito and Flor, became increasingly conscious of the usefulness of the camera to record and validate the moments of their lives, which was hardly a foreign notion in Mexico, where every public occasion finds street photographers memorializing the event for those who can afford it. But now they had cameras readily available, and they themselves were able to use them whenever and wherever the occasion demanded, as when we were all together on the day of Guanato's departure for Guadalajara. We waited with him that morning in the cavernous, sweltering bunker of a station, along with families still stretched out on blankets from the night before. Guanatos held his ticket tightly in one hand and a plastic shopping bag Ramona had packed with clothes and snacks in the other. We were at a loss as to what to do with the remaining moments when Flor, like a compulsive aunt at a wedding, began to arrange us for the photos. She had to have every possible shot of Guanatos, passing Davidcito around like a prop and making one after the other of us join or leave the photo. (2001: 63–4)

Besides their display in the shelter, most of the kids wanted other prints of their photos, either to carry with them, or to bring or send to family. I have already mentioned the time Jesús spirited away his portrait from the shelter before it could be framed and hung.

FIGURE 5: SHACK HOME IN COLONIA VIREYES

Months after that event I found it. I was up in the wild hills of Colonia los Vireyes, visiting the dirt-floored, windowless plywood shack built by an uncle, no longer in evidence, of Jesús. The rude shelter had been the rugged 'home' of about ten of the kids for about a year.

They had slept on the ground or on torn mattresses dragged from god-knows-where, and nothing else beyond a vinyl car seat or metal folding chair suggested human occupation. But on the occasion of this visit, all had changed. When Jesús swept aside the frayed curtain 'door' he bade me enter a far more domestic space. This was clearly meant to be a home. A couple of metal frame beds were pushed up against the walls. There was a calendar pinned above a simple chest of drawers to the side of the doorway, but another, far grander chest of drawers enjoyed a prominence on the back wall anyone entering would face. It was neatly covered by a piece of cloth and above it was a carefully framed and hung portrait of Jesús. 'Nice photo', I remarked. Jesús agreed, only slightly sheepishly, adding that he would like another for his father.

From that point on, whenever we discovered that any kid was in any kind of contact with his or

FIGURE 6: JESÚS

THE TUNNEL KIDS   133

her family, Maeve would produce and sometimes personally deliver portraits of their wayward children. In a sad reversal of this process, a grown woman approached Maeve one

FIGURE 7: EXTRAVIADO

day as she was photographing an entrance to the tunnel. She was looking for her lost eleven-year-old son, whose portrait was printed on a stack of flyers she was posting around the vicinity. In order to enhance the reach of that image, she asked Maeve to photograph her holding the flyer, hoping that a yet wider distribution might find someone who knew the whereabouts of her son.

While I would not want to over-estimate the significance of the use of these images, neither should we ignore the degree to which they functioned as powerful markers, reminders and perhaps even repairers of family relations.

Nothing of what I have described would be unique to the tunnel kids, of course, or even to Mexico. Family photos, even without the sacred dimension provided by the religious practices I have mentioned (common to many Mediterranean and Latin contexts), can and often do have the kind of power that animates their uses for the tunnel kids and their families. In American house fires, so we are often told, it is the photos that people try to rescue, or forever regret. I can remember vivid video footage of San Franciscans clutching photo albums that had somehow managed to survive the 1989 earthquake, found after many desperate hours of painful sifting through rubble. However, it is not typically imagined, it seems to me, that street children like the tunnel kids of El Barrio Libre are interested in photographic representations of themselves as individuals and group beyond the obvious gang signs and insignia; nor might one guess that the use of such photographic images would prove as variously meaningful and functional as it did. The last words Guanatos spoke to us, just before we parted company, were 'Send more photos of me!'

VIEWER RESPONSE

Our own use of the photographs in *Tunnel Kids* is of course a different matter, and another element in the complex interaction around photographic images I wish to explore. As mentioned earlier, Maeve took many candid as well as 'formal' portraits of the kids, but in the end she, our editor and I agreed that only the portraits should be included in the book. Our decision was made for both aesthetic and didactic reasons, not that we necessarily thought of those dimensions as wholly distinct. In either case, it was a matter of contrast. That is, the kids were 'pictured' in the text by me, and indeed by themselves when, as was frequently the case, their own words were used, in a way quite different from the way they were pictured in the photos. In the text they were active and usually together in groups. In the portraits they were 'still', and presented a self-considered version of themselves as individuals. As I look at them now, I would say that most of them have a typically Mexican, serious pose, though some with a definite tinge of gang-cool. A few, however, are smiling, and two or three might be described as 'sad', although I find the line between that and cool *calo palo* a narrow one.

In speaking of the portraits, Maeve remarks:

> I wanted them to have both an elegance and simplicity – a resting place if you like for the reader or viewer. The portraits are deliberately reflective and composed, providing a counterpoint to the text, a lively narrative about the kids and their hyperactivity, with one drama after another and a general sense of movement and restlessness. Using only portraits provided the opportunity to portray them differently: quietly and in a more open-ended manner.

Had there been greater similarity between the style of writing and the photographic content, the two may have been in danger of converging, indeed blending into each other, and readers would be less struck perhaps by the individuality of each of the portraits. I would hope that the juxtaposition in the book makes one think about what constitutes a photograph, because the image is looking at you, working on you very differently to the impact of the text. Ideally, this kind of positioning should guard against simply incorporating the images and text into a single story, a kind of collective image forming in the reader/viewer's mind comprising words and pictures. Instead s/he is confronted by a format that encourages awareness of and reflection on the very difference between photography and writing. Our decision to present the material in this way hopefully clarifies our collaboration and authorship as well. It's not simply a combination of photography with text; two different points of view and moods are conveyed throughout the book.

Of course, I cannot view the photos outside of my personal knowledge of the kids, which includes both a sense of the way they typically acted or looked and, in some cases, a familiarity with the particular 'pose' or expression. I am also familiar with the general 'posing' practice current in Mexico, which necessarily informs the postures struck by many of the kids. Other reader/viewers naturally come to the pictures with other kinds of knowledge and expectations, and hence 'read' the photographs differently. This reasoning is familiar enough from discussions of reader-response to texts, but if I can judge from the experience of our public presentations – to both academic and general public audiences in Tucson and Nogales, in Ireland, New York and Philadelphia – the range of 'reader-response' to photographs is, if anything, yet more volatile and unpredictable. Perhaps this fact is due to the less directive character of photographs; they don't arrive with instructions, as do descriptive texts. Another factor may be the 'face-to-face' interaction involved in the viewing of the portraits of the kids, most of whom might be described as having 'serious' expressions that leave a fair amount of room for interpretation. Whether listening to a presentation or reading *Tunnel Kids*, people, I have found, tend to have strong expectations of how such street children should look. When they see the pictures they may either read their expectations into them, or react with surprise that the pictures do not seem to conform. For example, only one of the kids could, I believe, be objectively described as pictured in dirty clothing: Marco Antonio, the new kid who came into the house described above.

FIGURE 9: MARCO ANTONIO

FIGURE 10: DAVID

All the others were in very to fairly clean clothing, which was their typical appearance on the streets, as they tended to wash their clothes, including their 'tennis', whenever they had the chance. Members of various kinds of audiences, viewing the slides and focusing in on the one or two visibly 'sad' expressions and the one kid with dirty clothing, would occasionally read all the photographs as depicting sad and dirty street children. More often, however, audiences would note with surprise the cleanliness of the kids, sometimes suspecting that they had been cleaned up and/or made to smile especially for the photographs.

Most striking however, has been the general audience tendency to sum up the photographs in one way or the other. They would see the kids as all sad, all happy, all dirty, or all clean. That is to say, viewers who have not read the text but only heard snippets in a presentation might be generally inclined to put together a single, coherent image to 'take away'. However, for readers of the text – and here I am judging especially from many student comments – the photographs are of people they are getting to know and hence are seen individually and complexly. Such readers may be less likely to generate a single, simple and collective image. For them, the text and photographs seem to interact in the way we had hoped, though of course even in cases of prolonged viewing/reading, expectations can triumph, producing opposite reactions which depend on where the viewer/reader is coming from.

When I say expectations, I mean of two sorts: of the subjects, and of photographs/photographers. In both dimensions there is of course an infinite individual variation, but one can usefully distinguish between the poles. At one end there is the naïve viewer, who assumes that the camera is simply capturing 'what is there', so that the photographer disappears from view. At the other extreme, there is the 'critical', often academic viewer, for whom it is rather the subjects who in a sense disappear. That is, the photograph is seen as a totally constructed product, an image not of the subject, but of the intentions, agendas, overt and covert perspectives and judgements of the photographer. The same can be said of the text. Following the reflexive critiques of ethnography as 'writing culture', one might charge that the tunnel kids, as both written and photographed, are a creation of the authors. Of course, this must be, at least to some extent, true. Unless we are to abandon both the ethnographic and the photographic representational act, however, such a critical perspective must be tempered by the belief that some way of knowing is possible. Can the final 'product' be constructed in such a way that space is left for the subjects to express themselves and for the photographer/writer to be identifiably present as selective interpreters without displacing the subjects as the focus of the book? I hope so, though I certainly view this a goal toward which to move modestly rather than one that can be achieved by means of any methodological formula. For me, as ethnographer/writer of *Tunnel Kids*, this meant showing the reader the interaction and dialogue between the kids and myself. For the photographer, so it eventually seemed to me, the portraits could be viewed as evidence of another sort of conversation, a communicative act between photographer and subject, that could and often did draw the attentive viewer into the conversation.

The conversation continued after the publication of *Tunnel Kids* in 2001. In that year, we returned to visit whomever we were able to locate, three years after the photos in the book were taken. Among a few others, we found Romel and La Flor, who no longer ranged the tunnels (for the moment apparently closed off to human but not drug traffic), but whose lives had hardly reached an easy plateau; little possibility of that had ever existed. [DVD REF 7: PHOTO] We have been devoting some of the modest profits of *Tunnel Kids* to aiding whoever is around with particular problems and projects, but it would be misleading to suggest that the impact has been great.

Tunnel Kids was not the last of my collaborations with Maeve Hickey. In our subsequent book, *Ambos Nogales: Intimate Portraits of the US/Mexico Border* (2002), a pictorial and narrative exploration of the twin border towns, which contained many photographs collected for but not published in *Tunnel Kids*, the weighting of images versus text was reversed, with nearly one hundred and fifty black-and-white photographs and a series of brief, mainly descriptive, written vignettes. The more general thematic focus of this work, as well as the predominance of high-production-value photographs, probably elicits a yet more wide-ranging set of viewing/readings than did *Tunnel Kids*. Since then Maeve and I have continued to work in the border region, but more or less separately. 'More or less' because, although we are working each on her/his own project, we continue to observe and discuss each other's work and this, along with the lasting impact of earlier collaborations, certainly continues to inform our respective goals and methods. We are currently completing a two-year field project during which we have lived among and travelled with members of the varied constituencies on both sides of the border that stretches two hundred or so miles west from Nogales. On the US side, this territory is in the main divided into vast tracts of public or Indian lands, including two National Wildlife Refuges, a National Park, the most important Air Force and Marine training ground and air-space in the US, and the Tohono O'odham Nation, the country's second largest Indian reservation. South of the border, the landscape is similar, but 'public' land exists only in the form of one large 'biosphere' – El Pinacate – and in the communal lands of dozens of widely scattered *ejidos*, Indian and Mestizo rural settlements. The western desert, which appears an empty wilderness to the visitor, is a deadly natural barrier, but it has not discouraged migrants. Many hundreds, possibly a few thousand, cross this border daily, typically walking all or most of a journey of forty, fifty or sixty miles through an awesome but cruel and largely waterless landscape; annual mortality has increased steadily, reaching more than two hundred in 2003.

My own work has centred not only on the migration, but on locations through which it moves, a highly contested space, full of places symbolically significant and politically explosive to Indians, expropriated ranchers, self-defined vigilantes and many others. How to explore and represent this dynamic world, where global process appears in the guise of a solitary woman walking through a desert, an empty water jug in one hand and a seven-year-old girl in the other? And how to convey that, alongside these desperate dramas, characters – remarkably creative, striving and often comically absurd – invent and reinvent themselves along the 'frontier' of their imaginations? I am currently writing a series of essays that explore these issues of place/movement/identity and am also completing a work of fiction. Reacting to the success with which *Tunnel Kids* has reached a largish audience and elicited engaged readings in and well beyond the classroom (there is currently a children's theatre adaptation underway), I wanted to step into another genre altogether with a series of what I call overlapping short stories that move along the western border from San Diego/Tijuana to Nogales.

Maeve Hickey, who has travelled through much the same geographical territory, is also working in two genres. She continues to do black-and-white photography not only of the borderland but further south into Sonora, for a work whose working title is 'Sonoran Notebooks'. Never having lost her 'sculptor's' eye, however, she has also created an exhibition of three-dimensional work entitled, *Lost and Found: Remnants of a Desert Passage* (2003). Shown to date in Tucson, Phoenix, Mexicali, Baltimore, Washington, DC and El Paso, Texas, this exhibition consists of a reconstructed migrant's desert campsite and sixteen Plexiglas containers – one very large, the others small boxes – in which she has composed assemblages using a vast array of objects discarded by migrants along their desert journey. Trash into art, anonymous and collective movement rendered personal and, according to many viewers, heartbreakingly poignant.

Bibliography

Clifford, J. and G. E. Marcus (eds) (1986) *Writing Culture: The Poetics and Politics of Ethnography*. Berkeley: University of California Press.

Hickey, M. and L. Taylor (2002) *Ambos Nogales: Intimate Portraits of the US/Mexico Border*. Santa Fe: SAR.

Taylor, L and Hickey, M. (1997) *The Road to Mexico*. Tuscon: University of Arizona Press.

_____ (2001) *Tunnel Kids*. Tucson: University of Arizona Press.

MIGRANT CHILDREN AND THE PERFORMANCE OF MEMORY: FILM FIELDWORK

Rossella Ragazzi

> There are people who belong to more than one world, speak more than one language (literally and metaphorically), inhabit more than one identity, have more than one home; who have learned to negotiate and translate between cultures, and who, because they are irrevocably the product of several interlocking histories and cultures, have learned to live with, and indeed to speak from, difference. They speak from the 'in-between' of different cultures, always unsettling the assumptions of one culture from the perspective of another, and thus finding ways of being both the same as and at the same time different from the others amongst whom they live.
>
> – Stuart Hall (1995: 206)

How do migrant children approaching adolescence link their place of origin with the location in Europe to which contemporary migration has brought them? For several years I have been conducting research engaging with both the real and the imagined, the symbolic and the lived experiences of such migration. How do children move from one kind of life to another? What happens when they enter a Western school system that takes no account of the place from which they came? As young newcomers negotiating an interstitial space, migrant children become the target of state educational discourses on interculturalism.

Children who have been in transit for long periods, or who 'finally' reach a new country in which their families hope to stay, experience on the one hand a 'geographical-cultural' shift, and on the other, by entering the Western school system, a 'disciplinary-collective' one. It is in this context, often marked by long silent periods of observation and withdrawal or conversely by hyperactivity and anxiety, that a psychic and physical journey towards so-called adulthood occurs, as the children become integrated linguistically, come to understand norms of behaviour and develop the skills necessary if they are to find employment and social acceptance. Migrant children, like settled ones, are not a homogeneous group; if their parents or carers are temporary/guest workers, travellers, refugees/asylum seekers or expatriates, investment in them and expectations for them vary considerably, affecting their identity formations in the host environment (Faulstich *et al.* 2001).

Through the accounts of migrant children and their relationships with those who care for them I have come to identify issues of 'memory', 'embodiment', 'silence' and 'resistance', the disciplinary formations and the performed identities that shape this limited but deep space-time while the child is adjusting to a new cultural context. In this chapter I intend to analyse via the use of filmic excerpts selective experiences of migrant children who find themselves in a liminal zone; their identity is gradually reshaping itself, but they have yet to put everything from their past life behind them. Fragmented recollections are revealed to the camera before being buried, perhaps forever.

Central to my visual ethnographic practice is the creation of a space 'surrounding' the camera (rather than having the camera search for events) so as to allow children's story-telling to emerge as a form of social articulation, especially in the case of those children who are testing out cultural boundaries and the limits of their cultural selves. It was by looking retrospectively at the various modes in which the child protagonists of these eth-nographies articulated their narratives that I began to 'map' out the various trajectories of their 'identities' – always emerging and in flux, but nonetheless situated in the space-time of the classroom and their own mixed memories of 'home', as mediated by themselves, their families, the 'host' environment in which they find themselves and the diverse 'ar-chives' that shape this environment.

In what follows I present two comparative accounts of two children: Mang Mang, an eleven-year-old girl from the People's Republic of China who I worked with in Paris,[1] and Tahar, a nine-year-old boy from Algeria who I met in Dublin in the context of my doctoral fieldwork.[2]

In Paris I was able pursue my research on migration and childhood by exploring the ways in which children recently arrived in France cope with building an identity during their first few weeks. During this time they are taught, among other things, new values, manners and rules of behaviour; in addition, since monolingualism is accorded great importance in the French educational system, they are hyper-stimulated to verbalise in French. In the case of Tahar, situated in the Irish classroom, the dialectical balance is bet-ween 'settled' children and migrant children and between teachers and children, parents and other related groups of individuals or persons involved in childcare. In Dublin I dis-covered tales that paralleled the Parisian ones, but with different inferences, textures and mediating sources (see Gupta & Ferguson 1997). My juxtaposition of visual ethnographies constructed in contemporary European nation-states is designed to provide not merely a comparative analysis, nor is there an underlying assumption that France possesses a vis-ible 'tradition' of hosting various ethnic minorities, political exiles and colonial subjects, while Ireland is a homogenous nation-state in which historically, emigration has been the norm and inward migration a recent phenomenon. This kind of macro assumption might preclude a productive comparison.[3] My aim is rather to reveal patterns of doxic discourse (see Bourdieu 1977) which contribute to the difficulties of perception and representation experienced by migrant subjects, especially young ones, in the society 'in progress' of the super nation-state that is federal Europe, where exchanges and perspectives on citizenship have to be thought through together and shared. Encounters with migrant children in the framework of this 'multi-sited' ethnography (Marcus 1995: 95) facilitates an understand-ing of the attempts made by young subjects to become citizens, in dynamic relation with the bonds of family, the educational system, their 'fresh' past and their sense of future.

FILM FIELDWORK IN PARIS: THE ELOQUENCE OF SILENCE

For any individual, memories of childhood years, overlain by other memories, fragments of memories and interpretations of later years, constitute an infinite resource for constructing 'a childhood'. Whether or not we accept the Freudian thesis that memory is total, that all experiences are somehow stored and variably

accessible, it can be still argued that memory is infinite. For any scene, image, individual feeling, or group sentiment that one recalls, it can be recollected from an infinite number of perspectives in an infinitely divisible number of ways.
– David Koester (1996:142)

In 'On Telling One's Own Story; or Memory and Narrative in Early Life-Writing' (1996), James Olney quotes from the autobiography of Maxine Hong Kingston titled *The Woman Warrior: Memoirs of a Girlhood among Ghosts* (1976). Remembering her schooldays, Kingston describes the learning process of a Chinese girl who had recently arrived in the USA. She had problems in reading 'I', the word that represents the Self, and was panic-stricken every time she was confronted with a text that contained that 'word'. This exposed her to all kinds of pressure, since 'I' is one of the most frequently recurring words in English. In the Chinese language, as Olney points out, the ideogram composed of one simple stroke (like the English 'I', a 'naked' line standing alone) means 'slave', while 'I' meaning 'myself', the first-person subject, is represented by an ideogram composed of seven strokes.

The symbolic fragility of the English 'I' was literally embodied by Maxine. This was not merely a metaphorical location for subliminal panic, but a process whereby the Chinese pupil was expressing, by means of resistance, the complicated relation she had with the construction of her new identity. Asian migrants laugh and joke about their inability to spell, but learning to spell 'I' is no mere phonetic or technical exercise; it is often, as in this case, the expression through stubbornness of a problem that is hard to decipher without a degree of intercultural understanding. This delicate balance between resisting change and the desire to overcome resistance created a new dynamic for this little Chinese girl, one which needed to be 'heard' by her teacher and subsequently be narrated as a distinctly intercultural phenomenon in her biography.

When I met Mang Mang, newly arrived from the Shanghai region of China, in the Cl.in class (a rapid 'total immersion' French-language classroom) in Paris, I was struck by her similarity to Maxine Hong Kingston as described by Olney. Sometimes anthropological descriptions of transcultural trials are as vivid as good literature. Observing the Chinese girl as she was urged to speak, I couldn't but feel a sense of empathy. Seen through the eyes of her teacher, Miss Pascale, who veered between anger and hopelessness, her paradoxical attitude seemed extreme, but there was an underlying logic, which Mang Mang tried to express.

Although she had arrived from China many months earlier, Mang Mang could not spell a single French word correctly. Sometimes she took five minutes to read a sentence. She trembled in panic and amazement when faced with exercises in orthography. Reading the word 'helicopter' caused huge difficulties, but at last the pedagogical relentlessness of her teacher triumphed and she finally said it – 'helicopter'. But Mang Mang did not know the meaning of the word that had caused so much trouble and when a Chinese friend

FIGURE 2: MANG MANG

translated it for her a disillusioned expression crossed her face seemingly saying: so much effort, only for that! [DVD REF 1: VIDEO]

The following day, during her first boxing session, a similar situation occurred. [DVD REF 2: VIDEO] She was not at all interested in boxing gloves, hits, knocks and the provocation implicit in this sport, but although reluctant to take the initiative, Mang Mang was both determined and impassive, exhibiting stereotypical 'Chinese endurance'. She seemed reluctant to aim a punch at her friend Nawel, who threw herself joyfully into the sport, putting on the gloves (so much bigger than her face), jumping into the ring like Charlie Chaplin in *City Lights*, adopting a burlesque attitude and playfully provoking her adversary (Mang Mang) who eventually started to respond. Little by little, the whole session turned into elation, dance and … relief! According to a pedagogical hypothesis, participation in sport has an effect on other skills, such as communication, social relationships, literacy and verbal fluency. As Mang Mang began to like boxing, she simultaneously began to spell and talk more easily. She felt the impact of her body on other bodies, she acquired the resolution necessary to aim and hit, and she (metonymically) protected her mouth (hand) with a big glove. Perhaps these parallel activities influenced each other; her spelling abilities certainly improved.

Spelling was not the only form of utterance that caused problems; there was also storytelling. Each time Mang Mang was invited by the teacher to 'tell' something (to explain the plot of a book by interpreting the illustrations, or to narrate a short story based on a sequence of cards), she resisted fiercely, like a torture victim whose words are extracted from her against her will. The following dialogue illustrates some of these points and makes her logic understandable in the light of her lived experience. It took place in a session in which the pupils were asked to describe their activities during the All Saints Day holiday in November:

Miss Pascale:	Mang Mang, it is your turn now! [She smiles because she knows that the Chinese girl is reluctant to talk in front of the class.] How did you spend your holidays?
Mang Mang:	Holidays?
Miss Pascale:	Yes. What did you do?
Mang Mang:	…
Miss Pascale:	Did you often go out for a walk?
Mang Mang:	[She shakes her head.]
Miss Pascale:	You never went out with your mummy for a walk?
Mang Mang:	No.
Miss Pascale:	Did you stay at home all the time?'
Mang Mang:	Yes.
Miss Pascale:	And what did you do at home alone? What do you usually do when you are at home?
Mang Mang:	…
Miss Pascale:	Did you watch TV?
Mang Mang:	[After a pause] Yes.
Miss Pascale:	What do you watch on TV?
Mang Mang:	…
Hedda:	Pascale, I believe she watches cartoons!
Miss Pascale:	I would like her to try to make one sentence. Up until now she has only answered 'yes' or 'no'! I would appreciate it if Mang Mang made the effort to say at least one short sentence in French!'
Mang Mang:	…
Miss Pascale:	What do you watch? First channel, second, third or Satellite TV? Chinese programmes perhaps?
Mang Mang:	[She becomes worried and scratches her cheek to show her perplexity. The whole class laughs.]
Miss Pascale:	What did you watch, what channels did you look at?'
Mang Mang:	…
Miss Pascale:	Do you like to watch cartoons, musicals, movies, do you look at Chinese shows?
Mang Mang:	…
Miss Pascale:	Do you know what you watch on TV, Mang Mang?
Mang Mang:	[She shakes her head.]
Miss Pascale:	Well, let's try it another way. If you watch TV, can you, at least, tell me please if they speak French or Chinese?'
Mang Mang:	…
Miss Pascale:	[Becoming more and more upset] Do they speak Chinese or

	French, Mang Mang?
Mang Mang:	They speak French.
Miss Pascale:	At last! So, then, what channel do you usually watch? The first? The second? The third?
Mang Mang:	[After reflection] First channel.
	[There is a pause while the children whisper about some programmes and then Miss Pascale begins again to press Mang Mang, who had thought the interrogation was over.]
Miss Pascale:	So, you did not go out at all during the holidays? Even in the evening, for a walk with your parents. Not even to the park, to the playground near your home? Not even to the Sacré Coeur park?
Mang Mang:	No.
Miss Pascale:	Do you have any sisters or brothers?
Mang Mang:	No, I don't have any sisters or brothers.
Miss Pascale:	[Perplexed and a little uneasy] Any friend, a girlfriend perhaps?
Mang Mang:	No.
Miss Pascale:	Do you ever get a visit from a friend? A friend who comes home to play with you?'
Mang Mang:	No.
Miss Pascale:	[Whispering to Kadiatou] Kadiatou, can't you do something with her?
Hedda:	Pascale, it is not true! I saw Mang Mang with someone a few days ago. A Chinese boy. At Sacré Coeur park.
Miss Pascale:	Is it true, Mang Mang? Who was he?
Mang Mang:	Well, he was something … only boy!
Hedda:	Yes, Pascale, she was playing with him.
Miss Pascale:	So you are not always home. Sometimes you do go out!
Mang Mang:	Yes.
Miss Pascale:	So, you can make a sentence out of it? Come on, let's make a sentence!
Mang Mang:	Sometimes I'm going to leave [for the] garden…
Miss Pascale:	[Correcting her] Repeat: sometimes I go to the Sacré Coeur garden!

This dialogue was similar to other conversations which had taken place in front of the class, while the principal had scolded Mang Mang for being so reluctant to find friends with whom she could speak French out of school. Miss Pascale even dared to ask her to speak French with her parents! Mang Mang was accused of speaking only Chinese when she left the class, and this was held to account for her slowness in learning the new language. [DVD REF 3: VIDEO] Although she had been in the Cl.in class longer than most of the other pupils (though not yet for a complete school year), she spoke less French than most of the newcomers, and when she tried to say something her sentences were never 'correct' or immediately comprehensible.

If one visited her at home, as I did, it became clear that her choices were limited, and this perhaps strengthened her resistance to the pressure put on her. Her parents, like many immigrants from the People's Republic of China, worked in a small firm engaged in garment production, managed by their co-nationals. The hours of work were long, ten to twelve hours a day, including Saturday. Mang Mang's parents spoke hardly any French, which they did not need in their daily life, surrounded as they were by other Chinese and doing their shopping in the local Chinese supermarkets. As in other diasporic Chinese communities, the social, cultural and economic practices effectively preserved the ethnolinguistic boundaries between the community's members and those outside it.

For Mang Mang it would have been humiliating to attempt to comply with Miss Pascale's request that she should speak French at home. It should be remembered that she had for many years been separated from her father, who had migrated to France to 'open' the way for the rest of the family. She had also spent a year and a half without her mother, who had come to France to be with her father. Mang Mang, their only child, as a result of Chinese birth control policy, had remained in China. She took care of her grandparents, hoping for her parents' return, but when her grandfather died, her father, who had come to China for the funeral, decided to take his daughter back to France. (He also took back a videotape of the burial ceremony.) Mang Mang, removed from one country to another, needed to re-establish an emotional connection with her parents, while at the same time contending with a school very different from the one she had attended in China, where she had been doing very well, especially in mathematics. When she arrived in Paris, she often watched the videotape of her grandfather's burial, the last images of a world that was disappearing. In Paris her family lived in a flat under the roof on the seventh floor, comprising two tiny rooms and a kitchen with a shower. There was no lift and the toilet was outside on the landing. In lacking private space, Paris was not really so unlike Chinkuan in China, but the interface between outdoor and indoor, the relationship with the neighbourhood and the life of the street, was of course very different.

Mang Mang's first preoccupation was probably to re-establish her position as a child, with less responsibility than she had had while living with two elderly relatives in China, but also with more difficulty in relating the home place to the surrounding society. Besides learning, like other migrant children, to accept that she had left the security of her original home, she had to acknowledge her new home as the foundation for a safe life in the new country to which migration had brought her. It was necessary to reintegrate the concept of home. School in China had been a space where Mang Mang was acknowledged to be clever, where she was well thought of; she had hoped to find herself in a similar position in France, but instead, because of her difficulties with French, her teachers considered her to be a loser. The school had presented the French language to her as a test; the need to structure her identity in the public sphere had to pass through that narrow door. The child was caught in what Gregory Bateson (1972) calls a 'double bind' between her desire to reconnect with her family on the one hand and the demands of the school on the other. For her, the process of integration was shadowed by confusion and a sense of loneliness, or even alienation.

The teacher's suggestion that she should speak French at home and watch French-language television made Mang Mang feel guilty and confused about revealing her family life. Her response could be interpreted as conveying two competing perspectives, one related to her female gender, the other more 'ethnically' influenced because it refers to her relationship with her co-national peers. When asked by the teacher whether she had any friends, she denied it not because she was deliberately lying, but because she thought that her teacher was only interested in French-speaking friends. When Hedda revealed that she had seen Mang Mang playing with a friend, Mang Mang replied that he was 'only boy'. If I understood her correctly, this category – 'boy' – fell outside the definition of 'friend'. Like her female classmates at the same stage of pre-puberty, she did not seek boys as friends, or at least was not meant to acknowledge them as such, even if she 'felt' a sense of friendship toward them. Then there was the language question: when she and the boy played together, they spoke their mother tongue, whereas the teacher had told her to find French-speaking playmates. The same was true for television: she denied watching programmes because they were Chinese-language programmes and as such not likely to be approved by her teacher. Hence her silence and her grimaces which so upset Miss Pascale and convinced her that Mang Mang had a basic handicap in verbal expression were strategies dictated by her need to acknowledge two worlds with different rules, tastes and taboos. In terms of language acquisition, she manifested a resistance which included aphasia, but showed nevertheless a strong awareness that she lived by bridging some 'paradoxical' gaps and that time was needed to integrate into a new life, to learn a new language. Moreover, because of her sense of moral devotion to the family in the larger sense, including her grandparents, she did not want to achieve integration at the expense of 'giving up' her parents' heritage, particularly the language. The request made at school that she should speak French at home appeared as a threat to her integrity vis-à-vis her parents, her past, her sense of belonging and moral views; it also involved repressing the only affective links she had so far in France. These are some of the aspects of the 'double bind' which migrant families face and which institutions in the hosting countries create, affecting particularly sensitive and loyal migrant children who find themselves in a situation calling for change and adaptation. Mang Mang, it seems, was at this time of her life such a person.

Although, through her experiences in the Cl.in class, Mang Mang realised that she was not the only one facing difficulties in bridging the gap between life within the family and life outside, she also saw that her classmates had more opportunities to speak French. In most cases they had siblings, they went out alone in the quarter, they strolled in the parks, and in some cases their parents already spoke the language well enough to be of help, at the oral level at least. This situation was reversed when some new Chinese children came to the Cl.in class in the second term. On this occasion, Mang Mang was asked by the principal to help in translating the school rules for the Chinese parents enrolling their sons. But Mang Mang, as it is possible to see in a sequence from *La Mémoire Dure*, refused to speak Chinese, pretending she had forgotten. The subsequent dialogue with the teacher shows how she tried to please both these antithetical worlds of hers by devising a new strategy. [DVD REF 4: VIDEO]

Significantly, Miss Pascale was also a complex agent in the chemistry of the school's life and in the facilitation of the learning process. Born in Tunisia she came from a family of 'Pieds Noirs' and her father was a graduate in the French army. Like hundreds of *colons*, they left prior to independence, and when they returned to France they were met with indifference, frustration and denial. Those who went through that historical and social experience of return and inward migration to their own 'unknown' country were often conscious of both a loss and lack of recognition of their identities. As Miss Pascale stated, she did not learn Arabic in Tunisia, but through the children of her Cl.in class – an in-

FIGURE 3: PASCAL MIMING

teresting point indicating her acknowledgement that any learning process is based on exchange and is therefore multidirectional. She too had been captured in a 'double bind', although as adult and leader she was perhaps meant or expected to be more 'autonomous' and aware of it.

Pupils compulsorily learning French in a Cl.in class are constantly urged to utter, to spell, to 'say it'. The teacher evaluates the pupil's speech; the pupil cannot remain silent; s/he cannot use non-verbal expressions. The educational system, which keeps a close eye on its members, required Miss Pascale to transmit knowledge according to a method which she had studied for many years, becoming a talented and highly visible teacher. Most of her colleagues admired her, especially the principal. In the years during which I observed and talked regularly to her she was authorised, even encouraged, to adopt a somewhat abrasive manner in handling children. Because of her genuine love for them, her behaviour did not attract blame, but on the contrary made her a more successful teacher. Most of her pupils reached an acceptable level and were prepared to face, more or less staunchly, their 'fate' in the French educational system.

If Mang Mang's 'silent mode' led me to explore the particular form of resistance that characterised her personality and her relational response at a given time and in a particular social context, I also came to qualify my interpretation by tracing back some of the forms of behaviour she brought to France to her upbringing in the Shanghai region. I also observed how her agency was expressed in the social context of her day-to-day education through reducing my interaction with her as much as possible, letting her relational modes emerge with others at school and home. In this way I could film without 'isolating' her as the main character, for school was a public arena in which she was not the sole person in focus. By visiting her at home, I developed a conversational, quiet way of being both together and apart. Often I did not film, for various reasons, but chiefly because we were usually alone in her home and I did not want to create an intrusive, unbalanced relationship based on the introduction of the camera into her intimate surroundings. I also wanted us both to relate to a physical proximity less intense than the one generated by filming. Mang Mang had never told me whether or not she liked to be filmed; she seemed almost indifferent to the gaze of the camera, acting in the same way whether I was filming her or not. She rarely talked, and I came to realise that her company was the most restful that I had ever experienced with a child. Not much hurry, few claims; anything that could generate tension was avoided by her. It was perhaps the behaviour of a very polite child who had grown up in the company of older people, within a cultural frame in which, if physical proximity leads to intimacy, this is not perceived as an abusive intrusion because each person adopts an introverted attitude and moves through the domestic space with a measured tempo and concentration. The counterpoint of school and home rendered visible the locus of Mang Mang's struggle in the French public sphere in which she was now located, while the time I spent at her home fed my understanding of her past and spare-time activities in 'solitaire' out of school, in her and our present.

LITTLE BY LITTLE THE BIRD MAKES ITS NEST: FILM FIELDWORK IN DUBLIN

The migrant children I got to know and film in the context of an all-boys Primary School in inner-city Dublin – children newly arrived from Eastern Europe, the Philippines and Nigeria – did not establish identical modalities in relation to our interaction. They showed me the space in which they preferred to act, while I tried to increase my understanding in the light of the locations and modes of socialisation they chose; children are likely to be more comfortable if they have chosen the loci in which the researcher is to observe them. This interactive positioning takes time (see Haraway 1991; Okeley 1992; Holtedahl 1993) and may lead to misunderstandings, but it is important to acknowledge that it is not a fixed, static process. In its adjustments a hypothesis is developed and results are achieved. This is why I prefer to call the children 'actors' and not 'informants', although I am aware that the use of a word transposed from the language of film could cause those in front of the camera to fall into the ambiguity of performing a professional role, while the readers of the text might mistakenly perceive the social actors as film actors. At the beginning of the film fieldwork, the children imagined themselves becoming movie stars, but once we had watched the rushes together, this dream faded away as they habituated to the presence of the camera (much to my relief).

Tahar: first encounter

The first day of term after the summer holidays: the school yard is crowded. The school is located in a former working-class district, where one generation seems to follow closely on another and motherhood is usually undertaken at an early age (16–19 years old).[4] The Irish constituency in this part of the city is today defined as an 'under class' living on welfare subsidies. Social deprivation, both overt and hidden, is on the increase and hope of a better future is rapidly diminishing. To me it seemed that, from the perspective of the inhabitants, one period had ended, leaving them without any clear idea of what was to follow. In this 'Irish-born' neighbourhood, a 'non-national' constituency has begun to develop in recent years:[5] immigrants sheltering in hostels, centres, temporary housing and gloomy flats below pavement level.

Manifestations of this new diversity are immediately apparent in the school. While its architecture is unchanged, inside, however, there are new signs and symbols displayed throughout the corridors. Parents, students, newly-enrolled children, siblings and even ex-pupils are chatting and, somewhat tensely, greeting the members of staff, some of whom are new acquaintances. Teachers tend not to stay long in these disadvantaged schools and there is a rapid turnover, giving a precarious air, apparent at first glance, to the socialising. Many young children are anxious on their first day at school, but in general the atmosphere is not too hectic. Almost everybody suspends judgement, oscillating between the fear of being singled out or, conversely, of being ignored. Very few children feel at ease and communicate freely among themselves.

This was not my first day at the school. I had begun my observations the year before and had already started to introduce the camera, so I knew who was new and which nationalities (by and large) were represented: in the previous semester (2003), 56 of the 126 pupils comprised a combination of 'non-nationals' and nationals who were not yet English-speaking. Waiting for the bell, delayed while the children were taught how to stay in line, I came across a parent – the only one – who was taking a picture of his son, a new pupil. I was struck by this caring act, by his pride in the boy's initiation into school and by some different quality in his behaviour. I noticed at once the elegant clothes and careful hairdressing of the mother. I saw that the younger sister stayed quiet to show respect for her older brother as he enrolled and that the boy attempted to hold a smile and a dignified pose for the portrait. The yard was grey, as is often in old schools, and the father was watching the sky, waiting for some sunshine. Suddenly he called to his son: 'Tahar! Tahar!' As the sun's rays pierced the clouds, Tahar's pose transcended the frenzied motion in the yard, capturing an instant of his own history, that first day at school in a new country.

In the following weeks, after I had negotiated consent with the school and with his parents, Tahar shaped the modalities of our encounters, introduc-

FIGURE 4: TAHAR'S FIRST DAY AT SCHOOL

ing me to his family and encouraging me to follow some of his daily routines. The boy seemed very aware of himself, of being only 'a child', but he also had the natural authority to ensure that he would be respected, protected and left in peace when he wished. Because he was at ease, sufficiently conscious of his identity and inner self to remain independent of both his teachers, peers and me, I never felt that I was pressurising him. He had already been at school for several days before anyone found a common language to speak with him; I spoke French to him, but he didn't really understand. He sat silent, observing, smiling sometimes, but mostly perplexed and locked in his own mood.[6] I was looking forward to speaking with one of the members of his family and finally, after a few weeks, I met his father in the yard. Mr Abane, from the Petite Kabylie area of Algeria, told me a great deal about the life of his Berber-speaking family during the very first conversation we had. He immediately understood the point of my research into the accounts, ways of integration and multiple identities of migrant children, and thought it a valuable project. As we talked on the way home from school, he revealed many of the feelings he had experienced as a refugee and shared with me in detail the long, desperate wait for his family to join him in Dublin. He had left Algeria when his youngest daughter was just a baby and it had been two and a half years before he had been able, the previous summer, to hug not only her but his son Tahar, his elder daughter Farida, his wife Khalida and his mother Madam Fatma.[7] For reasons which I learned later, his father had not been able to accompany them. Following this conversation I was allowed to film Tahar during his first days at school. [DVD REF 5: VIDEO]

During the autumn of 2003 the Irish government initiated reactionary measures against the so-called 'massive influx' of immigrants into Ireland. Similar trends were observable in other European Union member states as European governments contemplated the accession of ten new countries in May 2004. In Ireland the conditions for processing and extending residence permits were immediately tightened, in order to identify those with temporary permits, those without permits and those who did not fall within preselected domains of migrant labour. In addition, public opinion was called upon to debate the policies determining rights of citizenship.[8] The threat of deportation increased significantly upon the expiration of work permits and visas, each case scrutinised by the Departments of Justice, Equality and Law Reform and Enterprise, Trade and Development. In response multicultural newspaper *Metro Eireann*[9] published letters of protest from 'non-national' constituencies and individuals alike; the following excerpt is from a letter written by a group of Eastern European mothers addressed to Michael McDowell, Irish Minister of Justice:

> We are ordinary people trying to make a living in Ireland. We are all parents of little Irish citizens who want them to grow up and become builders, poets, pilots, farmers, singers, scientists and taxi drivers. Our children speak Gaeilge, play hurling and dance Irish dances. But there is one thing that makes us stand out from the rest: anxious waiting.[10]

This excerpt gives polished utterance, shaped into a 'call for tolerance', to the voice of a complex constituency; the words quoted above provide a real and immediate understanding of how quickly these migrant children could be integrated, as well as of the uncertainty with which their relatives have to live because they have a different national status.

What kind of challenge would Tahar's father encounter if a new child were born to him in Ireland following the family's recent reunion? How would issues of dual-citizenship be managed within the family when certain members obtained the rights of Irish citizenship, whereas others had refugee status? What relationship was there between issues to do with citizenship and the everyday realities of a changing cultural identity? These were questions I pondered as I tried to make sense of this family unit. As it stood, Tahar's father already felt conflicted about his identity in Ireland. At first Mr Abane seemed satisfied with Ireland and his Irish friends, but slowly it emerged that this was merely cosmetic, a way of disguising feelings of frustration, even bitterness, because he had lost his former status as a 'respected and influential man'. There had even been racist remarks in some of the pubs where he thought he had made new Irish friends. He admitted that he could not have endured living alone in Ireland without going regularly to the pub, socialising and drinking with new acquaintances. This was what had stopped him falling into a deep depression during his first months of exile. He explained that the material conditions of his stay in Dublin were so unbearable, in comparison with his previous lifestyle, that he needed the little pleasure afforded by the pubs. His wife now had a husband with new habits which had not been part of their common life in Algeria. He asked me not to enquire into the political reasons for and implications of his exile and I always respected this request, but aspects of the very dramatic sociopolitical conditions of his country of origin functioned as metaphors for the ideological 'untold'. One such aspect was the earthquake (discussed below) that destroyed their hometown, Regaya.

My position was delicately balanced, because the more I became acquainted with the family, the more a friendship developed which was outside the bounds of professional research; I was also well aware of what the ethnic group to which the family belonged had endured for more than a decade. On the other hand, since I was the recipient of a scholarship granted by the Irish state, it was possible that Mr Abane would consider me to be a government informant, operating under the cover of social scientific enquiry. All this made for an ambivalent situation. Images and film were not merely optional devices for furthering investigation or representation; in this case they took away the safe 'anonymity' with which, in order to protect both social actors and researchers, social scientific investigations usually operate (Bourdieu 1999).

Developing a relationship with Tahar and family

Even for a child memory is the cement which binds the elements of an improvised 'home'. One puts there visible and tangible artefacts of memory – still pictures, souvenirs – but the roof and walls protecting them are invisible, intangible and biographical.
    – John Berger (1999; my translation)

According to scholars (see, for example, Kristeva 1986; Berger 1999), and more recently a detailed study of integration and migration management in the context of civil liberty discourses,[11] people in conditions of exile are acutely aware that they have not chosen the country in which they live. Although thankful to have found a place of refuge in a host country – a sense of gratitude that often, so archetypal representations suggest, renders the exiled subject docile and withdrawn – it does not follow that the exile's sense of obligation will lead her/him towards integration into the new environment with its own language, dominant civil discourse and majority faith, or her/his stereotyped categorisation, as, for example, a 'dangerous Islamic fundamentalist'. For a subject like Tahar's father, accustomed to work as a respected lecturer in French and English, an influential person in his community of origin, a sports champion, life as a subsidised, isolated, single man in Dublin, doing small jobs and living in one underground room, was a shocking change.

Family members joining a close relation in exile often know little about their new environment except what they have learned from letters and pictures sent to them, usually describing a respectable life and exhibiting picturesque places. Whether new arrivals like the place or not can seem a secondary issue; what is important is quitting a life-threatening situation. At the beginning, everything is welcome and appreciated. This was the position of the Sadi family when I first met them; they were concerned to reconstitute themselves as a unit living together, finding a basis on which to build their future. Ramadan, occurring that year from October to late November, provided an opportunity to re-establish some of the family's customary religious practices. Prayers and special meals taken together determined the tempo of the days and nights and new learning processes took place, especially between the siblings. [DVD REF 7: VIDEO] I was invited by the family to document these moments.

The camera was easily accepted in the family home, especially by Mr Abane's wife, Khalida, and their oldest daughter, Farida, who wanted to send video footage of their present lives to relatives in Algeria. This arrangement or form of 'exchange value' characterised my film fieldwork with the Sadi family. A reciprocity developed in our relationship, though of course, as often happens during fieldwork, there were ups and downs, occasions when the boundaries between friendship and work became blurred. Tahar enjoyed being filmed and was intrigued by the camera. After some months, however, the family's interest in sending tapes to Regaya faded. They were happy to have a family archive, yet it had ceased to be a matter of urgency. I continued to film each time we met but the camera was no longer a catalyst for performance – the film, it seemed, was destined for a historiographic future.

Tahar took me on a tour of his home, where the whole life of the family, its agency and alchemy, were displayed and performed. He rapidly became the mediator between his family and myself. Although I struggled to keep him as my main character, the rest of the family continually 'intruded' into his space both on and off camera and I became bound up, at the boy's instigation, in the relational web woven by all six members of the Sadi family, a kind of revelatory agent of the inner paradigms of that small community. I was literally directing my camera lens at unfolding psychological bonds and formations in progress and, in a way, generating them by my ongoing attention.

Tahar's ethnographic portrait, originally conceived, as my work in Paris had led me to expect, as the figure of an individual struggling and performing in a world of adults and confronting new experiences, was vanishing little by little. Instead, he was asking to be seen within the context of his family home, where an attempt to rebuild both a real and a metaphysical hearth ('foyer') – a physical and mental location accommodating questions of history, gender, class and race in the migratory experience of exile – was 'happening' before the gaze of the camera and as a partial consequence of the persuasive presence of the camerawoman. Instead of the observational mode characterising my filming of Mang Mang in Paris, I came to use a more *vérité* style, a slightly stronger participant action, through filming various performances of loss, re-enacted remembrances (Benguigui 1997) and sensuous everyday practices and habits in a day-to-day, 'everyday is the same day' frame.

Reconfiguring intergenerational relations: earthquake in Algeria

On 21 May 2003 an earthquake of sudden and terrifying impact killed more than 2,300 people, leaving more than 7,000 injured and 130,000 homeless. It destroyed dozens of buildings in Regaya, the city where Tahar's father's family had lived for more than fifty years and where all Mr Abane's children were born. Recollections of this dramatic moment were performed spontaneously in front of the camera, in a multivocal session with echoes and counterpoint. [DVD REF 8: VIDEO] In a way, this performance illustrated an attempt to show that their beloved country was being destroyed not only by political paradoxes, but also by natural phenomena, which was perhaps easier to accept since it could be attributed to fate. The other family members added details and made corrections, and for the first time Tahar spoke at length in Algerian Arabic to the camera, describing the scene as his fifth-floor flat collapsed, while he, an onlooker, watched from below.

Tahar's life had been saved by chance; he had gone to the shops to buy a notebook. The moment in which he recalled the event, the sudden shift from shyness to exuberance, is visible in the DVD sequence. At the time, he was speechless and semi-paralysed for several hours. Worse, he was separated all night from the rest of the family, who were trapped in a hole underground. The succession of viewpoints during the experiential retelling of the earthquake disaster was therefore multi-layered. Mr Abane was particularly anxious to be the one to re-tell the tale, his desire to share this memorable turning-point with the rest of his family appearing stronger than concern for the credibility of his account. Behind him stood Tahar, who had also experienced the event from outside, impotently watching the terrible scene. The women, on the other hand, had in common the shared experience of being trapped, injured, under tons of rubble.

Neurologists and psychologists who assessed the rescued children and assembled the people in temporary camps suggested that their mother should send Tahar and Farida to the countryside, where their maternal grandparents could look after them, providing care and food and allowing them to speak of their experiences. The doctors had urged the children to verbalise their reactions, if possible to people close to them rather than in hospitals. In a few shaking minutes Tahar lost nineteen schoolmates who had gathered to watch a football match on TV in one of the highest flats. All of them had died in the desperate carnage as ceilings and walls collapsed.

Tahar's grandfather remained in Regaya, waiting to be allocated new accommodation. By staying there alone, he reduced the risk that the family would lose their chance of getting a permanent place of residence in the rebuilt city. Tahar's mother and her children were entitled to be re-housed because they were in Regaya at the time of the earthquake; had they already left for Ireland, they would have lost that entitlement. Gradually, the earthquake became the core experience, retold and shown on videotape or still pictures from the internet each time I visited the family. The tragedy became a locus of convergence for many other untold themes concerning the past and future of their country, their collective memory and social status, their loss and the constant threat and violence with which they had lived for decades.

Re-appropriating one's name

> To migrate means always to dismantle the centre of the world and to settle it again into a confusing, disorganised and fragmented world.
> – John Berger (1999; my translation)

On one of his first days at school Tahar's new Irish primary teacher, Miss Morris, asked him how to spell his family name correctly. [DVD REF 9: VIDEO] Such tact and attention is rarely shown to immigrant subjects and constitutes, in my interpretation, a crucial but often implicit understanding of a need to be acknowledged. Children can maintain continuity of identity by regarding their name as a visible piece of their body; in this they differ from adults, who know that names are or can become a convention. Many migrant children I have met (though not Tahar) have been forced by practical circumstances to change their names. Reasons vary: false passports, the need to smuggle subjects across borders, political persecution of family members, a more accessible spelling of names perceived as 'difficult' in the host environment, a quasi or complete 'assimilation' into the host language. The 'double' names of the children I worked with were sometimes revealed, sometimes hidden; it is a question I address with caution and determination after a long period spent in building trust and reciprocal confidentiality. It is a telling point, marking a tangible borderline between 'before' and 'after' migration; one name belongs to ancestry and the mother tongue, the other marks the migratory move to a new form of kinship, more imagined and idealised. The 'former', 'secret' name (which sometimes cannot be revealed) of many migrant children becomes the name of the 'former' self, the child before the journey, a protagonist of other stories, a twin in another space-time.

Tahar's name, unlike many foreign names, could easily be pronounced by Irish carers and peers, but he had a problem in accommodating it in terms of Western written forms. In an early visit to the family's one-room basement in Parnell Square (inner-city Dublin),

FIGURE 5: TAMAZIGHT ALPHABET: LETTER REPRESENTING 'Z'

I observed that Tahar could not hear and write 'T', the initial letter of his name. [DVD REF 10: VIDEO] While studying Berber phonetics and systems of notation, I had encountered the sound T (t) of Tamazight, and noticed that the phoneme 't' is attached as a prefix to the word Amazigh (a Berber) to make Tamazight (the Berber language). With Tahar's father's help, I learned further that, according to recent work under the auspices of the emerging Kabyl cultural-national movement (Kabylie is the name of the region where the family lived in Algeria and the variant of Berber spoken there is called Kabyl), that Amazigh probably meant 'free human being' in the ancient Berber language; the Berber letter representing the 'z' sound in Tamazight is the current symbol of the Kabyl liberation movement in the Maghreb, appearing on flags, CD covers and modern jewellery.

Ethnic identity, separation movements, cultural diasporic trends and Arabisation policies have provoked tensions in Morocco and Algeria for decades, and in Algeria they have exploded even more violently during the last ten years of civil war.[12] The Algerian-Berber diaspora is estimated at one million people in France alone. Many Kabyl musicians and poets from France have recently been murdered or imprisoned while touring in Algeria. Following the riots of 2003, the Algerian government has tried to come to terms with the Kabyl Independence Movement and there are indications that the government intends to introduce Tamazight as a second language in primary schools.[13]

On one occasion, Mr Abane mentioned the Kabyl cultural movement. [DVD REF 11: VIDEO] Since the family's Berber identity was emphasised, and also because I was interested, 'Kabylia-philia' became a theme performed by all the members of the family except Tahar. He had refused to speak Kabyl at home since arriving in Ireland, sticking instead to Arabic. There was a nostalgic moment during the fourth birthday celebrations for the 'baby growing older', Kahya, when unexpectedly all the onlookers started to listen to a CD of a famous Kabyl singer, the *chansonnier* Idir. [DVD REF 12: VIDEO] The song is powerfully nostalgic and draws attention, in very lyrical language, to the political oppression endured by the Kabyl people. It was sung first in Tamazight and then in French, bypassing Arabic, as Idir does intentionally in most of his songs. While they listened to the only CD they had brought with them to Ireland (everything else was lost in the earthquake), each person in the living-room seemed to be absorbed in his or her own mood. I wandered about with my camera, capturing this condition of suspended exile with great intensity.

The emerging sentiments from the various members of the family as they discussed their lost homeland – Kabylia, Algeria – in front of and for the camera, allowed for lyrical

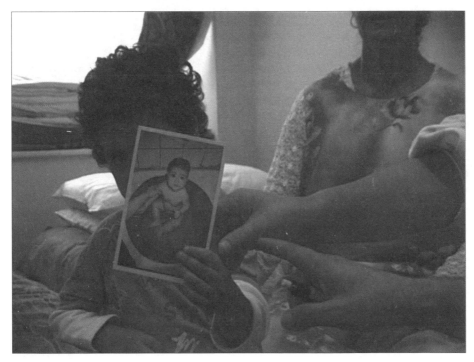

FIGURE 6: KAHYA

and open speculation about that imagined land as perceived by three different generations, for whom the song had very diverse meanings and evocations. Nothing was really discussed on the spot, apart from two swift comments from the mother: 'It is terrific, isn't it? It's gorgeous, but so sad,' and the daughter: 'It tells about a sad past, things which have faded away.' I captured the way it was expressed, experienced and re-enacted through the body language of the different members of the family, looking for or losing contact, coming together or drifting away, as well as through the feelings of solidarity evoked by the song: Tahar trying to get his sister to dance, the mother receiving and tenderly holding a doll from Kahya, the grandmother still melancholy, Farida observing, Kahya showing pictures of herself as a small child.

In the beginning I found Tahar's behaviour enigmatic; he directed my attention to his form of sociality through a very limited and episodic verbal address. He seemed to me to be expressing acceptance of his fate as being the only boy in the family, inheriting the values of a constructed virility. His father's expectations and his success as a son were bound up in his choice of a sport. In Regaya Tahar had been selected for national competitions and hoped to become a junior karate champion. His ability in this martial art (in contrast to Mang Mang's fear) showed him to be strong, able to overcome the traumatic experience of the earthquake and eager to let the body 'speak' through the postures of staged combat. In the short sequence with his father, [DVD REF 13: VIDEO] this playful moment of 'dialogue' through karate enacts a 'familiar lexicon', a common past and a passion for the same sport shared by father and son; it is also an attempt by Tahar to restore extra-linguistic communication with his father. The fact that his father had practised the same

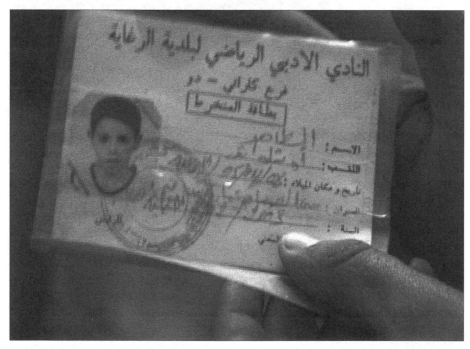

FIGURE 7: TAHAR'S KARATE CLUB MEMBERSHIP CARD

sport represented a bond between them. This bond was the living heritage which Tahar had brought with him, along with his karate club membership card from Regaya – his real passport and emblematic sign of continuity, a document which had meaning and in which his name sounded pleasant and full of praise, the initial letter restored: T+Ahar.

The domestic rebuilding of the 'foyer' became a central concern for Tahar. In time, he found new friends, speaking Algerian Arabic at home and the new English language, with its Dublin inflections, in the street and the school. In a follow-up visit to the family after they had moved to more spacious accommodation in County Dublin, [DVD REF 14: VIDEO] I was told by Tahar and Farida that he had fallen out of his new bed. He had finally got a room for himself, with a single bed, but he was used to sleeping in a big bed with his sister and grandmother. Unaccustomed to his new space and single mattress, he fell out while asleep. Farida commented that although the initial one-room accommodation they had had when they first came to Ireland was very cramped, she had felt more comfortable there than in their new, bigger house. Both she and Tahar stated upon returning to the underground flat in Parnell Square nine months later, they had only good memories of the place. Living downtown still had a fascination in their eyes because of the quantity of big, cheap stores, the oriental shops stocking Arab food, the commercial movie theatres and the social occasions which were much easier to access than from the residential, middle-class outskirts of the city, where they now lived. Good memories were visibly connected with that 'sentimentalised' space, which would otherwise have appeared gloomy and un-healthy. It seemed that the first days of reunion had already started to reflect the glow of an imagined family history, an idealised memory of happiness and novelty that was also emotionally connected with a sense of solidarity, of communal sharing, that the lack of space had allowed the family to feel again after years of separation, fear and despair. Situ-ations like the one in the sequence below, in which the Sadi family were able to sit and laugh together as they watched a comic English sketch, represent the re-instantiation of communal family life. [DVD REF 15: VIDEO]

THE CINEMATIC ENGAGEMENT

Contributions from the humanistic social sciences across the interdisciplinary fields of visual anthropology, historiography and media practice, drawing on fieldwork in schools and in locations where children interact with parents or peers, have facilitated a way to better understand recurrent (and sometimes contradictory) behavioural patterns, roles and power dynamics.[14] The researcher in the school or in the family has, because s/he is not a teacher, a relative or a carer, a particular status *vis-à-vis* children. Furthermore, when s/he holds a camera, the relation with children is of a particular type. The digital video camera – an instrument resembling a child's toy, all too familiar to migrant communi-ties in the context of circulating video tapes between separated communities – made my presence as filmmaker both fascinating and acceptable. Had I only observed and taken fieldnotes, the children would have experienced the medium – text – as strange and even threatening, a sort of perpetual 'homework'.

Film fieldwork requires far more time than documentary or reportage broadcast pro-duction. Throughout filming I deploy the 'participant observational' method, which derives from direct cinema involving a rigorous analysis of footage every week, since the narrative style and 'focus' can change shape, mutate and settle as the research develops. Given the lightness of digital video equipment and the lack of restrictions on the pace of work – in contrast to the production work of a full-scale film crew – it is therefore possible to develop a certain intimacy with the social actors and to find a comfortable footing, physically and mentally, within the community where the sequence is being filmed. The actors do not have to be 'hyper-stimulated' with questions about particular issues, involving the elicitation of their viewpoints and aspirations; their accounts can emerge gradually, informally and perhaps more spontaneously.

I had to listen on the sidelines and be prepared to guide, direct and consolidate the structure of the work in progress, while the relationship with the central actors developed, sometimes peacefully, sometimes discordantly, and 'reality' revealed, imposed and expressed itself through the dynamics of the relationships. To write a conventional treatment as one might for a documentary before shooting would be futile; in film fieldwork, the treatment has to be constantly re-adjusted and modified according to the new findings and stories generated by the ongoing (and often sustained) presence of the filmmaker in the ordinary life of the people being filmed, in the very locations where they live, act and socialise. A constant alertness to multiple dynamics – to the developing plot, to events and sudden recollections, or to the interactions of people being filmed – creates an entirely different rhythm and response. Once a definitive genre is established and maintained throughout, a self-reflexive style emerges, where the author/filmmaker is 'visible' behind the camera through his/her physical adjustments, emotions, distancing, misunderstandings, meddling and productive interventions.

Children, as they wait for the camera, have often stared questioningly at me wondering how and why I could be interested in such boring moments. This often happens with participant observational cinema when the actors' question to the filmmaker – 'why are you interested in this?' is the primary movement provoking the intersubjective engagement between filmmaker and subject(s). This intersubjective movement is arguably the reversal of the aggressive use of camera and microphone in many documentary productions. When the filmmaker only occasionally interrogates the actors, s/he ends up being interrogated in return; questions always unveil the filmmaker's presence, demanding that their intentions, plots and manipulations are rendered explicit. Above all, the filmmakers' self-reflexive awareness of their bias and ignorance is extremely important in any attempt to provoke a generative process of understanding. For this reason, I take issue with filmmakers who have yet to learn how to observe through the camera with empathy, modesty and humility, when they denigrate observational filmmaking with the stereotyped appellation 'fly on the wall'. To observe and learn, allowing imagined spectators to do the same 'together' with the filmmaker and the actors is a rare achievement, enabling ethnographic film to be as critically descriptive as it should be useful, unique and well crafted (see Ragazzi 2005; 2006).

In most cases ethnographic film is constructed in such a way that it is possible to follow the process by which the researcher/filmmaker learns, adapts and acquires relevant skills.[15] Questions that actors put to the filmmaker opens up a triangular formation (Holtedahl 1993; Altern & Holtedahl 1996), acknowledging, in cinematic terms, both the presence of an imagined viewer and the complicity of a shared, acceptable admission that not all the questions can be responded to at once. Ongoing reflection in the context of film fieldwork is a process informed by complex epistemological concerns in which I strive to find a voice to articulate this challenge, sometimes paying the price of being considered a hybrid, marginalised both 'inside', in the academic production of knowledge, and 'outside', in the commercial realm of media production and distribution. I have in fact been teased by the children at school, because I was neither making money nor making them famous. Sometimes I felt that I was confusing all the categories in a dangerous initiative from which nobody could benefit, not even myself.

My embodied film fieldwork practice is a craft compatible with telling, signifying and producing signs, as described by anthropologists (see, for example Ingold 2000 and Grasseni 2003); it is sustained almost entirely of my own labour, both technical and intellectual. The act of filming evokes a loom in which relations, actions and their inscriptions are woven: in a perceptive sense (because it was not staged) and a representational one (because the plot constantly evolved from this reciprocity). Filming is never exclusively an optical exercise, since it also involves motion and the caption and inscription of an emerging reality (MacDougall 1999; 2001; 2004; Holtedahl 2006). To see, as Maurice Merleau-Ponty explains, is to 'move toward' (1992: 6). By looking, learning and attuning oneself to the surrounding and unfolding reality, my sight seeks to comprehend relational phenomena. This is one of the parameters of what I call filmic engagement: an 'active observation' in which sight is not the sole sensory apparatus of our relational engagement with the world (Ingold 2000). In the wide palette of sounds surrounding the filmmaker, the voices of Others (organised into forms of speech that are perpetual and performative), together with the filmmaker's own voice and the tactile attempt at restoring the proximity with the Other, comprise a collective and constituent part of the act of filmmaking. Having the opportunity to film with children has allowed my practice to be imbued with inconsolable empathy (see Frank 1985; 1996), with amazement before the world of oblivious adults, with elation and sorrow but most of all with grace, the most necessary ingredient for engaging with realities which call for further understanding.

Notes

1   R. Ragazzi (*La Mémoire Dure*, 2000, 80 mins). Screened at numerous film festivals, among others: Nuoro International Film Festival, Italy (2000); Festival International du Cinema du Reel, Paris (2001); and Beeld voor Beeld, Amsterdam (2001).

2   I am grateful to the Irish Research Council for the Humanities and Social Sciences for the allocation of a doctoral research award in respect of this work (2002–05).

3   The extent to which the researcher is familiar with the original culture of migrants s/he seeks to portray is crucial. The difficulty of relying solely on doxic accounts is often conflated by the tendency of migrants to 'freeze' certain images of the past, offering a restricted level of 'truth' to the researcher. The assumptions of the researcher can further influence the response of migrant actors, reinforcing stereotypes about their 'origin' in the continuing construction of patterns through which culture is reinvented for the purposes of Western multiculturalism. This is why I think that researchers should try to learn about the life stories of the migrant actors in depth (see Gullestad 2003; 2004).

4   This is, paradoxically, the area where Dublin's most important maternity hospitals are located: the

Mater and the Rotunda, Europe's first public maternity hospital, established in 1745 and relocated in 1757 to its present site in Parnell Square.

5   The term 'non-national', referring to a person not born in Ireland to non-Irish parents, was first introduced into legislation in the 1999 Immigration Bill. Use of this term is problematic since there are few people living in Ireland who are without nationality and it continues to be misinterpreted to suggest that immigrants in Ireland are living in the country illegally, the majority of whom are clearly not. For these very reasons a spokeswoman from the Department of Justice announced in May 2006 that the term would be reviewed in the context of the new Immigration and Residence Bill.

6   In the first days at school, priority was given to the implementation of a strong disciplinary framework. Tahar, calm and obedient, was left more or less free to listen and tune into the situation, but was sometimes forgotten.

7   Tahar's grandparents on his father's side were both national heroes of the Front de Libération National d'Algérie (FLN); the grandfather spent two and half years in prison, while the grandmother, Madam Fatma, served three months of a life sentence but was freed by an amnesty. They were decorated after independence was proclaimed. Madam Fatma spoke metaphorically of the pain she experienced during the Second Algerian War: 'The vase', she said, 'was too full; it overflowed.' She suffers from Parkinson's disease and a chronic nerve condition and was semi-paralysed when she came to Dublin but, cared for by Mr Abane and his wife, her health and spirits improved. [DVD REF 6: VIDEO]

8   This discussion anticipated the call for a referendum on the then-existing constitutional (automatic) right to Irish citizenship of all children born in Ireland or with ancestors born in Ireland up to two generations back. The referendum of June 2004 resulted in a modification of that right, granting citizenship only to Irish-born children whose parents had lived for three out of four consecutive years in Ireland.

9   *Metro Eireann* is the first multicultural newspaper in Ireland. Established in 2000, it provides a forum for intercultural communication and debate and also organises annually the Media and Multicultural Awards in association with the national TV channel RTÉ.

10 *Metro Eireann*, November 2003.

11 See references to migration and integration in the United Nations *Human Development Report 2004*. Available at <http://hdr.undp.org/reports/global/2004/> [Accessed 18 March 2005].

12 In the early 1980s Algeria underwent both an economic and a political crisis. The FLN, in power since independence from French colonial rule was achieved in 1962, was under pressure, particularly from Islamic movements. In the elections of 1988 the Front Islamique du Salut (FIS) made gains and by 1991 had the backing of almost 50 per cent of the electorate. The government, fearing a takeover, suspended the democratic process. Violence was endemic and to outside observers Algeria became a theatre for the worst stereotypes of Islamic fundamentalism. In 1997, following a general amnesty, Kabyl movements renewed their struggle for recognition as an ethnic and linguistic minority. Algeria remains an area of conflict.

13 This has re-opened the controversy about the script in which Tamazight should be written; some favour Tafinagh (which developed in North Africa from 6 BCE and derived from Punic script), some the Arabic alphabet, but most scholars advocate the use of Latin characters, which give access to the internet and also to the 'Berberophone' communities in Europe, acccustomed to the Latin alphabet.

14 See, for example, Steedman (1987); Prout & Allison (1990); Toren (1993); Stephens (1995); Gullestad (1996); Corsaro (1997); MacDougall (1999; 2001; 2003; 2004; 2006); James *et al.* (1998); Christensen & James (2000); and Lidèn (2001).

15 For a selection of ethnographic films foregrounding methodologies of 'visible en-skillment' of film-

makers, see, for example: (Paggi 1996); (Holtedahl 1997); (Grasseni 1998); (Postma 1999); (Pourchez 2000); (Ragazzi 2000; 2003); (Arntsen 2001); (Djesa 2001); (Niglas 2001); and (Baba (2003).

Bibliography

Altern, I. and L. Holtedahl (1996) 'Kunnskap om oss og andre', *Norwegian Journal of Anthropology: Norsk Antropologisk Tidskrift*, 1: 4–20.

Bateson, G. (1972) *Steps to an Ecology of Mind*. New York: Ballantine Books.

Berger, J. (1999 [1985]) 'L' Exil. La Lettre Internationale' in *Péripheries: Journal Online*. Available at <http://www.peripheries.net/article195.html> [Accessed 20 October 2006].

Bourdieu, P. (1977) *Outline of a Theory of Practice*. Cambridge: Cambridge University Press.

_____ (1999) *The Weight of the World. Social Suffering in Contemporary Society*. Stanford: Stanford University Press.

Christensen, P. and A. James (2000) *Research with Children*. London: Falmer Press.

Corsaro, W. A. (1997) *The Sociology of Childhood*. London: Pine Forge Press.

De Certeau, M. (1993) *La Culture au Pluriel*. Paris: Edition du Seuil.

Faulstich M. O., B. Thorne, W. S. E. Lam and A. Chee (2001) 'Transnational Childhoods: The Participation of Children in Processes of Family Migration', *Social Problems*, 48 (4): 573–92.

Frank, G. (1985) '"Becoming the Other": Empathy and Biographical Interpretation', *Biography*, 8 (3): 189–210.

_____ (1996) 'Myths of Creation: Construction of Self in an Autobiographical Account of Birth and Infancy', in M. Gullestad (ed.) *Imagined Childhoods: Self and Society in Autobiographical Accounts*. Oslo: Scandinavian University Press.

Galand, L. (1979) *Langue et Litérature Berbères: Vingt cinq ans d'étude. (Chronique de l'Annuaire de l'Afrique du Nord.)* Paris: Editions du CNRS.

Grasseni, C. (2003) *Lo Sguardo della Mano. Pratiche della localitá e antropologia della visione in una comunitá montana lombarda*. Bergamo: Bergamo University Press.

Gullestad, M. (ed.) (1996) *Imagined Childhoods: Self and Society in Autobiographical Accounts*. Oslo: Scandinavian University Press.

_____ (2003) 'Fighting for a Sustainable Self-Image: The Role of Descent in Individualized Identitification', *European Journal of Social Anthropology*, 42: 23–30.

_____ (2004) 'Blind Slaves of our Prejudices: Debating "Culture" and "Race" in Norway', *Ethnos*, 69 (2): 177–203.

Gupta, A. and J. Ferguson (1997) *Anthropological Locations: Boundaries and Grounds of a Field Science*. Stanford: University of California Press.

Hall, S. (1995) 'New Cultures for Old', in D. Massey and P. Jess (eds.), *A Place in the World? Places, Cultures, and Globalization*. New York: Oxford University Press.

Haraway, D. (1991) *Simians, Cyborgs and Women: The Reinvention of Nature*. London: Free Books.

Holtedahl, L. (1993) 'Communication Problems in Social Research', in P. I. Crawford (ed.) *The Nordic Eye: Proceedings from NAFA 1*. Højbjerg: Intervention Press.

Human Development Report (2004) *Cultural Liberty in Today's Diverse World*. New York: United Nations Development Programme.

Ingold, T. (2000) *The Perception of the Environment: Essays in Livelihood, Dwelling and Skill*. London: Routledge.

Jackson, M. (2001) *The Politics of Storytelling. Violence, Transgression and Intersubjectivity*. Kobenhavn: Tusculanum Press.

James, A., C. Jenks and A. Prout (1998) *Theorising Childhood*. Cambridge: Cambridge Polity Press.

Koester, D. (1996) 'National Childhood: Expressions of Icelandic National Identity in Icelandic Life-Writing', in M. Gullestad (ed.) *Imagined Childhoods: Self and Society in Autobiographical Accounts*. Oslo: Scandinavian University Press.

Kristeva, J. (1986) *Etrangers à nous mêmes*. Paris: Editions Gallimard.

Lidèn, H. (2001) 'Barn og Kunnskapstilegnese i et Pluralistik Norge'. Unpublished PhD thesis, Norwegian University of Science and Technology (NTNU), Trondheim.

MacDougall, D. (1997) 'The Visual in Anthropology', in M. Banks and H. Morphy (eds) *Rethinking Visual Anthropology*. New Haven: Yale University Press.

____ (1998) *Transcultural Cinema*. Princeton: Princeton University Press.

____ (2006) *The Corporeal Image: Film, Ethnography and the Senses*. Princeton: Princeton University Press.

Marcus, G. E. (1995) 'Ethnography in/of the World System: The Emergence of Multi-Sited Ethnography', *Annual Review of Anthropology*, 24: 95–117.

Merleau-Ponty, M. (1990) *Le Visible et l'Invisible*. Paris: Editions Gallimard.

____ (1992) *L'Oeil et l'Esprit*. Paris: Editions Gallimard.

Olney, J. (1996) 'On Telling One's Own Story; or Memory and Narrative in Early Life-Writing', in M. Gullestad (ed.) *Imagined Childhoods: Self and Society in Autobiographical Accounts*. Oslo: Scandinavian University Press.

Okeley J. (1992) 'Participatory Experience and Embodied Knowledge', in J. Okeley and H. Callaway (eds) *Anthropology and Autobiography*. New York and London: Routledge.

Piault, M. H. (2000) *Anthropologie et Cinema. Passage à l'image. Passage par l'image*. Paris: Nathan.

Pourchez, L. (2000) 'Anthropologie de la petite enfance en société créole réunionnaise'. CD-Rom annexe PhD thesis, doctorat d'anthropologie, Ecole des Hautes Etudes en Sciences Sociales.

Prout, A. and J. Allison (eds) (1990) *Constructing and Reconstructing Childhood*. London: Falmer Press.

Ragazzi, R. (2005) 'Memory, Resistance and Speaking the 'Self': Migrant Children's Accounts of a Shifted Place-Time', in M. Postma and P. Crawford (eds) *Reflecting Visual Anthropology – Using the Camera in Anthropological Research*. Leiden: CNWS-Press and Intervention Press.

____ (2006) 'Living with Camera in between Barn and Kitchen: Phenomenological Perspectives on the Making of the Ethnographic Film Home *At Home in the World*', in E. Engelstadt and S. Gerrard (eds) *Challenging Situatedness: Gender, Culture and the Production of Knowledges*. Delft: Eburon.

Steedman, C. (1987) *The Tidy House: Little Girls Writing*. London: Virago.

Stephens, S. (1995) 'Children and the Politics of Culture in Late Capitalism', in S. Stephens (ed.) *Children and the Politics of Culture*. Princeton: Princeton University Press.

Stoller, P. (1992) *The Cinematic Griot: the Ethnography of Jean Rouch*. Chicago: University of Chicago Press.

Toren, C. (1993) 'Making History: The Significance of Childhood Cognition for a Comparative Anthropology of Mind', *Man*, 28 (3): 28–40.

Filmography

Age of Reason, The (2004), David MacDougall. Centre for Cross-Cultural Research, Australian National University, Australia, 87 mins.

At Home in the World (2003), Rossella Ragazzi. Visual Cultural Studies, University of Tromsø, Norway, 63 mins.

Brigade, The (2001), Liivio Niglas. F-Seitse & Liivio Niglas, 60 mins.

Castle in Africa, A (2006), Lisbet Holtedahl. Lisbet Film, Ethnographic Series, The Norwegian Research Council & Anthropos. 120 mins.

Ce gamin-la (1975), Victor Renaud. Les Films du Carrosse, 93 mins.

Ce qu'ils apprendront vaut-il ce qu'ils oublieront? (1997), Lisbet Holtedahl. The Norwegian Research Council, Lisbet Film and Antropos, 48 mins.

Chi non lavora non fa l'amore (1998), Cristina Grasseni. Granada Centre for Visual Anthropology, Manchester University, UK, 40 mins.

City Lights (1931), Charles Chaplin. Charlie Chaplin Productions/United Artists, 87 mins.

Cows are Better than Money (2003), Abdoullahi Baba. Visual Cultural Studies, University of Tromsø, Norway, 38 mins.

Doon School Chronicles (1999), David MacDougall. Centre for Cross-Cultural Research, Australian National University, Australia, 120 mins.

Fils de Jambe Tordue (1996), Silvia Paggi. Nanterre University, France, 50 mins.

Fish Come with the Rain, The (2001), Bjørn Arnsten. Visual Cultural Studies, University of Tromsø, Norway, Ethnographic film annexed to PhD, 45 mins.

La Mémoire Dure (2000), Rossella Ragazzi. Mémoire du Coquillage/Documentary Educational Resources, 82 mins.

Memoires d'Immigres (1997), Yamina Benguigui. Canal+, 173 mins.

Missionaries and Power (2001), Rachel Issa Djesa. Visual Cultural Studies, University of Tromsø, Norway, 42 mins.

New Boys, The (2003), David MacDougall. Centre for Cross-Cultural Research, Australian National University, Australia, 100 mins.

On Men and Mares (1999), Metje Postma, University of Leiden, Holland, 80 mins.

With Morning Hearts (2001), David MacDougall. Centre for Cross-Cultural Research, Australian National University, Australia, 110 mins.

sans titre/untitled: VIDEO INSTALLATION AS AN ACTIVE ARCHIVE[1]

Jayce Salloum

It was interesting to see the Soha tape along with the tape of the older man telling his story. It made for a complex layering of the notions of home and loss. The older man is narrative. And, the piece made me think about how narrative is a useful way to structure knowledge. The scene seemed almost pedagogical – he tells the story while the younger men listen. Narrative is also portable – it's what he's carried with him, and what he can give to those who are younger – a story of loss. The Soha piece is non-narrative – like any conversation, it's about breaks and pieces, interruptions and turning toward what the other said. I see that this was a good way to pull away from the narrative that dominates her – the martyr's narrative. Made me think of the problems with narrative, the fixing of one meaning (she resists the titling). This tape made me think differently about fragmentation, loss, and home. So, anyway, they were interesting together.

Love, Anne

'Postwar'

Lebanon, January 1992: the city is open and traversing it from east to west is again possible without fear of kidnapping or worse, at least for those of us distanced from the recent war and the still remote occupation in the south. Driving around, the slightly battered Fiat 128, looking somewhat the worse for wear, silver of sorts but covered in dust from years in the garage, makes its way hesitantly down one of the arteries leading into the core of Beirut – or one of them; for there are many centres here, old, new, destroyed, demolished, rebuilt, each act of construction part and parcel of a previous one of destruction. Walid [Ra'ad] drives, I shoot – video – gazing at the passing layers of modern and ancient architecture through the camera, using it like an appendage, as it inhales inadequate images of people, place: sites of historical and social signification, the fruit vendors, the shattered lives being pieced back together, more tattered buildings and ruins upon ruins.[2]

Posters of her are everywhere, on lampposts, in shop windows, in private homes in the place of honour next to the family's sons and daughters martyred in the war: Soha Bechara, member of the secular Lebanese National Resistance/Lebanese Resistance Front, captured on 7 November 1988 by the South Lebanon Army (SLA)[3] following her attempted assassination of their general, Antoine Lahad. She is framed on one side, the wounded Lahad on the other, floating on a pinkish background. Soha came close to assassinating the general, close enough to be an instant heroine, but not close enough to kill him. She was thrown into the 'living' hell-hole of El Khiam,[4] called a prison by those who knew nothing about it, while others who knew more referred to it, troublingly, as a concentration camp; colloquially here (or there) it was called something more benign: a *detention centre*. Soha was held there for ten years, six of which were spent in an isolation cell measuring 2½ x 6½ x 8 ft.

Before coming to Lebanon and during the year we spent there the Israeli occupation of the south was a predominant concern in our minds. I decided to focus one of the videotapes, *Up to the South* (Salloum & Ra'ad 1993), on this occupation.[5] The terms of its representation were inherent in discourses surrounding terrorism,[6] postcolonialism, occupation, collaboration, subjectivity, spokespeople, symbols, resistance, the land; in the history and structure of the documentary genre with regard to the representation of other cultures by the West in ethnographic enquiry and anthropological practices; and from the perspective of media practitioners. *Up to the South* challenged traditional documentary formats by positing representation itself as a politicised practice. We worked with the material drawn from our experiences of living in Lebanon, the emphasis being on a visible resistance to the acts of aggression in which documentary takes part and to the violence that is inherent in its means. The videotape developed a mediating 'language' of transposed experience in the guise of a 'reluctant documentary'. These methodologies were refined and developed further in some of the *untitled* videotapes,[7] which incorporate them in their own strategies and means, arrived at through labouring over the material collected. At some points in the working process these 'strategies and means' inform the development of the videotape/project and at others they arise from the material or process itself. Stylistically the parts and projects may appear to be drastically different from one another even within the same piece of work where an appropriateness of means is sought after, determined and utilised.

A clandestine evening in Paris

At some point in 1995 Moukhtar Kokache led me to his friend in Paris, Mireille Kassar, who arranged a clandestine screening of *Up to the South* one evening at the Institut du Monde Arabe (IMA). The IMA tries to avoid any overt embrace of politics, or at least attempts to place itself in a space of modernist neutrality; it does not recognise the impossibility of this effort or that its consequent position is one of complicity, co-dependency and conservatism. It therefore took no responsibility for the screening; the theatre space was quietly donated and one dark and stormy night we arrived to a packed house and a heated post-screening discussion. Fortuitously much of the audience was well versed in the issues with which the tape engages and a spark was generated that led to something much larger than the tape itself.

In the meantime

From 1992 onwards, concurrently with the production of the 'Lebanon' projects,[8] I gathered vast amounts of research material which during the process of accumulation became the subject of an installation, *Kan Ya Ma Kan/There was and there was not* (1995).[9] It was a transposition of a working studio, an exhausting study paralleling and exposing my projects in Lebanon. It called into question notions of history and research methodology, their role in the effacement of histories, and the mediated process inherent in the representation and (mis)understanding of another culture, in this case the construction of knowledge of the Middle East, while examining Lebanon as a site of production constructed in our collective and individual psyches. The audience was encouraged to have a hands-on

FIGURE 1: KAN YA MA KAN (DOSSIER ON BOTTOM RIGHT-HAND CORNER OF DESK)

encounter with the volumes of material in the seemingly endless threads of archives presented.[10] Although the fields and parameters were set out, viewers became part of the process, choosing their own paths, initially seduced, compelled and confronted, making decisions and in this manner being responsible for visualising and re-constructing their own cultural/political perceptions.[11]

Several months later a dossier arrives from Paris. Mireille has sent a substantial book of documents that was being used to solicit international support for the release of Soha and the other detainees of Khiam. I add it to the central desk element of *Kan Ya Ma Kan*.

The first version

1998: I am invited to participate in an exhibition to take place from October 2001 to March 2003 at the Canadian Museum of Civilization titled *The Lands Within Me: Expressions by Canadian Artists of Arab Origin*; the exhibition is to explore the themes of immigration and 'cultural intermixing'.[12] This seems a dry concept and has an opportunistic ring to it in the Canadian political climate, given the country's history of turning back asylum seekers, its escalation of closed borders (closed to people, not goods), and its less than repressed racism. There is also a renewed orientalism, or rather a neo-orientalism, at play. It is increasingly fashionable to have a token show with an Arab or Middle Eastern theme, one that avoids the complexities of subjectivity and identity. Initially I refuse to participate, but after continued requests from the curator I contemplate it further and see an opportunity to engage with a public outside the normative gallery or art museum mould and the potential for an experiment in community association. I decide to do a project dealing with concepts of movement (where it is permitted/restricted, desired or forced) in terms of specific histories, looking at something that is common to all our lives and at the base of this entity called globalisation. Subsequently I move to considerations of transition, a term/position we have devalued; the utmost prominence is usually given to the ends, both in and out of sight, of transition, while the 'in-betweenness' is ignored. This led me to focus on the notion of interstitiality, the interstitial subject and site, and the beginning of *untitled*.

untitled part 2

24 March 1999: NATO bombing of the Federal Republic of Yugoslavia (FRY) begins. I have been thinking a lot about interstitiality. Towards the end of summer I will have a break between exhibitions in Vienna and Brussels. I decide to make a trip from the top of the FRY to the bottom, taking time to visit the capital cities of each soon to be independent republic and start planning and emailing all individuals and lists I know with any connection to the region.[13] Searching through tapes and the initiation of the taping process commences at home. I start by recording conversations with a friend's mother Zenona Sava describing her survival of World War II, and Carmen Aguirre, a Chilean-Canadian actor about her struggles during the dictatorship of Augusto Pinochet and her current cultural battles in Canada. I don't know exactly what I'm searching for, but I intend to look at/record sites of emigration, places that people have left, are departing from or are immigrating to, and meet people who are living and/or theorising these threads of movement and change in trans/inter/intra-cultural settings.[14] On my way to Vienna I stop off in New York and tape Srdjan Jovanovic Weiss, an architect from Belgrade, Ammiel Alcalay, who discusses the Balkan region he knows so well, and Ella Shohat, who speaks about the colonisation of the Americas, the neo-colonial politics of the Middle East and the limits of identity-based politics. In Vienna, I tape exiles from the FRY, activists, artists and writer/theoretician Boris Buden, and finally I am on the train heading to Ljubljana, Slovenia, with subsequent stops in Zagreb, Sarajevo, Belgrade and Skopje. I offer to tape in any language but generally the preferred language of address is English. The conversations open a space for the contemplation of the present, the recent and more remote past and the implications for the future. We circle around life during and after Tito, the current reign of Milosevic and what may or will be coming. The subjects speak through the camera, through me, to some imaginary audience (Western? or somewhere else?) to formulate and send off missives, enquiries and speculations on what has happened. I have space to pause in the evenings and the between times, finding routes and transportation from person to city to new encounters. I tape these moments as well, the foggy indeterminate landscapes,[15] the jotting of notes while the bus bounces up and down, the passage through the checkpoints on new, old and reformulated borders; time and space stretch out, clarity is fleeting, elusive but not impossible. The juxtaposition of speakers stimulates patterns of thought; utterances of something this project might become, points of focus start to emerge through cycles and repetition. [DVD REF 3: VIDEO]

Eventually the conversations recorded, starting in Vancouver and ending in Skopje, were made into *untitled part 2: beauty and the east*. This videotape addresses issues of nationalism and the nation-state, alienation, the refusal and construction of political identities, ethno-fascism, the body as object and metaphor, agents, monsters and abjectness, subjective affinities and objective trusts. The subjects[16] come from a range of constituencies: im/migrants, refugees, asylum seekers, community groups, residents (permanent and transient), students, workers, cultural producers recounting experience, locating sites and events; the theorising of, and accounting for, issues at stake and associated ambient imagery form specific histories of locations, and locations of histories at the intersection of cultures in these particular places and times. The speakers are framed closely, creating a complicity with and acknowledgement of the constant framing/mediation. Moving landscapes and cityscapes are used to materialise the verbal and localise the discourse through levels of physicality, materiality and immateriality.

When finished in the southern reaches – Skopje, Macedonia, which is closer to the Middle East in feel and look then I imagined – I make my way to the airport, which is filled with NATO troops, fly to Germany[17] and take a couple of trains to Karlsruhe. The lecture I give there is on my as yet unbuilt website (rrrr.net), which could link up issues of representation, resistance and revolution and the discursive realities that enable or prevent such processes.

untitled part 1

Brussels a few days later: Mireille phones and tells me that an exhibition is being held in Paris of artworks made in Khiam and other Israeli detention centres, objects that were smuggled out over a period of ten years, and later brought out when the Red Cross was eventually permitted to visit in 1995: delicate carvings of soap, prayer beads and chess sets made from olive pits, embroideries from threads pulled from the inmates' clothes, fragile sculptures assembled from all kinds of scrounged materials and drawings made with burnt wood. These are tentative objects, clandestine carvings imbued with hope and faith. Mireille asks me to come and screen *Up to the South* at the gallery; she says Soha was released months earlier[18] and that after the screening she and Rabab (a former detainee recorded in *Up to the South*) could speak about the ongoing detentions in Khiam and Israel. It's a great surprise to find that Soha had been released; I had no prior knowledge that this was even close to being achieved. I make a deal with Mireille: if she comes to my opening we'll discuss what can be done. This could be the rare closing of a circle that started in 1992 with the work in the south. Mireille arrives and pulls me aside at the opening to mention discreetly that after the 1995 IMA screening of *Up to the South* she had instigated the formation of a committee to press for Soha's freedom and had worked, through newspaper ads in the major Paris journals and with help from activists and human rights lawyers in Europe, the Middle East and North Africa to mobilise worldwide support. Somehow the tape was complicit, adding to the momentum of the movement, a catalyst for what was undoubtedly already emerging.

A couple of days later we're in Paris. After the screening Rabab speaks about the ongoing torture and interrogation of the detainees, her present freedom, and life after Khiam. Soha discusses the continuing need to fight for the release of those left behind, the resistance to the occupation, and the struggles that are still going on. When the discussion ends she and I get away and talk over a Lebanese feast. I am reluctant, pondering whether or not to ask her to be taped. I am very ambivalent; she is being interviewed to death by the European and Arab press about the details of her captivity, the minutiae of her sur-

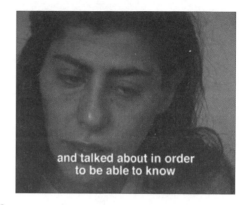

This history should be documented and preserved,

and talked about in order to be able to know

FIGURES 2 AND 3: FROM *UNTITLED PART1: EVERYTHING AND NOTHING*

viving it, the conditions in Khiam and the resistance. I can imagine her fatigue; after the ordeal of Khiam, she is faced with the pressures of being a 'living martyr'. But we get along well and so I succumb and ask; she thinks it's no big deal and invites me for breakfast the next day.

I go to her small dorm room on the edge of Paris (she is studying international law at the Sorbonne), not much bigger than her cell but with one large window. She sits on her bed. I ask her about the distance lived between Khiam and Paris and Beirut and Paris, about what she left in Khiam and what she brought with her, about flowers and how she never puts them in water [DVD REF 4: VIDEO]; about how it felt for her to be in such demand now and who is Soha Bechara? [DVD REF 5: VIDEO]. I don't ask her specifically about the torture she underwent or the trauma of detention. I am more interested in herself, her subjectivity and agency, her will to survive or, as she 'corrects' me, to live, how she enunciates her history and position, how she accounts for all that has happened, her philosophy of resistance then and what it means now on a daily basis. [DVD REF 6: VIDEO] I tape her before breakfast (kishk, a Lebanese yogurt and bulghar soup, something I grew up on and loved on special Sunday mornings). Afterwards, I felt there was something there in the tape but I didn't know what. It wasn't until six months to a year later, when Soha's text was translated, that I could read what had transpired. I knew that in those short hours a trust had developed, enabling her to accept my mediation. The material that I recorded of the time spent with her is not precious; it's just time, a conversation, and intense intimacy at a close and unbreachable distance.

One important element clarified by both the interview with Soha and the tapes filmed in the former Yugoslavia was the specificity of theme; the comprehension that the underlying thread of interstitiality could form the definite article or the object of this indefinite study, each part of the project addressing this in its own appropriate manner.

Figuring resistance

Upon first glance *untitled part 1: everything and nothing* appears unremarkable, shot and apparently edited out of one continuous take: a person on a bed speaking directly to the camera, the filmmaker behind the camera conversing with her. The tape only gradually becomes disarming; the viewer commits to several minutes of the conversation and an intimate connection is fashioned between politics and subjectivity. The engagement is latent but is carried relentlessly; this is one instance of the tape's subtle forms of resistance, a refusal to give in to the gratification of immediacy. More explicit references to various modes of resistance are made as the tape unfolds. With Soha it is necessary to look at her image as both a figure of resistance and a figure of *the* resistance, occupied by a history that is still being played out. This history grew into a near mythology and was used by contradictory forces to justify their aims. Her imagistic strength is superseded only by her actual life, making it even more problematic to try to do a piece with her and also a critical reading of her representational 'over exposure'. Her unwavering identification with the resistance (she expressed no critical relationship to it) helped her persevere; she claims a history of her own that is part and parcel of the secular resistance.[DVD REF 6: VIDEO] Soha is acutely aware of her role, her image and her mission, part of which is *talking about it*, a responsibility to speak out to a viewer anticipated but yet to be named. The (surviving) martyr's narrative is also ever-present, an overexposed and overshadowing structure. I try to permeate these layers by interruptions in the cadence with our in-between moments of banter, the immediacy of the medium, a specificity of language, technical denotations, structural breaks, time signified and a malleability of the image. [DVD REF 2: VIDEO] [DVD REF 4: VIDEO] [DVD REF 6: VIDEO]

Approaching distance

I asked Soha what she left behind and what she brought from Khiam to Beirut and Paris. [DVD REF 1: VIDEO] She answered: 'I left everything, and I left nothing, at the same time … I left martyrs who are still there, imprisoned by the Israelis, even as corpses. I left them but at the same time I didn't leave them…' There is a certain geographical distance involved here: Khiam, Beirut, Paris and the miles I traveled to meet Soha. She discusses what distance teaches and whether she is closer to the detainees now, thousands of kilometres away, or when she was in the cell next door. [DVD REF 7: VIDEO] The paradox of distance is also enacted linguistically, used as a trope and a means of approach. I pose the questions in a broken third language, French, fractured not only by my minimal fluency but more importantly by the intricate interior formulation needed to piece together the precise question, after her response in Arabic (practically unintelligible to me). She replies in French when the dialogue is less formal, during the in-between moments such as the discussion around a possible title for a project that wasn't yet a project, a tape that wasn't yet conceived. [DVD REF 2: VIDEO] She waits while I piece my language together; she is the speaking subject, I am the listener, except for these instances and for the tape where the subjects are other. This distance could also be seen as a form of productive alienation, perception (recognition of gaps, or the impossibility of understanding without which there would be no other), as constructive disjunction and as a provisional or analogous response to difference. The lifetimes of detention, the epoch of occupation, the period of shooting, editing time, 'real-time' videotape recorded, time spent with the footage and the factor of translation: distance is rooted in temporality, the two interchangeable at times. Temporal displacement is always required for an intelligent response; temporality provides a space for a visceral closeness throughout the tape, connecting viewers to subject to self.

The challenge of intimacy

Soha speaks quietly and directly into the camera (to a *listener*); this is juxtaposed against her silent self-listening (and her image, which is never silent). Some are unsettled by the intimacy of the encounter between subject and listener(s) (see Allan 2002), others find an empathy. Both reactions are engaged and complicit, but only the latter can lead to a type of awareness or consciousness. Video enhances, pixel by pixel, the emotive quality of the image and the nearness of the voice, lavalier mic at throat level, neck to ear through the encapsulated space, channeled into the privacy of headphones or loudspeakers; breathing mixed into the breathing of gallery/theatre (single-channel) viewers, their expressions and silences entwined. Intimacy is a determining cause in the possible impossibilities of representing the subject of resistance.

untitled part 3

Late in 2000, while rough editing the first two installation tapes, I realise that if articulating the condition of interstitiality as a subjective, political, or geographical state is to be the current focus of the project, it will be necessary to include a component on the Palestinians in Lebanon who have been residing in refugee camps of one form or another for close to sixty years. Most of them exist in a realm of interstitiality, unable to return to Palestine or to their villages (if they exist still) inside or outside the green line of Israel's borders. They are barred from working legally in over seventy professions in Lebanon and unable to obtain residency rights or citizenship (even if they desired to do so). Unable to return or to move forward, weighed down by their personal experiences of dispossession, several generations live in a state of permanent temporariness.

September 2000: I videotape in six refugee camps from the north to the south of Lebanon, the conversations being predominantly with Palestinian refugees from 1948, though some are with subsequent generations. The formal conventions are similar to *untitled part 2*, though the location and ambient imagery consist of more close-up and medium-range shots in the tight exterior and interior confines of the camps, as well as abstractions of flags, bodies during demonstrations and parades of martyrs. The conversations range from accounts of loss and displacement to memories of place, perceptions of absence and the violence of representation. In the first instalment of *untitled part 3a* I took excerpts from conversations with two elder Palestinians who had been living in refugee camps in Lebanon since 1948, Nameh Hussein Suleiman (in Baddawi camp, near Tripoli) and Abdel Majid Fadl Ali Hassan (in Bourg al Barajinah Camp, near Beirut). Nameh recounts leading her siblings on foot to exile in Lebanon (a monumental moment lasting years) and their present situation in a local and global context. Abdel Majid discusses absence and presence, recounting an eloquent poem by the ruins of his house in Palestine, which he was permitted to visit after his first thirty years of dispossession. During the Battle of Jenin in March and April 2002, I felt an overwhelming urge to say something, to make something; I took the central part of Abdel Majid's audio clip, where he locates the trees on the property as the audio/text for the single-channel tape, *untitled part 3b: (as if) beauty never ends*. [DVD REF 8: VIDEO] With ambient videotape – orchids blooming, plants growing, raw footage of the 1982 massacre at the Sabra and Shatila refugee camps in Lebanon,

- and then it asked me about

FIGURE 4: FROM *UNTITLED PART 3B: (AS IF) BEAUTY NEVER ENDS*

Times Square, Hubble space imagery, the Visible Body crosscuts and abstract shots of slow-motion water – this is a reflection on the past, its present context and its foreboding sense of the future. The tape permeates into an essay on dystopia in contemporary times. Working directly, viscerally and metaphorically it provides an elegiac response to the Palestinian dispossession. This material will ultimately be edited into the feature-length *untitled part 3*, a personalised confrontation of the Palestinian dispersion, the predicament of refugees (the representational equivalent of the interstitial state) and ethnic cleansing on a daily basis. This part of *untitled* continues the attempt to come to terms with the problem of representing something that is made unrepresentable by banal or sensational overexposure, lack of exposure, misrepresentation (to the point of absurdity), effacement, omission and repression.

Inside

Four parts of *untitled* (1, 2, 3a and 3b), and the three appendices (i, ii and iii) come together in the installation, extending the issues raised in the individual parts, building further relationships between the tapes and constructing an environment in which the spheres of histories are situated in a web of connectivity. It is a sculptural space that presents the effect of walking into the videotape itself: a stillness, a silence of moving images juxtaposed, flowing and colliding, waves of scan lines, an active meditativeness picturing the interstitial. Choices are made: to sit or stand, to use the headphones, closing off exterior sound and linking to the audio feed and the voice speaking from the image before you. The space is fixed and framed and the act of witnessing becomes confessional. The tapes and installation take time; they are demanding. Each part is projected on to its own screen area or emanates from a monitor in an atmosphere of visual collusion, collaboration, contextualisation, critical interference and mutual existence.

Telling

Narrative is mobile, travelling like well-worn suitcases, used often or stored and opened only occasionally to reveal cherished contents. Telling and retelling, writing and rewriting, narrative is appealing to use but, potentially formulaic and unprovocative, it is not to be relied upon as a convention. I am cautious about giving in to its authority. The narratives I'm interested in are either open or broken. Soha's conversation is broken, much more so than the English subtitles would suggest. She is cyclical in her dialogue, yet very clear.[19] She speaks elliptically; how can she speak otherwise? To describe her position there must be a certain amount of circling around the subject – herself – within the confines of the way in which 'resistance' situates her. The way she remembers is the way memory works, filling in gaps at each turn, writing in the spaces, reading the past from the context of the present, rewriting and speaking. With hours of unused videotape from other conversations, I've often thought about combining and rewriting the most absorbing parts in a script with a dense voice/textual overlay, intermittently reverting to a speaking subject on camera. I will incorporate this approach in the long format of *untitled part 3*.

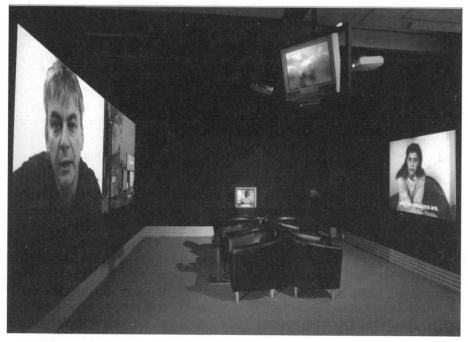

FIGURE 5: *UNTITLED* (INSTALLATION DETAIL), MUSEUM OF CIVILIZATION, 2001–03

VIDEO INSTALLATION AS AN ACTIVE ARCHIVE   173

FIGURE 6: FROM *UNTITLED PART 2: BEAUTY AND THE EAST*

A living archive

To amass an archive is a leap of faith, not in preservation but in the belief that there will be someone to use it, that the accumulation of these histories will continue to live, that there will be listeners. The taping of subjects is a collaborative process; we are both aware of the medium, of the dialogical aspects of the work, of transferring meaning and of the act of translating and editing that is at the core of subjects' expressions and my mediation. The material itself has a sense of 'living', a 'presentness', a relevance, excerpts of life resting in their context of extraction. A collaboration also exists with the viewer of the archive, taking on, unknowingly perhaps, a responsibility for the representations that are consumed. The viewer becomes part of the extended archive, collecting, preserving, sharing stories that could possibly disappear, and neglecting others that are disappearing. The archive is untitled, as is memory, as are the accounts of the subjects who refuse to be reducible. The individual parts of *untitled* follow this practice in their refusal of commodification. In the archive (*and* outside it) all viewing is incomplete; this is a living entity that rumbles along indefinitely, growing in stops and starts, mutating. You can walk into the vaults; there are files, stacks and shelves of material. The records are static but movement is written all over them.

Back to interstitiality

untitled seeks to articulate the conditions of living and moving, subjectivity strewn between or through borders, nationalisms, ideologies, polarities of culture, geography or histories. The visible act of concretising and valuing this interstitiality occurs while reconstituting and re-presenting the ephemeral and transitory demarcations in which it resides. These demarcations or, better yet, zones of being, are situated in the contested and conflicted notions of homeland, nation, diaspora, exile, travel, assimilation, refuge, native and other. Confronted as standard or anomaly, the subject may choose to intersect, suture, overlay, ameliorate, redefine, morph, hybridise, separate, erase, augment or rupture these constructions in a form of resistance or liberation from antagonising forces. Fixing the temporal, space and time become conflated. A sense of the momentary (living between or during events) stretches from a point of being into permanency, temporally or spatially bounded, which, as interstitial subjects know, can occupy significant moments or portions of our lives, and in some cases our entire lives.

Interstitial space can be seen as productive and tactical, not merely residing in the traumatic, devalued in the dysfunctional, rendered as anxiety, tentativeness or lack. *untitled* subjectively theorises interstitiality as a concrete entity, a place of living or a space/time of resistance or change; it explodes this notion, this site into discursive areas where it can be seen as a constructive space with increasingly important relevance to our public and private lives. Living the ephemeralisation of the fiction known as the concrete and concretising the ephemeral are two interrelated positions of these sometimes fragile, sometimes more than real polarities between which the interstitial subject or state exists – that state which we all occupy, more or less.

Ongoing/going on

> What I have seen of your work fascinates me especially because it insinuates a prelude to a much more complex politics, a preparation for something to come. The works that engage me, sometimes with a healthy degree of trepidation, create a space somewhere between a failure of politics and the agonized resolve to persist. And not just the persistence of a person or people but of an idea also; in other words, ideas too have their own biography.
> – Jawad Ali[20]

My methodological focus is one of constant research, rethinking and augmentation. This is intrinsic to all stages of production; reworking and learning from the material gathered leads the project instead of vice versa. I test out multiple forms and structures, metonymical chains, and formulate a detailed layout accounting for every frame of the piece. The editing stage is utilised as a forum of mediation and construction, where unanticipated and meaningful juxtapositions can be formed and the structure of the piece tweaked to its final shape. None of this is arbitrary, although it is occasionally affected by chance. The process becomes the product leading to the end result.

The 'syntax' structure developed is evident. The dialectical relationship of the speaker and the spoken is highlighted, the speech laid bare and layered between the story, the field of images, the suggested frames and the butted fictive and documentary process. Difference, articulated in and around the literal and metaphorical spaces of displacement and dwelling is viewed as a site of crucial social meanings rather than an extension of (an)other locale/space or subjective relationship. It is a dialectic of experience engaging a viscerality of substance.

These collaborations speak for themselves, the subjects in them speaking for both of us, I myself trying to avoid speaking for others. At times both paradox and solution, they are problematic and potentially full of possibilities for questioning and investigating each of our positions, for juxtaposing myself and the ostensible subjects (in front of the lens), the actual subject being both of us, investing in intersubjectivity, speaking in collaboration/conjunction, speaking through our articulations and mediations.

untitled has concerns common to all its parts, addressed at different times in diverse ways. Each part has its own themes which are brought to the forefront, like a juggler who drops some of the objects circling to focus on the ones in hand. These themes include the disintegrating nation/body, body as nation, nation as metaphor, dysfunction and crisis, abject geographies, agents and monsters, ethno-fascism, displacement and dispossession, the self in interstitial space, refusal as a claim of the subject, and the perseverance of will. A key focus of the project is borders, physical and metaphorical, imaginary and ontological; how they are constructed and defined and how they inscribe, control, restrict, shield and screen us. Borders are seen as barriers, margins and occasionally zones of autonomy. Their emplacement, reflecting apparent necessity or uselessness, belies their histories and permanence/impermanence, porousness (to the movement of goods and capital) and impermeability (to the movement of peoples). When meaning slips around and through borders, frontiers are crossed and new associations made; without that movement, the body public disintegrates.

Inherent and critical references to conventional documentary (and ethnographic representations) are woven into the tapes as a subtext. Some of these are made visible through the structure, elements, techniques and aesthetics utilised. Only available light is used; interior location shots, public settings and abstracted direct imagery are layered underneath and around the textual elements. There is no detached authoritative voice dictating what to see or think. Asynchronous voices are edited from the material recorded. This audio carries its own content (and form), which parallels the video component, forming relationships of the oblique, directional and expansionary, delineating and speculative. Working outside an essentialising gaze, the audio/text/image configurations selectively release levels and layers of information from shifting positions for specific purposes and at times for specific publics, with more vernacular or fluent 'readings' dependent on language and affiliation. Entry points are multiple, as are means of access. No monikers (restrictive forms of identification) of the subjects are used; there is no overdetermined representation of the sites, no artifice of 'objectivity' or naturalising discourse of seamless realism, no 'grand' summarising narrative or imposition of closure. With no beginning or end texts to package and objectify the tapes, each is part of one continuous endless whole; confused at times and semi-raw, the project incorporates this even as the end product is less raw and more finished. The tape/installation's unwieldiness is analogical to the provisionality of the process.

A relationship to reality can only be arrived at through the subjective. The basis of objectivity is where subjectivity is placed and how it is revealed in the issues at stake and the circumstances of the lives lived. *untitled* is situated firmly between genres on the margins of the margins in an unstable and unsettling placement, establishing this in-between state as a critical position to elucidate a context or contexts, look at historic and present-day realities and engage in the transference of lived experiences.

This project renders different forms of resistance: the figure of the resistance fighter struggling for self-determination and liberation; resistance in a broader sense as part of a daily struggle against a predetermining hegemony; the act of staying on the ground or in a more domestic sphere and working within; and survival as an act of resistance. I attempt to have my work function as a form of resistance, which affects social, political or personal change. The pivotal relationship is that of individual to community. This is an intrinsic part of all forms of resistance (and identity). The acts of taking apart, building and dismantling to build again is more than an exercise in laying bare the elements, process and motivations of power. It is an attempt to articulate the conditions of a subject's individual life and the forces that confront our individual and common realities.

Opening a fissure/filling a void

In the triangulation of histories and positions between countries, cultures and subjectivities, *untitled* continues to build on previous production and curatorial projects of mine (see Salloum 1998, 2001a, 2001b), aiming to implode existing barriers, chipping away at the structure until it dissipates, identifying a space to locate difference in forms of articulation, filling these (intentional and unintentional) gaps in representation, intervening in these spaces between spaces, messing them up with deliberated contentions, then leaving others to clean them up and to refine and reflect upon them. Massive amounts of material and a density of meaning are imperative; an exigency of excess is required in the demand to be heard/listened to, in the opening of spaces for silenced or negated voices to emerge. These are politicised spaces where one is challenged to respond (or challenging responses) and one's perceptions and understandings are confronted. These openings are productive interstices where possibilities exist to engage, encounter, reflect and act upon the forces that act upon us all the days of our lives.

Is it enough sometimes to provoke and at other times to provide a meditative space claiming a calmness in the midst of anxiety? It is in a way a set-up, the polarities contesting each other to create an active space in which the viewer can be placed, a space that is questioning, unresolved, at times lucid, always open, but open with angst, pleasure, contemplation, anger, frustration or sadness. These projects often fall between the cracks of genre and of attention. There is a price to be paid for not heeding cautionary tales, for breaking rules, pushing the conservatism and limits of institutions, providing layers of realities, tactile, juxtaposed in correlation and contradiction with dominant motifs: a price of denial and censure.

Histories of the self

Who are we allowed to be? Who allows us to be who we are? Where is this power usurped from? What constructs us as human beings, what informs our psyche, what shapes how we perceive each other and the world around us? This is a question not of identity but of subjectivity and agency, where we are placed, where we choose to position ourselves, how the world acts upon us and how we act upon the world. Place is defined by the people who live it (or have lived it) daily; without this, there is no place, no sense of place and no geographic local(e) existing in the real or the imaginary.

Many of us want to claim a space for fluidity of self, an identity that is determined contextually, a subjectivity that is unimpeded. Others seek to hold on to or regain a land, a nation, with all that entails. The right to be self-inscribed spans a flexible local identity and the trans-local, the particularities of each, the movement between the two, the split and the interconnectedness, and the usurpation of either. One searches to make sense of things, to have something static to grab on to, whether a set of images, or beliefs, or ways of perceiving which are grounded in the real. [DVD REF 9: VIDEO] This project's fragments of narrative have a coherency and a positioning that question the grand narrative(s) that put/set things in order; it aims to deeply disrupt/interrupt unified notions of nationalism, empire and identity. These are experienced through the body. [DVD REF 3: VIDEO] We are all transnational subjects, entwined globally, in assault, complicit with, directly or indirectly affecting all, at risk of being affected by each other at any time, both those we choose to identify with and those we ignore. As viewers and consumers of culture(s), we need to challenge our existing assumptions and preconceptions. We are implicated within these constructions; our histories are present there and here, our projections firmly entrenched.

Re-presenting accounts of experience over a range of locations and contexts, the act of videotaping is used as a direct way of tracing lives, revelations of the self and the realities around us, as well as a tool for looking at issues of representation, governing paradigms and the construction of meaning. The subjective enunciatory experience is central to this. Working, from very local positions, with representations that respect the individual subject and are immersed in the complexities of culture(s), models can be developed that confront and theorise the representation of politics and the politics of representation as part of the mandate and mode of production. This critique of all hierarchic forms of information, corporatism and systems of overarching authority is part of a larger analysis of political and economic strategies and the effects of corporate globalism and the military-industrial complex. This project provides a heterogeneous engagement with the facilitation of a means of contemplation that can counter the imposition of consent.

untitled brings the intensely personal space of the dialogue moment into the context of the intrinsic social and political site, a different process for each subject but with overlapping and overarching points of contention, correspondence, senses of place, notions of community, domains of discursivity, legacies of conflict and capital, disenfranchisement and ties of transnational concurrence. This project is not about difference per se but about separateness and a connective web. Sometimes I wonder how I carry a 'presentness' of home with me, working where others found and lost theirs. How can one, building in the political discrepancies of the present, move forward without ignoring the traces of the past? In the words of Soha Bechara:

> We have no boundaries. Our boundaries should be the love that continues forward. If we want to define that movement, it goes beyond acceptance, beyond tolerance, it is the capacity to reach an empathy with the other in a way that encompasses everyone, democratically, with liberty, equality and justice, and it's the creating and maintaining of a system that asserts itself without attacking, and without assaulting the other on a daily basis. [DVD REF 6: VIDEO]

Notes

1   The installation's title derives from one segment of the interview with Soha Bechara in *untitled part 1: everything and nothing*. [DVD REF 1: VIDEO] The subtitle derives from another segment of the interview. [DVD REF 2: VIDEO] The installation also has a pre-title, which changes for each version, for example, *everything and nothing and other works from the ongoing video installation, 'untitled', 1999–2004*.

2   During the year spent in Lebanon over 200 hours of Hi-8, Regular 8 and VHS videotape were recorded and collected, thousands of photographs made and half a ton of documents, objects and found film salvaged. From this were produced two videotapes, *This is Not Beirut* (1994) and *Up to the South/Talaeen a Junuub* (1993); an installation, *Kan Ya Ma Kan/There was and there was not* (1995); and a photographic series, *(sites +) demarcations* (1992–94). We also set up a media studio in which people produced videoworks of their own.

3   A predominately Christian right-wing militia created, controlled and funded by Israel to administer south Lebanon and give a Lebanese façade to the occupation of the south. A surrogate force such as the SLA had been planned by prominent figures in the Israeli government since the early 1950s; see Rokach (1982) and Sharett (1996).

4   For purposes of this text El Khiam (or Al Khyam) detention centre is referred to as Khiam, which is also the name of the village in south Lebanon where the centre is located. Set up by the Israeli Defence Forces (IDF) in 1982, it was administered by the SLA under IDF supervision. Khiam detainees were not held under due process of law, detentions were arbitrary at the whim of the IDF or the SLA. There were 150–300 detainees at any one time, ranging from 15 to 60 years old, detained for periods of three days to ten years. Torture inflicted upon the detainees included electric shock, beatings, solitary confinement, and long-term sleep deprivation. Khiam was liberated along with most of south Lebanon in May 2000.

5   The Israeli occupation (1978–2000) of south Lebanon was a very sophisticated form of terror and colonisation. The occupied area covered about 500 sq. miles/1500 sq. km., approximately 10 per cent of the country, fluctuating in size according to the political climate in Israel and generally containing between 1,500 and 3,000 Israeli soldiers. Approximately 180,000 Lebanese lived in the occupation zone.

6   The terms 'terrorism' or 'terrorist' are assigned to those with whose actions we disagree. We have stopped looking critically at the historical context in which they are used; reinvented, they serve to obscure the roots of political conflict and to nullify a multitude of ways of thinking and living resistance.

7   The *untitled* videotape components are: *untitled part 1: everything and nothing* (2002); *untitled part 2: beauty and the east* (2003); *untitled part 3b: (as if) beauty never ends* (2004); *appendix i: lands* (2001); *appendix ii: clouds* (2001); *appendix iii: other* (2001).

8   See n. 2.

9   For full description and installation images, see <http://www.111101.net/Artworks/jaycesalloum/> and <http://www.lot.at/politics/contributions/s_jayce1.htm> [Both accessed 10 February 2005].

10 Museum guards revealed that it was the first time they had been asked to encourage visitors to handle displayed objects, leaf through files, remove dossiers from the walls and shelves and make themselves 'at home' in an exhibition. They also admitted they enjoyed the comfort of the sofas while taking their lunch.

11 The *untitled* installation follows on from this but inverts the relationship of initial form and content. It is not modeled on the viewing of art (i.e. an exhibition of paintings) but on a subjective approach to re-

search/reading of an active archive, or sets of walk-in, expanding systems of files, CDs or hypertexted DVD-ROMs.

12 Following their viewing of the exhibits, my video installation *untitled* among them, the museum authorities attempted to cancel the exhibition, but were forced by public outcry and political and media pressure to reconsider, although they reneged on a commitment to an international tour. They also closed the museum's Mid-East/South-West Asia department, the director proclaiming that he was not interested in 'conflictual histories'.

13 The former Syndicate (before it morphed into Spectre and the *new* Syndicate) and Nettime lists figured most prominently in making connections; see <http://www.nettime.org> [Accessed 13 February 2005].

14 In post-war zones I found temporary spaces open to seemingly countless possibilities. At such a time, when everyone is scrambling for survival and laws and regulations have yet to come inevitably into place, sense of some kind is often made of the recent past.

15 These became the predominant footage in the installation tape *appendix i: lands*, a silent projection of images shot from bus/train rides and shown next to the *untitled part 2* projection screen, alternatively colliding and running parallel to the literal and metaphorical references of the speakers. From very close croppings of detailed edges and shapes to distant views disclosing colour and form, these shots provide associative imagery: cityscapes and landscapes, ribbons of rivers, dishevelled fields, arrays of forests and rolling hills and valleys blanketed in heavy fog, where only occasional glimpses of ephemeral objects and abstract homes/houses pierce through.

16 Among those featured are Boris Buden, Marina Grzinic, Eda Cufer, Renata Salecl, Dunja Blazevic, Zarana Papic, Slavica Indzevska, Mihajlo Acimovic, Ella Shohat, Ammiel Alcalay and Carmen Aguirre.

17 I add to the footage clouds taped from airplane windows, mostly after take-off and before landing, when you pass through the layer of clouds into the sunlight or descend into what waits below; the intermediary stage that suspends you for a moment, distant shots and close views, disintegrating forms and substantive yet fleeting shapes floating on ground and/or space(s). These are used in the installation tape *untitled appendix ii: clouds*, depicted via a silent monitor hung at the entrance to the space at a height simulating airport arrival and departure monitors.

18 Soha was released from the detention centre on 3 September 1998.

19 Five translators provided me with fairly different interpretations of her Arabic account upon which I drew when writing the English subtitles.

20 Co-founder of the Levantine Cultural Centre, Los Angeles, who moderated a screening of my video work titled *everything and nothing and other works, from the ongoing video project, 'untitled' (1999–2002)*, in the context of the programme 'In/tangible Cartographies: New Arab Video', held at UCLA Television and Film Archive Theatre, November 2002.

Bibliography

Allan, M. (2002) 'The Location of Lebanon: Portraits and Places in the Videography of Jayce Salloum' *Parachute*, 108: 165–177.

Dion, F., M. Hankwitz, W. Ra'ad and J. Salloum, J. (1996) *There was and there was not (Kan Ya Ma Kan)*. Montréal: Optica Gallery.

Marks, L. et al. (2003) *The Lands Within Me: Expressions by Canadian Artists of Arab Origin*. Gatineau: Canadian Museum of Civilization. Available from: <http://www.civilisations.ca/cultur/cespays/payinte.

html> [Accessed 10 February 2005].

Rokach, L. (1982) *Israel's Sacred Terrorism: A Study Based on Moshe Sharett's Personal Diary and Other Documents*. Belmont: Association of Arab-American University Graduates. Available at <http://www.radioislam.org/historia/zionism/rokach.html> [Accessed 3 March 2005].

Salloum, J. (1992-94) *(sites +) demarcations*. Lebanon [Photo installation].

_____ (1995) *Kan Ya Ma Kan/There was and there was not*. [Mixed media installation]. Available from: http://www.111101.net/Artworks/JayceSalloum/index.html?http:///www.111101.net/Artworks/JayceSalloum/kanyamakan/index.html [Accessed 10 February 2005]; <http://www.lot.at/politics/contributions/s_jayce1.htm> [Accessed 10 February 2005].

_____ (1998) *...east of here ... (upon arrival)*, in J. Salloum (ed.) *...east of here ... (re)imagining the 'orient'*. Toronto: YYZ Artists' Outlet.

_____ (2001a) 'History of our present: new arab film and video', in P. Willemsen (ed.) *Argos Festival 2001*. Brussel: Argos Editions. Available at <http://www.rouge.com.au/1/arab.html> [Accessed 14 February 2005].

_____ (2001b) *in/tangible cartographies: new arab video*. Amsterdam: WWVF. Available at <http://www.wwvf.nl/2001/0newarabvideo.htm> [Accessed 14 February 2005].

Salloum, J. and M. Hankwitz (2002) 'Occupied Territories: Mapping the Transgressions of Cultural Terrain'. *Framework*, Fall, 43 (2): 85–103; reprinted in A. Kafetsi (ed.) (2003) *Testimonies: Between Fiction and Reality*. Athens: National Museum of Contemporary Art, 163–82. Available from: <http://www.111101.net/Writings/Author/Jayce_Salloum/> [Accessed 3 March 2005].

Sharett, M. (1996) *Personal Diaries*, trans. Ahmad Khalifeh. Beirut: Institute for Palestine Studies.

Videography

Up to the South/Talaeen a Junuub (1993), Jayce Salloum and Walid Ra'ad. Lebanon, videotape 60 mins. Available from <http://www.lot.at/politics/contributions/s_jayce2.htm>; <http://www.vdb.org/smackn.acgi$tapedetail?TALAEENAJU>;<http://www.111101.net/Artworks/JayceSalloum/index.html?http://www.111101.net/Artworks/JayceSalloum/uptothesouth/index.html>.

This is Not Beirut (1994), Jayce Salloum. Lebanon/New York, videotape 49 mins. Available from: <http://www.vdb.org/smackn.acgi$tapedetail?THISISNOTB>; <http://www.111101.net/Artworks/JayceSalloum/index.html?http://www.111101.net/Artworks/JayceSalloum/thisisnotbeirut/index.html> .

untitled part 1: everything and nothing (1999–2002), Jayce Salloum. France/Canada, videotape 40 mins 40 secs. Available from: <http://www.111101.net/Artworks/JayceSalloum/index.html?http://www.111101.net/Artworks/JayceSalloum/untitled/index.html>; <http://www.vdb.org/smackn.acgi$tapedetail?UNTITLEDPA>.

untitled part 2: beauty and the east (1999–2003), Jayce Salloum. Former Yugoslavia (Bosnia-Herzegovina, Croatia, Macedonia, Serbia and Montenegro, Slovenia), Austria, USA, Canada, videotape 50 mins 15 secs. Available from: <http://www.vdb.org/smackn.acgi$tapedetail?UNTITLEDPA_002>; <http://www.111101.net/Artworks/JayceSalloum/index.html?http://www.111101.net/Artworks/JayceSalloum/untitled/index.html>.

untitled part 3b: (as if) beauty never ends ... (2002–04), Jayce Salloum. Lebanon/Canada, videotape 11 mins 22 secs. Available from: <http://www.111101.net/Artworks/JayceSalloum/index.html?http://www.111101.net/Artworks/JayceSalloum/untitled/index.html>.

untitled appendix i: lands (2001), Jayce Salloum. Former Yugoslavia (Bosnia-Herzegovina, Croatia, Macedonia, Serbia and Montenegro, Slovenia), Austria, USA, Canada, videotape 20 mins silent loop. Available from: http://www.civilisations.ca/cultur/cespays/images/pay2_20p5.jpg.

untitled appendix ii: clouds (2001), Jayce Salloum from various aeroplane flights, videotape 15 mins 35 secs silent loop]. Available from: <http://www.civilisations.ca/cultur/cespays/images/pay2_20p5.jpg>.

untitled appendix iii: other (2001), Jayce Salloum. Austria, Germany, Macedonia, videotape 6 mins silent loop.

Video Distribution

Argos, Werfstraat 13, Brussel B-1000, Belgium, ph: (32) 2 229-0003, fx: 223-7331, info@argosarts.org, www.argosarts.org

Heure Exquise!, B.P. 113-59370 Mons En Baroeul, France ph:(33)20-04-95-74, exquise@nordnet.fr, www.exquise.org

Lux, 3rd Flr, 18 Shacklewell Ln, London E8 2EZ, England, ph: 44 207 503 3980, info@lux.org.uk, www.lux.org.uk

Video Data Bank, 112 S. Michigan Ave, Chicago, IL 60603, (312) 345-3550, fx: (312) 541-8073, info@vdb.org, www.vdb.org

Video Out, 1965 Main St., Vancouver, BC, Canada, V5T 3C1 ph:(604)872-8337, videoout@telus.net, www.videoout.ca

V Tape, 401 Richmond St. W., #452, Toronto, Ont., Canada M5V3A8, ph:(416) 351-1317, distribution@vtape.org, www.vtape.org

TEXTUALISING RADIO PRACTICE: SOUNDING OUT A CHANGING IRELAND

Harry Browne and Chinedu Onyejelem

HOME FROM HOME: IMMIGRATION AND THE IRISH MEDIA

This chapter addresses a combined documentary and book project, *Home from Home*, being undertaken by Harry Browne, a journalist, lecturer and Irish citizen born in Italy and raised in the United States, and Chinedu Onyejelem, a migrant cultural producer, journalist and naturalised Irish citizen from Nigeria. The collaborators have previously worked together on the *Irish Times*, where Browne was a member of staff and Onyejelem, then a recent migrant, was exploring his opportunities in Irish journalism. They continue to work together (Browne on a part-time basis) on the weekly 'multicultural' newspaper edited and published by Onyejelem, *Metro Eireann*.[1]

The changing ethnic constituencies of the population are among the most dramatic developments to affect the economic, religious and social life of Ireland since the early 1990s. A number of efforts, journalistic and academic, have been made to summarise and comment upon this phenomenon, but most of them have hinged on the question of 'racism';[2] *Home from Home* is among the first wholly devoted to the stories and views of those who have lived through and embodied those changes[3] – predominantly immigrants themselves, but also members of minority groups who were in Ireland prior to the 'Celtic Tiger' economic boom that started in the mid-1990s, and other Irish-born people who have been closely associated with the changes, their causes and their effects through work and/or activism.

To initiate an essentially public project such as this one requires an engagement with and understanding of the wider discourse about immigration, race and 'intercultural-ism' (the term often now preferred to 'multiculturalism') that exists within Irish society, especially in its public spheres. *Home from Home* is intended to be a populist interven-tion with widespread media publicity and direct access to the airwaves through its radio incarnation. Radio, the most technologically adaptable approach to such a project, is also the most important medium or sphere in Ireland both for popular discourse on issues of public importance and for the narration of personal stories.

The project draws upon one-to-two-hour interviews with at least forty people, chosen to be as representative as such a small 'sample' can be with regard to gender, economic po-sition, ethnic origin and language (translators are used as needed). The interviews range from biographical detail to political outlook and all points between. Rather than adver-tising for interviewees, we proceed via the journalistic method, whereby contacts beget contacts. For example, a chance encounter on a Kerry hillside resulted in an interview between former colleagues Browne and Hester Storm, which moves across many shared experiences and is rather awkwardly and audibly pervaded by a sense of friendly 'catch-ing-up'. [DVD REF 1: AUDIO] This might well have been disastrous if the interview were being presented as a coherent whole; it posed fewer difficulties in light of the editorial methodology outlined below. Nonetheless, this sort of *ad hoc* sourcing of subjects clearly has dangers, in terms of yielding 'findings' based on an essentially closed, albeit large, circle of subjects. Care is taken in this respect, and such findings as we present will be duly contingent and particular, avoiding unsupportable generalisation.

The book will not present the interviews serially but will use excerpts, ranging generally from about forty to four hundred words, arranged in thematic chapters; this chapter structure will, in turn, generate thematic programmes for a radio series. In as much as the project crosses media, it attempts to adopt a single editorial strategy for both book and audio form; radio audiences should, for the most part, be able to 'read along' by referring to the book. The idea is to get a number of 'voices' (at least eight per chapter/programme) talking about a particular subject or category of experience, implicitly developing, commenting upon and even contradicting each other. Such a method should allow for certain 'big picture' ideas to emerge organically, while at the same time clearly emphasising the diversity, complexity and subjectivity of people's experiences.

This has a significant bearing methodologically. The fundamental building block of the finished product will be words rather than voices; excerpts will be joined together based on what the interviewees say rather than how they say it. This dictates that auditory effects conjuring particular spaces will be absent, or at least homogenised as much as possible, and even what might conventionally be regarded as the dangers to listenership of, for example, a series of heavily-accented voices in succession will be ignored. The rhythm, too, will be uneven, with clips ranging in length from only ten seconds to several minutes. This should not be seen as the subordination of the form of this project to the literary one; on the contrary, the concept of succeeding and contending voices is one that can be said to derive from the tradition of the radio documentary more than from any print medium. German documentarist Helmut Kopetsky believes 'that the competition between strong opinions is a vital and driving force in feature programmes' (cited in Crook 1999: 213).

Interviewees will be clearly identified except where legal or personal considerations dictate anonymity; we envisage too that only 'legal or personal' considerations would lead to any significant editorial alteration from the transcribed interviews, though these would of course be subject in general to some cutting and 'smoothing' to ensure they are lively and readable. But the dual-media format does place some limitations on that process. The more limited editing possible in audio as compared to print helps to keep the finished product 'honest'; for example, when Haseeb Ahmed from Pakistan talks about his experience working in the Holiday Inn, the result is necessarily and awkwardly idiomatic. [DVD REF 2: AUDIO]

At present fewer than half the interviews and one sample chapter, on experiences of employment in Ireland, have been completed. Most interviews have been free-flowing, relaxed and forthright. The tone and temperament of the book is emerging in large part from what its subjects have to say about themselves and, crucially, about Ireland. On the basis of material generated so far, it should include some sharp and negative comments about the state and society of Ireland as they confront a diverse new population in pursuit of the 'Irish Dream'.

Between 1996 and 2002, a period of unprecedented economic growth, the state had a *net* immigration of more than 150,000 people (Central Statistics Office 2002: 10–11), a huge figure for a population of slightly below four million, though returning Irish-born emigrants make up roughly half of in-migrants. Close analysis of the 2002 census suggests that the number of residents born elsewhere was 137,000 greater than in 1996, with perhaps 20,000 of these being Irish nationals born abroad (Fitzgerald 2003). Arguments continue about the reliability of data on some immigrant populations, with estimates of the number of Chinese-born residents ranging from 6,000 to several times that number. Nigerians, officially estimated in 2002 at about 10,000, were the largest foreign-born community apart from Americans and Britons; since then Ireland, with only one per cent of the EU's total population, has continued to be the most significant single European destination for asylum seekers from Nigeria. More recently, the expansion of the European Union in 2004 and 2007 has changed the character of immigration in Ireland, with the large majority now coming from the accession states.

The reliability of the asylum figures as an indication of non-work-permit and non-visa immigration has probably declined, as it becomes clear that Ireland's asylum system offers few opportunities for success or employment. The number of people living outside the state's statistical net has undoubtedly grown. Despite successive governments' efforts at geographic dispersal (meant to have a discouraging effect on would-be asylum seekers who might like Dublin but hate Longford), the capital, in particular its poorer residential and commercial districts, is where the new diversity is most evident.

Since *Home from Home* is intended to be both a popular book and a populist intervention on radio, our practice requires a critical engagement with mass-media practice more than it does with academic output. The context for any such engagement is the extraordinary continuing absence of non-white, non-Irish practitioners in virtually all Irish media, despite the presence of many experienced journalists among recent immigrants to the country. The reasons for this failure to open the columns and airwaves are manifold, and certainly not all sinister. They include the increased 'professionalisation' of media practice, whereby entry to employment comes largely through third-level courses accessed through a centralised process that reifies performance on a standard examination based on a set curriculum. As a result, classrooms full of future journalists and documentarians remain almost exclusively white and Irish.

Access by immigrants to professional training would not, however, be sufficient to open up the Irish media environment, which – perhaps incongruously, given its professionalisation – does often operate on the basis of close-knit and long-established social networks. The presence in Dublin of several well-run and highly respected 'national' media organisations may, for observers, obscure the fact that they exist in a relatively small capital city of only one million people, often likened to a 'village' by its elite. Breaking into the village media elite is far from impossible, but both *Home from Home* creators are, as immigrants, familiar with the opportunities and suspicions it offers to outsiders. (Nonetheless, both have stepped sufficiently far 'inside' to make this project reasonably attractive to publishers and broadcasters.)

In the latter half of 2004, a process began with a view to licensing a Multi-Cultural Broad Format Sound Broadcasting Service for Dublin. The Broadcasting Commission of Ireland (BCI) received two applications. Failte FM, a proposed co-operative, said its programme service would be 'based around the principle of multiculturalism and empowerment' and would aim to 'develop a strategy of training and capacity building to promote the participation and integration of refugees, asylum seekers, immigrants and travellers within the wider Dublin society'.[4] Global94.9 FM, submitted by *Metro Eireann*, targetted the 'new Irish, old Irish, the hidden people, the invisible people, tourists, the person beside you on the bus'.[5] According to the promoters, it would 'be a voice for all the diverse peoples of Dublin'; it would aim 'to promote cross-cultural understanding and co-operation among the various different cultures in our capital city and part county [and to serve] as a tool for creating cross-cultural bridges, empowering ethnic minority groups, encouraging self-reliance and fostering a positive outlook'. The innovative aims and objectives outlined in these applications were destined to remain unfulfilled; the state's regulator decided that the time had not yet come to license a new 'multicultural' radio service.

At this point it is worth noting that the period of economic boom, and therefore labour-market pressure, has meant that significant sections of government and media here see the 'flexibility' provided by immigration as an essential element of growth. In recent governments this tendency was personified politically by the small, centre-right Progressive Democrat (PD) party, largely liberal on social policy but free-market ideologues. The PD leader, Mary Harney, consistently pushed in the late 1990s for higher numbers of work permits and visas to serve the needs of Irish and multinational industry; her colleague Liz O'Donnell simultaneously used her junior-ministerial post as a platform for a 'compassionate' attitude to immigrants. Both were conspicuously in opposition to the more hardline attitudes emanating from the Department of Justice. In recent years the party's face on this issue has been the harder one of Michael McDowell, the Minister for Justice responsible for introducing in 2004, following a referendum, constitutional change to deny the babies of immigrants the automatic right to Irish citizenship.

The mainstream print and broadcast media, in which PD thinking is often said to have disproportionate influence, has been slow to embrace the tougher, McDowell posture; however, one does hear fewer 'liberal' complaints about, for example, asylum seekers being barred from taking paid employment, a recurrent theme in the late 1990s. The year 2004, with its referendum on citizenship, may yet be seen as a landmark in the evolution of racialised discourse in Irish media. An ongoing project, 'Conflation, Construction and Content',[6] has subjected the dominant media's production, content and reception, in respect of new migrants, to critical sociological scrutiny. Eoin Devereux and Michael Breen argue that 'the problematising of immigrants [in terms of crime or welfare fraud, for example] within Irish media discourse conforms to the wider tendency of the mainstream media always to demonise the most marginalised in society' (2004: 185). They offer, however, only scant anecdotal evidence of such problematising/demonising, drawn largely on research carried out in the 1990s by journalist Andy Pollak (1999). Indeed, they state that 'the Irish people are well served ... by the high quality of journalism found in radio, television and the broadsheet newspapers' (2004: 171). While not inclined to concur on the general excellence of Irish journalism, we would argue that the media record to date is no more shameful than might have been expected.

Although social activists may rightly complain about effective and structural anti-immigrant bias in the dominant media, and some critiques have identified clear if narrow areas of concern about effectively racist practice (see Pollak 1998, 1999; and Reilly 2004), broadcast media are a distinctly mixed bag in which there are often many 'positive' ingredients. This is not particularly brave on the media's part: there is, as yet, no significant, identifiable constituency that genuinely and deeply perceives immigration as a threat, either socially, culturally or economically; anti-immigration political candidates, such as those attached to the much-abused Immigration Control Platform, have performed very poorly in elections. The deeply racialised discourse about immigration, and asylum in particular, that splashes across the British tabloid media is relatively speaking invisible in Irish media – although not in Ireland, given the daily availability of many British papers.

Media such as talk-radio do like to pose issues in terms of 'for' and 'against'. That means that in order to set up a 'debate' about race and immigration it is considered important to have someone who is, objectively, racist to take one side of the issue. For years, radio broadcasts in Ireland have been content to observe this unappetising convention in relation to the native population of nomadic Travellers. The shocking levels of invective and (effectively racial) stereotyping that have characterised this debate have only occasionally been repeated in relation to immigrants; most broadcasters, it seems, would rather avoid the 'debate' entirely than pursue its ugly possibilities.

To say that the discourse which does appear is usually, in the end, 'about' and cautiously 'pro' immigrants and members of ethnic minority groups is not at all the same as saying that it is 'by' and 'for' them. This is in large part where enterprises such as *Metro Eireann* and *Home from Home* come in. But it is too simplistic to posit that what we are doing is a straightforward 'corrective' to otherwise well-meaning but hopelessly ignorant and uninvolved media peers. Our work is indeed 'by' immigrants, in the sense that we both grew up outside Ireland, but we are integrated citizens, playing full roles in what might be called the 'host society' as well as pursuing, to varying degrees (Onyejelem far more than Browne), subcultural projects; this immediately differentiates us from many or most of our immigrant peers. Although one can imagine a publicity campaign that suggested otherwise, our book and radio series will not be 'by' those people who are interviewed; however much we strive to respect their views and experiences, the process of selection and editing inevitably alienates it from their words – words that have themselves been coaxed out in interview.

It is not in the nature of a project such as *Home from Home* to agonise excessively about these limitations. As is standard journalistic practice, subjects consent to having their words and voices used, under our complete editorial control, and this is assumed from the moment they agree to be interviewed, within the constraints imposed by a request that some material be anonymous or 'off the record'. While it might be desirable to show material to subjects prior to publication/broadcast – as was Susan Knight's (2001) practice – it is not feasible in this case, given the montage uses to which we are putting even short snatches of speech. It is unlikely that at any point we will produce full transcripts of each interview from which to select material; journalistically, we cut straight to the selection.

While we might like to think of immigrants and members of ethnic minorities as a potential audience for this project, no commercial publisher would dare to get involved in a venture in which such a group would be the limit or even the mainstay of the would-be market. As we have heard on more than one occasion from potential commissioners of this work, the project must not be 'about' interculturalism, nor simply 'about' the people whose words will appear in print and be sounded on the airwaves. It must be 'about' Ireland.

The recent history of radio confirms similar priorities; immigrants may be the material from which this discourse is constructed, but they are not its subject. Thus, for example, a blandly unobjectionable and, inevitably, prize-winning radio documentary series made in 1999 about immigrant families was called, absurdly, *The New Irish* – a moniker that turned up again in an *Irish Times* print series in 2004. Much as we might like to think of our project as breaking new ground in this regard, it is unlikely to progress without at least some strong 'new Ireland' component. There is nothing particularly smug about this self-conscious requirement that one says something about 'Irishness'; the national drama is likely to take centre stage in any small, postcolonial country with a significant history of 'loss' through oppression and out-migration. Our challenge is to find a practice that both recognises this narrative convention – we do, after all, intend to put this work in the marketplace – while simultaneously acknowledging its limitations. At the same time, being coherently 'about' anything other than Ireland is a difficult matter given the sheer diversity of migrant constituencies, ranging from Africans in the irregular economy through Vietnamese refugees from the 1970s and Indian computer programmers on work visas to EU citizens from outside Ireland. The notion of distilling any singular experience of displacement and migration is dispelled quickly when, in an interview for *Home from Home*, recent arrival Emiliana Volpe from Italy rather unpersuasively explained her move to Ireland as simply a case of late post-adolescent, world-is-my-oyster indecisiveness. [DVD REF 3: AUDIO]

Our interviewing process and editing plans suggest a method that is rather *ad hoc*. Our interviews are wandering affairs, with people encouraged to speak about what they like, to follow tangents wherever they may go, but that won't be the form in which the interviews eventually appear. A thematic organisation of our material will mean that stories will, literally, be taken out of context; that juxtapositions will be used to create effects not intended by any of the interviewees; that a composite 'big picture' will be painted, in which an individual's story may provide no more than a couple of brushstrokes. This won't be an accidental consequence of the process; it's what we're hoping to achieve, both because 'coherence' and accessibility are critical necessities when presenting our work to a wider public, and because, one hopes, some arguments are likely to emerge.

The adaptation of this project into a radio format is entirely appropriate, given the widespread consumption of radio in a relatively small island such as Ireland. David Hendy's archetypal comment about the medium globally – 'its profile in the social landscape is small and its *influence* large' (2000: 3) – is arguably only half-true in Ireland, where radio's profile in the social landscape is considerable. For example, the uncertain prospect of a minor scheduling change more than a year ahead at RTÉ Radio 1, the flagship radio service of the state broadcaster, was treated as front-page news in the country's highest-circulation newspaper (see Nolan & Cusack 2003).

Interestingly, given the discussion about radio's role for immigrants and as a tool for integration, it has been seen in the past as a force for social disintegration. In the 1950s, it was cited in an official government document as a significant factor in encouraging Irish out-migration, and in 1956 a report by a government commission on emigration stated that, because of radio, 'people [are] becoming aware of the contrast between their way of life and that of other countries, especially in urban centres' (quoted in Brown 1985: 184). Nowadays, while radio listenership in Ireland is predictably divided according to class and age demographics, with younger and poorer listeners tending to prefer pop-music stations, speech radio is the most broadly popular radio format; almost all the highest-rated programmes are variations on the news or current affairs theme, and almost all are broadcast on RTÉ Radio 1. Up to 20 per cent of the adult population tunes in to some part of the two-hour *Morning Ireland* programme on any given day. Even on RTÉ's pop-music service, 2FM, the top-rated *Gerry Ryan Show* is dominated by current-affairs-based interviews and phone-ins rather than music; although the material tends to be light, 'lifestyle' oriented or 'human interest', this programme has often featured discussion of 'serious' global topics such as the wars in the Middle East or the issues associated with immigration.

While Ryan is occasionally opinionated in a populist way, presenters with overt political convictions are very much the exception in Irish radio, not only on RTÉ but on local and national commercial stations as well. The culture is one of studied 'neutrality' – a posture that of course tends to reify the *status quo ante*, although not to the point of explicit nostalgia for a period prior to the 'waves' of in-migration that began in the early 1990s. In 1997 Eamon Dunphy, a presenter on a national commercial station, broke the taboo against opinions on an evening drivetime programme when the discussion was about immigration: 'There is the position,' he commented, 'and this would be closest to my own point of view, that Ireland is too small, it does not have the economy or the infrastructure to support large numbers of immigrants...'[7] This was probably as near as any national presenter came to 'hate radio' – certainly far short of the sort of talk, from the likes of Rush Limbaugh, with which US listeners are familiar. However, at the time Dunphy's programme was a 'two-hander', with an openly 'liberal' co-host, and his posturing could conceivably be justified in terms of 'balance'. When Dunphy took over sole presenting of the programme, he didn't repeat such a statement, and indeed his programme's popular comedy sketches occasionally dealt with immigration in ways that were highly sympathetic to asylum-seekers (portraying them as passive victims of an insensitive system).

The taboo on opinionated presenters, however, has not entirely prevented variations on 'hate radio' from taking hold in Ireland. In what is probably best described as an unhappy coincidence, the late 1990s, a period of unprecedented in-migration, were golden years in Dublin local radio for free-wheeling late-night phone-in programmes. Again, the presenters – most famously Chris Barry and Adrian Kennedy – adopted postures of 'neutrality', but this rarely extended to the insertion of accurate information into the bitter and often abusive discourse supplied by 'callers' (often, in fact, carefully pre-programmed provocateurs). In the shout-filled midnight hours of these briefly popular and influential programmes, 'sponger' was synonymous with 'refugee', and 'immigrant' was the rhetorical equivalent of 'asylum-seeker'. These programmes were the home of many persistent urban myths concerning luxury items such as cars, homes and mobile phones purchased by the state for 'these people'. Occasionally, one of 'these people' was allowed on-air to speak about persecution in his or her country of origin, or the desire to work rather than depend on social welfare in Ireland, but it was easy for other callers, and listeners, to accommodate these presumably 'exceptional' individuals in an otherwise thoroughly racist worldview. Indeed, it was not uncommon for the immigrant caller to end up differentiating him/herself from less-principled peers.

By late 2003, such radio discussions had largely disappeared from the airwaves. In fact, in December of that year, on RTÉ's own late-night talk show, *Tonight with Vincent Browne*, the presenter unhesitatedly labelled a guest a 'racist'.[8] Browne's relatively easy target was Justin Barrett, well known anti-immigration (and anti-abortion, and anti-EU) campaigner, who was expressing views that would have put him on the liberal wing of the Dublin phone-in shows five years earlier. Such 'progress' needs to be measured in the context of, on the one hand, a persistently monocultural broadcasting environment, and, on the other, the complex cultural politics of immigration and representation. It is a well known media-world 'fact' that an English accent is a virtual bar to regular on-air employment in the Irish broadcast media. (The often rather anglicised accents of many upper-class Irish people are only slightly more welcome). Rodney Rice, presenter and producer of RTÉ's *World Apart* programme, argued that accent was also one of the factors militating against the inclusion of immigrants in the broadcast media.[9] However generalisations about accents and the under-representation of immigrants and ethnic minorities in the media should not lead us to make hasty assumptions about the pervasiveness of racist discourse; whenever Nelson Mandela or Archbishop Desmond Tutu speak in public or on radio in Ireland they receive a thunderous ovation.

BROADCASTING PRACTICE: CONVENTIONS AND TABOOS

The broadcasting environment in Ireland is more open than those of us who like to imagine ourselves in heroic resistance to hegemonic forms of cultural oppression want to imagine. Conservatives would certainly argue that the hegemony may even run the other way: an annual prize for 'media and multicultural' initiatives to 'promote cross-cultural understanding', initiated by *Metro Eireann*, has won sponsorship from RTÉ, the *Irish Times* and even the state's own Reception and Integration Agency, a division of the oft-demonised Department of Justice. This is not simply a matter of 'liberals' strategically placed in RTÉ, the *Irish Times* and elsewhere. The discourse of labour-market flexibility already discussed has a considerable hold on broadcast media. For as long as spokespeople for the employers' organisation, the Irish Business and Employers Confederation (IBEC), can be heard complaining about the difficulties of obtaining work permits for immigrants, there remains a reasonable fit between broadcasting practice in the current affairs realm (in which IBEC is a privileged 'source' of news and views) and liberal 'compassion'.

It is no exaggeration to say this gives rise to a rhetorical farrago when immigration is being defended: confusion about whether to highlight human rights, global justice, cultural diversity or capitalist opportunity often means that words evoking all four spill out together. From this jumble, extraordinary generalisations emerge. For example, in 2003 RTÉ radio presenter Pat Kenny, interviewing former Irish President and UN Human Rights Commissioner Mary Robinson, spoke admiringly of the 'docility' of immigrants: 'If you tell them that what they have to do to get on here in Ireland is go on social welfare, they'll go on social welfare; if you tell them they have to work twenty-three hours a day, they'll work twenty-three hours a day.'[10] The implication that immigrants should be allowed to exercise the latter option was clear, and Robinson did not contradict it.

Those who wish to exploit immigrant labour have had remarkable success, especially in broadcast media, in portraying this desire as a matter of extending rights to 'non-Irish nationals'. Only a decade after immigration began to rise dramatically, it is now a media truism that 'immigrants do the jobs Irish people won't do' – jobs Irish people were doing in the living memory even of Irish teenagers. The elementary economic facts of this matter – that temporary work permits for migrant labourers help to keep wages depressed in low-skill occupations, perpetuating the unattractiveness of such jobs to Irish workers; that a 'black economy' of immigrants without work permits has further low-wage effects – are rarely acknowledged, even by Irish trade unionists. It is only occasionally acknowledged that 'non-nationals' tend to be working well below their level of skill and training, or that the system whereby employers control work permits is a licence for exploitation.

The disproportionate number of immigrants caught up in the criminal-justice system is also a subject that is largely taboo. In Ireland (unlike Britain) ascribing racism, individually or structurally, to police and the courts is very rare, and the question of crime and punishment for migrants and other minorities faces not only that discursive bottleneck but also the more liberal fear of appearing to suggest that members of ethnic minorities are more prone to crime. (Irish people have, of course, been on the receiving end of both racist practice and stereotyping in other jurisdictions, especially Britain.) *Home from Home* is attempting to confront this issue, and at least one chapter/programme will deal with experiences of 'justice'. So far, one interviewee, Guylaine Klaus-Corsini, has told stories based on her experience as an unconventional teacher in Mountjoy women's prison, where the guards were alternately curious, condescending and cruel. [DVD REF 4: AUDIO]

It's not surprising that pro-immigration campaigners, and multicultural newspaper *Metro Eireann* as their most directly accessible medium, take whatever rhetorical opportunities come their way, whether it's patronisingly ascribing 'cultural vibrancy' to every African woman who buys a yam on Parnell Street,[11] or accepting a strategic alliance with employers seeking the freedom to draw on a globalised reserve army of unemployed. There is an underlying assumption in much media discussion of immigration, *Home from Home* potentially included, that such reportage is intended to persuade a white Irish audience that immigration should be more acceptable. Ironically, in 'seeking to be socially responsible', as practitioners sometimes describe it, they may actually eschew the complexity and questioning that a genuinely responsible practice demands. For example, while some few liberal journalists have probed at the alliance with employers and exposed workplace abuse of migrants by white Irish bosses, class division and exploitation within immigrant communities in Ireland remains an almost entirely prohibited subject. In the course of our research we found that many immigrants working in immigrant businesses face appalling levels of exploitation (see, for example, Onyejelem 2003). The taboo on this very serious and delicate issue extends to academic discussion as well as mass-media coverage of immigration issues. It's a taboo we are especially keen to break with *Home from Home*.

Radio is a particularly crucial forum for multiculturalist 'persuasion' of white Irish listeners, and for the portraits of Irish society that are the preferred format for such persuasion. As Stephen Barnard has pointed out, its capacity as an instrument of hegemonic ideas of the 'nation' have often been the stuff of sinister fiction: 'Throughout literature, film and popular culture in general, radio has traditionally been seen as a repressive influence, controlling thought processes and inspiring either mindless compliance or apathy' (2000:

219). Barnard also argues that the medium has only a limited capacity to treat social problems as being anything more than an accumulation of individual problems, perhaps to be overcome with a spirited argument and a timely editorial intervention: 'Individualism ... finds its most potent expression in radio programming through a focus on aspiration and achievement, on solving problems...' (2000: 224).

The aura of 'persuasion' in programming on ethnic-minority issues is highlighted by the fact that, at the BBC – serving a far more developed and coherent set of immigrant and ethnic communities than exist in Ireland – such shows are funded from the education budget. Yet as Barnard argues, 'there remains an unmistakable sense of dispensed liberal favour about the programmes that result' (ibid.). Barbara Savage's (2002) study of the history of an important US radio show, *Town Meeting of the Air*, reveals how such favour was dispensed rather freely during World War II, with spirited discussion programmes about race in America, then withheld for three years after the war's end. Such manipulation is scarcely surprising: during the nation's anti-fascist crusade, there was heightened consciousness of the need to view the US as being on its own march toward greater freedom and equality, while the anti-communist crusade that followed the war made civil rights campaigners rather more suspect. Savage cites the difficulties faced even during the latter part of the war by the African-American writer Langston Hughes:

> Recounting that 'liberal' network executives lacked the political resolve to air a dramatic series about African Americans which he had repeatedly proposed to them, Hughes concluded: 'I DO NOT LIKE RADIO, and I feel that it is almost as far from being a free medium of expression for Negro writers as Hitler's air-lanes are for the Jews.' (2002: 235)

Of course, for every citation of radio as an instrument of genocide (as in Rwanda in 1994), the medium has been seen as offering opportunities for revolutionary mobilization. Commenting on the situation in Algeria, Frantz Fanon wrote: 'Suddenly radio has become just as necessary as arms for the people in the struggle against French colonialism' (cited in Lewis & Booth 1989: 139). The manifesto of French Radio Alice, one of the anarchist-oriented 'free-radio' movements in Europe in the 1970s, stated: 'We did not see radio as solely a political means but also a possibility of organising the experience of homogeneous communities' (cited in Lewis & Booth 1989: 143).

But what about heterogeneous communities? In his study of British broadcasting in the early-to-mid 1990s, Paddy Scannell writes:

> British Asians and Caribbeans have often been arbitrarily yoked together in 'ethnic minority' programmes in attempts to satisfy both ... An intrinsic difficulty for mainstream broadcasting is that ... it is hard to avoid the ghetto effect – of bracketing out the minorities in special 'minority' programmes that are ignored by the majority and do not always appeal to the minority. On the other hand, it is often unclear what kind of representation is being demanded. (1995: 35)

The alternative that he saw emerge in mid-decade was self-produced, licensed, 'ghetto' broadcasting.

In Ireland, RTÉ's stuttering effort, beginning early in 2000, to create a catch-all Radio One World for all immigrants in Ireland was a resounding failure. For reasons internal to RTÉ and with disastrous editorial consequences, the new service was based in Cork rather than Dublin, and for two hours each weeknight it broadcast a hotchpotch of speech and music on a little-known medium-wave frequency. Its marketing among ethnic minorities was poor, and the most that can be said is that it provided some broadcasting opportunities for a few people otherwise conspicuously excluded from the state's airwaves. The service disappeared within two years, replaced by an occasional wandering weekly half-hour programme on RTÉ Radio 1. This gave way in 2003 to the still vaguer and more watery *Different Voices*, which by abandoning a 'global' remit and instead simply 'embracing diversity' was able to do away with foreign-sounding presenters in favour of the unthreatening voice of a 'nice Irish woman'. Relaunched in 2004 as a 12-part series, it once again adopted a more 'global' approach and was presented by Cameroonian Guy Bertrand Nimpa.[12] It was succeeded in 2006/7 by Spectrum, a distinctly mild-mannered programme submerged in the low-listening ghetto of Sunday evening. A far more successful site of 'inclusion' in Irish radio has been the not-for-profit community-radio sector. Beset by 'amateurism' and poor resourcing, the best of these stations have nonetheless developed some 'subcultural' visibility among immigrants. An interesting example is on the northside of Dublin, where community-station NEAR FM has developed some African listenership, partly with local programming such as *Majority World*, but also by re-transmitting Radio France Internationale, a service that particularly targets francophone African listeners in Africa and elsewhere.

There is no little irony, of course, in the fact that a small Dublin station reaches a local audience of recent immigrants by re-broadcasting this most global of radio services direct from Paris, one of the old centres of the European global empire. If, as Hendy has written, 'creating a *sense of place* is one recurring theme of radio's meaningfulness in modern life' (2000: 177), it becomes necessary to ask how the phenomenon of migration, within and across national frontiers, affects our 'localised' perception of the medium's role. After all, as Hendy continues:

[T]here is also our sense of *space* to be considered: that in transmitting its signals over many hundreds of miles, and in allowing us in our domestic lives to be 'connected' to events and people beyond physical reach, radio somehow transforms our sense of space *between* different places. (Ibid.)

Quoting Judy Berland and her writing on radio as a 'space-binding' medium, Hendy writes:

[Radio], permitting rapid dissemination of information across ever larger areas, also 'erode[s] local memory and the self-determination of peripheral groups ... People's feelings about community, about territory, work and weekends, roads and traffic, memory and play, and what might be happening across town' are seized by radio so that it can 'map our symbolic and social environment'. (2000: 188)

But radio, while perhaps eroding the identity of peripheral groups, can only cope with so much change. The medium is likely to be less successful in mapping those regions of a symbolic environment that are home to real-life re-location and, indeed, dislocation. The movement of people, therefore, poses particular difficulties for radio's role in binding space and creating a sense of place.

LIFE STORIES

How then are questions of space and place addressed in *Home from Home*, with its emphasis on 'oral history'? How can we validly take individual autobiographical testimony and fit it into larger questions about group behaviour and social change in early twenty-first-century Ireland? In previous eras and across different cultures, it might have been taken for granted that stories of particular individuals could not be abstracted from wider social issues. Much recent sociological work using autobiographical methods, while based on individually-told stories, nonetheless treats families, groups or communities, rather than the individuals themselves, as the irreducible subject. This has arisen partly through a conjunction of the rising interest in social history and a sort of campaigning social work: 'It was oral historians, some of whom were or became social practitioners, who already in the early 1980s adopted life-history methods as an emancipatory tool, and launched the concept of "empowerment" as a key concept in welfare practice' (Chamberlayne *et al.* 2000: 2). At the same time, academic postmodernism has surely done away with the essentialist assumptions about the 'typicality' of individuals, and the breezy non-concern with the researcher's mediation, that we find in a previous generation of social researchers, as in Charles H. Cooley's classic summary from the first half of the twentieth century:

> We may study closely actual person [sic] or groups and use the perspective thus gained as a core upon which to build an understanding of other persons or groups, and eventually of the whole complex. In somewhat the way a naturalist hidden in a tree-top with his camera watches and records the nesting behaviour of a pair of birds, hoping by a series of such studies to understand those of the species. (1930: 331)

This might still act as a mission statement for some journalists (for whom the taxi-driver is generally the archetype of the species), but social scientists will be more wary. Ken Plummer speaks for a later age when he describes the approach of Cooley and other 1930s researchers in the 'Chicago School' of 'symbolic interactionists' as 'important but in the end untenably naïve' (2001: 115).

Following the terminological guidelines set by Daniel Bertaux (1981) and Stephen Tagg (1985), our own approach follows a 'life story' method, as opposed to 'life history', 'autobiographical' or 'case history', because it relies solely on the interviewee's oral account. The cautiousness in Tagg's general endorsement of life-story interviewing is particularly applicable to *Home from Home*: 'The method ... can present problems, for example ... when a series of stories are to be combined or contrasted' (1985: 163). One such problem our practice raises, of course, is whether what was at the time it took place a life-story interview can still go by that name once it has been chopped and changed and combined with other similar interviews to create some effect external to its own original logic.

A provisional answer is provided by Bertaux, who points to a larger purpose in such methodology. In the course of perhaps the most coherent, and probably the most passionate, case for life stories as an alternative to quantitative social-research methods, he writes, 'this approach yields ... a direct access to the level of *social relations* which constitute, after all, the very substance of sociological knowledge' (1981: 30). For Bertaux, 'social relations' roughly equates to 'structures of domination', and he insists that the best way to see inside these structures is with the direct assistance of those living inside them. This call to arms reasonably summarises the thinking and method behind *Home from Home*, and its methodology. As Bertaux writes: 'If given a chance to talk freely, people appear to know a lot about what is going on; a lot more, sometimes, than sociologists' (1981: 38). Or, as one of Bertaux's colloborators puts it: 'When people tell their life stories, culture speaks through their mouths' (Bertaux-Wiame 1981: 259).

Immigrants are in some ways the quintessential tools for a life-story approach to social questions, falling as they do into Plummer's category of 'Strangers/Outsiders/Marginal People' (2001: 134), rather romantically seen as the sorts of people whose fate reveals most about the underlying nature of a society. The Stranger is 'a person who may be in society but not of it' with a life lived 'at a cultural crossroads' (ibid.). So, for example, when Onyejelem interviewed Sahr Yambusu from Sierra Leone, the middle-aged subject highlighted his own rather dramatic shift in status upon migration, which enabled him to view Irish society in a way that was impossible for a native Irish person, a way in which he could never have seen his home society, where his 'place' was stable. [DVD REF 5: AUDIO]

Home from Home's editing strategy – its intention to break apart individual stories and interweave different voices around particular themes – is both a means of throwing light on the cultural order and of avoiding what Franco Ferrarotti calls 'the literary danger inherent' in autobiographical narrative and the tendency 'to interpret the specific biography as an absolute and irreducible destiny' (1981: 19). In his own work in rural southern Italy, he writes, 'I was very careful to try to connect individual biographies to the global characteristics of a precisely dated, experienced historical situation' (ibid.). For Ferrarotti the notion of saying anything coherent and meaningful about an individual is too complicated for a mere sociologist: 'the individual is not the founder of the social, but rather its sophisticated product' (1981: 26). Why not, he asks, 'substitute the biography of the primary group [rather than of an individual] as the basic heuristic unit of a renewed biographical method?' (1981: 24). One senses in Ferrarotti that the choice to foreground the 'primary group' (workplace, extended family) is something of a methodological shot in the dark, in the absence, in either sociology or Marxist theory, of what Sartre calls 'a hierarchy of mediation' (cited in Ferrarotti 1981: 23).

Nonetheless, Ferrarotti's call to locate biographical method clearly in the dialectic between individuals and social systems offers useful guidance even to research-driven journalism. The same goes for his important observations on the dialectics of interviewing:

The observer is radically implicated in his research ... [the interviewee] far from being passive, constantly modifies his behaviour according to the behaviour of the observer. The circular feedback process renders any presumption of objective knowledge simply ridiculous. [Instead, any knowledge gained will be] mutually shared knowledge rooted in the intersubjectivity of the interaction ... The price to be paid by the observer … will be to be reciprocally known just as thoroughly … Knowledge thus becomes what sociological methodology has always wished to avoid: a risk. (1981: 20).

It is within an acknowledged realm of risk, then, that we should ask ourselves the sort of questions posed by Tagg: 'To what extent should the interviewer explore the details of particular remembered events? Should the interviewer differentiate the typical from the exceptional, and how should the interviewer encourage elaboration?' (1985: 168). Ferrarotti's formula suggests that there cannot possibly be any 'correct' answer to these questions in the context of a given 'circular feedback process' (1981: 20), though they must surely also be revisited in the course of transcribing, compiling and editing the work – bearing in mind too that 'all actors are incompletely conscious of the conditions, meanings and outcomes of their actions' (Chamberlayne et al. 2000: 9).

CONCLUSION

Even once we accept, for the sake of argument, that we can gain some socially useful knowledge from a life-story project such as *Home from Home*, some questions remain, enunciated by other life-story researchers: 'It is precisely its possibilities for bringing private understanding and emotions about the private and the public into the public arena as textual narratives that raise ethical questions about the use of autobiography for the researcher' (Harrison & Lyon 1993: 103). For most journalists who work in the 'social affairs' realm, necessitating intimate discussion with 'ordinary people', these questions – essentially about the 'use' of people's lives – have to be pushed aside, for the greater good either of the journalistic enterprise or of some larger cause that is served by the telling of a private story. While the authors of the above insist that 'contexts such as political intentions' do not 'necessarily invalidate autobiography as a research resource or topic' (ibid.), their warning puts such rationalisations in an important ethical context.

Nonetheless, and with all cautions duly noted, the *Home from Home* project fits within the most optimistic and engaged view of the capacity of the biographical method as a means of challenging elite notions of social organisation, and the discriminatory practices and discourses that often flow from these. Indeed, in as much as it must be 'about the New Ireland', it may serve to define that Ireland as comprising precisely those notions, practices and discourses. Biography, in this view, is 'an alternative narrative … a means to challenge a system which substitutes efficiency for sociability, economy for need, and public panic for individual experience (Chamberlayne et al. 2000: 29). The words are particular apt in relation to the potential role of life stories in the arguments, in Ireland and elsewhere, about immigration.

Notes

1   A tabloid newspaper founded in 2000 and, at the time of writing, the only self-consciously 'multicultural' periodical in Ireland.

2   See, for example, Cullen (2000), Farrell & Watt (2001), Fanning (2002) and Lentin & McVeigh (2002).

3   The nearest, partial analogue is Susan Knight's (2001) book of interviews with female immigrants.

4   See Broadcasting Commission of Ireland (2005) *Failte FM*. Available at <http://www.bci.ie/failte%fm_table.html> [Accessed 27 January, 2005].

5   See Broadcasting Commission of Ireland (2005) *Global94.9 FM* Available at <http://www.bci.ie/global%2094.9fm_table.html> [Accessed 27 January, 2005]. The practice of establishing radio stations for ethnic/multicultural audiences is not new in Europe. Radio Multikulti came on the air in Berlin in September 1994: 'Broadcast media in Berlin have recently been the focus of considerable public attention concerning potential trajectories for the future of the city's ethnic diversity' (Vertovec 2000: 14).

6   See <http://www.ul.ie/sociology/conflation.html> [Accessed 27 January 2005].

7   Quote based on Browne's near-contemporaneous notes of the broadcast.

8   Irish defamation laws mean that calling someone a racist, even in the midst of spirited argument, is a risky business in broadcasting.

9   A talk given on the occasion of the Africa Solidarity Centre Annual Public Lecture, titled 'Imaging and Representing Africa in the Western Media' (2004).

10 Quote based on near-contemporaneous notes.

11 Certain low-rent commercial streets of Dublin's north inner-city have filled with immigrant businesses, most notably Moore Street, where cheap short leases have been available due to uncertainties about large-scale redevelopment.

12 See RTÉ Radio 1 (2005) *Different Voices*. Available at <www.rté.ie/radio1/differentvoices/> [Accessed 31 January, 2005].

Bibliography

Barnard, S. (2000) *Studying Radio*. London: Arnold.

Bertaux, D. (1981) 'From the Life History Approach to the Transformation of Sociological Practice', in D. Bertaux (ed.) *Biography and Society: The Life History Approach in the Social Sciences*. London: Sage.

Bertaux-Wiame, I. (1981) 'The Life History Approach to the Study of Internal Migration', in D. Bertaux (ed.) *Biography and Society: The Life History Approach in the Social Sciences*. London: Sage.

Broadcasting Commission of Ireland (2004) *Multi-Cultural Broad Format Sound Broadcasting Services*, Dublin. Available at <http://www.bci.ie> [Accessed 27 January 2005].

Brown, T. (1985) *Ireland: A Social and Cultural History, 1922–1985*. London: Fontana.

Central Statistics Office (2002) *Census 2002: Preliminary Report*. Dublin: Stationery Office.

Chamberlayne, P., T. Wengraf and J. Bornat (eds) (2000) *The Turn to Biographical Methods in Social Science: Comparative Issues and Examples*. London: Routledge.

Cooley, C. H. (1930) *Sociological Theory and Social Research*. New York: Henry Holt.

Crook, T. (1999) *Radio Drama: Theory and Practice*. London: Routledge.

Cullen, P. (2000) *Refugees and Asylum Seekers in Ireland*. Cork: Cork University Press.

Devereux, E. and M. Breen (2004) 'No Racists Here? Public Opinion, Immigrants and the Media', in N. Collins and T. Cradden (eds) *Political Issues in Ireland Today* (third edition). Manchester: Manchester University Press.

Fanning, B. (2002) *Racism and Social Change in the Republic of Ireland*. Manchester: Manchester University

Press.

Farrell, F. and P. Watt (eds) (2001) *Responding to Racism in Ireland*. Dublin: Veritas.

Ferrarotti, F. (1981) 'On the Autonomy of the Biographical Method', in D. Bertaux (ed.) *Biography and Society: The Life History Approach in the Social Sciences*. London: Sage.

Fitzgerald, G. (2003) 'Comings and Goings are More than We Thought', *Irish Times*, 8 November.

Harrison, B. and E. Stina Lyon (1993) 'A Note on Ethical Issues in the Use of Autobiography in Sociological Research', *Sociology*, 27 (1): 101–9.

Hendy, D. (2000) *Radio in the Global Age*. Cambridge: Polity Press.

Knight, S. (ed.) (2001) *Where the Grass in Greener: Voices of Immigrant Women in Ireland*. Dublin: Oak Tree Press.

Lentin, R. and R. McVeigh (eds) (2002) *Racism and Anti-Racism in Ireland*. Belfast: Beyond the Pale.

Lewis, P. M. and J. Booth (1989) *The Invisible Medium: Public, Commercial and Community Radio*. London: Macmillan.

Nolan, L. and J. Cusack (2003) 'Marian's Outrage as RTÉ to Give Her the Chop', *Sunday Independent*, 30 November.

Onyejelem, C. (2003) 'How Black People Feel About Media Representation'. Unpublished M.Phil. dissertation, Trinity College, Dublin.

Plummer, K. (2003) *Documents of Life 2: An Invitation to a Critical Humanism*. London: Sage.

Pollak, A. (1998) 'Refugees and Racism', *Irish Times*, 25 February.

_____ (1999) 'An Invitation to Racism? Irish Daily Newspaper Coverage of the Refugee Issue', in D. Kiberd (ed.) *Media in Ireland: The Search for Ethical Journalism*. Dublin: Open Air.

Reilly, C. (2004) 'Mirror, Mirror, Off the Wall: Coverage of Refugees and Asylum Seekers in the *Irish Daily Mirror*'. Unpublished MA dissertation, Dublin Institute of Technology.

Savage, B. (2002) 'Radio and the Political Discourse of Racial Equality', in M. Hilmes and J. Loviglio (eds) *Radio Reader: Essays in the Cultural History of Radio*. New York and London: Routledge.

Scannell, P. (1995) 'Britain: Public Service Broadcasting, from National Culture to Multiculturalism', in *Public Broadcasting for the 21ˢᵗ Century*. London: Acamedia Research Seminar 17.

Tagg, S. K. (1985) 'Life Story Interviews and Their Interpretation', in M. Brenner, J. Brown and D. Canter (eds) *The Research Interview: Uses and Approaches*. London: Academic Press.

Vertovec, S. (2000) *Fostering Cosmopolitanisms: A Conceptual Survey and a Media Experiment in Berlin*. Available at http://www.transcomm.ox.ac.uk/working_papers.htm.

BACK ROUTES: HISTORICAL ARTICULATION IN MULTIMEDIA PRODUCTION

Roshini Kempadoo

You might like to view and experience the artwork prior to reading this chapter. Launch Back Routes from the DVD ensuring the computer speakers are on. Please feel free to explore, using combinations of rollover and clicking actions. Use the (Esc) key to exit piece.
If you would like to experience all aspects of the artwork as you read, follow the grey italicised comments as they appear in the chapter.

> Like personal memory, social memory is highly selective. It highlights and fore-grounds, imposes beginnings, middles and ends on the random and contingent. But equally, it fore-shortens, silences, disavows, forgets, elides many episodes which – from another perspective – could be the start of a different narrative.
> – Stuart Hall (1999: 15)

> To view collectively Kempadoo's intricate photo-constructions produced over the last decade is to encounter a dense, multi-media labyrinthian flow of still images, through which the diasporic artist interrupts and recontextualises the present.
> – Ashwani Sharma (2004: 5)

In 2002 seven artists, whose work focused on exploring territories, boundaries, cultural and physical landscapes and national identity, were commissioned 'to produce an artwork in response to a location of his or her choice in Britain' (Griffiths 2002: 7) for the exhibition 'Travelogue' at the Whitworth Art Gallery, Manchester. *Back Routes* was one of the commissioned artworks.[1]

Launch the artwork and leave it running idle, without any keyboard or mouse activity.

This chapter will closely examine and analyse the research and production process undertaken in creating *Back Routes*, one of my earlier digital media artworks,[2] produced

FIGURE 1: DETAIL FROM *BACK ROUTES*, 2002

as an 'interactive'[3] and digitised projection of sound and imagery specifically for a gallery space. In order to locate my work, I will outline the main historical and contextual events and issues that have affected my documentary photographic/digital media practice. *Back Routes* emerges from a central concern for the black Caribbean colonial subject and my own relationship as a practitioner to the colonial narratives of the transatlantic trade routes and the concept of the 'Black Atlantic' (Gilroy 1992: 19). I consider my practice to be based on a partly autobiographical artistic exploration by a person with origins in the Caribbean who has experienced an exilic, migratory experience. I signal the principal issues and concerns underlying my practice through textual analysis of *Back Routes*, in particular the conceptual, technical and aesthetic explorations made in producing it, and explore ways in which contextualising historical frameworks may mark contemporary everyday British experience.

BLACK REPRESENTATIONAL PRACTICES

> The history of black photographic image-making has been obsessed with opening up the apparently fixed meanings of images. Where documentary photography carries a claim to truth, with the meta message of *this is how it really was … a* number of black photographers began to explore questions of identification, the issue of how best to contest dominant regimes of representation … This mode goes against the grain of realism: indeed it opens up realism and exposes it as a particular genre and privileges instead non-realist modes such as formalism, modernism and surrealism, which can be grouped together under the rubric of avant-gardism.
> – Stuart Hall and David A. Bailey (1992: 18)

In the late 1970s I returned to the UK from Guyana; by the mid-1980s I had completed my degree course and was working as a documentary photographer in the West Midlands. The technique and compositional qualities of photographers such as Bill Brandt or Henri Cartier-Bresson (particularly his influential genre of the 'decisive moment' (1952)) served as early influences on my work, but later I became interested in a more critical dimension of the photographic which I found in critics such as John Berger and Roland Barthes.

The question of British representation of the Caribbean had been the main focus of my interest in the study of photography and visual culture/communications. Stuart Hall's writings on cultural identity in the 1990s, in which he explores representations that position 'the black subject at the centre' and implicates 'the positions from which we speak or write – the positions of *enunciation*' (1990: 222), resonated with my original intention of working with visual photographic representations as a means of interrogating the historical mediation of Carribean discourse and culture. As a first-generation British Guyanese whose parents, optimistic about the prospects of post-independence Guyana, had made the *return journey* to the Caribbean in the 1970s, I wished to explore British Caribbean/ Caribbean identity, engaging in 'passionate research … directed by the secret hope of discovering beyond the misery of today, beyond self-contempt, resignation and abjuration, some very beautiful and splendid era whose existence rehabilitates us both in regard to ourselves and in regard to others' (Fanon 1963: 170).

The period from the mid-1980s to the late 1990s was particularly important for me. I became involved in questioning the societal and cultural space within which the photograph worked and the practice of photography itself, as well as in the articulation of an independent critical practice defined by a distinctly black arts/photographic/film formation and development.[4] Separate autonomous spaces were opened up for the critical engagement of media with the black presence in Britain. Debate, advocacy, exhibition and production in the arts were reflections of and responses to the wider racialised events of strikes, marches, demonstrations and street riots, in turn associated with and mostly created by the Conservative political climate. It is not within the scope of this chapter to enter into the complexity of the political and social backdrop against which the work of black practitioners emerged, but nationally and internationally photographers (including myself), filmmakers, critics, intellectuals and curators – Monika Baker, Deborah Willis, Kellie Jones, bell hooks, Sunil Gupta, Marc Boothe, Vanley Burke, Ingrid Pollard, Chila Burman, Pratibha Parmar, Armet Francis, Eddie Chambers, Lola Young, David A. Bailey, Stuart Hall and John Akomfrah – formed the basis of this intervention. Collective groups and resource bases such as the Black Audio Film Collective (1983), Autograph ABP (1988), AVAA (1989) and IVA (1994) were formed, supported by a combination of public funds and freelance independent, autonomous and voluntary efforts, while the agencies and the individuals running them pressed for the key issues of equality of opportunity, voice, visibility and access to be taken up by art film and television institutions. Journals such as *Screen Education* (1974–82), *Framework* (1975–92), *October* (1976–), *Ten.8* (1979–92) and *Third Text* (1987–), together with publications such as *There Ain't No Black in the Union Jack* (Gilroy 1987), *Disrupted Borders* (Gupta 1993) and Stuart Hall's writings were key contributions to and reflections of the debates of the time, while a series of key themed and issue-based shows exhibited work that explored historical and contemporary articulations of what it meant to be black and living in Britain. Films, screenings and festivals also marked this period of formation, creativity and articulation.

It cannot be argued that a coherency or consistency of approach, style and content defined the work produced by the black practitioners mentioned, which reflected a wide and varied range of autobiographical, intimate and public perspectives. Questions and critiques included thematics such as subjectivity, cultural specificity and a critical engagement with the economic, social and cultural power structures inherent or normalised in the contemporary British experience and in media practice itself. An intrinsic part of what Hall and Bailey called the 'critical decade' (1992: 4) was an increasing international and diasporic perspective and the establishment of a network between black individuals and groups. The articulation of a black presence in Britain through a diasporic legacy necessitated wider international support and an infrastructure not limited by geographical borders. I became increasingly familiar with the work of photographers who would act as influences, catalysts, milestones and mentors in the struggle for a black presence within photographic practice.

Significant to my own photographic practice was *The Sweet Flypaper of Life* (1967, reprinted 1984), a combination of black-and-white photographs by Roy DeCarava and prose by Langston Hughes. This far-reaching and intimate photographic work revealed the extent to which an articulation of difference can reveal itself through the production process. Difference and particularity were inscribed in the combinations of photographs and text; the layout, the textures and tones of the images, the informal intimate prose written by Hughes, suggest different ways of seeing and reading:

> Yes, you can set in your window anywhere in Harlem and see plenty . . . I never did like looking backwards nohow. I always believe in looking out front – looking ahead – which is why I's worried about Rodney. (1984: 98)

This extract and the accompanying photograph of a young African American man with glasses reading a book in the window bay illustrate some of the conceptual and aesthetic strategies that continue to provide inspiration and reflection for my own practice. There is the intricate and interwoven use of fictional, informal and nuanced African American-style prose and its relationship to a documentary style of black-and-white photography representative of the African American experience in Harlem during the 1950s. The particularity of the location (Harlem), the intimacy of the home environment forming the visual backdrop of the publication, the introduction of characters both visually and referenced in textual form, combine to enhance the interpretation of the publication as being of and about an African American community. DeCarava's practice of working from and stretching out the darker tonal zone of the black-and-white photograph in representing African American skin tones is illustrative of his aesthetic style and approach and of the relationship between technique and process.

The high-street aesthetic of the Harlem photographer Van der Zee, who worked in the 1930s, also greatly influenced my practice. His style in the vernacular and everyday studio photography of African Americans in Harlem opened up an important space for family and studio portraits – the ameliorative photograph of the high street, representing black communities, articulating lifestyles and bestowing a dignity on individual African Americans which society at large had rarely offered. Van der Zee's unique retouching – introducing wealth and accoutrements for the African American sitter in the frame – reflected the possibility (in my view, necessity) of establishing creative, fictional detail for a marginalised and brutalised African American population. In *The Harlem Book of the Dead* (1978), his darkroom technique used superimposed multiple negatives to construct portraits of deceased relatives, revealing the possibilities of a more instrumental and direct way of opening up the documentary studio image to an imaginative space that signified memories, loss and melancholia, and worked against a linearity of past and present, presence and absence.

NETWORKS AND EXCHANGES

International networks and exchanges, particularly between the African American and Black British practitioners and curators, were crucial in consolidating and defining a more collective approach to ways of producing and creating. The African American curator/photographer Deborah Willis was especially relevant to my own professional development as a photographer, both because I worked with her as an intern at the Schomburg Center for Research in Black Culture in New York[5] and because she was instrumental in the development of Autograph, of which I was an active member.

The London-based women's picture agency Format[6] provided an outlet for my work documenting the social concerns, interests, political activities and events of black communities and focusing in particular on groups concerned with black women's issues. I was photographing in a political climate where workforces were becoming increasingly vocalised and visible: labour unions, separate black caucus conferences, anti-racist marches and demonstrations. I was also documenting specific everyday events and experiences of Caribbean and Asian communities in Leicester, Birmingham and Coventry. The general lack of visibility of black communities and the stereotyped images in the popular media were of immediate concern, particularly in the context of the riots of the early 1980s. The social documentary genre – its relationship to historical and archival material and to contemporary celebration – played an important role, highlighting the different lifestyles of Britain's black populations, while inscribing a personal authorship that situated the black photographer behind the camera.

Marking the deep, significant and complex differences between black communities and black individuals, whether of Asian, African or Caribbean origin, signified a cultural shift. My interest in taking control of the context and determining the conceptual framework for the 35mm format colour and black-and-white photographs meant developing a photographic style that had implications for where it was to be viewed and published. My work was concurrently being exhibited in gallery spaces; *My Daughter's Mind* (1986),[7] one of the first exhibitions, was at the Ikon Gallery and there were commissions for group shows such as *Fabled Territories* (1989), *Autoportraits* (1990) and *Black Markets* (1990).

The artistic context of my photography allowed for experimentation in a new direction and an aesthetic that was more autobiographical, constructed, layered and multiple. As a photographer simultaneously concerned with the two aspects/practices that Hall identifies as a concern for opening up 'fixed meanings' in the documentary image while going against the 'grain of realism' (1992: 19), my artistic practice took on a more exploratory and imaginative position in relation to representation. What became significant was examining the limitations of a documentary genre that designated 'otherness' as representative of what Okwui Enwezor calls the 'object of fetishistic fascination and disturbance' (1997: 3) caught in the gaze of imperial visual structures. The work represented a significant shift, as I came to 'construct' photographic images through the expanded use of a range of photographic genres (most importantly the family album image).

FIGURE 2: DETAIL FROM THE BACKGROUND IMAGE FOR *BACK ROUTES*, 2002

I explored the notion of expanding the parameters of photography through interventions with other media, attempting to use text as a medium to 'clarify the reception of the single image, grounding ideology and meaning and leaving less chance for misinterpretation' while 'expanding the meaning of the single image [and] chang[ing] the traditional relationship between the photographer and the subject' (Jones 1990: 133). Most importantly, I began the process of distilling the particularities of a British/Caribbean culture from an autobiographical perspective, using the experience of growing up literally in two spaces (Britain and the Caribbean) and exploring simultaneously the concepts of migration and states of being as belonging 'to a future as much as to the past' (Hall 1990: 225).

Excavating and maintaining an ambivalence towards the territorial sites and situatedness of Trinidad/Guyana and Britain in my practice led me to explore the trauma and signification of the colonial experience as a means *through* which I could expand and comment on a contemporary British lived/live social experience. The specificity of the Caribbean colonial experience is based on transportation, migration and relocation. Expressing and uncovering British/Caribbean narratives, as I have in *Back Routes*, meant exploring the notion of migration as upheaval, the displacement and uprooting of African and Indian populations from one place to another. I highlight the condition of the continuous migrant, for whom slavery and subsequently indentureship[8] in the Caribbean meant removal from a place of origin to a new world, the colonial black subject being inserted into the space of the plantation and the symbolic economy of the West (see Hall 1990).

RESEARCHING AND PRODUCING FRAME I: MIGRATORY SPACES

In researching and producing *Back Routes*, I established a core perspective of what I consider to be a Caribbean experience, one that is based on a series of past and present migratory and cross-cultural events and spaces. Reflecting past colonial narratives through a contemporary and imaginary space, the artwork is primarily a photographic representation presented, to suggest a more ambivalent perspective and starting point, in a multimedia experience. Using multimedia enabled me to reflect a series of contradictions and a more complex series of relationships. It became possible to encompass contradictory positions of time, a temporality that fluctuates between past, present and future accounts and events; to create a hybrid space, articulating a fluidity of movement between territories, nations and locations; to view slippery and contradictory moments in memory and in historical accounts, where the overarching factual, normalised histories can be problematised through an imaginary network of fictional narratives.

There are three main strands to the interactive artwork, made up of combinations of visual and aural components: the background, combining a series of landscape images; an aural and written short story appearing on the left-hand side of the projection; and fragmentary components of an aural and visual experience of an artefact known as the Drake Cup, accessible on the right-hand side of the screen.

When the viewer/user enters the gallery space, the main focus of the work is the continuous background landscape image moving pixel by pixel as a projection. It is a hybrid

Caribbean/British landscape of here/there, made up of borders, edges and distant views, with the sea as a mesmerising space of longing and nostalgia, as well as the redolent and perpetually rehearsing Atlantic slavery metaphors for trauma, loss and tragedy. The ambivalence of the here/there migratory experience resonates in the composition of the image. It employs two conceptual strategies. The first uses uneven splices and snippets of images, sometimes seamlessly merging from one still image to another, at other times with juxtaposed images abruptly making use of an overt edit or jump cut. The second strategy uses the in-between space of movement and stillness actualised through the digital process. The digitised perpetual image is on the one hand in movement but on the other resistant to the notion of speed, acceleration and exaggeration – concepts associated with the digital and computerised productions of the popular mainstream cinematic experience. The image is neither bound by associations with the digital nor bound up in the intense signification of the single frame.

The still landscape images are devoid of people, in particular of representations of the black colonial subject. As mentioned earlier, the context and development of my photographic practice is an integral part of my current multimedia productions; the contemporary construction of the black subject in photography is therefore an ongoing concern and focus. Becoming equally important, as I concentrate on the representation of the historical Caribbean subject, is the portrayal of the black subject through historical material. The problematic continues to be the relationship photography has had to the anthropological view of culture. As Nicholas Mirzoeff suggests:

> The anthropological view of culture depended upon a clear distinction being drawn between 'their' culture and 'our' civilization. It was the anthropologist's task to research and discover the wholly different ways in which these cultures were organized. (1999: 130)

The first recognisable anthropological organisations in Britain were founded at the same time as the earliest photographic processes were formed.[9] The technological European apparatus of the camera helped formulate the anthropological view of the black colonial subject as the primitive and exotic other. It was through anthropology that the power of knowing was transformed into a 'rationalisation of colonial domination and … gave the weight of scientific truth to assumptions of racial character (Edwards 1992: 6). Mimesis became the motif for both anthropology and the photograph. Representations of the black colonial subject are haunted by the idea of creating an image that mirrors life without any distortion and is believable as truth, yet in *Back Routes* I looked for strategies of absence, for ways to remove entirely the visibility of the black subject on the screen or in the frame.

The digitised still images in *Back Routes* make it possible for the image to be seen in a transitory state, one of becoming, evolving or in a process of temporary actualisation. Since *Back Routes* is a projection, the digitising of the photographic or the electronic image can be distinguished from a conventional analogue photographic print. The artwork presents the still image as one that erodes the efficacy of the photograph, with an emphasis placed on movement through animation and video post-production effects, and an ambivalence surrounding the image as legal evidence or the embodiment of believability.

The intensification of the visual through a digitised form combining the cinematic mode of projection and computerised manipulation, montage and construction implies a more fleeting computerised optical form. In other words, *Back Routes* makes use of a process or mode of production that facilitates what Roy Ascott describes as 'various interests … evidently and potently invested more in what cannot be seen at the surface level of reality, in what is invisible, fluid, and transient: human relationships, systems, forces and fields as they are at work in nature, politics and culture' (1996: 166).

Activate the artwork using the computer mouse in a rollover action when a semi-transparent image appears on the right of the screen. Explore the right-hand side of the screen.

RESEARCHING AND PRODUCING FRAME II: ARTEFACTS AS CAPITAL

I discussed above the importance of displacing the notion of a fixed territorial location in *Back Routes*. It also became necessary to problematise the presentation and presence of colonial narratives. I researched the possible use of an artefact or object as a way of referencing a historical context relating to the English-speaking Caribbean islands, currently part of the Commonwealth, and symbolic of a legacy of British dominance. I was interested in concentrating on the object or artefact as symbolic of a historical moment and yet referential of a wider notion of colonial commercial enterprise – the transactions, goods and capital that mobilised colonialism.

I was directed to an object entitled 'The Drake Cup' (*c.*1580): a cup formed from a coconut and held in place by silver-gilt mounts. Its historical significance and multifaceted detail are described in the catalogue of the 'Treasures of the North' exhibition held in 2000 at the Whitworth Gallery:

> The Drake Cup is traditionally held to have been presented to Sir Francis Drake from a grateful Queen on his return from his three-year circumnavigation of the globe. He landed at Plymouth in September 1580 with a vast booty … He was knighted by Queen Elizabeth in April 1581, when the Queen came to Deptford to attend a banquet given by Drake in her honour … Lady Elliot-Drake in *The Family and Heirs of Sir Francis Drake*, London, 1911, suggests that it was around this time that the Queen presented Drake with the cup. The bowl, formed from a coconut, is finely carved with the arms of Queen Elizabeth, the arms of Sir Francis Drake with the date 1580, and a representation of the Golden Hind being towed towards the Isles of the Moluccas. The vase-shaped stem is supported by the figure of a dragon, perhaps alluding to the arms used by Drake before the new grant given with his knighthood. The domed cover is chased with sea-monsters and ships and is surmounted by a model of the Golden Hind on a globe.

This sixteenth-century curiosity is acknowledged as a treasure of national and historical importance, valued and authenticated by the direct descendants of the Drake family and the auction house Christie's. Contractual arrangements between the owner and public institutions ensure that it is publicly displayed for some six months every year. As with many other privately-owned artefacts deemed of national significance, this arrangement is based on a tax relief scheme acceptable to both parties. The cup had already been exhibited in the Victoria and Albert Museum and the National Maritime Museum, Greenwich. Following negotiations between the Whitworth Gallery and the owner, I was given permission to photograph it and did so at the owner's residence in Hampshire. I was interested in considering the artefact as a commodity embodying value and having what Arjun Appadurai describes as 'particular types of social potential' (1986: 6) and in exploring its cultural biography within a colonial and post-colonial regime of value and exchange.

Roll over the semi-transparent image of the cup on the right to explore the fragmentary images in more detail and to listen to the various aural aspects that are triggered.

A semi-transparent single image of the cup appears as a register or a resultant image on the screen, enabling the viewer/user in the installation seating area of the gallery to access the work by using the mouse available to them. Animated by a rollover movement, the artefact appears as fragmentary images, dissected and broken in a series of close-ups revealing the details engraved on the cup. When accessed, each fragment triggers an aural extract – a short commentary by a valuations expert from Christie's. In the interview I conducted with the expert, he refers to the cup's origins, historical significance and craftsmanship. Combined, the aural commentary and photographic fragments act as symbols of a historical moment and refer to the object itself. The cup refers to the embodied yet contested value of a commodity – an item whose valuation is based on its circulation as an object of economic exchange (Appadurai 1986: 16).

Listen to and experience more details of the cup by using the rollover action repeatedly. Move the mouse out of and back into the right-hand side of the screen, exploring the top, middle and bottom areas of the screen.

Through its make-up and materiality, the Drake Cup embodies the notion of transnational enterprise and transaction. Physically it is a hybrid: a cup in the form of a coconut said to have been carved by a sailor, presumed to have been brought from the 'colonies' and supported by silver-gilt holders fashioned by Flemish craftsmen. In its current context as a museum object of national significance, the Cup references and articulates the transnational economic relationship which was to develop between Europe and its colonies. Its materiality and craftsmanship straddle the divide between Europe, perceived as more refined, valuable and modern, and the 'new' world, seen as exotic, 'rudimentary' and 'primitive'. As an artefact, the cup commemorates the circumnavigation of the globe while bestowing on the explorer Drake reward and recognition from the Crown and by implication from the nation. I was interested in the circumnavigation of the globe as a visual and aural metaphor for the *ambition* of the colonialist and the *consequence* for the colonial subject.

The cup may be regarded as anticipating and signifying the intention of the individuals and populations who were later to define and determine the British Empire. It references the scope and ambition of the British colonial project and illustrates the British/European perspective of economic expansion in the Americas, based on the exhilaration of discovery, curiosity about the exotic and new, the zeal for commercial enterprise and the domination of other territories.

The fragmented form of the cup, the related commentary appearing in the artwork and its relationship to the narrated Creolese story invoke the direct and devastating legacy of British colonial authority for the surviving black colonial subject and labourer, whether of African, Indian or indigenous American origin. *Back Routes* draws on the cultural practices of the survivors of this period of expansion, slavery and indentureship as opposed to those simply and inhumanely killed by the system. Forcibly transported from Africa and India to the Caribbean, the surviving populations suffered a brutal upheaval, which severed links with their original homelands, families and livelihoods. A minority of the indigenous people of the Caribbean also survived, displaced and contained in restricted areas of the islands.

RESEARCHING AND PRODUCING FRAME III: CREOLISING HISTORY

Historical accounts are never straightforward; they always require authentication, analysis and interpretation. According to a spokeswoman for the Drake Exploration Society,[10] there are in existence three or four cups that can be associated with Sir Francis Drake, his relationship to the Queen and the recognition of his circumnavigation of the globe. It was this that aroused my fascination and curiosity; the cup came to symbolise and encompass the unstable space of interpretation and evaluation. At the point of interpretation, translation and meaning for the private owner and wider public, the Drake Cup embodies conflicting and competing 'truths'.

I began to think of the artwork as inhabiting an ambivalent space, somewhere between fictional and factual discourses that might critique a colonial history using an imaginary narrative. I wanted to open up and create a wholly fictional space for absent narratives that then questioned the evidentiality of the images and text; in other words, to problematise the factual proximity surrounding the materiality of the cup, to produce a 'just suppose' point of production. In my view, this would be the best way to extend and situate representations of a British colonial legacy from the perspective of the absent Caribbean colonial labourer whose story, trauma and loss begins with the slave trade between West Africa and the Caribbean.

How could the authenticity, authority and value of the cup be temporarily transferred to the other story, to the position of the colonial subject? How could the artwork refer to the missing narrative of the slaves? How could it reflect the hideous Atlantic crossing, the absence of the mass of people who did not survive, the broken family ties, the hazards of survival in the new world? I worked with the idea of there being another cup, in another place, time and space, a concept articulated not solely through photographic representations, but also through the use of English Creole in a written and aural form.

The short story *Fruit and Ting*, written in English Creole by Marc Matthews, was commissioned for *Back Routes* with the aim of actualising it as both a written and an aural experience. Marc is an influential artist from Guyana who has performed dub poetry around the Caribbean. His work over the years has explored oral storytelling traditions – in the different dialects of Trinidad, Guyana, Barbados or Jamaica – with other performers and writers such as Ken Corsbie, John Agard and Henry Muttoo. Their poetry, music, drama and comedy, accessible through performance and radio, were key contributors to the recognition of English Creole culture as a distinct and unique part of the Caribbean heritage and their work popularised what Edward Kamau Brathwaite calls 'Creole society'.[11] In the 1950s a canon of Caribbean literature had been established, written and published in the Caribbean and in Britain, and by the early 1970s the Caribbean curriculum was established and recognised, Caribbean culture found expression in literature, music and the performing arts and English Creole usage gained recognition through the education system.

Marc Matthews's work for *Back Routes* is based on research into and discussion of my initial idea and response to my photographic work and the material I gathered. His Creolese short story *Fruit and Ting* is experienced in a written form on the screen, with related still images hyperlinked to phrases and words, and as an aural narrative continuously heard in the gallery space, providing a prominent pivotal focus for the viewer/user:

> An dis is wah all you see hea is more dan coconut, wuh you see hea is ah man life.
> From he born. From how get capture.
> How dem pack dem tight like cotton.
> How dem pack up an lock down in room without sun like tomb inna burial groun.
> How dem get bundle an pitch in punt
> How dem get plant like cane, like cotton like annatto.

The story is based on another cup and its owner, an elderly Caribbean woman called Nenneh Tooky, and set in an imaginary Caribbean village. Written in the third-person, it tells of the cup being seen by a museum curator and photographer. Nenneh chooses to relate the provenance of the cup itself and the slave story inscribed in it to the other members in the village, rather than hand it over to a museum collection. Apart from the narration of the transatlantic crossing, the story comments on two aspects. The first is the notion of archive and national heritage, particularly as it relates to the archival practice of a colonial legacy. Interestingly, the narrative reflects two principles that Jacques Derrida identifies as of importance in understanding a historical collection or archive – 'commencement and commandment' (1996: 1), the way in which conditional structures govern the collection, processing and maintenance of the colonial archive. The other aspect is the different values attributed to the cup by the characters in the story as they explore the tension between the cup as a commodity for exchange and the cup as representing the social and cultural values of exchange.

The written form of the fictional short story is further embellished by stylistic considerations relating to the text itself and its aural form: how and when the text appears on the screen, the concept and construction of the hyperlinked visuals to words and phrases, and when and how the aural text might be activated by the user, particularly in relation to the counterpart sound element of the valuation expert from Christie's.

I wanted to create a micro-space in the piece, where further associated material could be articulated and related to the story, and to explore the possibility of the narrative being read in a way that could be partly instigated by the viewer/user in the gallery. I pursued the possibility of the artwork providing a more uncertain relationship to the authorial position of the artist and user/viewer in the gallery space.

Trigger the other level of related visual material by clicking on the hyperlinked text (purple in colour) of narration on the left-hand side of the screen.

The still-image animations hyperlinked to the short story, appearing for a fixed transitory time on the screen, are activated by a mouse-click by the user/viewer. They are combinations of Caribbean landscapes, using digital techniques of manipulation, sampling

FIGURE 3: DETAIL FROM THE HYPERLINKED TEXT, *BACK ROUTES*, 2002

and seamless montage. They appear almost as diary snapshots that may come from, or be associated with, Nenneh Tooky's localised sense of space and location. I am interested and challenged by the space of the vernacular and the everyday, whilst disrupting it through a more digitalised production form and aesthetic. In the layering, pace and appearance of the animations, I attempt to maintain a certainty and reliance on photography's position of signification, its indexicality to the 'real' and its function and purpose in recalling memories, symbolic of the memorial and ameliorative photographic images of death, loss and commemoration.

The micro-space of the short story then presents a Creole framework for an audience that is both Caribbean and English and either willing to engage or familiar with Caribbean dialect and usage. It situates Caribbean cultural specificity within the frame, dominating the overall aural experience and appearing in a dialogic relation to the fragmentary aural and visual representations of the Drake Cup.

Matthews' story *Fruit and Ting* gives the Caribbean an unrelenting presence. It is ever present in both an aural and a visual sense on screen and in the gallery space, acting as a continuous reminder of and metaphor for the disruption of a historicised British hegemonic discourse. Its presence questions and critiques the operation of societal power and authority on British historical narratives in both Britain and the Caribbean, detracting from and often disguising the brutal legacy of the British colonial system.

The use of Creole posits the way in which historical Caribbean narratives are and should continue to be an inclusive part of a wider historic and British cultural heritage.[12] On the other hand, the artwork illustrates the creativity and distinctiveness of Creole usage as something contributing to the formation of Caribbean identity, with the signatures of common histories of slavery and indentureship creating an imaginary coherence across different races and Caribbean populations. The Creole framework for *Back Routes* proposes a transcultural notion of heritage, making use of a digitised experience to delimit and facilitate a more layered presentation of a British/Caribbean colonial legacy. The symbolic references to the sea, shorelines, distant views, horizons and spaces between land and sea, situate the migration, slavery, loss and trauma of the colonial Caribbean labourer. The Creole short story of Nenneh Tooky and the cup ensures the continuous presence of the Caribbean/Creole in the artwork, while commenting on the way in which historical accounts come to be legitimated and validated. The fragmentary representations of the Drake Cup as a cultural artefact of national value are placed in the frame as a way of exposing the limits and limitations of the societal and cultural authenticity of such an artefact. The artwork seeks transference of the symbolic authority and legitimisation posed by the Drake Cup to another, creolised, space and experience.

Back Routes is one of a series of artworks through which I am extending the notion of creolisation/*créolité* – two established concepts of Creole culture and cultural mixing that have been significant components of Caribbean discourse since the early 1970s – into a digital artistic practice. They have become synchronous with post-colonial discourses associated with English- and French-speaking Caribbean intellectual thought.[13] While there are deep divisions between the two con-cepts, the debates have nearly always centred on polysemic formations and inherent structures of creolised Caribbean literature and language in written and spoken form. Both recognise and are underpinned by the primal scene of tragedy and the brutality of plantation and slavery. Dis-cussion and development of these concepts by writers and theorists such as Édouard Glissant and Françoise Vergès have influenced my more recent work,[14] leading me to explore further the means by which the concept of creolisation and/or *créolité* can operate at a more integrated level in all aspects of artwork and to define the ways in which such hybrid, transcultural forma-tions can be identified or articulated through a multimedia artwork that situates the experience and presence of the plantation labourer.

FIGURE 4: DETAIL FROM *BACK ROUTES*, 2002

Central to the creative production process of *Back Routes* has been a critique and analysis of the research and subject matter. The Caribbean migrant experience is inextricably linked to and referential of a colonial legacy of forced migration and relocation and the experience of slavery and indentureship. The challenge then is to foreground the invisible and unknown individual experience of trauma and loss while maintaining a legitimacy and currency for the historical accounts of the period. I want to continue to explore ways in which artwork can seek out and expose the conven-tions through which 'truths' are produced and yet survive within an increasingly popu-larised and fictional space of production. I am also concerned to examine how repeated migratory experiences of dislocation, displacement and relocation resonate in the forma-tion and development of Caribbean nation-states and Caribbean identity in Britain.

Notes

1   Curated by Mary Griffiths, the concept of the exhibition originated partly in response to the Whit-worth's collection of late eighteenth- and early nineteenth-century British landscape watercolours 'ini-tially produced for the upper classes ... construct[ing] a vision of Britishness' and thereby endorsing 'a particular patrician view of national identity' (Griffiths 2002: 7). The exhibition further coincided with

the Commonwealth Games held in Manchester that year.

2 I have been working with digital media and networked environments since 1992. My early work was with digital still images, printed in photographic form for exhibition. The web piece *Sweetness and Light* (1996) was my first screen-based artwork. For further comment on and viewing of my work, see catalogues produced by *OVA* (1994) and *Autograph* (1997), together with a selection of essays by, among others, Giertsberg (1992/93); Doy (2000); Hall & Sealy (2001); Fehily *et al.* (2001); Finley (2004); and Berry Slater (2004).

3 This term, originally linked with other disciplines, has become increasingly associated with digital media since the 1990s. Within computer technology it describes a procedure (interactive mode) whereby large amounts of data can be processed simultaneously with other processes and is often associated with thinkers and inventors such as Alan Kay and Vannevar Bush, who saw interactive computer databases as a way of achieving an improved management of information. Within a capitalist construct, the term is associated with the notion of consumer choice. Cybertheorists associate interactivity with shifting the emphasis of authorship from the producer to the reader or consumer (Landow 1992), a theory first associated with poststructualism and the notion of the death of the author.

4 The term 'black', widely used during this period by black activists, politicians, theorists, producers to describe individuals and communities of African, Asian and Caribbean origin, was marked by the notion of solidarity, commitment and political/social agency.

5 A historically significant and national research library that collects, preserves and provides access to resources documenting the experiences of peoples of African descent, predominantly within the US. 'The Center's collections first won international acclaim in 1926 when the personal collection of the distinguished Puerto Rican-born black scholar and bibliophile, Arturo Alfonso Schomburg, was added to the Division of Negro Literature, History and Prints of the 135th Street Branch of the New York Public Library' (<http://www.nypl.org/research/sc/about/history.html> [Accessed 23 December 2005]).

6 Maggie Murray, Sally Greenhill and Val Wilmer founded Format, the first female photographers' agency in Britain, in 1983. I joined Format on leaving university in 1985 actively contributing for some ten years.

7 *My Daughter's Mind* was a series of documentary images of an extended family, three generations of women of Asian origin living in the Walsall area. It explored notions of belonging, identity and difference from one generation to another. The images were combined with a selection of quotes from the women photographed.

8 Indentureship was a labour system introduced to the British Caribbean between 1830 and 1917. Some half a million Indian and Chinese immigrants were indentured to work as labourers for approximately five years on sugar plantations, often replacing and competing with former slaves. The essence of the contract labourer's obligation was his/her surrender for a specified period of the freedom to quit his/her work and employer. Other stipulations covered such matters as repayment of the costs of transportation, housing, training and other living expenses (see Tinker 1974).

9 'The Aborigines Protection Society and the Ethnological Society of London were founded in 1837 and 1843 respectively; the first successful daguerrotype was made in 1837 and Fox Talbot's "photogenic drawing" was announced to the public in 1839' (Pinney *et al.* 1995: 7).

10 The Drake Exploration Society, founded in 1996, aims to perpetuate Drake's memory through research, fieldwork, lectures and publications.

11 For a more detailed discussion on Brathwaite's notion of Creole society see Shepherd & Richards (2002).

12 Creole has been used in many works since the early 1950s; see, for example, Lamming (1953); Selvon, (1956); Johnson (1974; 1975); and Dabydeen (1996).

13 Jean Bernabé, Patrick Chamoiseau, Raphaël Confiant and Édouard Glissant are associated with establishing the notion of *créolité*. Edward Kamau Brathwaite can be seen as instrumental in establishing the English Caribbean definition of Creole society in his seminal text *The Development of Creole Society in Jamaica 1770–1820* (1971). More recent publications and events, such as Documenta11_Platform 3, held in St Lucia, West Indies in January 2002 and the resultant publication, continue the debate; key contributors include Stuart Hall, Derek Walcott, Annie Paul and Françoise Vergès.

14 *Ghosting* (2004), commissioned by the Peepul Centre and Leicester City Art Gallery and *Endless Prospects* (2004), commissioned by Pitzhanger Manor and Gallery, London, both for the OVA touring exhibition *Roshini Kempadoo: Works 1990–2004*.

Bibliography

Appadurai, A. (1986) 'Introduction: Commodities and the Politics of Value', in A. Appadurai (ed.) *The Social Life of Things: Commodities in Cultural Perspective*. Cambridge: Cambridge University Press.

Ascott, R. (1996) 'Photography at the Interface', in T. Druckrey (ed.) *Electronic Culture: Technology and Visual Representation*. New York: Aperture.

Autograph (ed.) (1997) *Roshini Kempadoo: Monograph*. Autograph: London.

Berry Slater, J. (2004) 'White Lies: On the Question of "Identity" in New Media Art Made in Britain', in L. Kimbell (ed.) *New Media Art: Practice and Context in the UK 1994–2004*. London: Arts Council of England.

Brathwaite, E. K. (1971) *The Development of Creole Society in Jamaica 1770–1820*. Oxford: Clarendon Press.

Cartier-Bresson, H. (1952) *The Decisive Moment*. New York: Simon and Schuster.

Dabydeen, D. (1996) *The Counting House*. London: Jonathan Cape.

DeCarava, R. and L. Hughes (1984 [1967]) *The Sweet Flypaper of Life*. Washington DC: Howard University Press.

Derrida, J. (1996) *Archive Fever: A Freudian Impression*. Chicago: University of Chicago Press.

Doy, G. (1995) *Seeing Consciousness: Women, Class and Representation*. Oxford: Berg.

_____ (2000) *Black Visual Culture*. London: I.B. Tauris.

Edwards, E. (ed.) (1992) *Anthropology and Photography 1860–1920*. New Haven: Yale University Press.

Enwezor, O. (1997) 'Reframing the Black Subject', in O. Enwezor (ed.), *Catalogue for 2nd Johannesburg Biennale, Trade Routes: History and Geography*. South Africa: Johannesburg Biennale.

Fanon, F. (1963) *The Wretched of the Earth*. New York: Grove Press.

Fehily, C., K. Newton and L. Wells (eds) (2001) *Shifting Horizons: Women's Landscapes Photography Now*. London: I.B. Tauris.

Finley, C. (2004) in OVA (ed.) *Roshini Kempadoo: Work 1990–2004*. London: OVA.

Giertsberg, F. (1992/93) 'Roshini Kempadoo – Cultural Identity and Representation', *Perspektief Magazine*, 7–18.

Gilroy (1987) *There Ain't No Black in the Union Jack: The Cultural Politics of Race and Nation*. London: Hutchinson.

_____ (1992) *The Black Atlantic: Modernity and Double Consciousness*. Cambridge: Havard University Press.

Griffiths, M. (ed.) (2002) *Travelogue: Views of Britian by Seven Contemporary Artists*. Manchester: Whitworth Art Gallery.

Gupta, S. (ed.) (1993) *Disrupted Borders: An Intervention in Definitions of Boundaries*. London: River Oram Press.

Hall, S. (1990) 'Cultural Identity and Diaspora', in J. Rutherford (ed.) *Identity: Community, Culture and Difference*. London: Lawrence and Wishart.

____ (1999) 'Un-Settling "the Heritage": Re-Imagining the Post-Nation', in *Whose Heritage? The Impact of Cultural Diversity on Britain's Living Heritage*. Manchester: Arts Council of England.

Hall, S. and D. A. Bailey (1992) 'The Vertigo of Displacement: Shifts within Black Documentary Practices', *Critical Decade Ten*.8, 2 (3):14–23.

Hall, S. and M. Sealy (2001) *Different. A Historical Context: Contemporary Photographers and Black Identity*. London: Phaidon Press.

Johnson, L. K. (1974) *Voice of the Living and the Dead*. London: Race Today.

____ (1975) *Dread Beat and Blood*. London: Bogle L'Ouveerture.

Jones, K. (1990) 'In Their Own Image: Black Women Artists Who Combine Text With Photography', *Art-Forum*, 29: 132–8.

Lamming, G. (1953) *In the Castle of My Skin*. New York: McGraw Hill.

Landow, G. P. (1992) *Hypertext: The Convergence of Contemporary Critical Theory and Technology*. Baltimore: Johns Hopkins University Press.

Mirzoeff, N. (1999) *An Introduction to Visual Culture*. Routledge: London.

OVA (ed.) (2004) *Roshini Kempadoo: Work 1990–2004*. London: OVA.

Pinney, C., R. Charity, C. Wright and R. Poignant (eds) (1995) The Impossible Science of Being: Dialogues Between Anthropology and Photography. London: The Photographers' Gallery.

Selvon, S. (1956) *The Lonely Londoners*. White Plains: Longmans.

Sharma, A. (2004) in OVA (ed.) *Roshini Kempadoo: Work 1990–2004*. London: OVA.

Shepherd, V. and G. Richards (eds) (2002) *Questioning Creole: Creolisation Discourses in Caribbean Culture*. Kingston: Ian Randle/Oxford: James Currey.

Tinker, H. (1974) *A New System of Slavery: The Export of Indian Labour Overseas 1830–1920*. London: Institute of Race Relations.

Van der Zee, J. (1978) *The Harlem Book of the Dead*. New York: Morgan and Morgan.

Williamson, J. (1994) *Decoding Advertisements: Ideology and Meaning in Advertising*. London: Marion Boyars.

Willis, D. (2002) *Reflections in Black: A History of Black Photographers, 1840 to the Present*. New York, London: W. W. Norton and Company.

Willis, D. and C. Williams (2002) *The Black Female Body: A Photographic History*. Philadelphia: Temple University Press.

PRESENTING THEMSELVES BEFORE THE CAMERA: THE SOMALI ELDERS PROJECT IN CARDIFF

Glenn Jordan

The decolonised peoples of Jamaica, Trinidad, Barbados, Guyana, India, Pakistan, Bangladesh and other once colonies of the Empire [e.g. Somalia] who have made their home in Britain, together with their children and their children's children, act as a perpetual reminder of the ways in which the once metropolis is intimately connected to its 'peripheries'. Both colonists and colonised are linked through their histories, histories which are forgotten in the desire to throw off the embarrassing reminders of Empire.

  – Catherine Hall (1996: 67)

Wales … has always been – and will always be – a multicultural, multi-ethnic society. Multiculturalism is one element of historical continuity, an enduring quality of this small but ancient nation. Nevertheless, recognition of the fact of multiculturalism and any systematic response to it has been patchy and contradictory.

  – Chris Williams, Nick Evans and Paul O'Leary (2003: 1–2)

Whose history matters? Is the history of Wales only a history of people who are called white? What is at stake in the ways immigrants and minorities are portrayed? Do they have the right to present themselves as they wish to be seen?

The Somali Elders Project is a cultural-political intervention combining humanist portrait photography, collaborative ethnography and oral history.[1] Based in Cardiff, Wales – a key site in the Somali diaspora – it is a mode of socially-concerned research, photography and presentation in which previously marginalised voices, images and experiences are brought to the fore, with the subjects actively participating in the process. It is an exercise in cultural democracy that takes seriously the admonition that all human beings, especially those excluded from power and privilege by virtue of their class, racial or cultural background, should be treated with dignity and respect. It is a cultural-political practice that challenges and seeks to subvert hegemonic images, narratives and meanings. It is, unashamedly, an exercise in anti-racist education and an appreciation of cultural diversity in these times of great difficulty between 'Islam' and 'the West'.

If one hears a racist statement in Cardiff, it is likely to be about Somalis. In the larger society, they are an ethnic group with very low status. In mainstream history, art and culture, their presence is virtually invisible. The intent of the Somali Elders Project is to reverse this trend, to render visible this community, its history and present. Given Butetown History & Art Centre's commitment to 'history from below' (see Jordan & Weedon 2000; Jordan 2003), to foregrounding histories and experiences that have been marginalised and excluded, this initiative is particularly appropriate for us. The fact that three of the elders whom I photographed – Elmi Jama Handulleh, Mohamed Ali Mohamed and Said Ismail Ali – died before the exhibition was completed underscores the moral imperative of this work.

I usually conduct research and write. Why, this time, have I privileged photography? Photography often shows us things – people, places, faces, everyday life – that we have failed to notice before. It has the ability to help us see what our unseeing eyes have missed. Through humanist, empathetic portraits of older Somali men, we confront stereotypes and misrepresentations.

When the Somali Elders Project was initially conceived in 2000/1, it was expected that three products would result: an exhibition; an accompanying catalogue combining photographs and text; and an anthology of life stories. The exhibition and its bilingual catalogue are both called *Somali Elders: Portraits from Wales/Odeyada Soomaalida: Muuqaalo ka yimid Welishka* (2004). The photographs were taken by me and I authored the catalogue with the assistance of two Somali researchers, Akli Ahmed and Abdihakim Arwo. The exhibition was opened on 18 July 2004 at Butetown History & Arts Centre; the event attracted a large, enthusiastic crowd.[2] [DVD REF 1: VIDEO] [DVD REF 2: VIDEO]

Perhaps you are wondering: Why Somalis? What have their images, voices and memories to do with Wales and the British Isles?

IDENTITY OR DIFFERENCE?

Look at Figure 1 (overleaf). Who is this man? What do you see when you look at this image? How does the subject present himself to the camera? How does he address you, the viewer? Taken in 2001, this is of one of my first photographs of a Somali elder. The subject was 92 years old at the time. Born in a town called Berbera, in the northern region of Somali, Said Shuqule[3] lived in Wales – in Newport, a city only ten miles from Cardiff – for some 56 years before his death in 2002. The following is an extract from his life story, or rather a biographical statement about him constructed by my research assistant, Abdihakim Arwo, from various sources, including an article in a local newspaper and interviews with members of Shuqule's family:[4]

> Said Ismail Ali participated in World War II and, forty years later, in the Falklands War. He left his hometown of Berbera, where he used to work for his brother who owned a coffee shop, in 1939. He worked on both Royal Navy and Merchant Navy ships. 'There was little work and I had a young family to bring up. The sea meant at least a steady wage, but I do not hold any romantic notions about it all. It was simply a job.' Said did many jobs on board ship, ranging from donkeyman, greaser, fireman and storeman to trimmer. Just after he arrived in Britain, he became involved in World War II aboard warships. The Italians invaded his country in 1940 and it was relieved by British troops six months later. During the war, on his voyages to supply the British Army, his ship called *Beaver* was sunk. As a young mess boy he tried to save the lives of his shipmates, taking them to lifeboats. On that day he lost his Somali shipmate called Hassan Mohammed, who died. In 1946, Said brought his family to Newport and lived there until his death in 2002. He used to say: 'There was a small community in Newport. I decided to settle here and bring my family.' (Jordan 2004: 188)

FIGURE 1: SAID ISMAIL ALI ('SAID SHUQULE') ON THE WALL, WITH HIS MEDALS, CARDIFF, 2001

Although a Somali by birth, Said Shuqule lived most of his adult life in Wales. With that background in mind, I now invite you to look again at his photograph and consider the question: Do his image and life story belong more to the history of Wales or to that of Somaliland? Where does he belong?

ON THE SOMALI PRESENCE IN WALES

Where are they from? And how have they come to be here?

There is a worldwide diaspora of Somalis living in Europe, North America and the Gulf States. Tens of thousands of Somalis now live in the UK, scattered in cities such as London, Cardiff, Liverpool, Sheffield, Manchester, Birmingham, Bristol, Hull, Middlesborough, Leicester and Newport. London Docklands (the East End) and Cardiff have the longest-established Somali communities in Britain. No accurate census has been conducted (and the census reports do not mention the word 'Somali'), but estimates put the Somali population in Wales at around 7,000, with some 5,000 in Cardiff. Nonetheless, their history and presence and the sacrifices they have made in the service of the UK remain largely unknown.

Somalis are a single ethnic group (divided into clans) who share a common culture, religion (they are Sunni Muslims) and language. Culturally and linguistically they belong to the Cushitic-speaking family, a branch of the Hamito-Semitic family, which also includes Semitic, Berber and Egyptian. With an estimated population of 8–10 million, their homeland is in the eastern corner of the Horn of Africa, a vast area 3,000 kilometres long and 1,000 kilometres across bordered by Kenya, Ethiopia, Djibouti, the Gulf of Aden and the Indian Ocean. People from the various areas of the Somali diaspora often visit each other; during marriage festivals whole extended families in the UK gather together and sometimes members come from Europe, America and the Gulf States. During such gatherings, the sense that there is a connected diaspora is tangibly felt.

Traditionally, Somalis have been a pastoral nomadic people, herding camel, sheep and goats for thousands of years: cattle herding is a more recent phenomenon. The nomadic life entailed constant movement of people and livestock in search of better pasture and water. This nomadic tradition seems still to exert its influence today: whether as seamen or refugees, Somalis are a people who move:

A man who has not travelled does not have eyes.
– A well-known Somali proverb

Being a nomad, I am always picking myself up and moving on. It makes you resilient.
– Eid Ali Ahmed (Cardiff, August 2001)

In the last quarter of the nineteenth century, the Somali nation was divided up between three European colonial powers, Britain (which took control of the northern coastal area), France (which took the area now known as Djibouti) and Italy (which controlled the largest territory, in the south), as well as two African states, Egypt and Ethiopia (both of which took areas adjacent to their own territories).[5] Nearly all the Somali elders in Wales are from the north, the territory formerly known as British Somaliland. For most of their existence in Wales, the Somali community has comprised perhaps half a dozen different clans, the largest being the Isaq clan. Since the 1990s, the community in Wales has been becoming more diverse; Cardiff and Newport are now home to Somalis from the south – for example, Mogadishu – as well as from the north. In Cardiff the community, which is concentrated in the Butetown, Grangetown and Riverside areas (there are also significant numbers in Splott, Rumney and St Mellons), can be considered as consisting of two basic groups, seamen and refugees, along with their families and descendants. Although British-born Somalis are a significant group (Cardiff has the largest British-born Somali population in the UK), they are not the focus of our current project.

Most of the elderly Somalis now living in Wales are men who came to the UK between 1937 and 1961, especially during World War II and the following years of post-war reconstruction. These seamen left their country, a British colony, intending to earn some money and return home. Most were hoping to use their earnings to buy more livestock, but things rarely turned out as they had planned. For example, in an interview for the exhibition, Ibrahim Ahmed Hassan tells how he was brought to the UK in 1958 by his father, who served as a merchant seaman in the two world wars. He returned to Somalia in 1983 after 23 years at sea, but was back in Cardiff two years later and back at sea from 1987 to 1995.

In addition to the seamen, a large proportion of the Somali community in Cardiff are refugees who joined family members who were already living here. Most of these refugees have gone through the settlement phases and are now struggling to adapt to their new lives.

It is sometimes observed, especially by members of the larger society, that Somalis

FIGURE 2: IBRAHIM AHMED HASSAN IN A CLASSIC SOMALI ELDER'S POSE, CARDIFF, 2001

rarely interact socially with others and seem to confine their social activities to themselves. Partly, the issue has to do with language; many members of the Somali community do not have good English-language skills. Those such as former seamen, who have travelled widely and interacted with other societies, tend to have attained higher levels of proficiency, while refugees who make friends with locally-born Somalis tend to become fluent English speakers. As more and more Somali students attend local schools, the number of English speakers is on the increase. Perhaps social interaction between Somalis and other groups will also increase, although currently there is often some antagonism.

SOMALI SEAMEN IN CARDIFF: A HUNDRED YEARS OF (UNRECORDED) HISTORY

I was born in Arabsiyo. I'm 92 years old. Arabsiyo is a small town west of Hargeisa and is famous for its farms. My father used to have lots of horses. I was born near a famous tree called Agamso. We used to live in a traditional Somali tent. I moved to Djibouti when I was 12 years old. My uncle was living there and I joined him … I entered the Quranic School and, when I finished, I went to the French school where I learned the French language…

I saw a lot of people going to France to get jobs and I decided to follow them there. I sold my boat and went to France. I stayed in Marseilles and worked in

FIGURE 3: MOHAMOUD KALINLE WITH HIS WAR MEDALS, CARDIFF, 2001

factories and sometimes on the ships. We used to sail to all over the world. I left Marseilles and went to Paris and from there I caught the train and went to Le Havre, where I boarded the ferry to Dover. From there I came to Cardiff in 1937 and stayed here since then. I joined the Merchant Navy and later the Royal Navy and worked as fireman and donkeyman in the engine-room. There were lots of Somalis who have now died and all of them were either in the Merchant Navy or the Royal Navy. I travelled here with a man called Abdi Osman who was my best friend but who is now dead. He wanted to join his uncle in Cardiff and I had a cousin in Cardiff. I worked on ships and also on some destroyers. I was in World War II and destroyed some ships and two fighter aircrafts in Malta. We used to carry food and a lot of military equipment to the front line during World War II. I was also a member of the National Union of Seamen.

– From interview with Mohamoud Kalinle (Cardiff, May 2004)
[DVD REF 3: PHOTO; PDF]

The nineteenth century was a period of great migration throughout the world, when tens of millions left their homelands in search of work. Somalis, a nomadic people accustomed to movement, were no exception. By the mid-1830s, many had travelled across the sea to neighbouring Arab and Asian countries. Following the opening of the Suez Canal in 1869 Somalis journeyed to different parts of Europe. There was a Somali presence in Wales before the end of the century.

Somali seamen in Cardiff tended to move to the 'Tiger Bay' or Butetown area, where they joined what was rapidly becoming one of the most cosmopolitan communities in the world:

The Butetown district, an area approximately a mile long and a quarter of a mile wide located on the southern end of Cardiff – an area which locals referred to as 'Tiger Bay' and 'The Docks' – was particularly favoured as a home away from home for new immigrants and minorities. It is often said that, during its heyday, from the latter 1800s to the mid-1900s, it included people 'from the four corners of the earth'. In the 1940s some 45 to 50 nations, and many more ethnic groups, were represented in a population of around five thousand … This population of immigrants and minorities included the following:

- Greeks, Turks and Cypriots
- Spanish, Italians, Portuguese and Maltese
- Colonial Portuguese (mainly Cape Verdeans)
- Yemenis, Egyptians and Somalis
- Welsh, Irish, English and Scots
- West Africans (Nigerians, Sierra Leoneans and others)
- West Indians (Jamaicans, Barbadians, Trinidadians, St. Lucians, St. Kittsians and others)
- British Hondurans, Panamanians and Guyanese
- French, Mauritians, Colonial French
- Chinese, Malays and Indians (i.e., people from what is now India, Pakistan and Bangladesh)
- Poles, Ukranians and Eastern European Jews
- Estonians, Latvians and Lithuanians
- Germans, Norwegians, Finns, Swedes and Danes
- North Americans, South Americans
- And a few more… (Jordan 2001: 9–10)[6]

The skills and abilities nurtured by one culture can be transferred to another setting and the harsh pastoral life had given the Somalis diverse skills and a sense of adventure. Travel across the sea to other lands was an important concept in Somali culture, and Somalis often refer to themselves as a travelling people.[7]

Before 1914 the number of black people in Cardiff was not large. However, the outbreak of World War I led to a dramatic increase in the number of Somali and other 'coloured' seamen. As local white men left the Merchant Navy to join the Royal Navy, more Merchant Navymen were badly need. The Somalis settled in Cardiff passed this information on to their relatives and clan members and new streams of seamen flocked to the coal-exporting port. A substantial community of male Somalis in Wales dates from that period. The outbreak of the World War II resulted in a further dramatic increase in the Somali community in Wales, as labour was badly needed on the tramp steamers and in factories to support the war effort. It was during this time that official attitudes towards the black population were modified to such an extent that many Somalis joined the Royal Navy, while the number of those joining the Merchant Navy also grew significantly. Postwar reconstruction attracted more Somalis into the area. Many of the present elders in Wales worked as both labourers and seamen.

For decades no Somali women came to Britain and Somali men married or befriended women who were white or mixed-race or married at home and visited their families during their holidays.

The situation began to change in the 1970s. Somali men were encouraged to bring their families to Britain by the fact that men from other Muslim communities had started

FIGURE 4: MARRIAGE OF MOHAMED HASSAN AND KATIE LINK, C.1925

to do so, and it was in the areas where these Muslim communities were concentrated or significant that the first nucleus of Somali families grew. However, the first Somali families in Wales settled not in Cardiff but in Newport.

In addition to changes in the family, there have also been changes in religious practices and beliefs. There is a strong Somali religious group in Cardiff with its base at the Nuur al-Islam Mosque. Within the Muslim world, there are many different, often competing interpretations of Islam. Although Somalis historically have had a tradition of Sufism, modern trends and outside influences are having their effect, especially among the young. The ideas of the Muslim Brotherhood in Egypt, the Wahabi doctrine of Saudi Arabia and other militant Islamic organisations now have some influence among certain sections of the local Somali community. In Cardiff, the Wahabi influence is clearly visible, to such an extent that a number of the elders feel uncomfortable and prefer to pray mainly at the 'Yemeni mosque' (the South Wales Islamic Centre), whose imam is the moderate community leader Sheikh Said Hassan Ismail.

As a result of the shift towards a more fundamentalist Islam, there was some opposition, on religious grounds, to participation in the Somali Elders Project. One young man, who had had his picture taken with his uncle, returned about twenty minutes later to tell me that he had just found out that 'It's against my religion'. He asked that his photograph should not be exhibited or published and, of course, we honoured his wish. His uncle, who was eighty, had no objection whatsoever. He loved the photograph I took of him and returned to the Centre during the exhibition to ask me to take another, as he had grown a beard.

THE SUBJECTS: FACES, MEMORIES, VOICES

Of all the modes of photographic expression, the most difficult to resolve successfully would seem to be the portrait. A portrait photograph immediately triggers such profoundly personal responses in the viewer, emotive, paradoxical, and
not always rational. The issues raised are complex, challenging, even treacherous,
centring upon the self and its representation, upon identity and immortality ...
[The photo-portrait] is fully capable of mythologising and immortalising. It can
confer acknowledgement and bestow dignity. It can also stereotype, debase and
dehumanise. The portraitist, therefore, should harbour a clear moral mandate, for
his [or her] powers to misrepresent are wide. He has been entrusted, no less, with
his sitter's identity. And the act of portrait making ... is inherently perilous ...
But if the moral injunction is recognised, and accepted, then the photographic
portrait at best might reinforce our positive sense of collective and individual humanity. Thus for me the best photo-portraitists invariably have been humanists.
And if they themselves have not been outright moralists, their work nevertheless
has been moral.

  – Gerry Badger (1988: 125)[8]

Forty-seven elders are depicted in the exhibition and its accompanying publication. The
youngest is in his mid-fifties; the two oldest are in their nineties; most are in their seventies
or eighties. [DVD REF 4: VIDEO] They were all born in what was then British Somaliland.
Most of them are from in or around Hargeisa, Buroa, Arabsiyo or Berbera. For the most
part, they came to the UK between 1937 and 1961. They were not the first generation of

Somali immigrants to come here; there were
earlier pioneers. I have interviewed people
who remember Somali seamen who came to
Cardiff prior to World War I. One of them
was Abdi Nuur, known locally by his nickname 'Abdi Gurri', whom I knew well. When
he died in 1992, he was approximately one
hundred years old.[9]

The majority of the Somali elders in this
project are economic migrants who came to
Wales and joined that invisible, marginalised
group that Karl Marx aptly called the 'reserve
army of labour'. Some, like the Irish immigrants before them, worked in heavy industry, including the steel works, the mines and
the docks. They did hard manual labour and
a number of them sustained serious injuries
in the process.

I include a number of their biographies/
stories with the tellers' photographs. These
stories are slightly edited written texts, not

FIGURE 5: OMAR NOOR KIBAR, CARDIFF, 2004

the original spoken narratives, because all of the interviews were conducted in Somali.[10] I insist on naming them, using both the English and Somali versions of their names, as a matter of recognition:

- Ibrahim Ahmed Hassan/Ibraahim Axmed Xasan [DVD REF 5: PHOTO; PDF]
- Mohamoud Kalinle/Maxamuud Qalinle [DVD REF 6: PHOTO; PDF]
- Omar Noor Kibar/Cumar Nwuur Kibear [DVD REF 7: PHOTO; PDF]
- Said Ismail Ali/Saciid Ismaaciil Cali [DVD REF 8: PHOTO; PDF]
- Abdi Adan Mohamed/Cabdi Aadan Maxamed [DVD REF 9: PHOTO; PDF]
- Adan Samater Yusuf/Aadan Samatar Yuusuf [DVD REF 10: PHOTO; PDF]
- Ahmed Mohamed Adan/Axmed Maxamed Aadan [DVD REF 11: PHOTO; PDF]
- Ahmed Yonis Awalleh/Axmed Yoonis Cawaale [DVD REF 12: PHOTO; PDF]
- Hassan Ahmed Essa/Xasan Axmed Ciise [DVD REF 13: PHOTO; PDF]
- Hussein Ismael Abdi/Xuseen Ismaaciil Abdi [DVD REF 14: PHOTO; PDF]
- Ibrahim Hussein Abby/Ibraahim Xuseen Caabi [DVD REF 15: PHOTO; PDF]
- Ismael Ali Gass/Ismaaciil Cali Gaas [DVD REF 16: PHOTO; PDF]
- Mahamud Jama Mohamed/Maxamuud Jaamac Maxamed [DVD REF 17: PHOTO; PDF]
- Mohamed Abdi Ahmed/Maxamed Cabdi Axmed [DVD REF 18: PHOTO; PDF]
- Mohamed Adan Ahmed/Maxamed Aadan Axmed [DVD REF 19: PHOTO; PDF]
- Mohamed Hashi Halig/Maxamed Xaashi Haalig [DVD REF 20: PHOTO; PDF]
- Omar Yussuf Essa/Cumar Yuusuf Ciise [DVD REF 21: PHOTO; PDF]

Having introduced the voices of the elders, let us listen to the photographer, as he is being interviewed by the author of this chapter. The dialogue took place in 2004 when the exhibition was in the final stage of preparation.[11]

Author: Were there any Somali elders who refused to have their photographs taken?

Photographer: Yes, of course, but they were very much in the minority. Interestingly, it is younger Somalis who are most likely to raise objections, on religious grounds, to having their photographs taken and displayed. In Wales, and, I suspect, in many other places as well, fundamentalist Islam has a much greater grip on the young than it does on the old.

Author: Is it possible to categorise the elders who refused?

Photographer: One category would consist of those Somali elders who, like many of us, do not like to have their photographs taken; these are not people who have principled objections to being photographed – they don't object on moral, religious or political grounds – and thus, as one might expect, some of them eventually agreed to participate. The best example is that of Esa Mohamed Omar.

When I arrived to photograph him in Rothesay House, the local nursing home, he was in bed. One of his countrymen spent ten minutes or so persuading him – in Somali – to be photographed. He got out of bed, put on his jacket and sat on a chair. (I covered the back of the chair with his jumper to conceal from the viewer the not-so-lovely floral pattern of the cushions.)

Another example is Ahmed Mohamed Adan, known in the Somali community in Wales as 'Barry Dock', because he used to live in Barry and work in the docks, cleaning the decks and engine-rooms of the ships. He only agreed after Vera Johnson, an old friend of his who happens to be a volunteer at Butetown History & Arts Centre, talked to him. As it turned out, he seemed thoroughly to enjoy the process of being photographed, and he brought his daughter and grandchildren to the opening of the exhibition. I photographed them all there together, with his portrait in the background, towering over them.

Perhaps the most interesting category was those men, perhaps three or four, who insisted on being paid. Presumably, they regard photography as a mode of exploitation and they wanted to ensure that they would be at least partial beneficiaries. In any event, those who demanded money as a condition of their participation in the project were not included.

The final category consists of one man who seems to have felt, with absolute certainty, that I was some kind of spy! He adamantly insisted that I was 'from the government' and even said so in English when I was standing nearby. He was not included either, although my researcher tried to persuade him of the importance of the project and the moral credentials of the photographer.

Author: So, what status do the Somali elders have here?

Photographer: The elders are regarded as the traditional leaders in Somali society. They are much revered. Recognised as having accumulated years of rich experience, wisdom and judgement, they are regularly consulted on clan affairs, and they

FIGURE 6: ESA MOHAMED OMAR, CARDIFF, 2004

FIGURE 7: AHMED MOHAMED ADAN WITH DAUGHTER AND GRANDCHILDREN, *SOMALI ELDERS* EXHIBITION OPENING, CARDIFF, 18 JULY 2004

usually have the final say in consultative meetings, where every adult male has the right to speak. Although many of them have had only basic schooling, the elders are experts on the local environment, culture, genealogy, history and oral poetry; some have called them 'walking encyclopaedias'. The respect they receive from their own society gives them esteem, pride and self-confidence.

Most of the elderly Somalis in Wales, especially those who have been here for a long time, formerly worked as seamen. Many suffer from illnesses connected to their work at sea and some have not been compensated for these illnesses and injuries. Despite the respect they receive from their own society, there is a general feeling that officialdom in Cardiff and elsewhere in the UK has failed not only to ensure that they have proper access to health and social services but also, crucially, to acknowledge their contributions to British society, in particular, their contributions during World War II. Recently, government has begun to respond to this situation; Red Sea House, a residence for Somali men, has been opened and some of the elders pictured in this exhibition live there. The exhibition and its catalogue represent a small step towards giving these men visibility and respect in the larger community.

Author: I notice that many of the men have walking sticks and that most of them have fine hats with beautiful embroidery. Can you explain the significance of these items?

Photographer: I'll try, although let me say at the outset that I'm not an expert on Somali history, society and culture. The presence of the hats is easy to explain; traditionally, Muslim men tend to wear such hats. Regarding the walking sticks, my suspicion is that they are a modern appropriation of an ancient tradition. The people of northern Somalia have been pastoralists, specifically camel herders, for hundreds, even thousands of years and as such would carry staffs. Also, note that it is the elders, specifically, who carry the walking sticks. This suggests that the sticks may also be signifiers of status and honour, as well as, where necessary, mobility aids.

Author: On the other hand, look at Ali Mohamed Ahmed[12] using his umbrella as a prop. [DVD REF 22: PHOTO] What does this suggest?

Photographer: It suggests that the walking sticks may be a matter not only of status but also of style. In any event, it is interesting that a number of the men who carried the sticks seemed to walk perfectly well without them.

Author: Why are there no women in these photographs?

Photographer: I'm glad you noticed that; it would be upsetting if viewers did not. The reasons women are not present in these images are to do with history and everyday social life in the Somali community. Let me take history first. It is only in the last thirty years or so that Somali women have begun coming to Cardiff. Thus, older Somali women do not belong to the history of Somalis in Wales in the way that the men do. The second point has to do with culture. As a male photographer, it would be difficult, if not impossible, for me to do portraits of Muslim women. I think there should be such a project for Muslim women in Wales and have discussed the idea with a female photographer who has worked in Islamic countries.

Incidentally, when I said to my Somali community researcher that I wanted to do a photographic project on 'Somali elders', I did not specify whether the participants should be male or female. As it turned out, all the people who came to be photographed were male. This was the case even when two of the elders brought along a few of their descendants; one brought his son and grandson; the other brought his nephew and nephew-in-law. All cultures have rules regarding what males and females should or should not do.

Author: A lot of these men in your photographs are all dressed up, some of them in beautiful robes, others in suits, etc. Why is that? [DVD REF 23: PHOTO]

Photographer: Almost all these photographs were taken on Friday afternoons after prayers at the mosque. Just as a lot of people dress up to go to church, many Muslims dress up to go to the mosque.

Author: Perhaps you would wish to argue that, in a sense, your photographs aren't really authentic. They don't really show us how these men look most of the time.

Photographer: I don't think it's very helpful to get into a debate about what is or is not an 'authentic' photograph. In any case, I never claimed that these images are of Somali elders as they look everyday. There are a few exceptions, photographs in which the men are in their everyday apparel. Look at the photograph of Ali Mohamed Ahmed in his woollen cap and chequered shirt. [DVD REF 24: PHOTO] Those photographs were taken, as I recall, on a Tuesday. Anyway, I don't have a problem with people dressing up as they choose and presenting themselves to be photographed. Portrait photographs are co-productions and, morally and ethically, the subjects should have rights when it comes to how they will be portrayed.

Author: A lot of these men seem to be staring at you or the camera. Why is that?

Photographer: I'm not entirely sure why so many of them appear to be staring at the camera. You'd have to ask them and see if you can get a satisfactory answer. In her book *On Photography*, Susan Sontag argues that the people of non-industrialised countries still feel apprehensive about having their pictures taken (1979: 161). I don't know whether this statement helps us at all. It may simply be that they are adhering to different conventions regarding the pose one assumes when one's photograph is being taken. Perhaps they have their own understandings of portrait photography – clearly, most of them have.

Consider, by way of comparison, the formal stances, the body language and faces, of the subjects in studio photographs taken in the West during the Victorian and Edwardian periods. They are similar, although I think it is fair to say that viewers may find some of these photographs more confrontational; the subjects stare back with greater vigour. Perhaps earning the right to look is one of the benefits of being an elder; perhaps it is a matter of their status and power.

In any event, I would suggest that some of their poses have an elegant stillness. Consider, for example, the portrait of Mohamed Abdi Ahmed [DVD REF 18: PHOTO] which is another of my favourites, although some viewers find it troubling. There are photographs here where the subject seems to be very comfortable with the camera. One such example might be the photograph of Elmi Jama Handulleh, who local Somalis called 'Sultan'. [DVD REF 25: PHOTO] Another example is the picture of Ibrahim Hussein Abby, where he is standing at an angle to the wall with his face turned to the photographic lens. [DVD REF

26: PHOTO] I remember taking that; Ibrahim Hussein Abby just walked up to the wall and assumed that pose, which was unexpected. It was the first photo that I took of him. Clearly, he was very comfortable with the camera, as was the eighty-year-old Ismael Ali Gass. [DVD REF 27: PHOTO] With his suave clothes, careful poses and dark glasses, I am tempted to call him 'Mr Cool'; on seeing the photographs I took of him, two members of my staff nicknamed him 'The Godfather'. And then there is his cousin, Hussein Ismael Abdi, who, after seeing and admiring a work print of Ismael Ali Gass, came back and asked me to re-take his photograph. [DVD REF 28: PHOTO]

But notwithstanding these examples, I think many of them were not comfortable. I suspect they have not bought into the Western convention that you should smile when the camera turns towards you. Whatever the reasons, I'm glad most of them did not smile. In some cases I think the result has been the production of very powerful images, which they, more than I, made. Consider, for example, the portraits of Adan Samater Yusuf, Hasan Hadji Yusuf, Saeed Ali Abyan and Said Ismail Ali. [DVD REF 29: PHOTO]

There are a few subjects who are not properly looking at the camera. [DVD REF 30: PHOTO] Some of these images were taken for aesthetic reasons. For example, the photograph of Mohamed Adan Abdi is, in my view, an absolutely beautiful image. Perhaps the most interesting of the subjects who do not return the viewer's gaze is Ahmed Yonis Awaleh. [DVD REF 31: PHOTO] He's nearly blind. Thus, he allows the viewer to look without being challenged. Nonetheless, his eyes, I would suggest, have a definite power. If you don't believe me, I invite you to look closely at them.

Author: How are we to read these photographs, these visual statements?

Photographer: One of my favourite portraits is that of Said Shuqule. [DVD REF 8: PHOTO] I have shown large prints of it to various visitors to Butetown History & Arts Centre. The predominant response is, 'What a sad face'. I had not anticipated this; I was struck by the power of his gaze, not the sadness of his face. Viewers feel that, by virtue of our status as fellow human beings, we can discern or deduce what emotions, attitudes and experience lie behind or beneath photographed facial expressions. We look at faces and we see kindness, contentment, sorrow and pain, self-satisfaction, longing and desperate disappointment. We invariably seek to read faces and to create narratives about the lives of those whose essence we feel we have deciphered.

Author: But can we read these faces? What do they say?

Photographer: Different viewers, occupying different social positions and having different experiences, will decode them in different ways. Nonetheless, I would suggest that we – certainly those of us in the West – share certain cultural beliefs about the human face and photographic representations of it. We know that facial expressions signify, that they play a crucial role in communication. We believe that the camera can 'capture' more than a likeness of its subjects, that the successful portrait 'unmasks' the face – penetrates the veil – to reveal inner character, inner being. When we look at portraits, especially of old people, we see the story of their lives written in their faces, in their eyes, in the wrinkles of their skin, in their apparently characteristic expressions.

I think that the assumptions underlying this view are far too simplistic, reductionist and essentialist. Arnold Newman, the distinguished portrait photographer, once said, 'It seems to me that no one picture can ever be a final summation of a personality. There are so many facets in every human being that it is impossible to present them all in one photograph' (quoted in Sobieszek 1999: 23). Moreover, I am not quite sure what to make of some of the Somali elders' expressions. I suspect that they often have more to do with conventions of portraiture prevalent in the sitters' community than with their own personal expressions. Compare Faras (Hassan Ahmed Essa) laughing with his more formal pose. [DVD REF 32: PHOTO] One could ask, 'Which one is really him?' But the question would not really make sense.

Some time in the 1980s, Richard Avedon, the widely acclaimed fashion and portrait photographer, said, 'You can't get at the thing itself, the real nature of the sitter, by stripping away the surface. The surface is all you've got' (quoted in Sobieszek 1999: 25). I know enough about modernist art, poststructuralism and postmodernism to know that I should be wary of the view that the camera 'reveals inner character and emotional states'. Nonetheless, when I look at a number of these photographs I feel some central dimensions of emotion and character are made manifest. I am prepared to accept the possibility that I am deluding myself, that the general public and I are simply wrong, but somehow, I don't think so.

Author: Whose viewpoint is depicted in this work? Do we see these men through your eyes or their own?

Photographer: Through both, of course. But the point is that I did not want to make my vision predominant. I wanted the images to be the product of a kind of collaboration – and for the sophisticated viewer to see them as such.

Author: Is the Somali Elders Project an exercise in the production of 'positive images'?

Photographer: I can see at least two reasons why one might say this. First, three of the men are wearing medals, which points to their involvement in World War II and other war efforts. This counters the stereotype that immigrants are simply scroungers who, to quote popular ideology, 'come here and live at our expense'. Secondly, the Somali elders appear as a diverse group. Their images reveal considerable diversity in terms of physical appearance (phenotype), dress and self-presentation. Also, their biographical sketches reveal differences in terms of social background. This counters the homogenising tendency that is characteristic of racist and other stereotyping.[13] Nonetheless, I am somewhat uncomfortable with the term 'positive images' because it has certain connotations. Among clever, well-informed cultural practitioners it is *passé*, denoting a practice widely used by black artists in the 1960s and 1970s but considered a bit suspect now.

Author: Why? What do you mean?

Photographer: 'Positive images' is a concept that depends on its opposite, 'negative images', for its meaning; it involves a strategy of reversal. For example, in response to three hundred years of imagery in which black people were represented as ugly and stupid, Black Americans, in the context of the Black Power movement of the 1960s and early 1970s, declared 'Black is Beautiful' and black artists, intellectuals and writers began creating new images and texts in which our beauty, intelligence and humanity were affirmed. Our physical features, our history as slaves, our African ancestry – all of this was reconstructed as a source of pride.

I was there and I experienced this development as profoundly liberating; obviously, the effects of this reversal have been predominantly good. Nonetheless, I think that the binary thinking that underlies the 'positive images' concept can be dangerous. It remains reductionist; it assumes that racial, ethnic and national groups are more homogeneous than they are, it fails to understand that identity is not simple but complex and it can lead to ethnocentrism and racial chauvinism. So, although I would accept that the Somali Elders Project can be understood as an exercise in the creation of positive images of a black and Islamic people, I am not fully comfortable with the term.

Author: I note that in addition to the portraits you took in 2001 and 2004, the publication accompanying the exhibition includes some earlier portraits and documents. What are these and why are they included? It is it simply a matter of providing the viewer with glimpses of now and then?

Photographer: Everybody likes old photographs, but that is not why I included them. [DVD REF 33: PHOTO] The section in the exhibition catalogue consisting of old photographs and documents, which includes new portraits on either side of it, is intended to make a number of points. By providing photographs of these men as elders and as young men, I wish to call attention to the fact that identities are *complex*, *plural* and *changing*. In the early photographs, all these men are 'Western' in appearance; one even wears an Afro and a Black Panther-style leather coat (the photograph is from the 1970s). Some who are now devout Muslims drank and gambled as younger men. Many had relationships with British and/or other European women. Many have bi-cultural families that include non-Muslim wives and children. Moreover, a number of them served as seamen in both the Merchant Navy and Royal Navy and contributed to various war efforts, especially World War II but also the first Gulf War and the Falklands War. The Somali elders are not absolute 'others'; on the contrary, they belong to 'our' history and culture: ironically, their contributions to Wales and Britain far exceed those of many who would seek to exclude them. It is high time that this fact is properly acknowledged. Finally, the old portraits remind us of a universal point about human existence: we all age. Here, if nowhere else, all of us can identify with the elders.

CODA

In closing, I want to introduce the voice of Abdikarim Adan, Director of the Somali Advice & Information Centre in Cardiff, speaking at the opening of the *Somali Elders: Portraits from Wales* exhibition at Butetown History & Arts Centre. [DVD REF 1: VIDEO] Abdikarim Adan, despite his relative youth, is one of the most prominent members of the

Somali community in Wales. The concluding remarks he makes are very generous. Why does he make such comments? It is true that we are friends, that we have known each other a long time and that we respect the work that each of us is trying to do. But it is more than this; he is convinced of the great importance of this project, which ensures that the history in Wales and Britain of the community to which he belongs is not forgotten. I watched dozens of Somali people look at the images when they were on our gallery wall. They loved the images and many expressed their gratitude to me for doing the project. It is this response that means most to me. It signals that the project has been a success – that it has achieved at least part of its moral mandate.

Notes

1 Extracts of this chapter are taken from the exhibition catalogue: *Somali Elders: Portraits from Wales/ Odeyada Soomaalida: Muuqaalo ka yimid Welishka* (2004), Glenn Jordan with Akli Ahmed and Abdihakim Arwo. All photographs referred to are by permission of Butetown History & Arts Centre. The video clips are from *Somali Elders: Portraits from Wales – Celebrating the Opening of a Powerful Photographic Exhibition*, a video made by Alpha Bah for Butetown History & Arts Centre. Alpha Bah was a successful portrait photographer in Sierra Leone before he became a refugee. He now lives in Cardiff and works as a freelance video cameraman.

2 By Alun Michael, MP for Cardiff South and Penarth and formerly a youth and community worker in Butetown. Michael has a long association with the local community. He also has longstanding ties to the Somali community in south Wales and over the years has assisted a number of local Somalis with immigration problems.

3 Virtually all Somalis have nicknames, which are used by other Somalis. Said Ismail Ali's nickname is 'Said Shuqule'. Since I knew only the nickname until three years after I took this picture, when we needed to ensure that the subjects' proper names were inscribed in the *Somali Elders* exhibition catalogue, I continue to use it here.

4 The reader may have noted that I have not given a specific reference for the newspaper in question; I don't know the date or even its name. A member of Shuqule's immediate family allowed us to borrow and scan his papers as a contribution to our work on the history of Somalis in Cardiff. Among them was a newspaper article, yellow with age but legible almost throughout, folded and preserved. Entitled 'Wars of Newport's Seafaring Somali', it was a short feature story on Shuqule (see Jordan 2004 *et al.*: plate 49).

5 For an overview of the history of Somalia from colonialism to the present, see I. M. Lewis (2002). Lewis is widely regarded as the leading expert on Somali history, society and culture. Many Somalis don't agree, not least because Professor Lewis cannot speak Somali.

6 The most informative book on the history and presence of ethnic minorities in Wales is Williams *et al.* (2003).

7 In the mid-1990s, a Somali community newsletter was published in Cardiff. Its title, interestingly, was *Dal Mar*, which literally means 'The Traveller'.

8 This passage, from an essay by Gerry Badger on Richard Avedon (1988), outlines my position precisely.

9 'Abdi Gurri' literally means 'left-handed Abdi'. There is a photogtaph in the *Somali Elders* catalogue of Glenn Jordan and Abdi Nuur, taken in 1989 in the Butetown Community Centre (2004: 190).

10   The interviews were done by Abdihakim Arwo, who works as a Somali community historian at Bute-
     town History & Arts Centre. He also translated the texts, which were then edited by Glenn Jordan and
     Chris Weedon. The stories included on the DVD, and other additional ones, are contained in a section
     of the *Somali Elders* catalogue entitled 'Faces, Memories, Voices' (2004: 169–91).

11   A more complete version of this dialogue occurs in the *Somali Elders* catalogue; see 'What Kind of
     Photographs Are These? A Dialogue between Author and Photographer' (2004: 30–55).

12   Not long after this photograph was taken, Ali Mohamed Ahmed went into a coma.

13   For an excellent discussion of racial stereotyping, see Hall (1997).

Bibliography

Adan, A. (2004) 'Foreword/Gudbin', in G. Jordan with A. Ahmed and A. Arwo, *Somali Elders: Portraits from Wales/Odeyada Soomaalida: Muuqaalo ka yimid Welishka*. Cardiff: Butetown History & Arts Centre.

Badger, G. (1988) 'Richard Avedon: I Want to Be an Artist Like Diane', in P. Turner and G. Badger, *Photo Texts*. London: Travelling Light.

Hall, C. (1996) 'Histories, Empires and the Post-colonial Moment', in I. Chambers and L. Curti (eds) *The Post-colonial Question*. London and New York, Routledge.

Hall, S. (1997) 'The Spectacle of the Other', in S. Hall (ed.) *Representation: Cultural Representations and Signifying Practices*. London: Sage.

Jordan, G. (2001) 'Tiger Bay, Picture Post and the Politics of Representation', in G. Jordan (ed.) *Down the Bay: Picture Post, Humanist Photography and Images of 1950s Cardiff*. Cardiff: Butetown History & Arts Centre, 9–21.

_____ (2003) 'Voices from Below: Doing People's History in Cardiff Docklands', in S. Berger, H. Feldner and K. Passmore (eds) *Writing History: Theory and Practice*. London: Arnold.

Jordan, G. and C. Weedon (2000) 'When the Subalterns Speak, What Do They Say? Radical Cultural Politics in Cardiff Docklands', in P. Gilroy, L. Grossberg and A. McRobbie (eds) *Without Guarantees: In Honour of Stuart Hall*. London: Verso.

Jordan, G. with A. Ahmed and A. Arwo (2004) *Somali Elders: Portraits from Wales/Odeyada Soomaalida: Muuqaalo ka yimid Welishka*. Cardiff: Butetown History and Arts Centre.

Lewis, I. M. (2002) *A Modern History of the Somali: Nation and State in the Horn of Africa* (second edition). Boulder: Westview Press.

Sobieszek, R. (1999) *Ghost in the Shell: Photography and the Human Soul*. Cambridge: MIT Press.

Sontag, S. (1979) *On Photography*. London: Penguin Books.

Williams, C., N. Evans and P. O'Leary (2003) 'Introduction', in C. Williams, N. Evans and P. O'Leary (eds), *A Tolerant Nation? Exploring Ethnic Diversity in Wales*. Cardiff: University of Wales Press, 1–13.

INDEX

GUIDELINES FOR DVD-ROM

The DVD-ROM included is designed as an essential and integrated component of this book, offering the reader a viewing source of all moving image, photographic, audio and pdf materials referenced in the introduction and each of the eleven chapters. We would encourage the reader therefore to work closely with both text and DVD media content simultaneously.

The book's cross-links to the DVD-ROM are embedded within chapters, designated by a corresponding numerical DVD reference, together with one or more of a combination of the following descriptive media types: video, photo, audio and pdf. These cross-links may also appear in chapter footnotes. While appearing in sequential order, authors will occasionally refer back to previously cited DVD references, retaining the numerical and medium specificity of the cross-link.

Double-clicking on the **ProjectingMigration.exe** (PC) or **ProjectingMigration** (Mac) icon launches the contents menu of the DVD-ROM in which the introduction, chapter titles and authors are presented; clicking on a selected chapter activates its submenu. On the PC the DVD-ROM will auto-launch once the disc has been recognised by the system; there is no auto-launch on the Mac. The DVD-ROM can be exited on either PC or Mac by using the **quit** button found in the top right-hand corner.

Layout and navigation structure of chapter submenu:

– The **references** section is automatically selected, providing a corresponding list of numbers (and titles) of DVD references cited in each chapter, together with their written colour-coded media types: video (blue); photography (yellow); audio (green); pdf (red). Click on a reference to open its media content. Navigate between references via **previous** and **next** or by clicking on **references**. Note that the stage size is fixed and cannot be enlarged to full screen.

– Click on the **figures** option to browse sequentially numbered illustrations used in chapters. These are reproduced for convenience of the reader to view figures in their original format and are presented as a slideshow sequence. The dropdown titles of chapter figures appear only when the cursor is placed on the image; this same principle applies when viewing series of photographs in references.

– The **author biography** option contains photographs of authors, together with brief biographical statements.

– Click on **chapters** to return to contents menu.

Minimum requirements: Windows 2000 or later; Mac OS X; DVD-ROM Drive; monitor resolution 800 x 600; and desktop speakers.